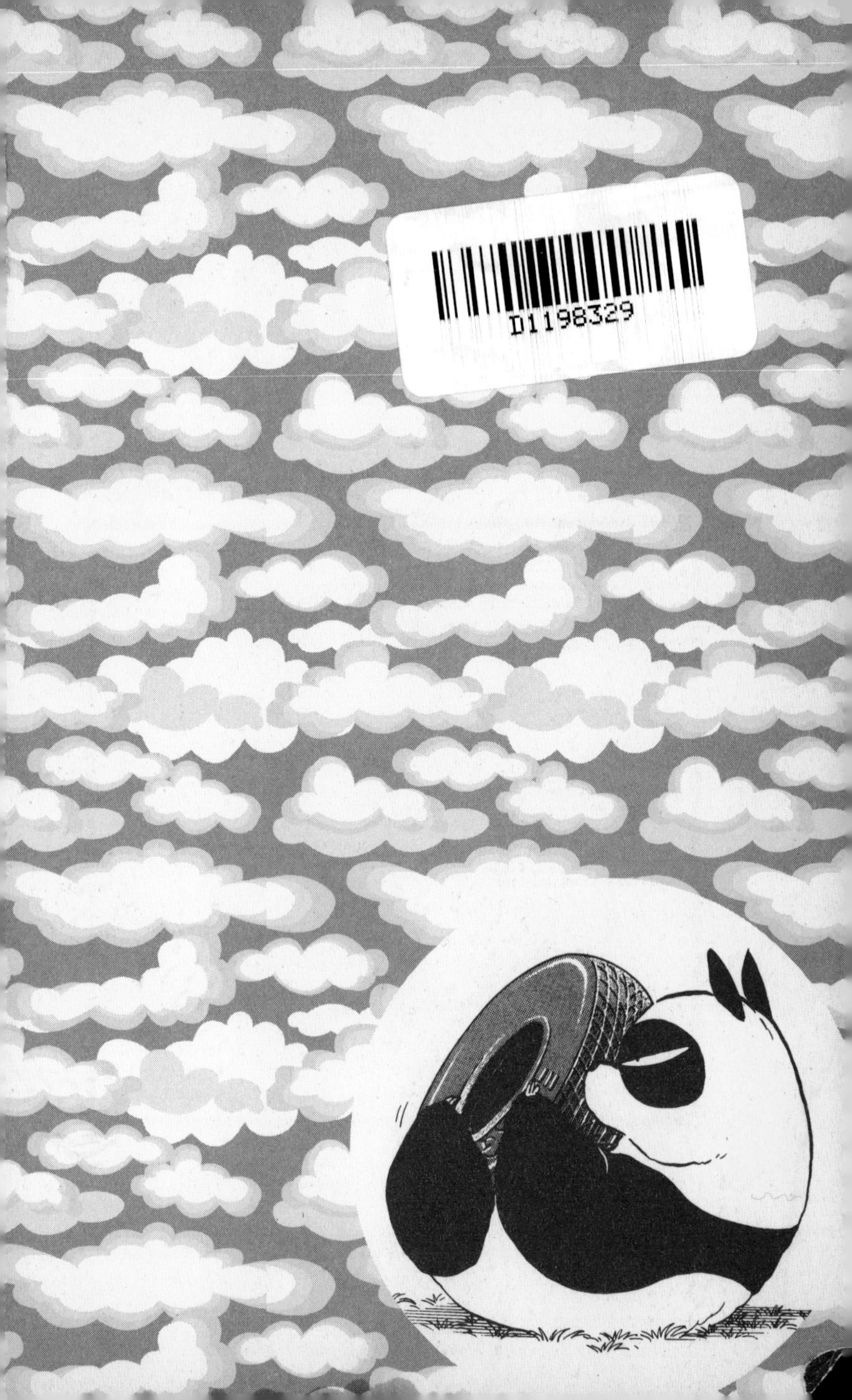

Ranma 1/2

VOL. 7 Action Edition

STORY & ART BY

RUMIKO TAKAHASHI

Ranma 1/2

VOL. 7
Action Edition

Story and Art by
RUMIKO TAKAHASHI

English Adaptation by Gerard Jones & Toshifumi Yoshida
Touch-Up Art & Lettering/Wayne Truman
Cover and Interior Design & Graphics/Yuki Ameda
Editor (1st Edition)/Trish Ledoux
Editor (Action Edition)/Julie Davis

Managing Editor/Annette Roman
Editor in Chief/William Flanagan
Production Manager/Noboru Watanabe
Sr. Dir. of Licensing & Acquisitions/Rika Inouye
VP of Marketing/Liza Coppola
Sr. VP of Editorial/Hyoe Narita
Publisher/Seiji Horibuchi

RANMA 1/2 is rated "T+" for Older Teens. It may contain violence, language, alcohol or tobacco use, or suggestive situations.

Printed in Canada.

Published by VIZ, LLC
P.O. Box 77010
San Francisco, CA 94107

1st Edition published 1996

Action Edition
10 9 8 7 6 5 4 3 2 1
First printing, January 2004

store.viz.com

STORY THUS FAR

The Tendos are an average, run-of-the-mill Japanese family—at least on the surface, that is. Soun Tendo is the owner and proprietor of the Tendo Dojo, where "Anything-Goes Martial Arts" is practiced. Like the name says, anything goes, and usually does.

When Soun's old friend Genma Saotome comes to visit, Soun's three lovely young daughters—Akane, Nabiki, and Kasumi—are told that it's time for one of them to become the fiancée of Genma's teenage son, as per an agreement made between the two fathers years ago. Youngest daughter Akane—who says she hates boys—is quickly nominated for bridal duty by her sisters.

Unfortunately, Ranma and his father have suffered a strange accident. While training in China, both plunged into one of many "accursed" springs at the legendary martial arts training ground of Jusenkyo. These springs transform the unlucky dunkee into whoever—or whatever—drowned there hundreds of years ago.

From now on, a splash of cold water turns Ranma's father into a giant panda, and Ranma becomes a beautiful, busty young woman. Hot water reverses the effect...but only until next time.

Ranma and Genma weren't the only ones to take the Jusenkyo plunge—it isn't long before they meet several other members of the "cursed." And although their parents are still determined to see Ranma and Akane marry and carry on the training hall, Ranma seems to have a strange talent for accumulating extra fiancées, and Akane has a few suitors of her own. Will the two ever work out their differences, get rid of all these extra people, or just call the whole thing off? And will Ranma ever get rid of his curse?

CAST OF CHARACTERS

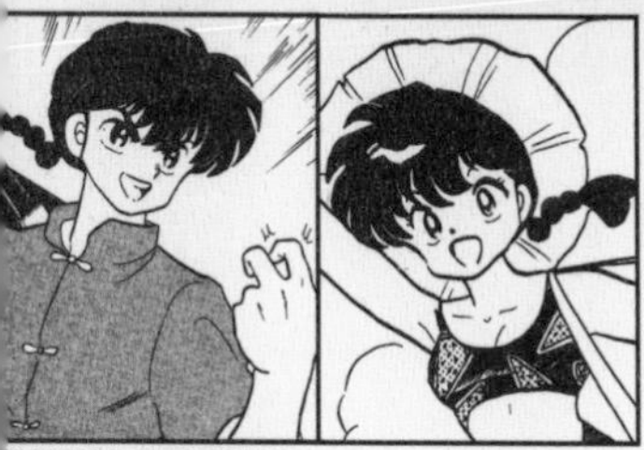

RANMA SAOTOME
Martial artist with far too many fiancées, and an ego that won't let him take defeat easily. He changes into a girl when splashed with cold water.

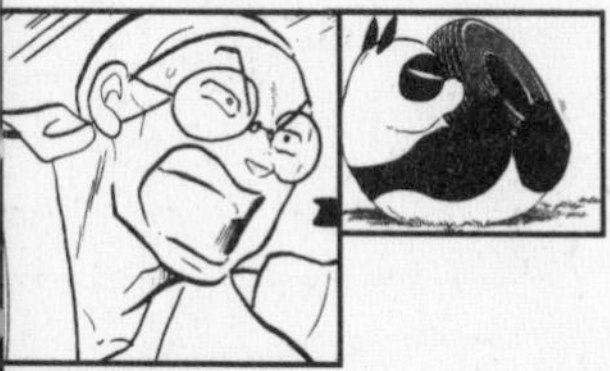

GENMA SAOTOME
Ranma's lazy father, who left his home and wife years ago with his young son to train in the martial arts. He changes into a panda.

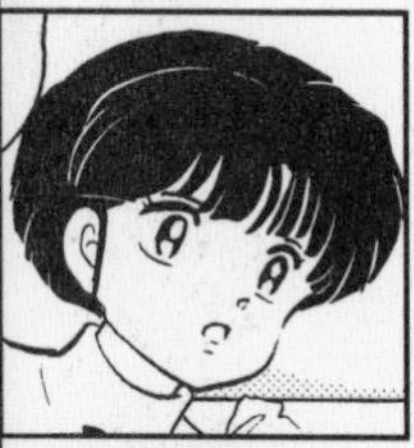

AKANE TENDO
A martial artist, tomboy, and Ranma's fiancée by parental arrangement. She has no clue how much Ryoga likes her, or what relation he has to her pet black pig, P-chan.

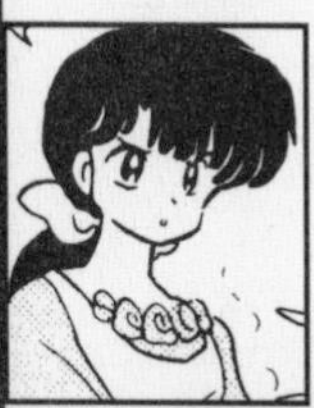

KASUMI TENDO
The oldest Tendo daughter, a happy homemaker.

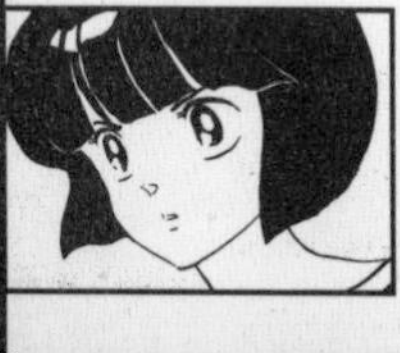

NABIKI TENDO
The middle Tendo daughter, who can always find a way to make a few yen from any situation.

RYOGA HIBIKI
A melancholy martial artist with no sense of direction, a crush on Akane, and a grudge against Ranma. He changes into a small, black pig Akane calls "P-chan."

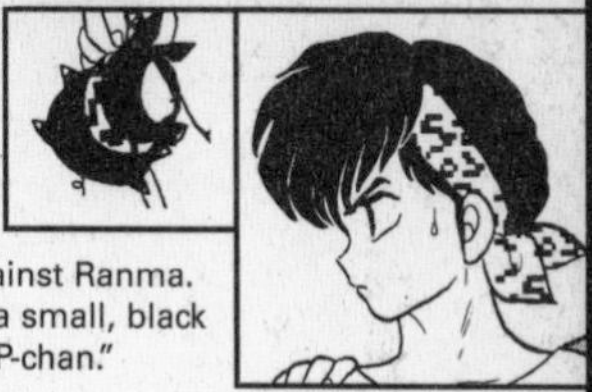

TATEWAKI KUNO
Furinkan High's *kendo* club president, Kuno can't decide which girl he likes best—Ranma (in girl form, a.k.a. the "pigtailed girl") or Akane.

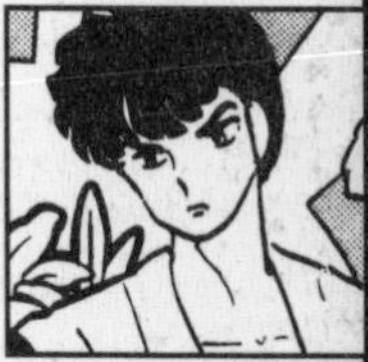

KODACHI KUNO
A diabolical gymnast, Kodachi is Kuno's demented sister. She is determined to make Ranma her own.

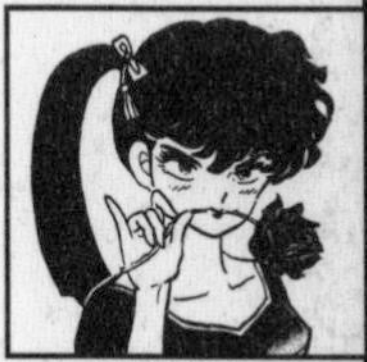

GOSUNKUGI
A spooky young man with a crush on Akane. For obvious reasons, he hates Ranma.

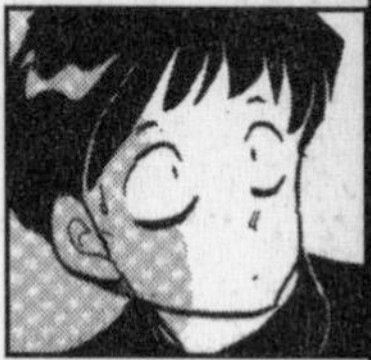

HAPPOSAI
The martial arts master who trained both Genma and Soun. Also a world-class pervert.

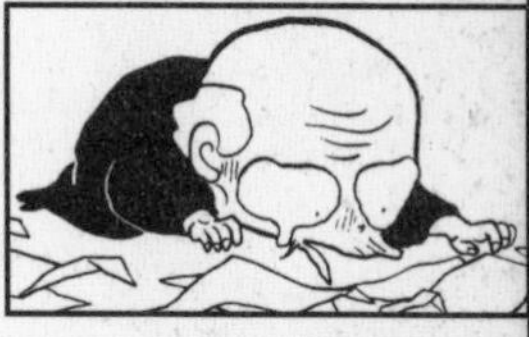

SOUN TENDO
The head of the Tendo household and owner of the Tendo Dojo.

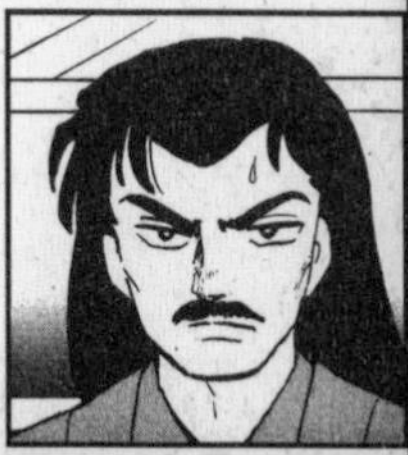

CONTENTS

Part 1

WHEREFORE ART THOU, ROMEO?

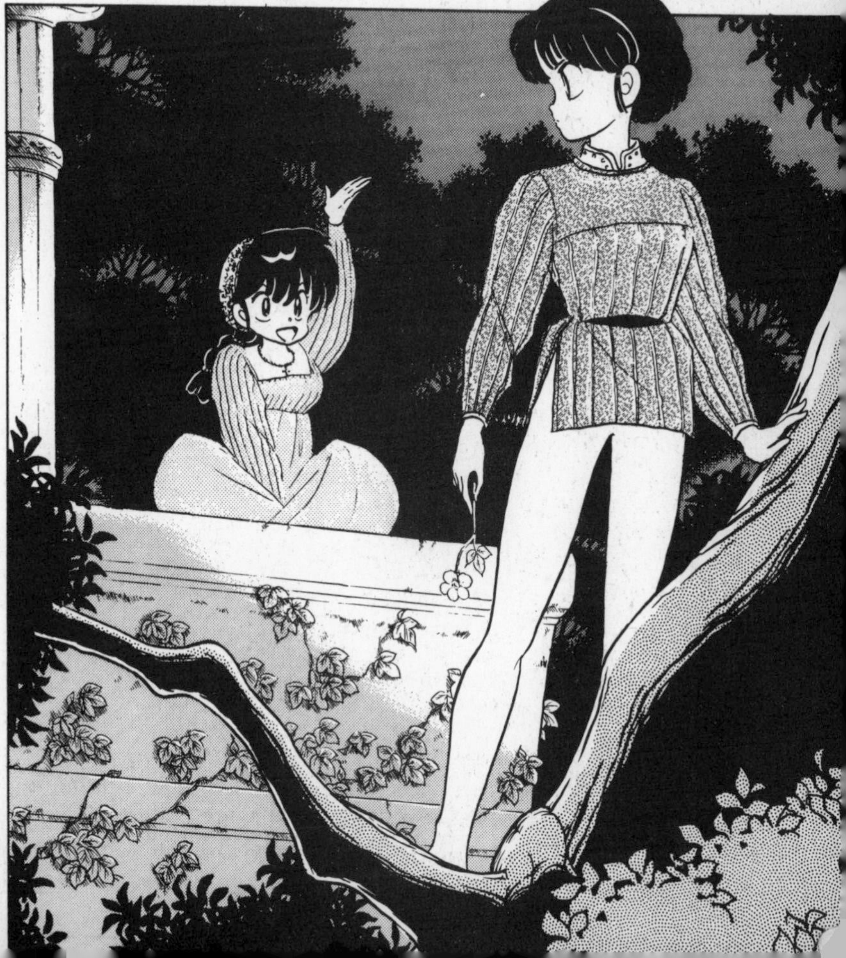

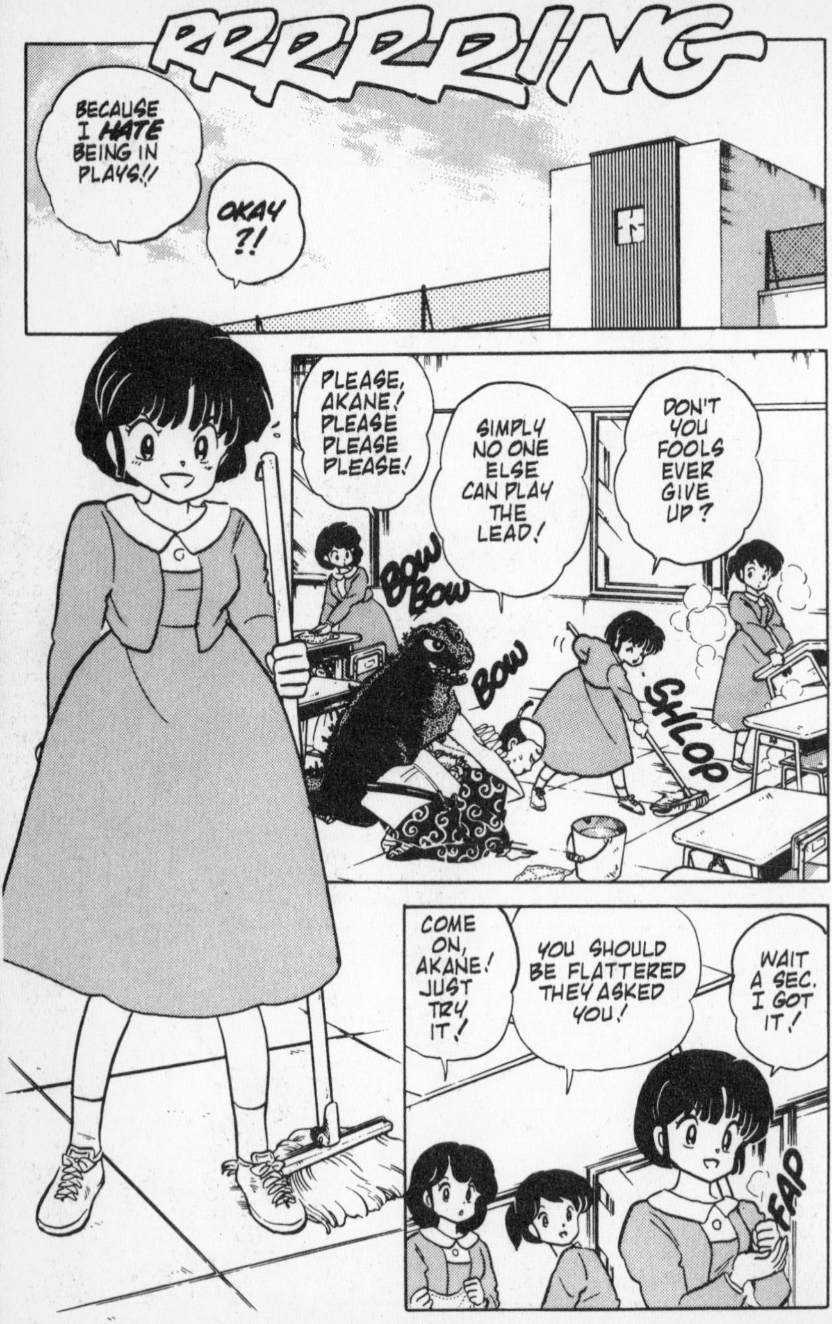
RRRRRING
BECAUSE I HATE BEING IN PLAYS!!
OKAY ?!
PLEASE, AKANE! PLEASE PLEASE PLEASE!
BOW BOW
SIMPLY NO ONE ELSE CAN PLAY THE LEAD!
BOW
DON'T YOU FOOLS EVER GIVE UP?
SHLOP
COME ON, AKANE! JUST TRY IT!
YOU SHOULD BE FLATTERED THEY ASKED YOU!
WAIT A SEC. I GOT IT!
FAP

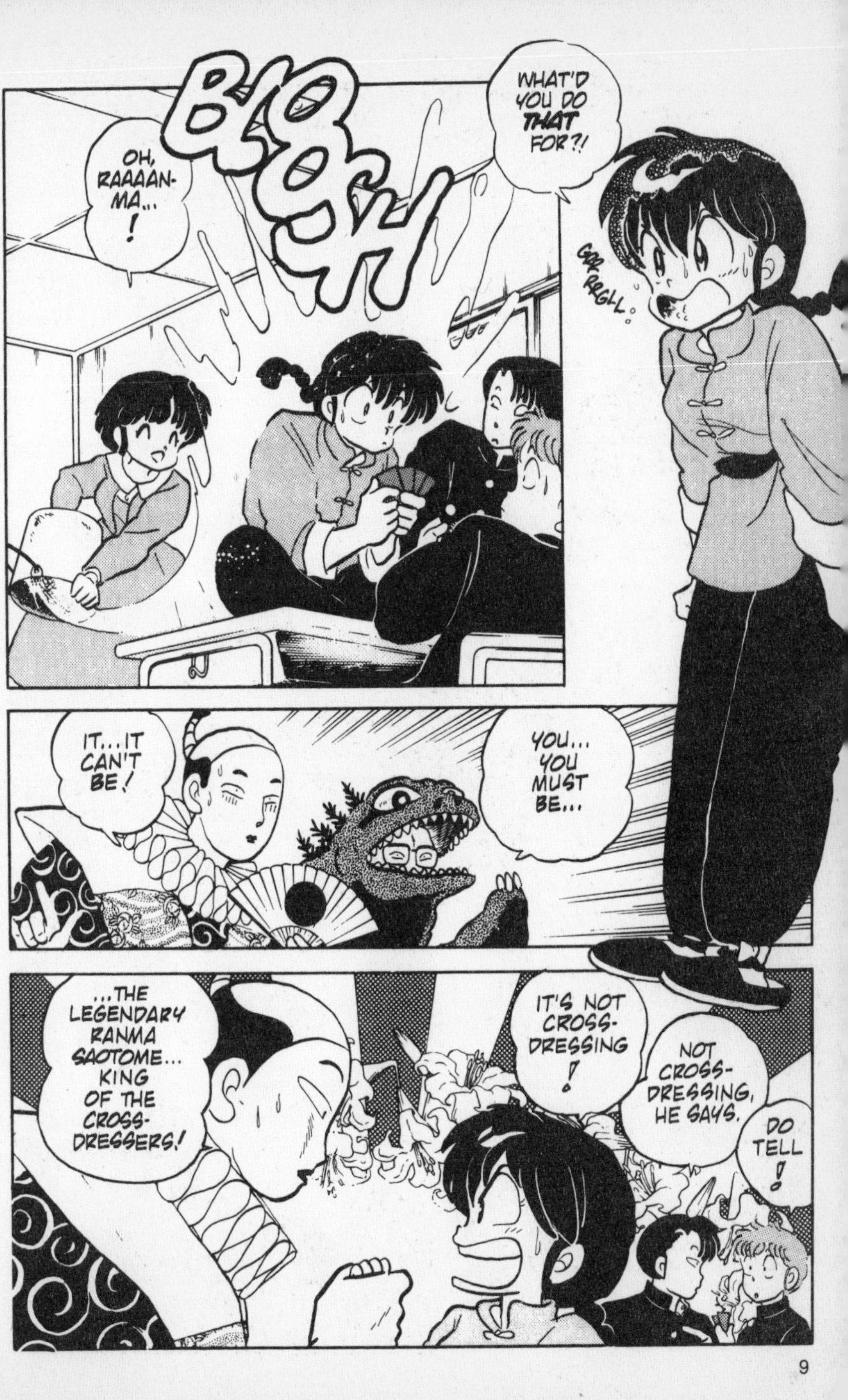
BLOOOSH
OH, RAAAAN-MA...!
WHAT'D YOU DO THAT FOR?!
GRR RRGLL
IT... IT CAN'T BE!
YOU... YOU MUST BE...
...THE LEGENDARY RANMA SAOTOME... KING OF THE CROSS-DRESSERS!
IT'S NOT CROSS-DRESSING!
NOT CROSS-DRESSING, HE SAYS.
DO TELL!

HE DOES AERIAL FLIPS.

CRUSHES ROCKS BAREHANDED.

AND HE LEARNS NEW TRICKS EVEN QUICKER THAN LASSIE.

HEY!

WHY DON'T YOU WANT THE ROLE, AKANE?

IT'S THE LEAD! IT'S...

LET ME GUESS.

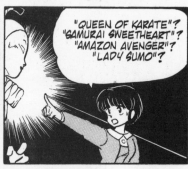

"QUEEN OF KARATE"? "SAMURAI SWEETHEART"? "AMAZON AVENGER"? "LADY SUMO"?

GO FOR IT, AKANE! YOU WERE BORN FOR THE ROLE!

WHISH

WHOA!

BUT, AKANE, IF YOU'D ONLY LET ME--

BOOM

I SAID **NO** AND I MEAN **NO!**

BOOM

DO WE HAVE A CHOICE?

I THINK WE DON'T.

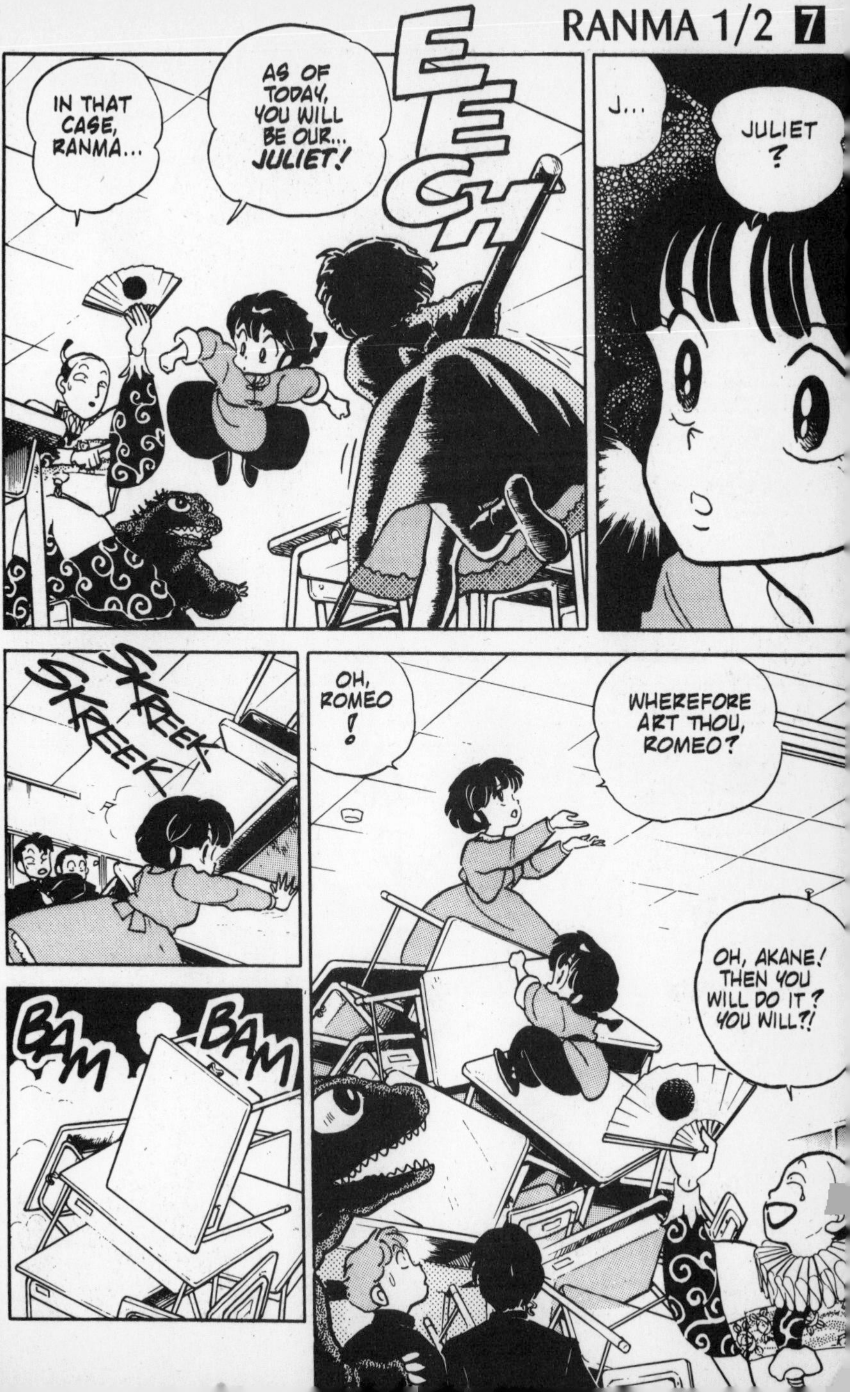
IN THAT CASE, RANMA...
AS OF TODAY, YOU WILL BE OUR... JULIET!
EEECH
J...
JULIET?
SKREEK SKREEK
OH, ROMEO!
WHEREFORE ART THOU, ROMEO?
OH, AKANE! THEN YOU WILL DO IT? YOU WILL?!
BAM BAM

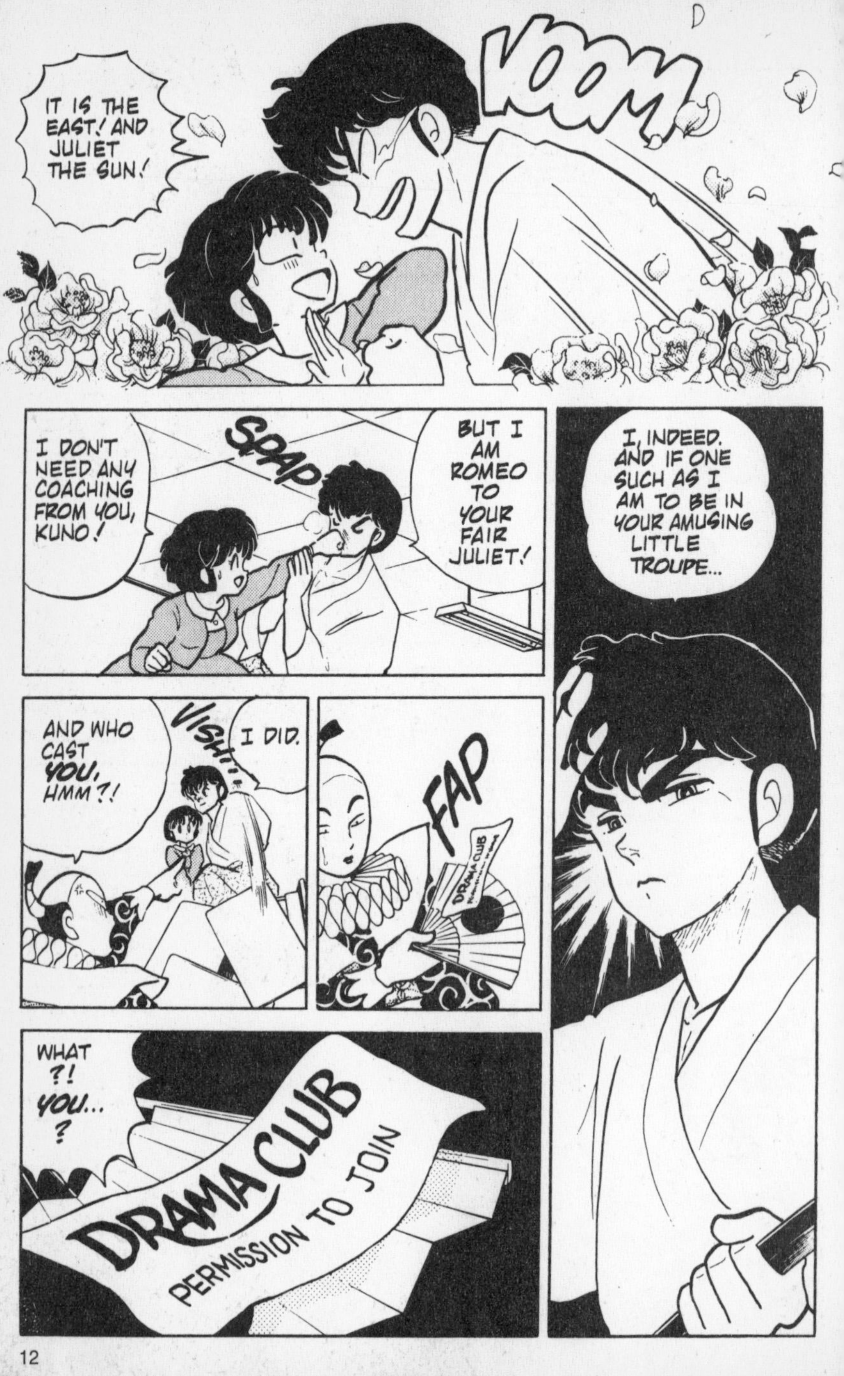
VOOM
IT IS THE EAST! AND JULIET THE SUN!
I DON'T NEED ANY COACHING FROM YOU, KUNO!
SPAP
BUT I AM ROMEO TO YOUR FAIR JULIET!
AND WHO CAST YOU, HMM?!
VISH...
I DID.
FAP
DRAMA CLUB
WHAT?! YOU...?
DRAMA CLUB
PERMISSION TO JOIN
I, INDEED. AND IF ONE SUCH AS I AM TO BE IN YOUR AMUSING LITTLE TROUPE...

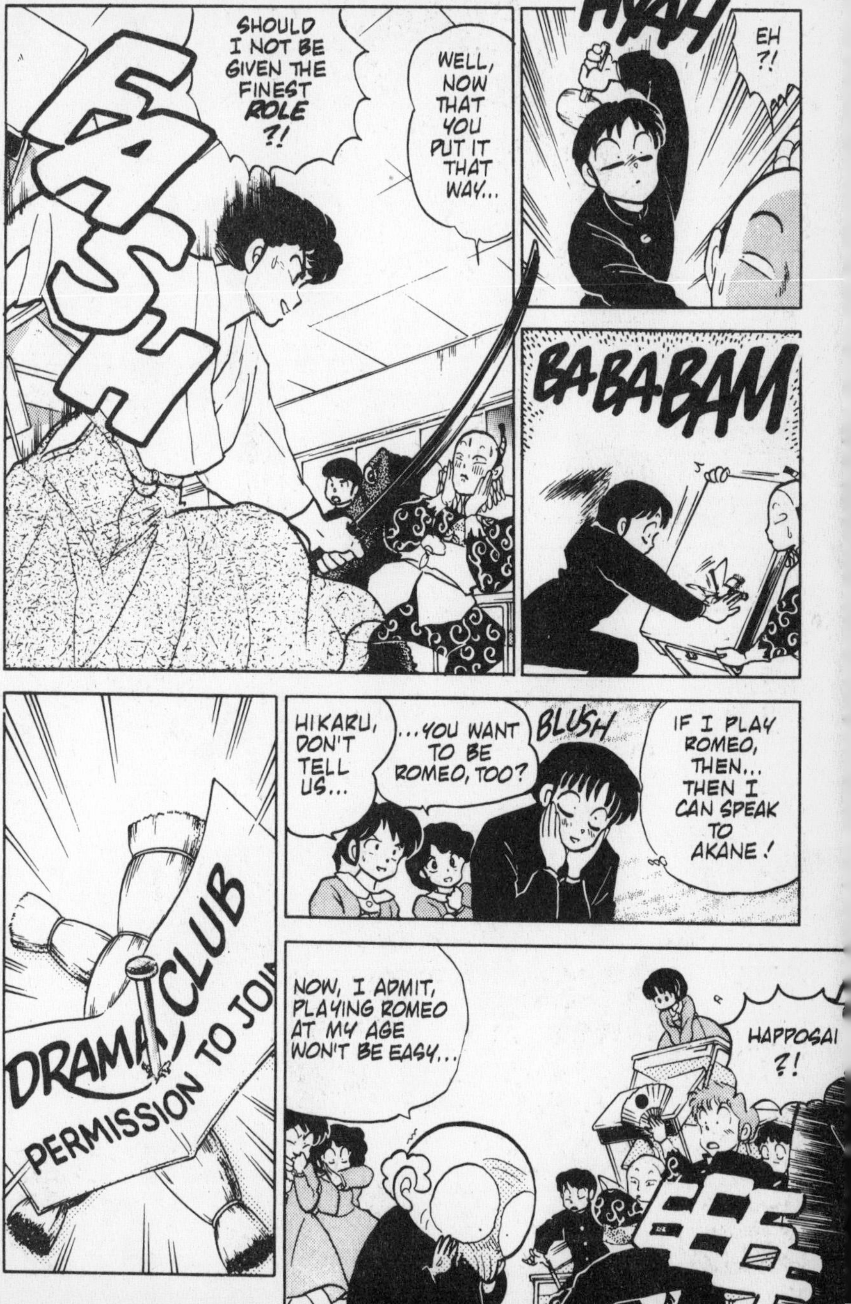
SHOULD I NOT BE GIVEN THE FINEST ROLE ?!
WELL, NOW THAT YOU PUT IT THAT WAY...
HYAH
EH ?!
BA-BA-BAM
DRAMA CLUB
PERMISSION TO JOI
HIKARU, DON'T TELL US...
...YOU WANT TO BE ROMEO, TOO?
BLUSH
IF I PLAY ROMEO, THEN... THEN I CAN SPEAK TO AKANE!
NOW, I ADMIT, PLAYING ROMEO AT MY AGE WON'T BE EASY...
HAPPOSAI ?!

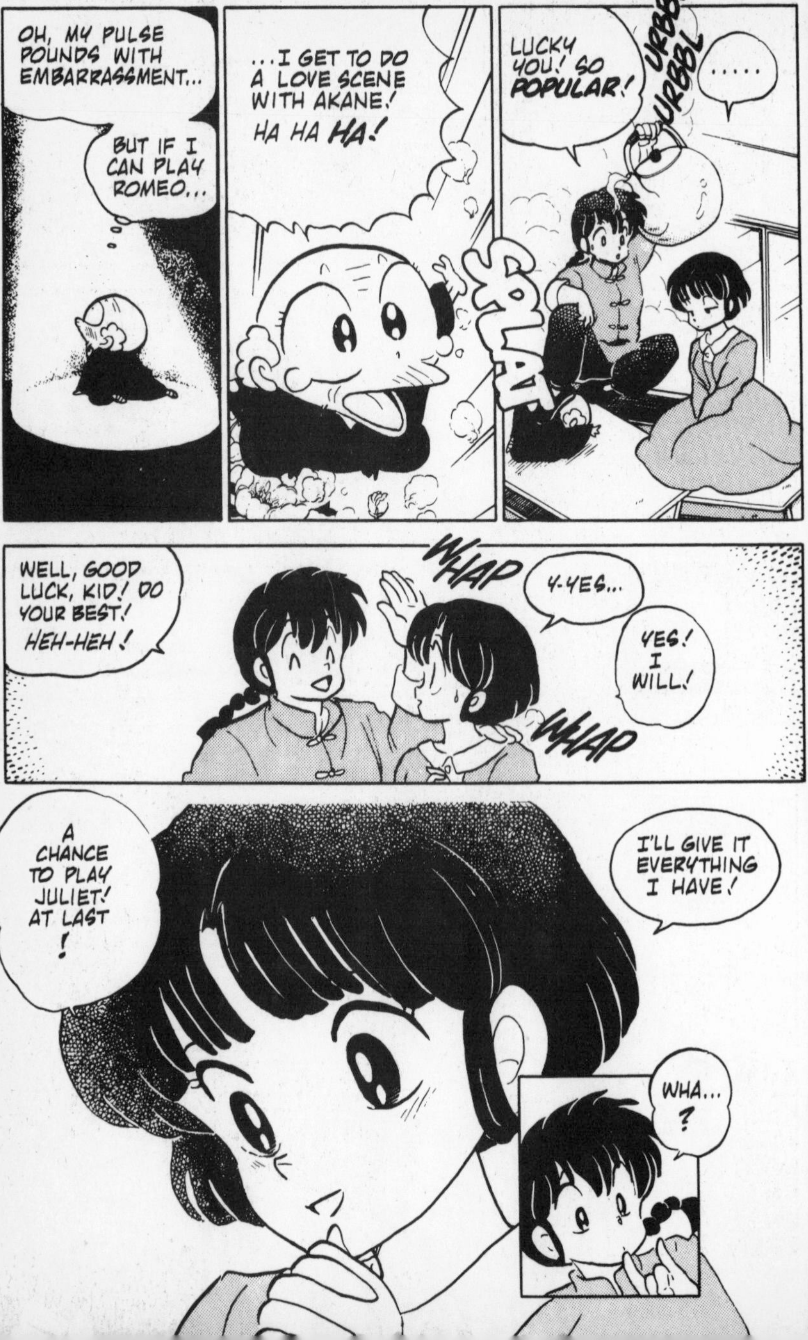
OH, MY PULSE POUNDS WITH EMBARRASSMENT...
BUT IF I CAN PLAY ROMEO...
...I GET TO DO A LOVE SCENE WITH AKANE!
HA HA HA!
SPLAT
LUCKY YOU! SO POPULAR!
URBBL URBBL
.....
WELL, GOOD LUCK, KID! DO YOUR BEST! HEH-HEH!
WHAP
Y-YES...
YES! I WILL!
WHAP
A CHANCE TO PLAY JULIET! AT LAST!
I'LL GIVE IT EVERYTHING I HAVE!
WHA...?

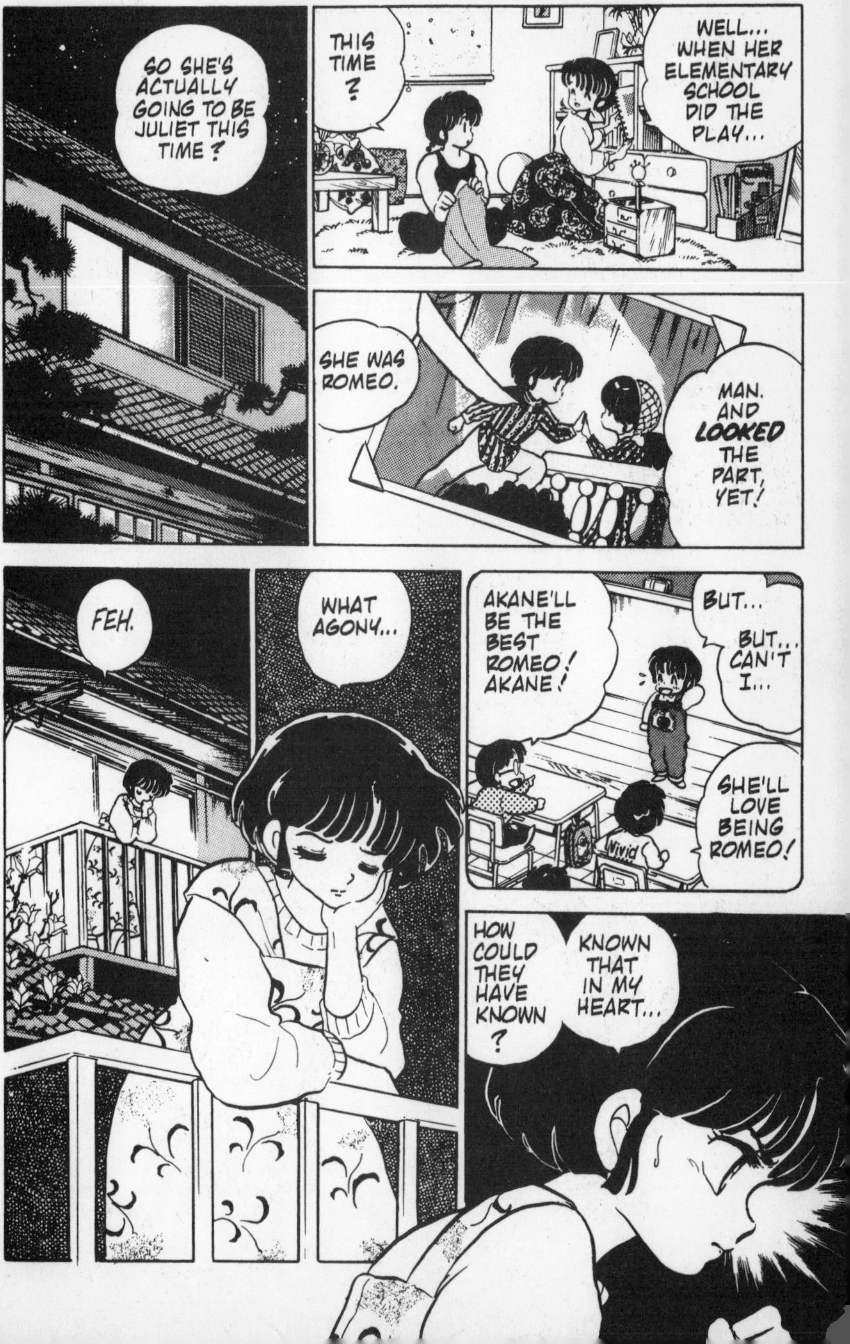
SO SHE'S ACTUALLY GOING TO BE JULIET THIS TIME?
THIS TIME ?
WELL... WHEN HER ELEMENTARY SCHOOL DID THE PLAY...
SHE WAS ROMEO.
MAN. AND LOOKED THE PART, YET!
FEH.
WHAT AGONY...
AKANE'LL BE THE BEST ROMEO! AKANE!
BUT...
BUT... CAN'T I...
SHE'LL LOVE BEING ROMEO!
Nivid
HOW COULD THEY HAVE KNOWN ?
KNOWN THAT IN MY HEART...

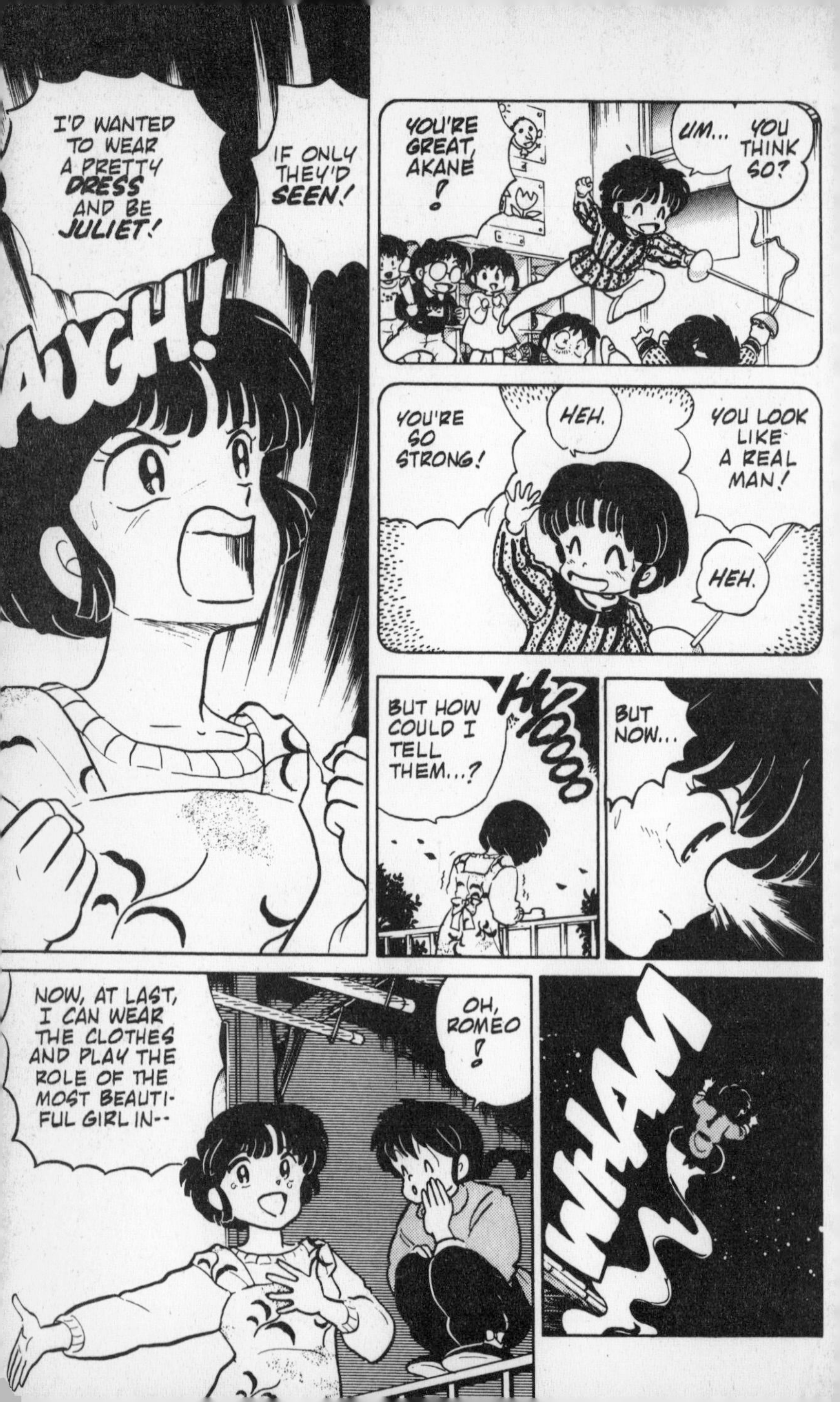
I'D WANTED TO WEAR A PRETTY DRESS AND BE JULIET!
IF ONLY THEY'D SEEN!
AUGH!
YOU'RE GREAT, AKANE!
UM... YOU THINK SO?
YOU'RE SO STRONG!
HEH.
YOU LOOK LIKE A REAL MAN!
HEH.
BUT HOW COULD I TELL THEM...?
HIYOOOOO
BUT NOW...
NOW, AT LAST, I CAN WEAR THE CLOTHES AND PLAY THE ROLE OF THE MOST BEAUTIFUL GIRL IN--
OH, ROMEO!
WHAM

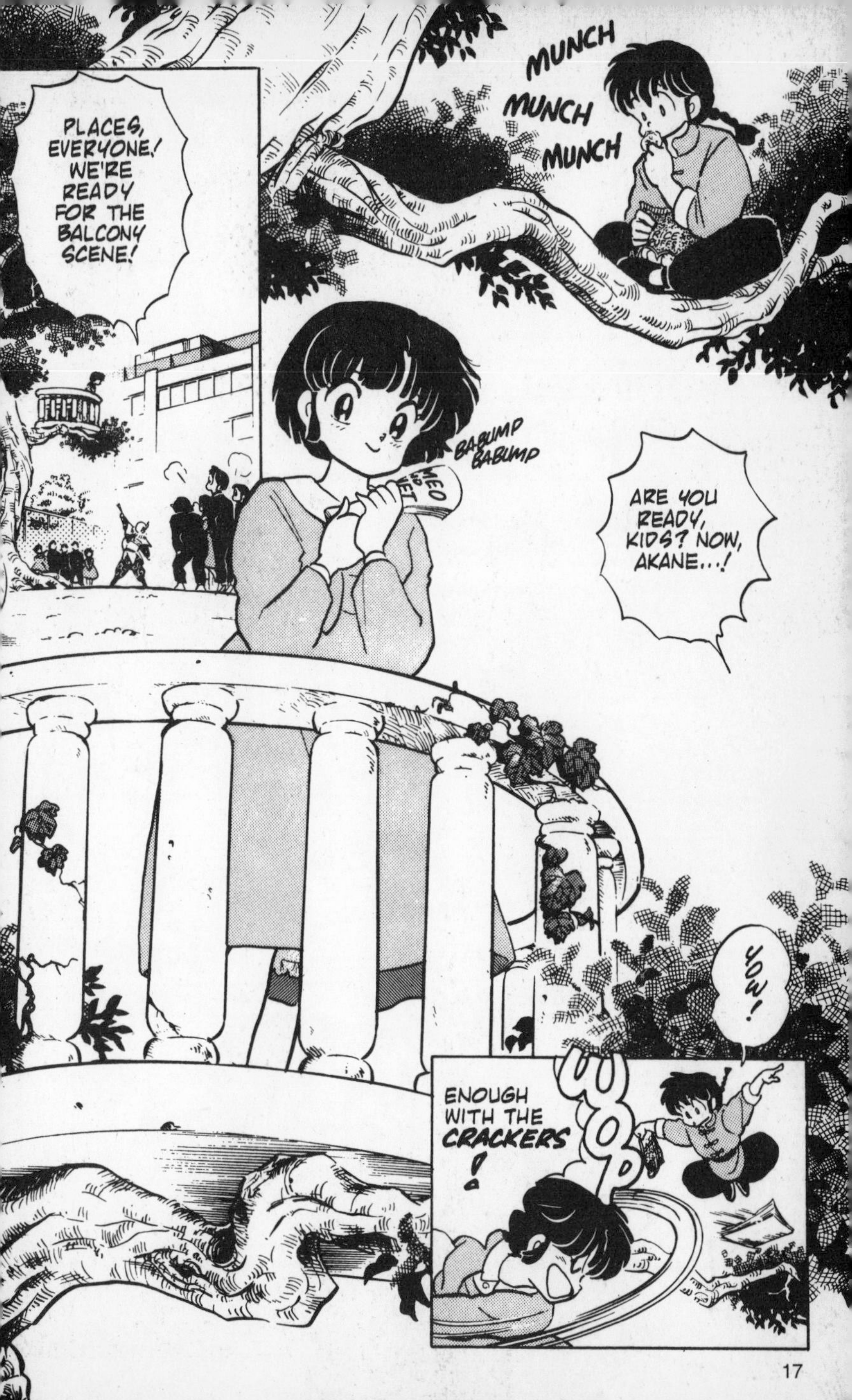
PLACES, EVERYONE! WE'RE READY FOR THE BALCONY SCENE!
MUNCH
MUNCH
MUNCH
BABUMP BABUMP
ARE YOU READY, KIDS? NOW, AKANE...!
YOW!
ENOUGH WITH THE CRACKERS!
BOP

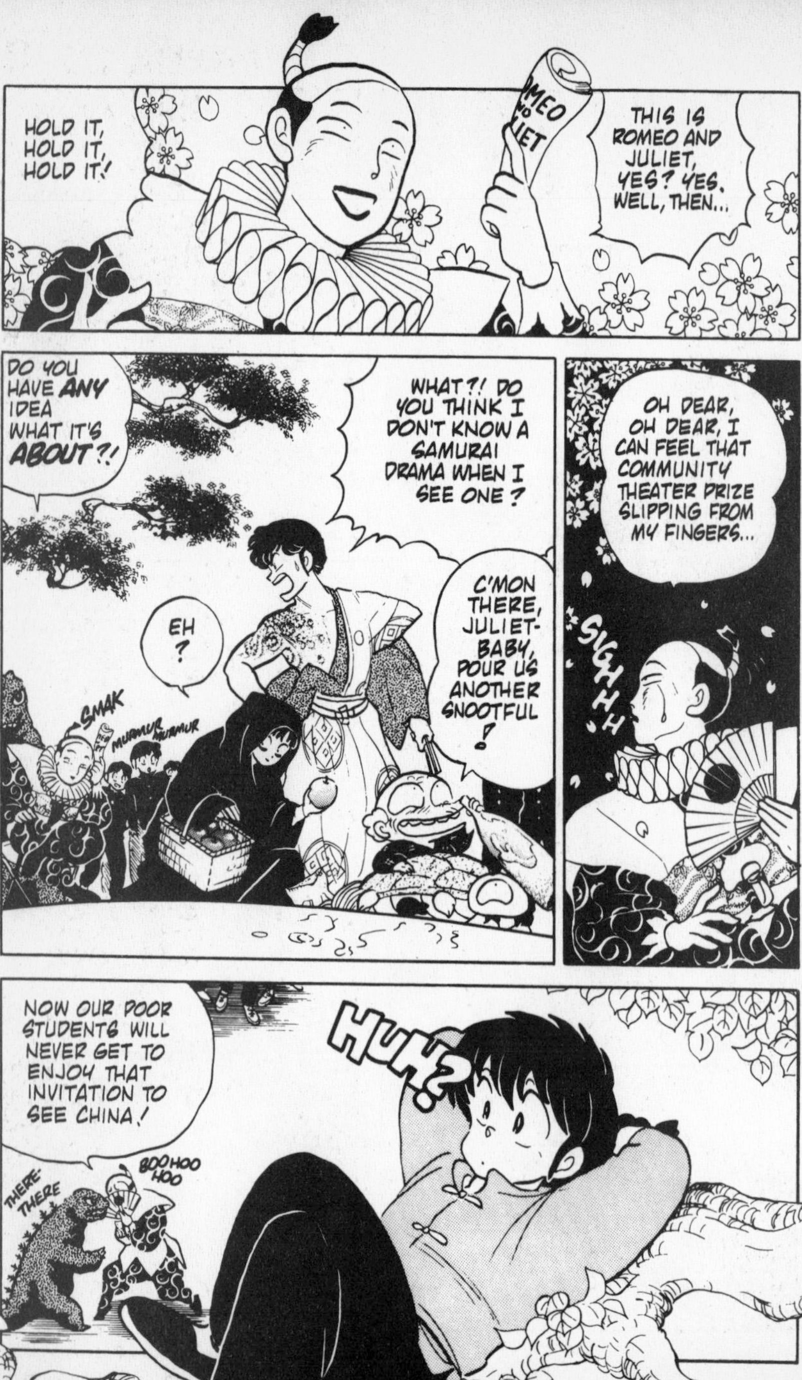
ROMEO NO JULIET
HOLD IT, HOLD IT, HOLD IT!
THIS IS ROMEO AND JULIET, YES? YES. WELL, THEN...
DO YOU HAVE ANY IDEA WHAT IT'S ABOUT?!
WHAT?! DO YOU THINK I DON'T KNOW A SAMURAI DRAMA WHEN I SEE ONE?
EH?
SMAK
MURMUR MURMUR
C'MON THERE, JULIET-BABY, POUR US ANOTHER SNOOTFUL!
OH DEAR, OH DEAR, I CAN FEEL THAT COMMUNITY THEATER PRIZE SLIPPING FROM MY FINGERS...
SIGHHH
NOW OUR POOR STUDENTS WILL NEVER GET TO ENJOY THAT INVITATION TO SEE CHINA!
THERE THERE
BOO HOO HOO
HUH?

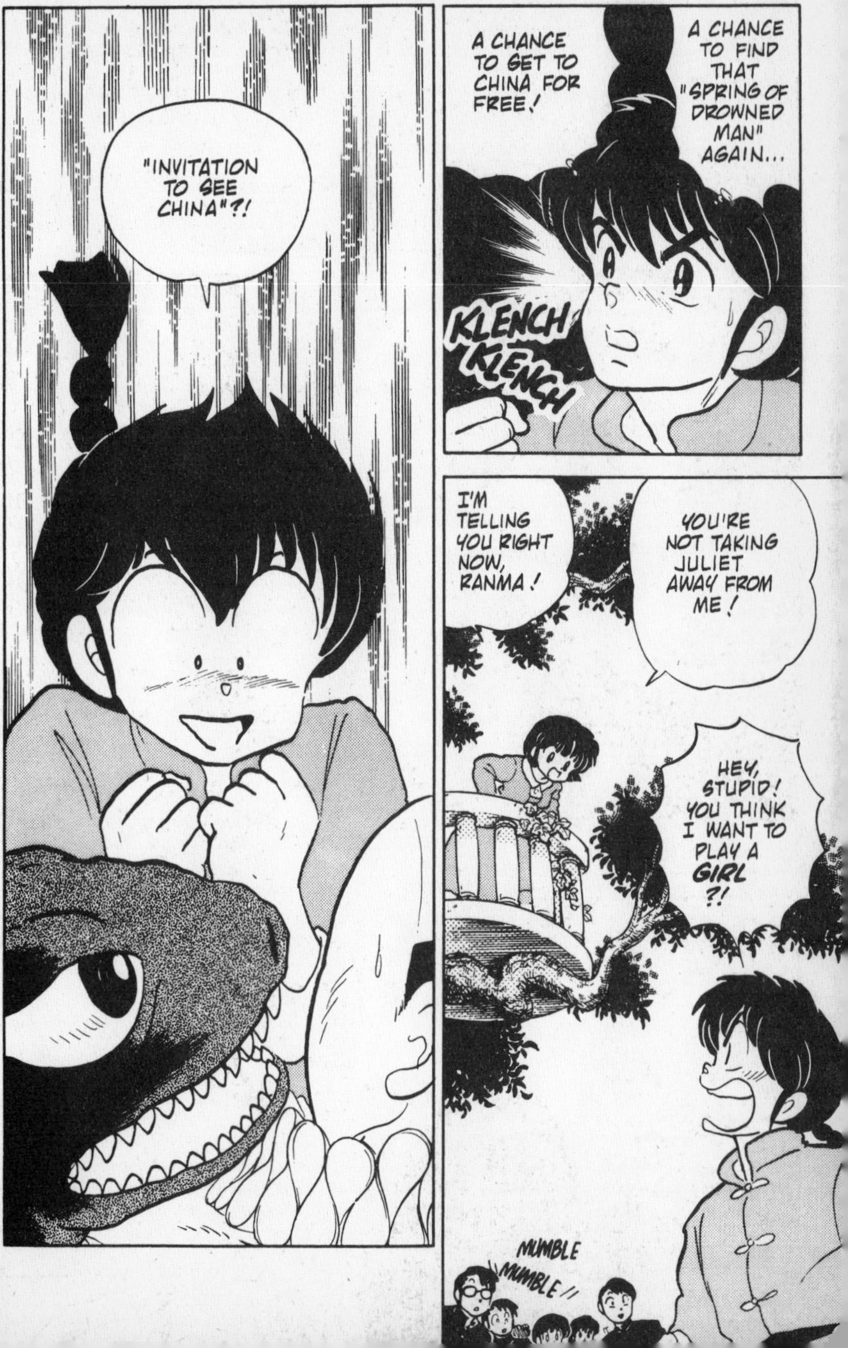
"INVITATION TO SEE CHINA"?!
A CHANCE TO GET TO CHINA FOR FREE!
A CHANCE TO FIND THAT "SPRING OF DROWNED MAN" AGAIN...
KLENCH
KLENCH
I'M TELLING YOU RIGHT NOW, RANMA!
YOU'RE NOT TAKING JULIET AWAY FROM ME!
HEY, STUPID! YOU THINK I WANT TO PLAY A GIRL?!
MUMBLE
MUMBLE

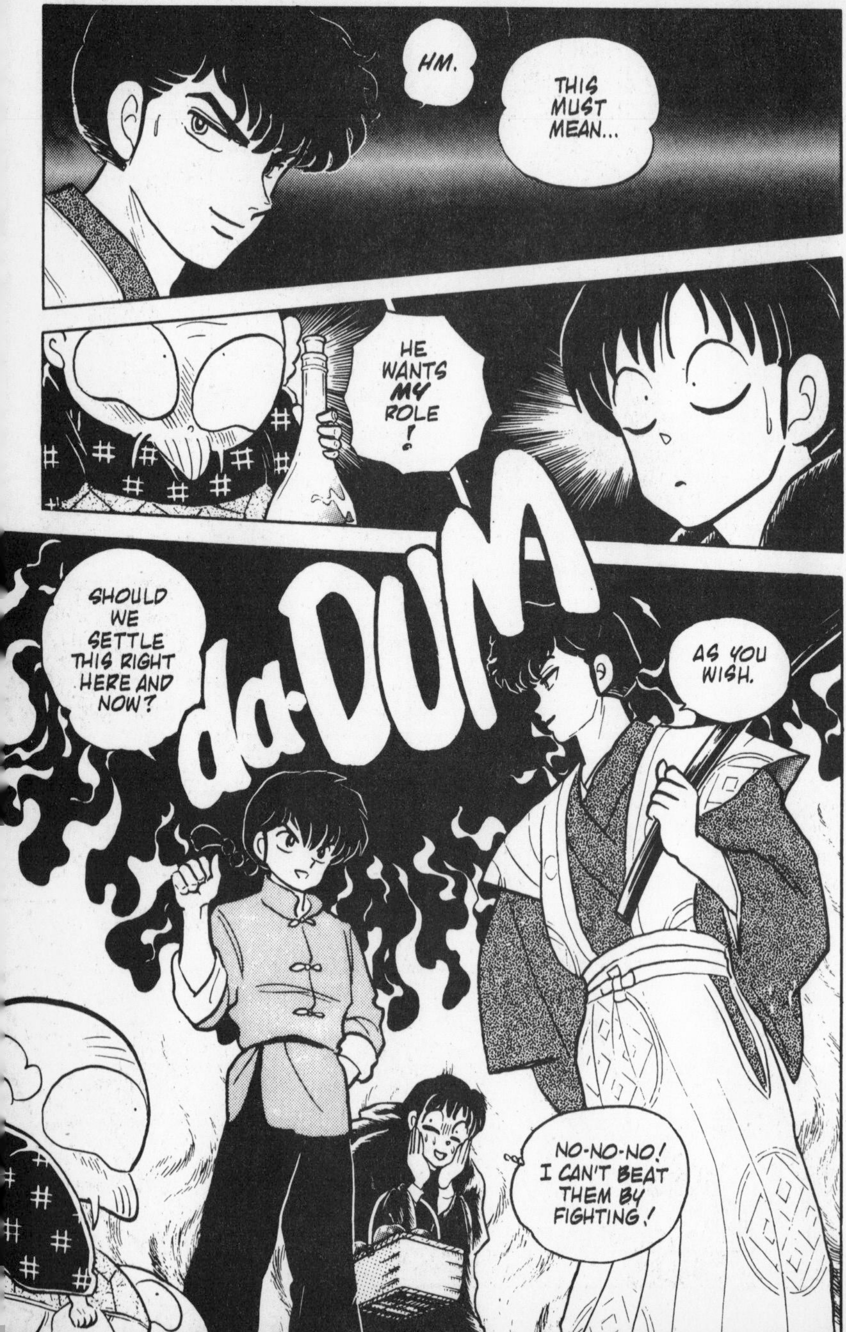

HM.
THIS MUST MEAN...
HE WANTS MY ROLE!
SHOULD WE SETTLE THIS RIGHT HERE AND NOW?
da-DUM
AS YOU WISH.
NO-NO-NO! I CAN'T BEAT THEM BY FIGHTING!

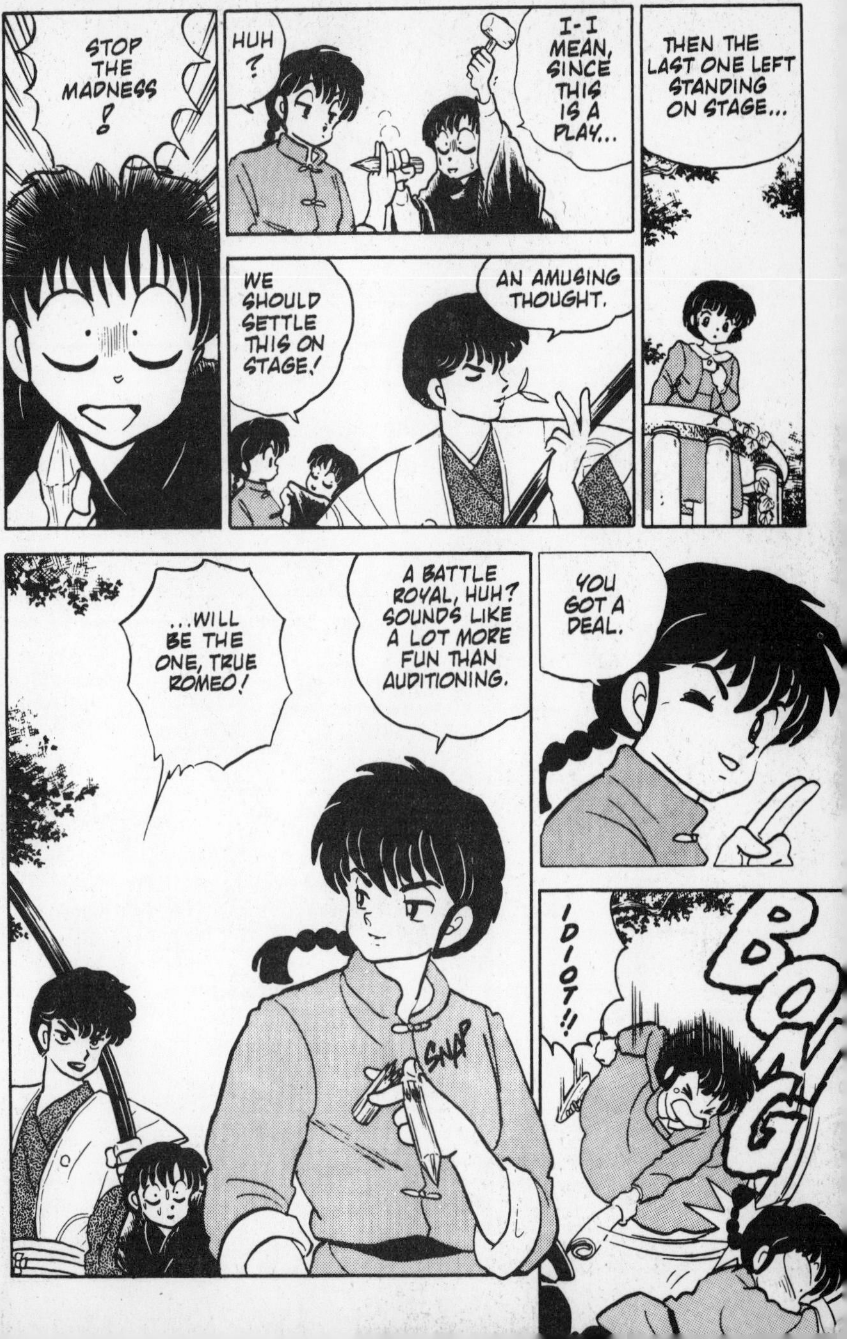
STOP THE MADNESS!
HUH?
I-I MEAN, SINCE THIS IS A PLAY...
WE SHOULD SETTLE THIS ON STAGE!
AN AMUSING THOUGHT.
THEN THE LAST ONE LEFT STANDING ON STAGE...
...WILL BE THE ONE, TRUE ROMEO!
A BATTLE ROYAL, HUH? SOUNDS LIKE A LOT MORE FUN THAN AUDITIONING.
SNAP
YOU GOT A DEAL.
IDIOT!!
BONG

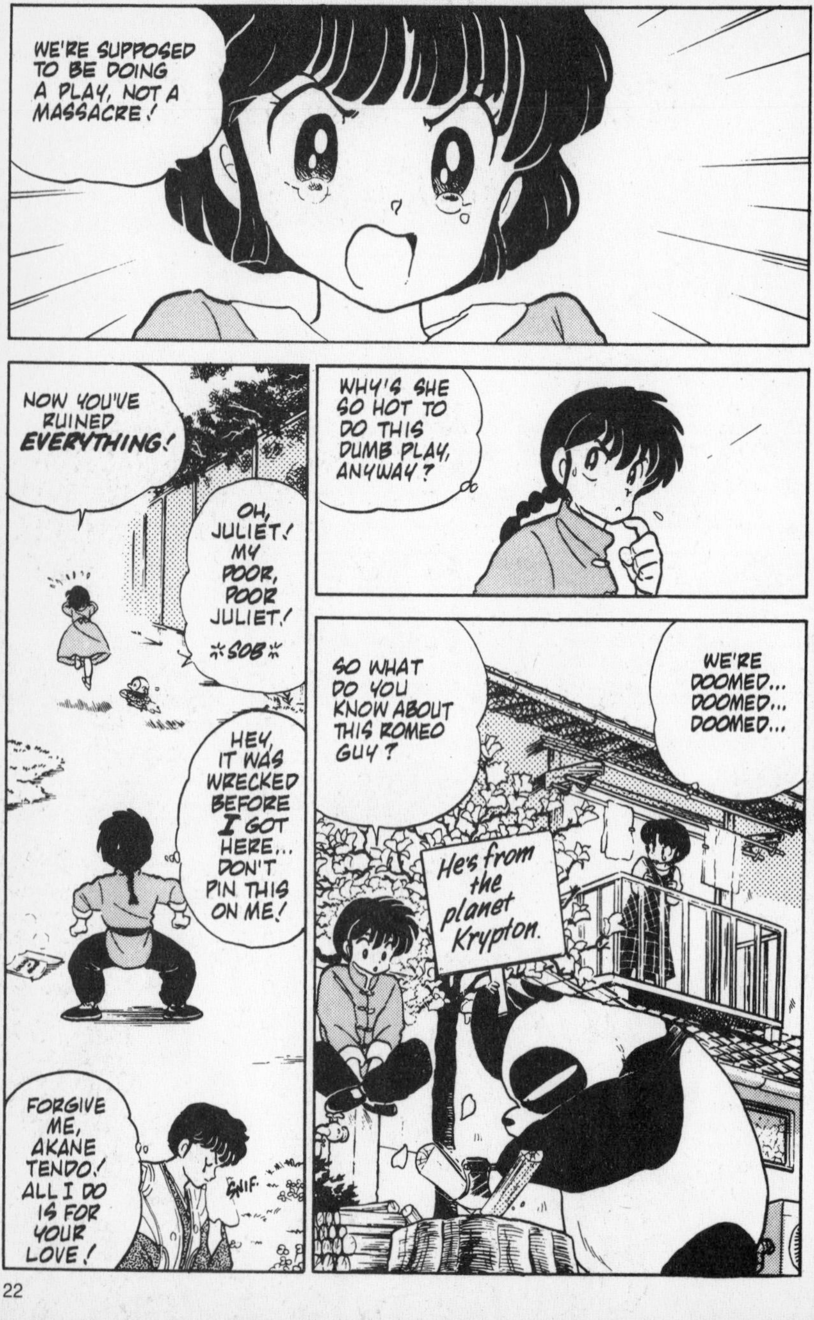
WE'RE SUPPOSED TO BE DOING A PLAY, NOT A MASSACRE!
NOW YOU'VE RUINED EVERYTHING!
OH, JULIET! MY POOR, POOR JULIET!
SOB
HEY, IT WAS WRECKED BEFORE I GOT HERE... DON'T PIN THIS ON ME!
FORGIVE ME, AKANE TENDO! ALL I DO IS FOR YOUR LOVE!
SNIF
WHY'S SHE SO HOT TO DO THIS DUMB PLAY, ANYWAY?
SO WHAT DO YOU KNOW ABOUT THIS ROMEO GUY?
He's from the planet Krypton.
WE'RE DOOMED... DOOMED... DOOMED...

Part 2

ROMEO? ROMEO? ROMEO!?

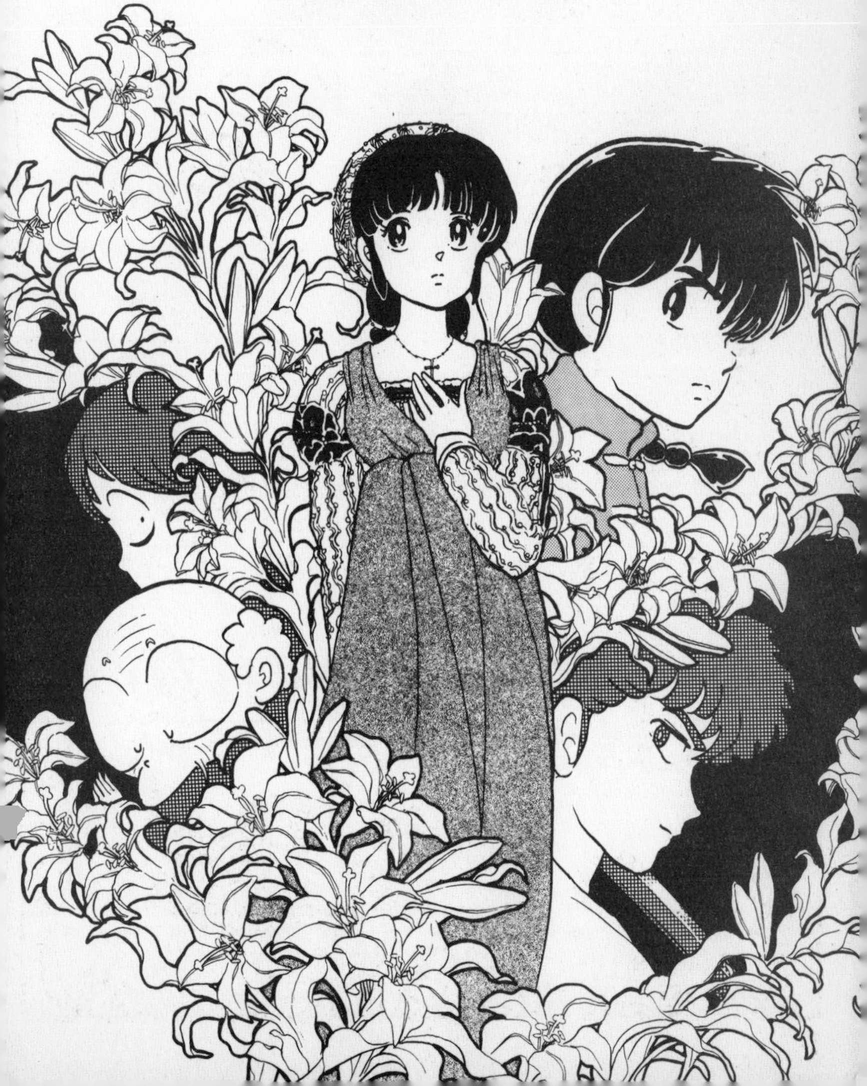

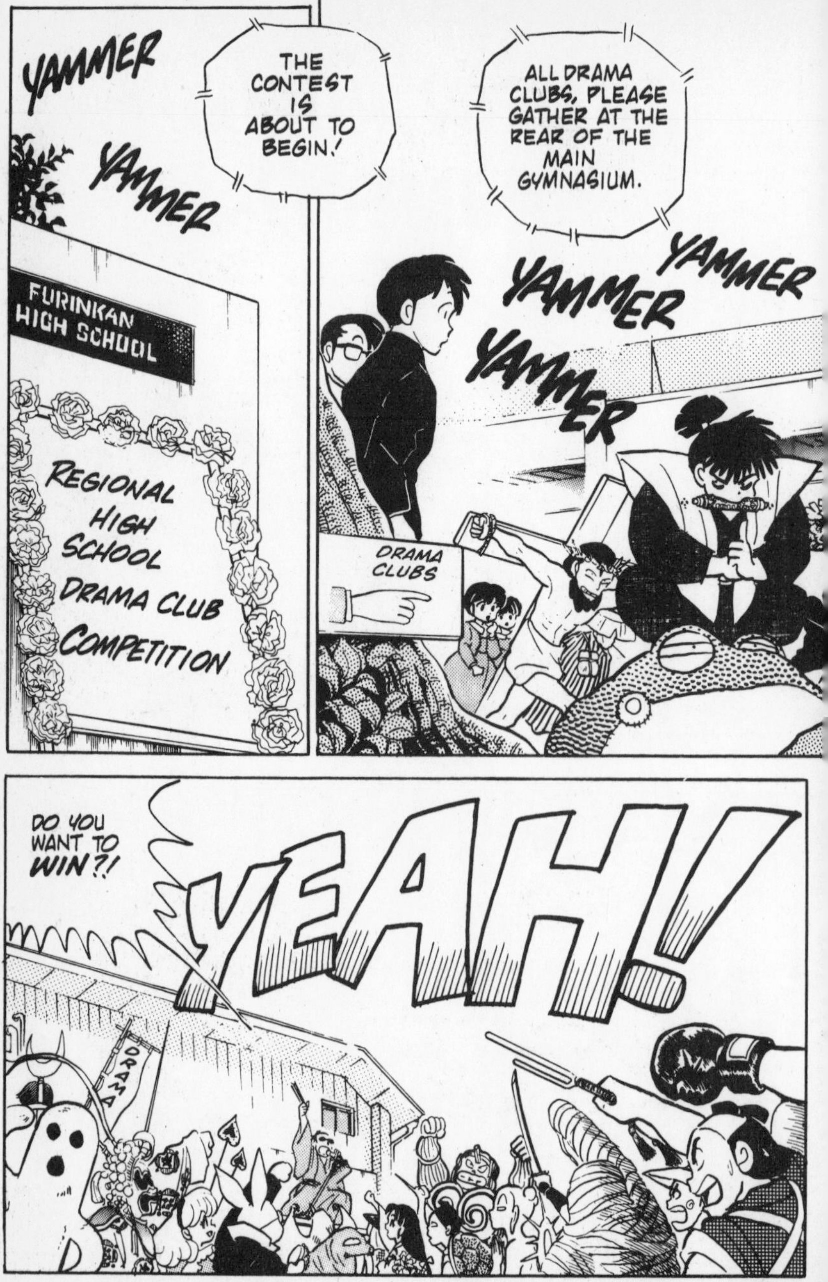
YAMMER
YAMMER
FURINKAN HIGH SCHOOL
REGIONAL HIGH SCHOOL DRAMA CLUB COMPETITION
THE CONTEST IS ABOUT TO BEGIN!
ALL DRAMA CLUBS, PLEASE GATHER AT THE REAR OF THE MAIN GYMNASIUM.
YAMMER
YAMMER
YAMMER
DRAMA CLUBS
DO YOU WANT TO WIN?!
YEAH!
DRAMA

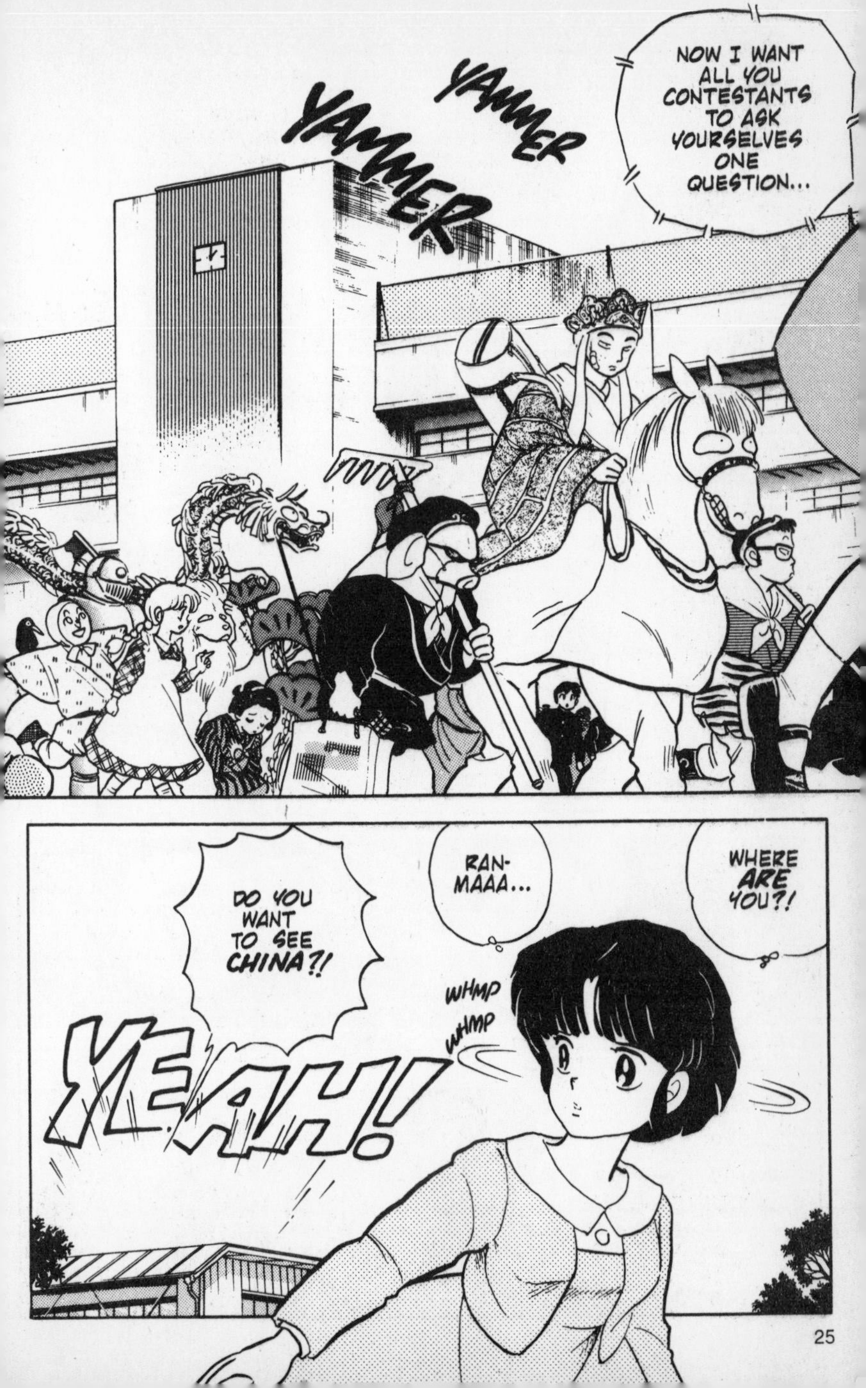
YAMMER
YAMMER
NOW I WANT ALL YOU CONTESTANTS TO ASK YOURSELVES ONE QUESTION...
DO YOU WANT TO SEE **CHINA**?!
YEAH!
RAN-MAAA...
WHMP
WHMP
WHERE **ARE** YOU?!

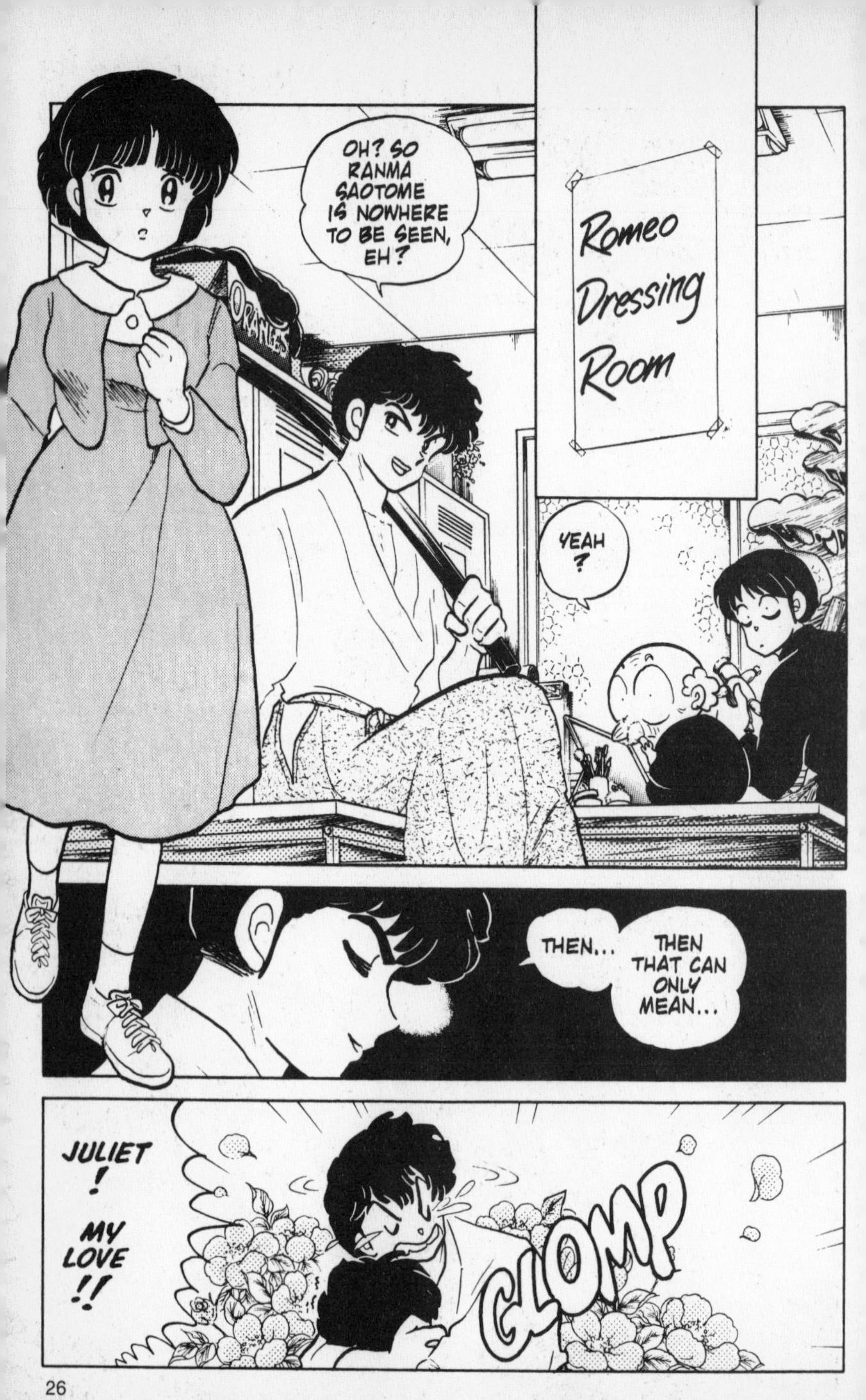

OH? SO RANMA SAOTOME IS NOWHERE TO BE SEEN, EH?
Romeo Dressing Room
YEAH?
THEN...
THEN THAT CAN ONLY MEAN...
JULIET! MY LOVE!!
CLOMP

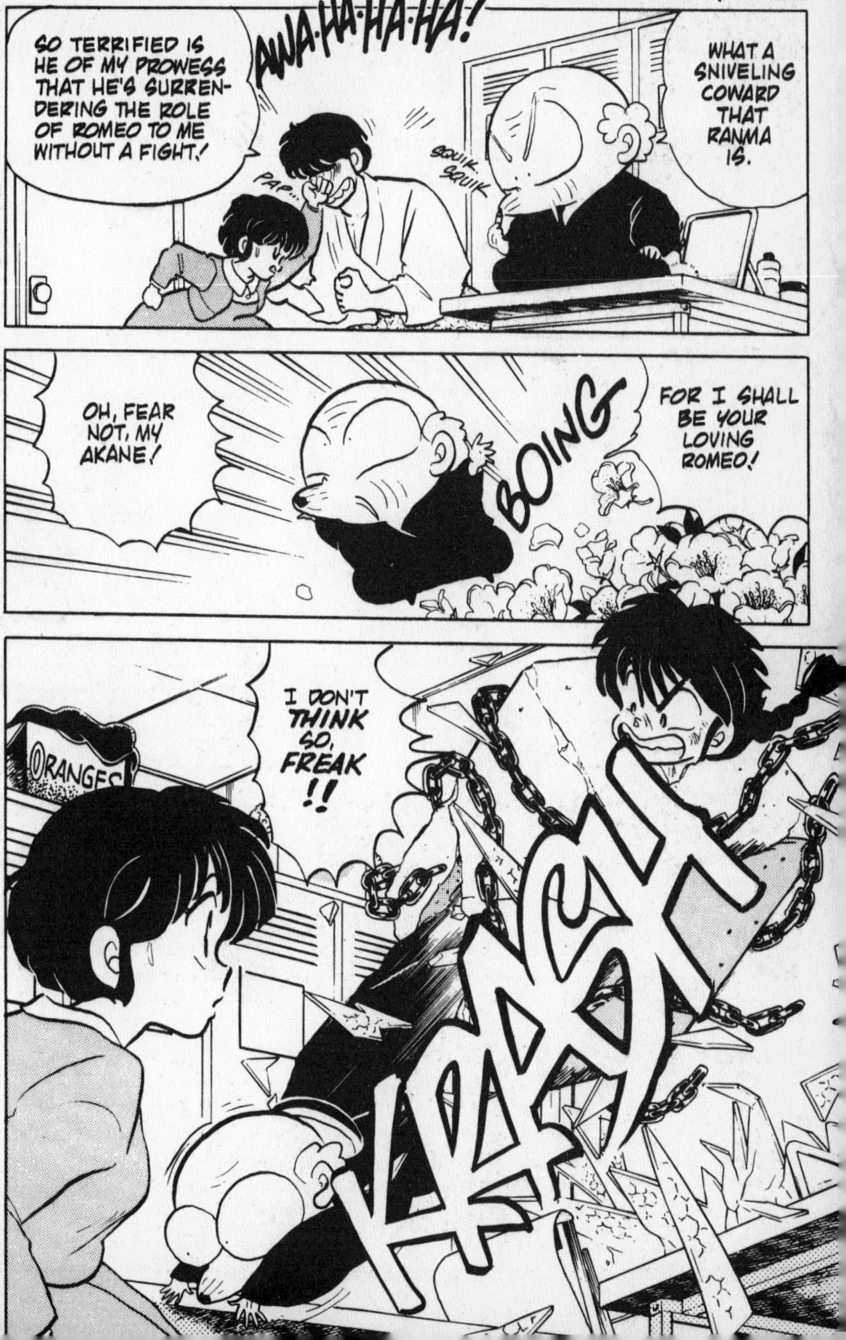
SO TERRIFIED IS HE OF MY PROWESS THAT HE'S SURREN-DERING THE ROLE OF ROMEO TO ME WITHOUT A FIGHT!
AWA-HA-HA-HA!
PAP...
SQUIK SQUIK
WHAT A SNIVELING COWARD THAT RANMA IS.
OH, FEAR NOT, MY AKANE!
BOING
FOR I SHALL BE YOUR LOVING ROMEO!
ORANGES
I DON'T THINK SO, FREAK!!
KRASH

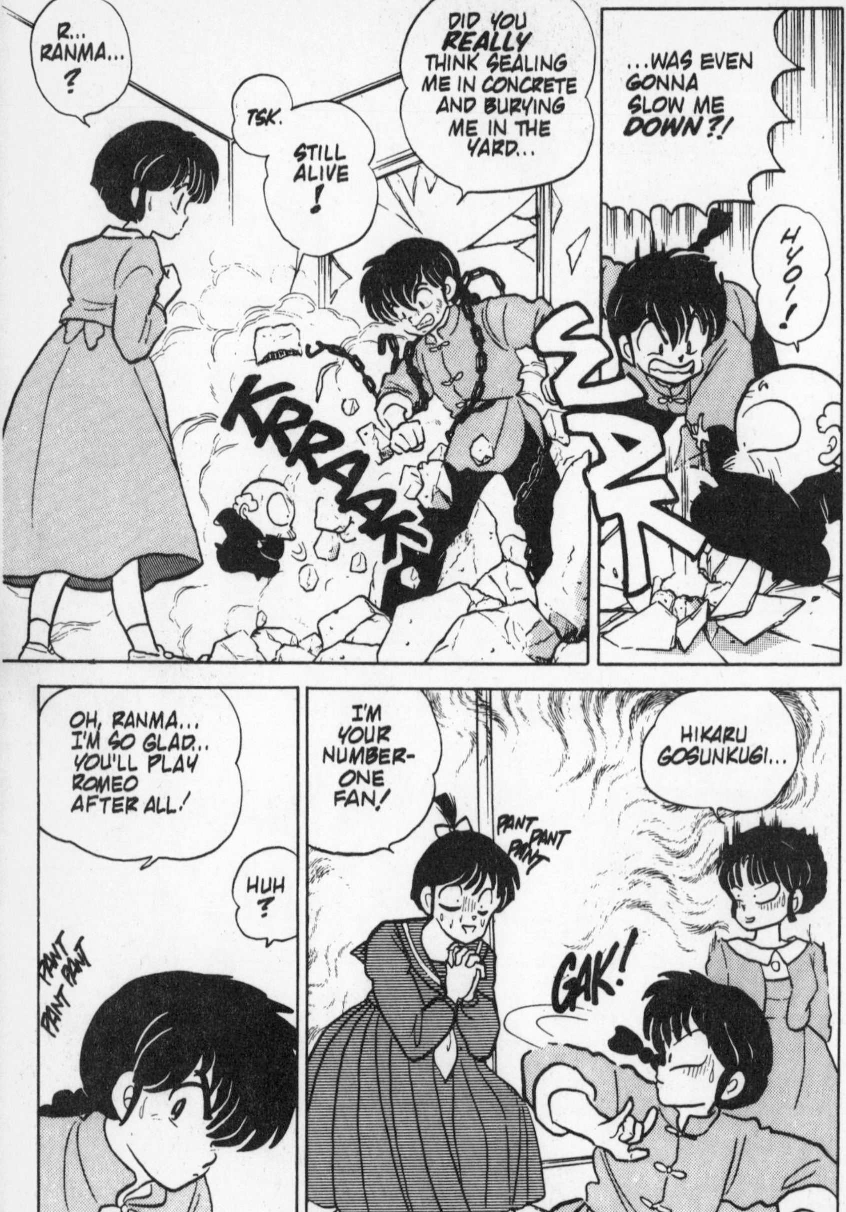
R... RANMA...?
TSK.
STILL ALIVE!
DID YOU REALLY THINK SEALING ME IN CONCRETE AND BURYING ME IN THE YARD...
KRRAAK!
...WAS EVEN GONNA SLOW ME DOWN?!
HYOI!
OH, RANMA... I'M SO GLAD... YOU'LL PLAY ROMEO AFTER ALL!
HUH?
PANT PANT PANT
I'M YOUR NUMBER-ONE FAN!
PANT PANT PANT
HIKARU GOSUNKUGI...
GAK!

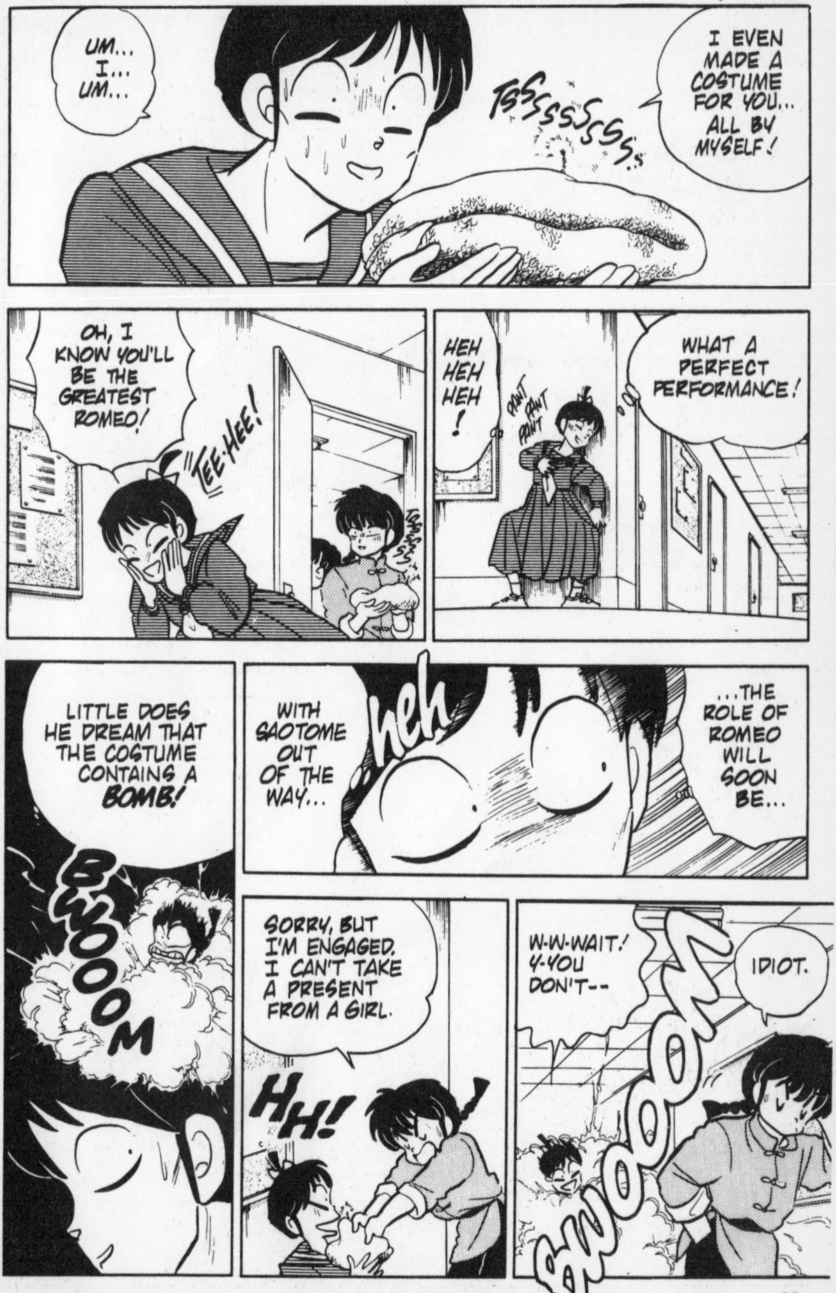
UM... I... UM...
TSSSSSSSSS
I EVEN MADE A COSTUME FOR YOU... ALL BY MYSELF!
OH, I KNOW YOU'LL BE THE GREATEST ROMEO!
TEE-HEE!
HEH HEH HEH!
PANT PANT PANT
WHAT A PERFECT PERFORMANCE!
LITTLE DOES HE DREAM THAT THE COSTUME CONTAINS A BOMB!
BWOOOM
WITH SAOTOME OUT OF THE WAY...
heh
...THE ROLE OF ROMEO WILL SOON BE...
SORRY, BUT I'M ENGAGED. I CAN'T TAKE A PRESENT FROM A GIRL.
HH!
W-W-WAIT! Y-YOU DON'T--
BWOOOM
IDIOT.

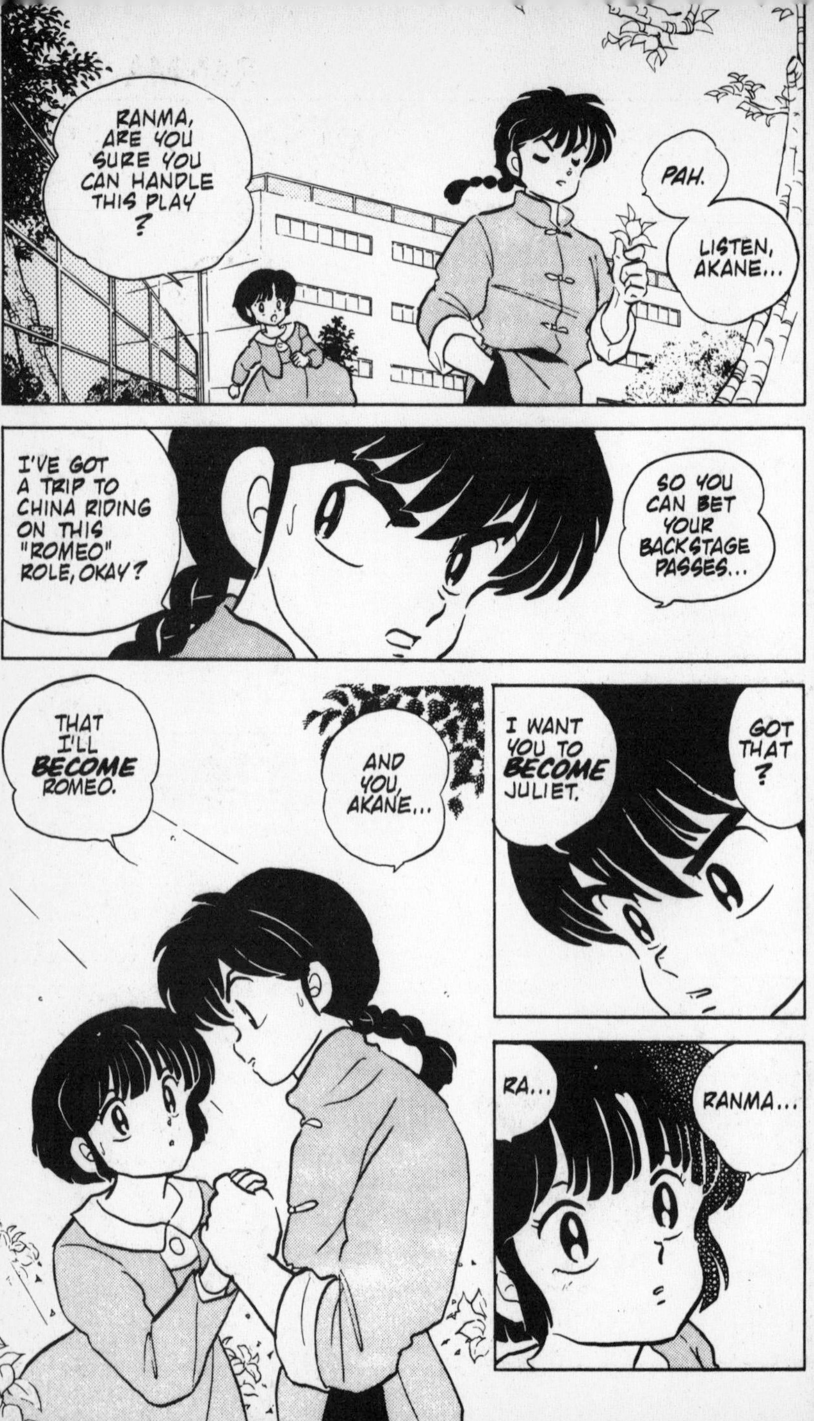
RANMA, ARE YOU SURE YOU CAN HANDLE THIS PLAY ?
PAH.
LISTEN, AKANE...
I'VE GOT A TRIP TO CHINA RIDING ON THIS "ROMEO" ROLE, OKAY?
SO YOU CAN BET YOUR BACKSTAGE PASSES...
THAT I'LL **BECOME** ROMEO.
AND YOU, AKANE...
I WANT YOU TO **BECOME** JULIET.
GOT THAT ?
RA...
RANMA...

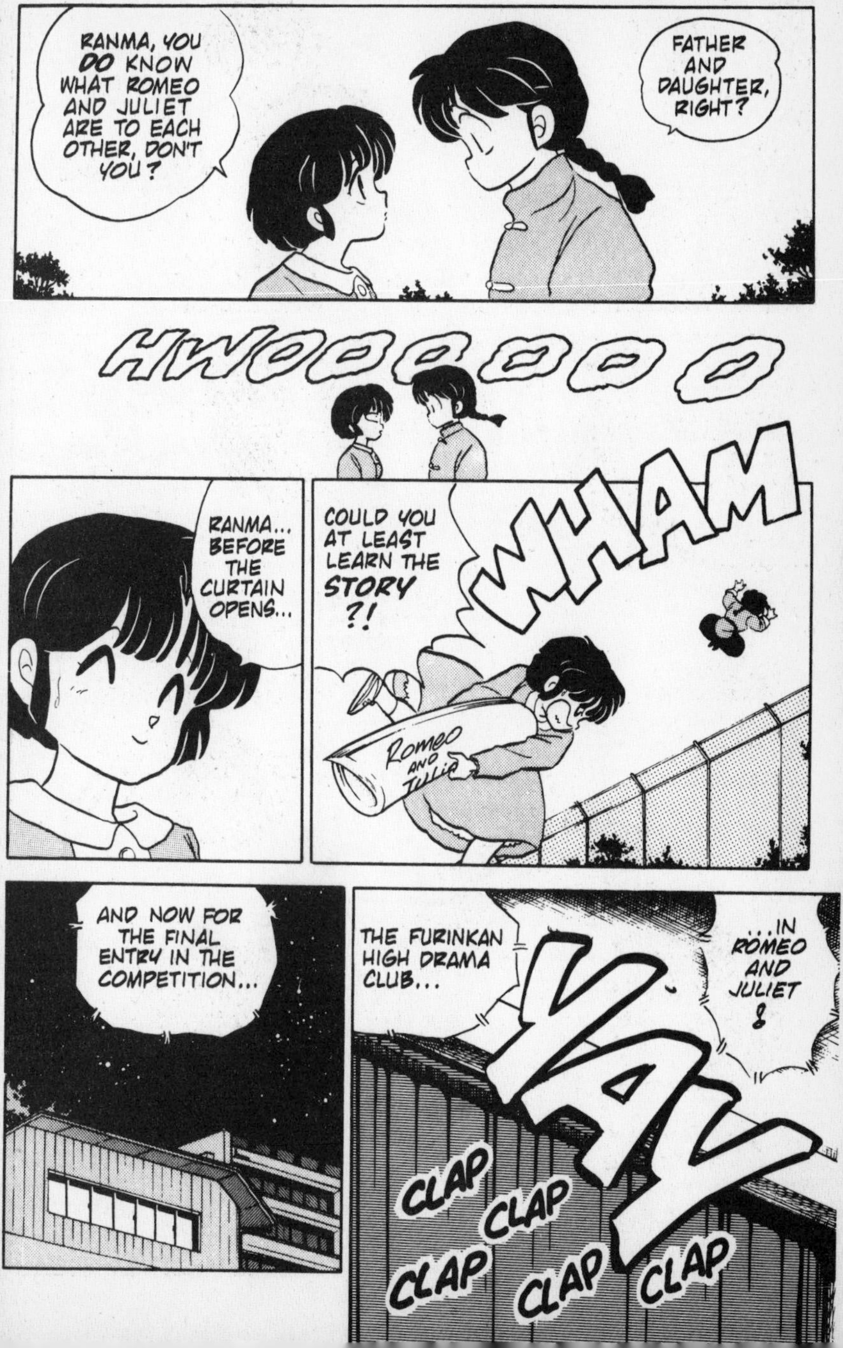
RANMA, YOU DO KNOW WHAT ROMEO AND JULIET ARE TO EACH OTHER, DON'T YOU?
FATHER AND DAUGHTER, RIGHT?
HWOOOOOOO
RANMA... BEFORE THE CURTAIN OPENS...
COULD YOU AT LEAST LEARN THE STORY ?!
WHAM
Romeo and Juliet
AND NOW FOR THE FINAL ENTRY IN THE COMPETITION...
THE FURINKAN HIGH DRAMA CLUB...
...IN ROMEO AND JULIET!
YAY
CLAP CLAP CLAP CLAP CLAP CLAP

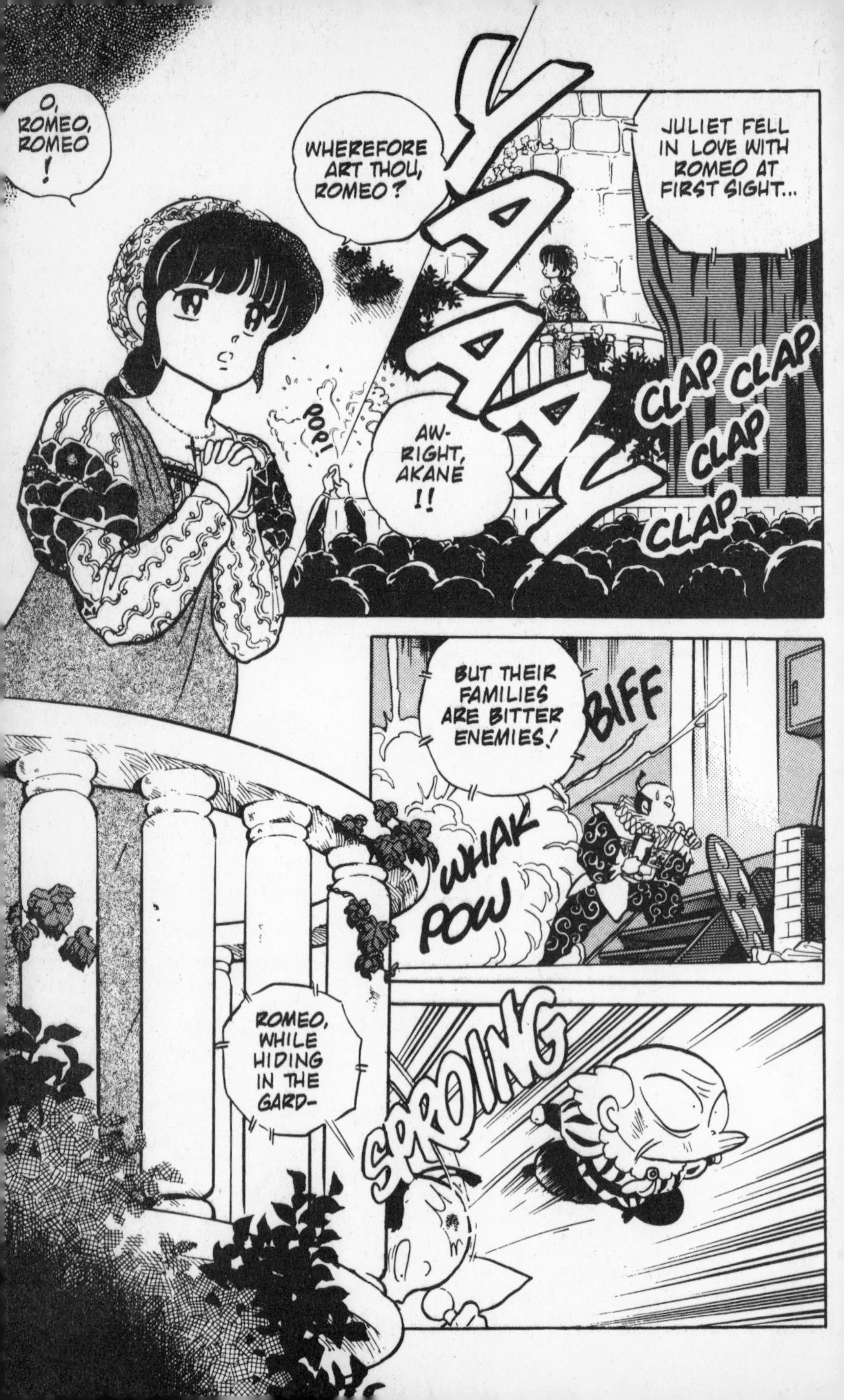
O, ROMEO, ROMEO!
ROMEO, WHILE HIDING IN THE GARD-
WHEREFORE ART THOU, ROMEO?
YAAAY
JULIET FELL IN LOVE WITH ROMEO AT FIRST SIGHT...
POP!
AW-RIGHT, AKANE!!
CLAP CLAP CLAP CLAP CLAP
BUT THEIR FAMILIES ARE BITTER ENEMIES!
BIFF
WHAK
POW
SPROING

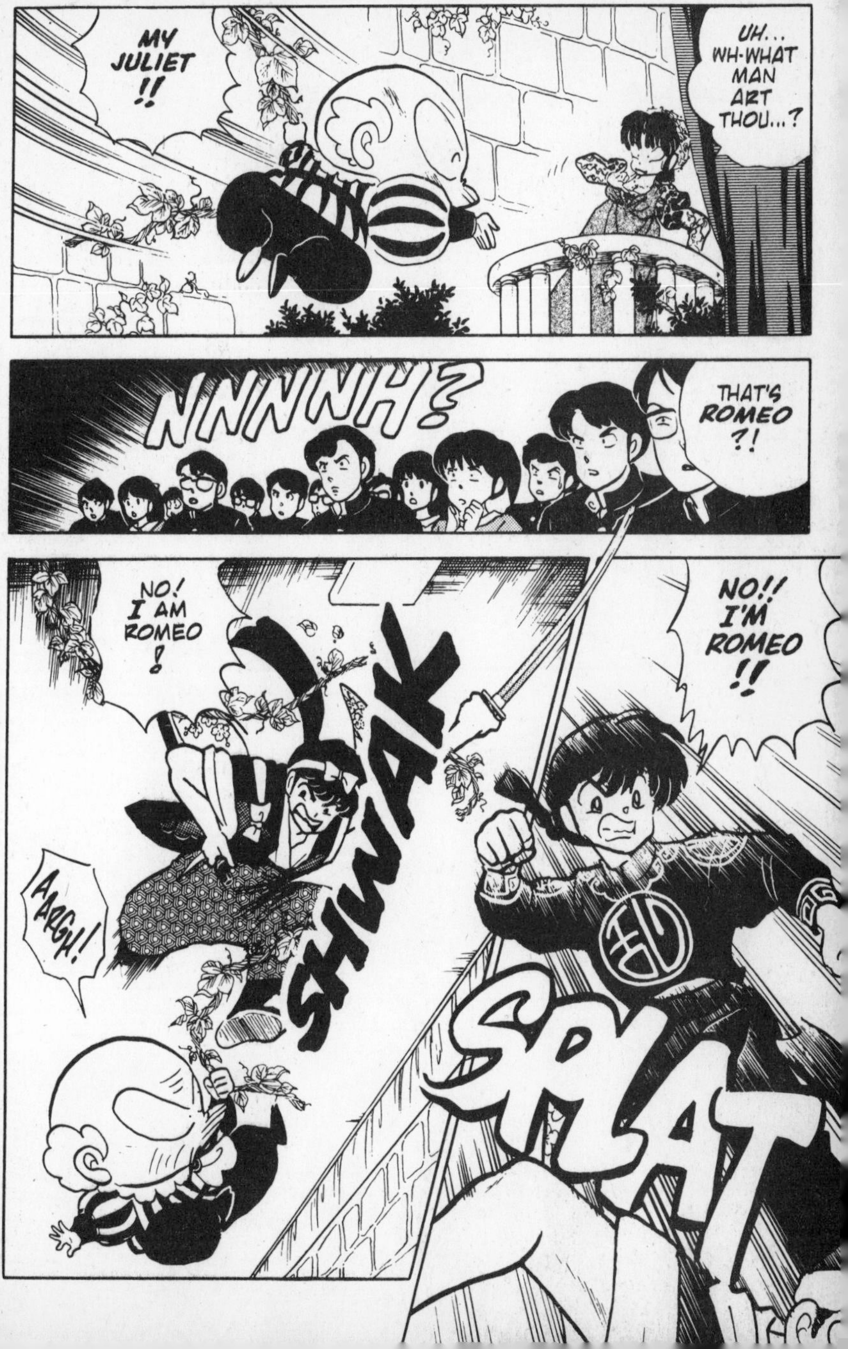
MY JULIET !!
UH... WH-WHAT MAN ART THOU...?
NNNNH?
THAT'S ROMEO ?!
NO! I AM ROMEO !
NO!! I'M ROMEO !!
SHWAK
AARGH!
SPLAT

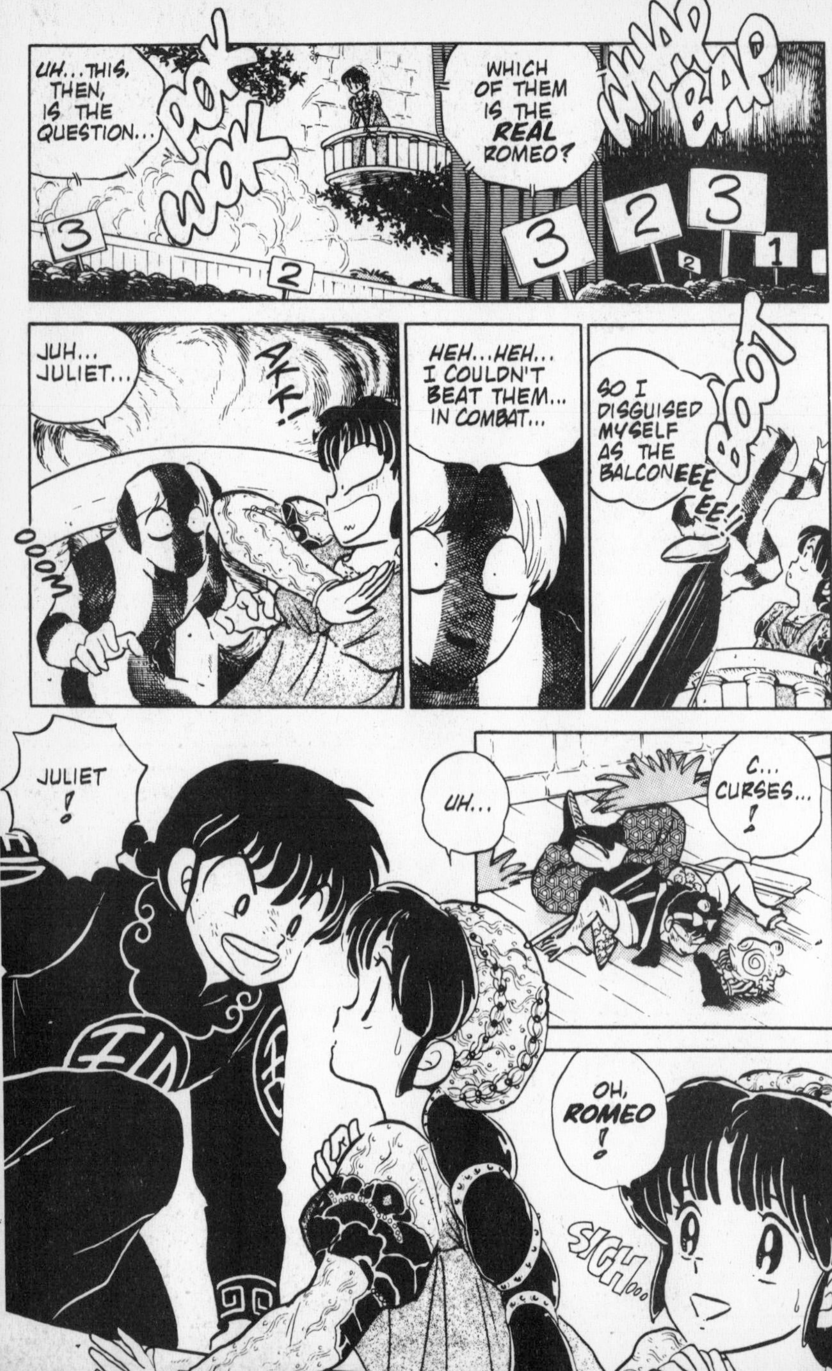
UH...THIS, THEN, IS THE QUESTION...
POK WOK
WHICH OF THEM IS THE REAL ROMEO?
WHAP BAP
3
2
3
2
3
2
1
JUH... JULIET...
AKK!!
OOOM
HEH...HEH... I COULDN'T BEAT THEM... IN COMBAT...
SO I DISGUISED MYSELF AS THE BALCONEEE EE!!
BOOT
JULIET!
UH...
C... CURSES...!
OH, ROMEO!
SIGH...

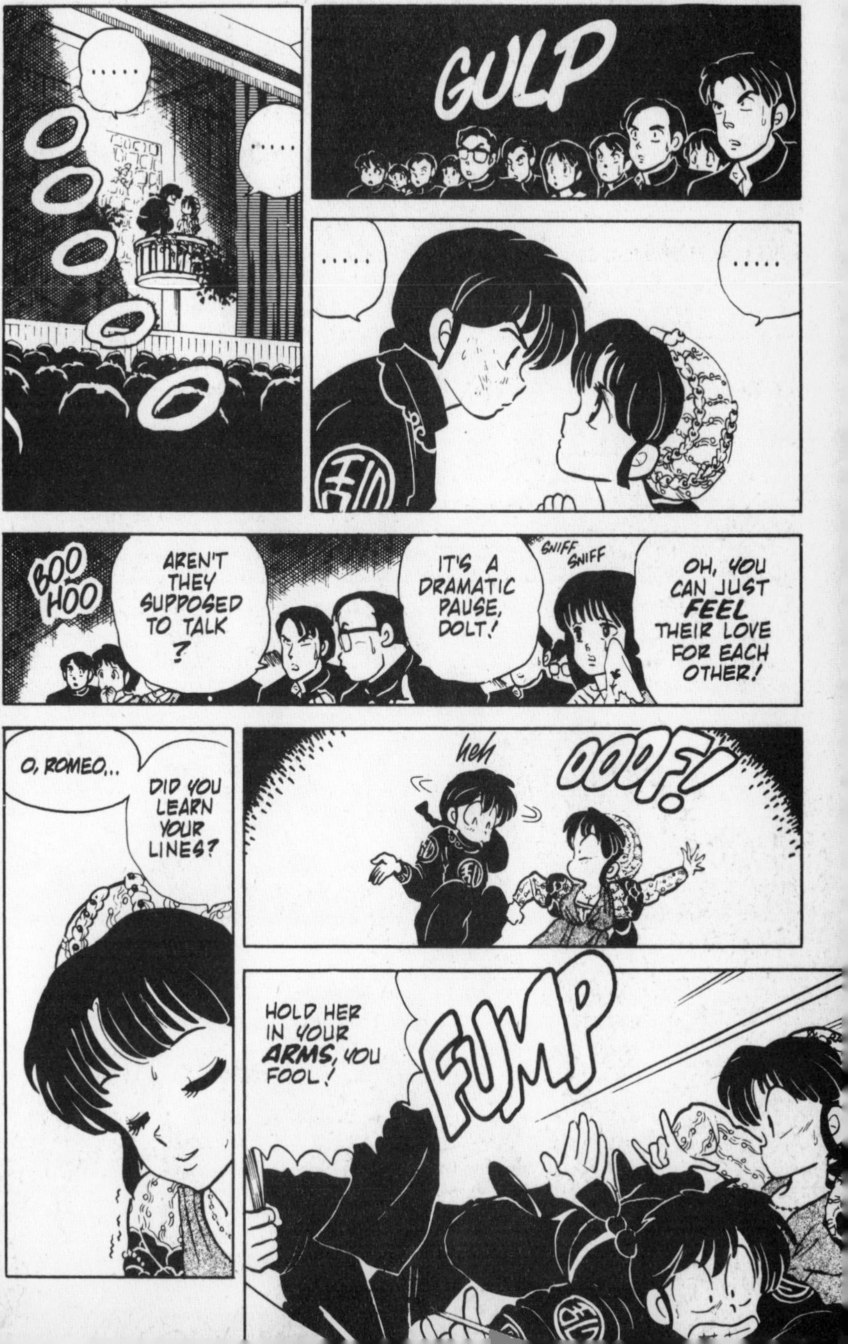

......
......
GULP
......
......
BOO HOO
AREN'T THEY SUPPOSED TO TALK ?
IT'S A DRAMATIC PAUSE, DOLT!
SNIFF SNIFF
OH, YOU CAN JUST FEEL THEIR LOVE FOR EACH OTHER!
O, ROMEO...
DID YOU LEARN YOUR LINES?
heh
OOOF!
HOLD HER IN YOUR ARMS, YOU FOOL!
FUMP

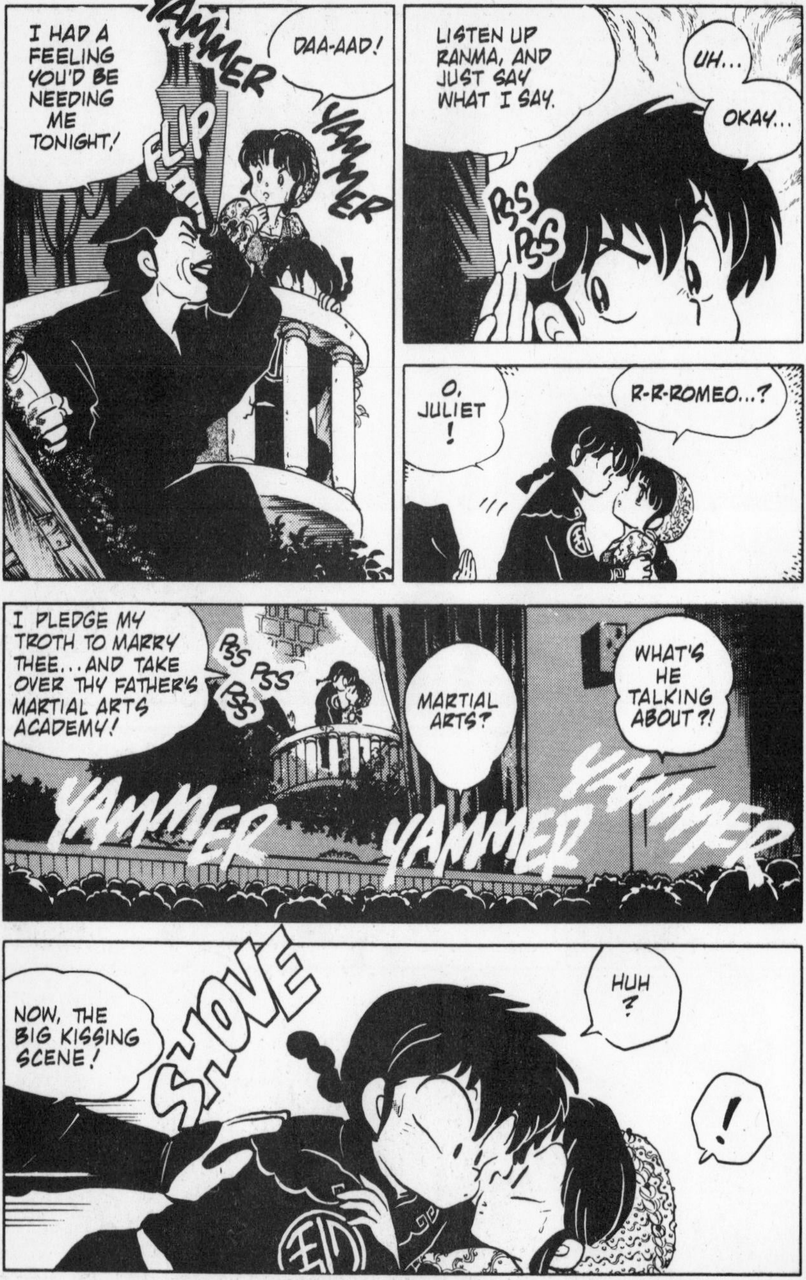
I HAD A FEELING YOU'D BE NEEDING ME TONIGHT!
YAMMER
DAA-AAD!
YAMMER
FLIP
LISTEN UP RANMA, AND JUST SAY WHAT I SAY.
UH...
OKAY...
PSS PSS
O, JULIET!
R-R-ROMEO...?
I PLEDGE MY TROTH TO MARRY THEE... AND TAKE OVER THY FATHER'S MARTIAL ARTS ACADEMY!
PSS PSS PSS
MARTIAL ARTS?
WHAT'S HE TALKING ABOUT?!
YAMMER
YAMMER
YAMMER
NOW, THE BIG KISSING SCENE!
SHOVE
HUH?
!

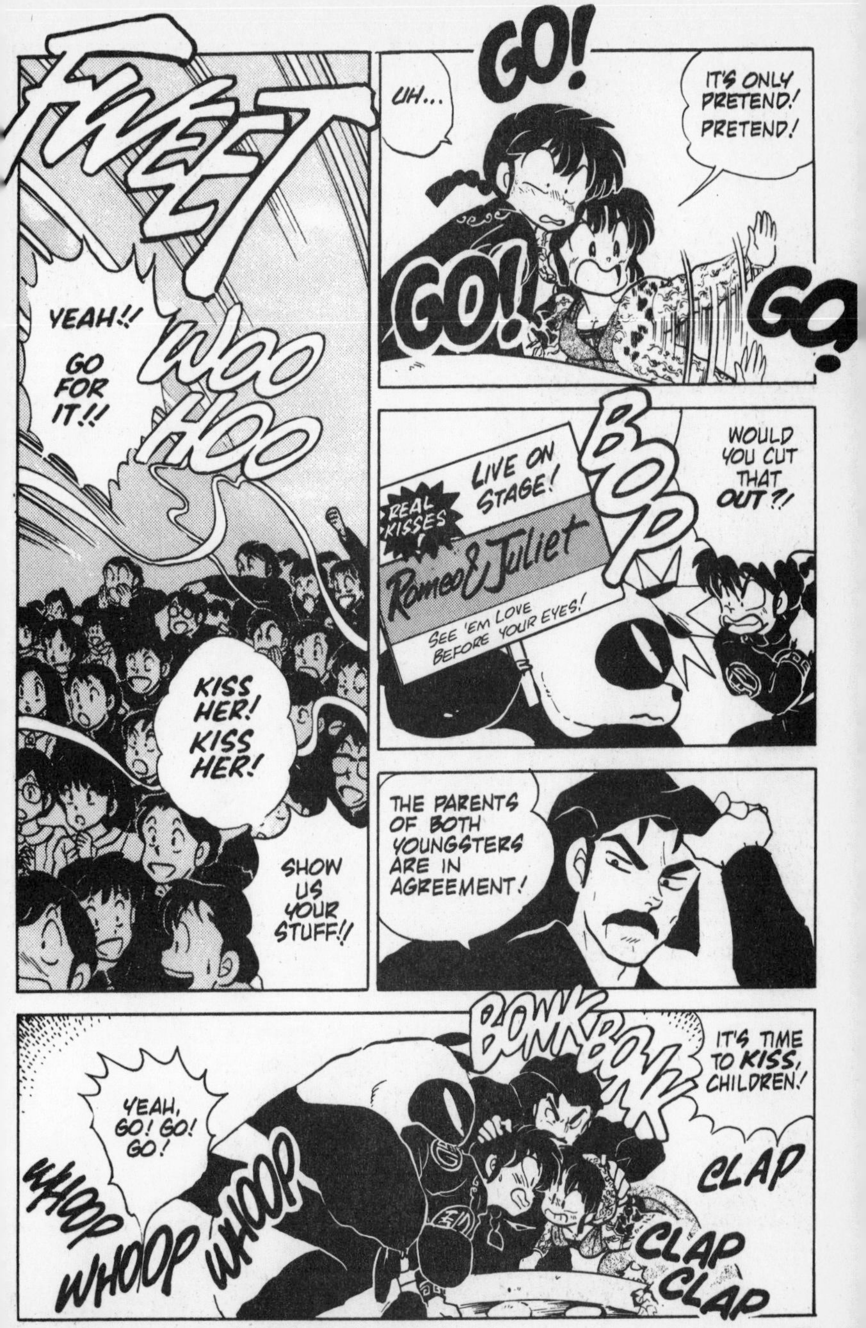
FWEET
YEAH!!
GO FOR IT!!
WOO HOO
KISS HER! KISS HER!
SHOW US YOUR STUFF!!
GO!
UH...
IT'S ONLY PRETEND! PRETEND!
GO!
GO!
REAL KISSES!
LIVE ON STAGE!
Romeo & Juliet
SEE 'EM LOVE BEFORE YOUR EYES!
BOOP
WOULD YOU CUT THAT OUT?!
THE PARENTS OF BOTH YOUNGSTERS ARE IN AGREEMENT!
BONK BONK
IT'S TIME TO KISS, CHILDREN!
YEAH, GO! GO! GO!
WHOOP
WHOOP
WHOOP
CLAP
CLAP
CLAP

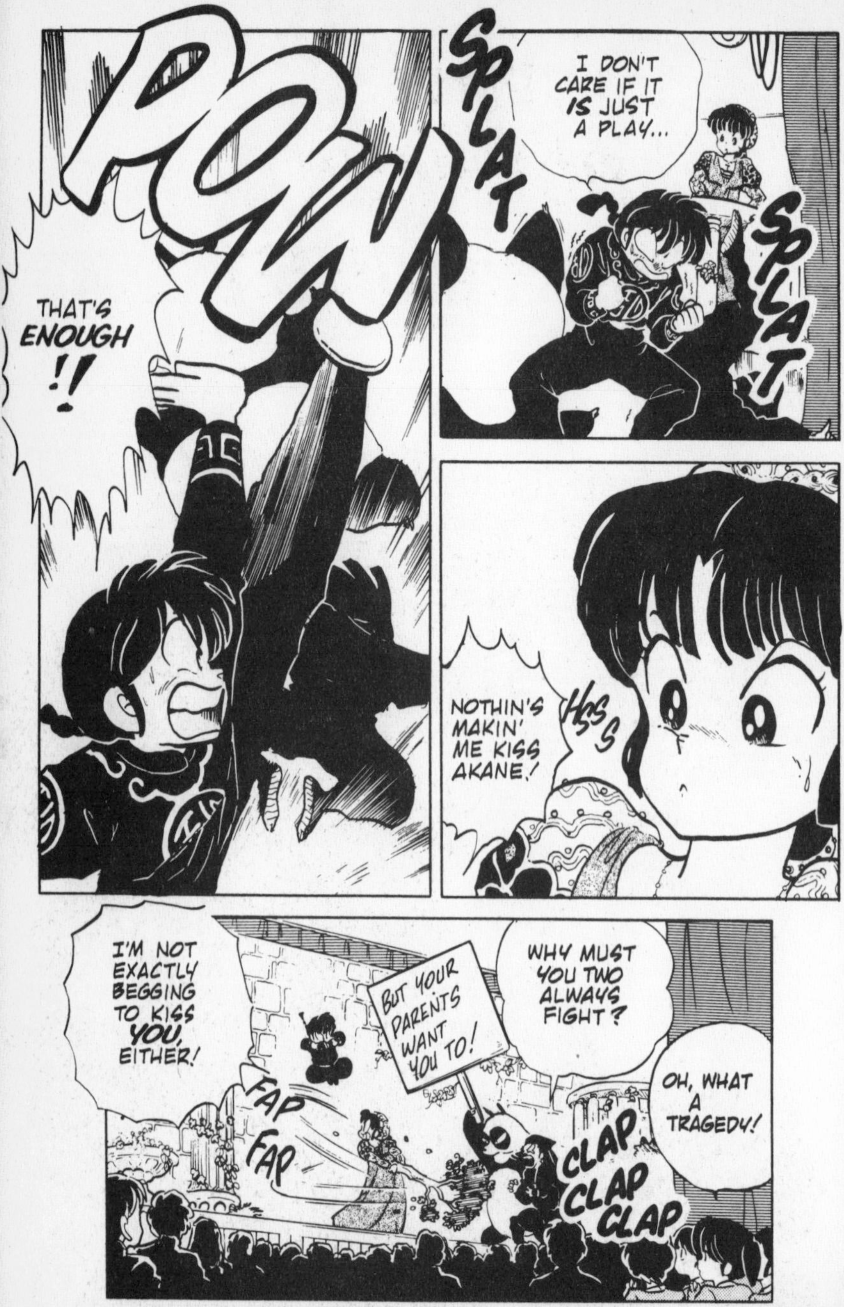
POW
THAT'S ENOUGH !!
SPLAT
I DON'T CARE IF IT IS JUST A PLAY...
SPLAT
NOTHIN'S MAKIN' ME KISS AKANE!
HSSS
I'M NOT EXACTLY BEGGING TO KISS YOU, EITHER!
BUT YOUR PARENTS WANT YOU TO!
FAP FAP
WHY MUST YOU TWO ALWAYS FIGHT?
OH, WHAT A TRAGEDY!
CLAP CLAP CLAP

Part 3
NOT YOUR TYPICAL JULIET

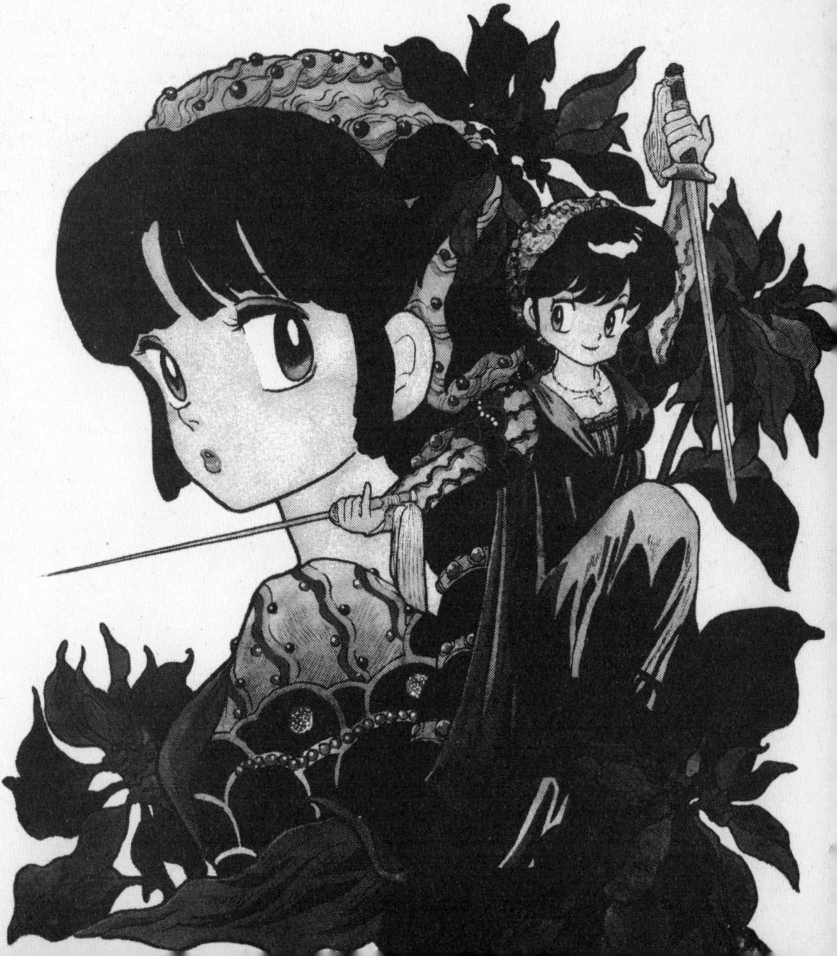

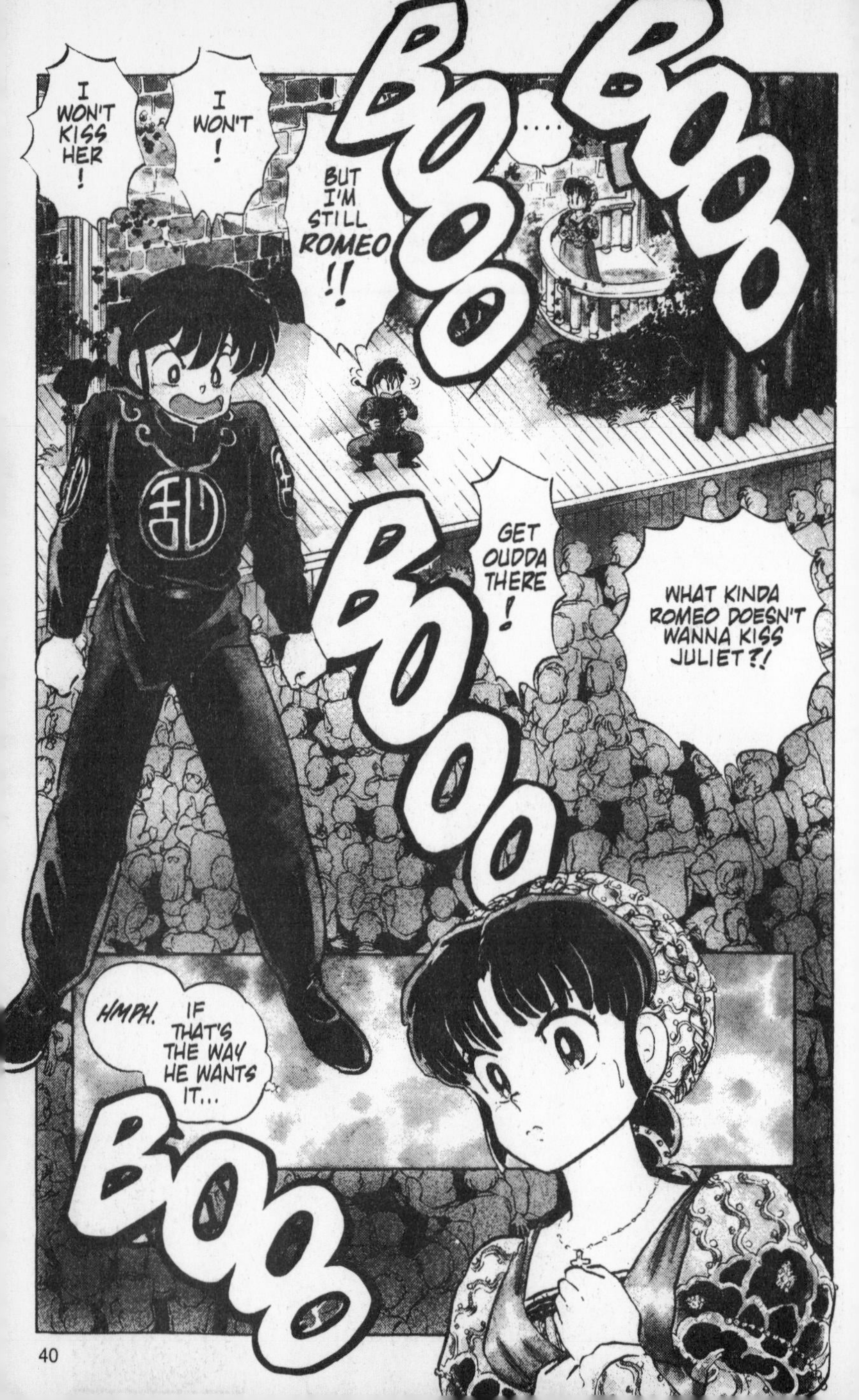
I WON'T KISS HER !
I WON'T !
BOOOO
.....
BOOOO
BUT I'M STILL ROMEO !!
GET OUDDA THERE !
WHAT KINDA ROMEO DOESN'T WANNA KISS JULIET ?!
BOOOOO
HMPH. IF THAT'S THE WAY HE WANTS IT...
BOOO

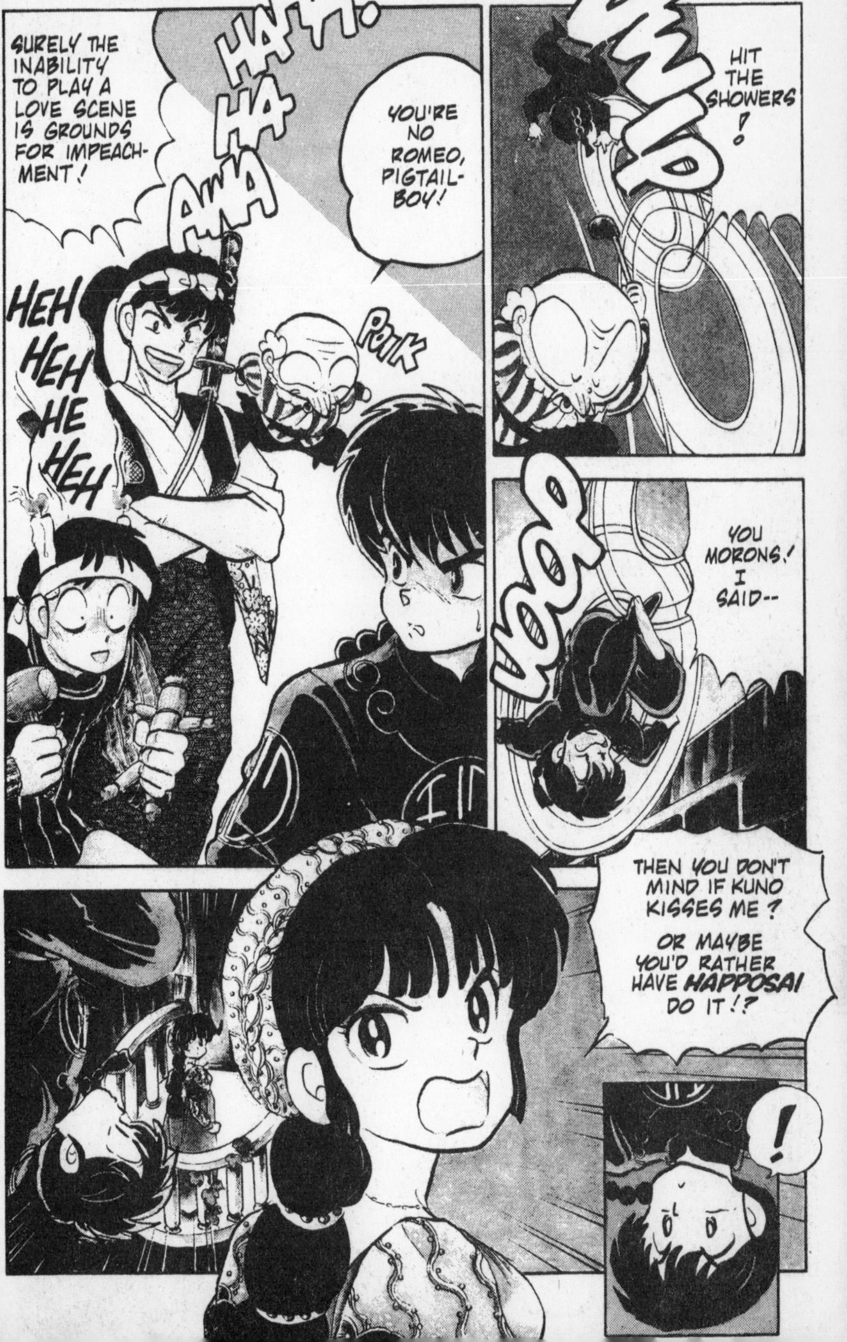

SURELY THE INABILITY TO PLAY A LOVE SCENE IS GROUNDS FOR IMPEACHMENT!
AHA HA HAHA!
YOU'RE NO ROMEO, PIGTAIL-BOY!
HEH HEH HE HEH
POK
WHIP
HIT THE SHOWERS!
WOOP
YOU MORONS! I SAID--
THEN YOU DON'T MIND IF KUNO KISSES ME?
OR MAYBE YOU'D RATHER HAVE **HAPPOSAI** DO IT!?
!

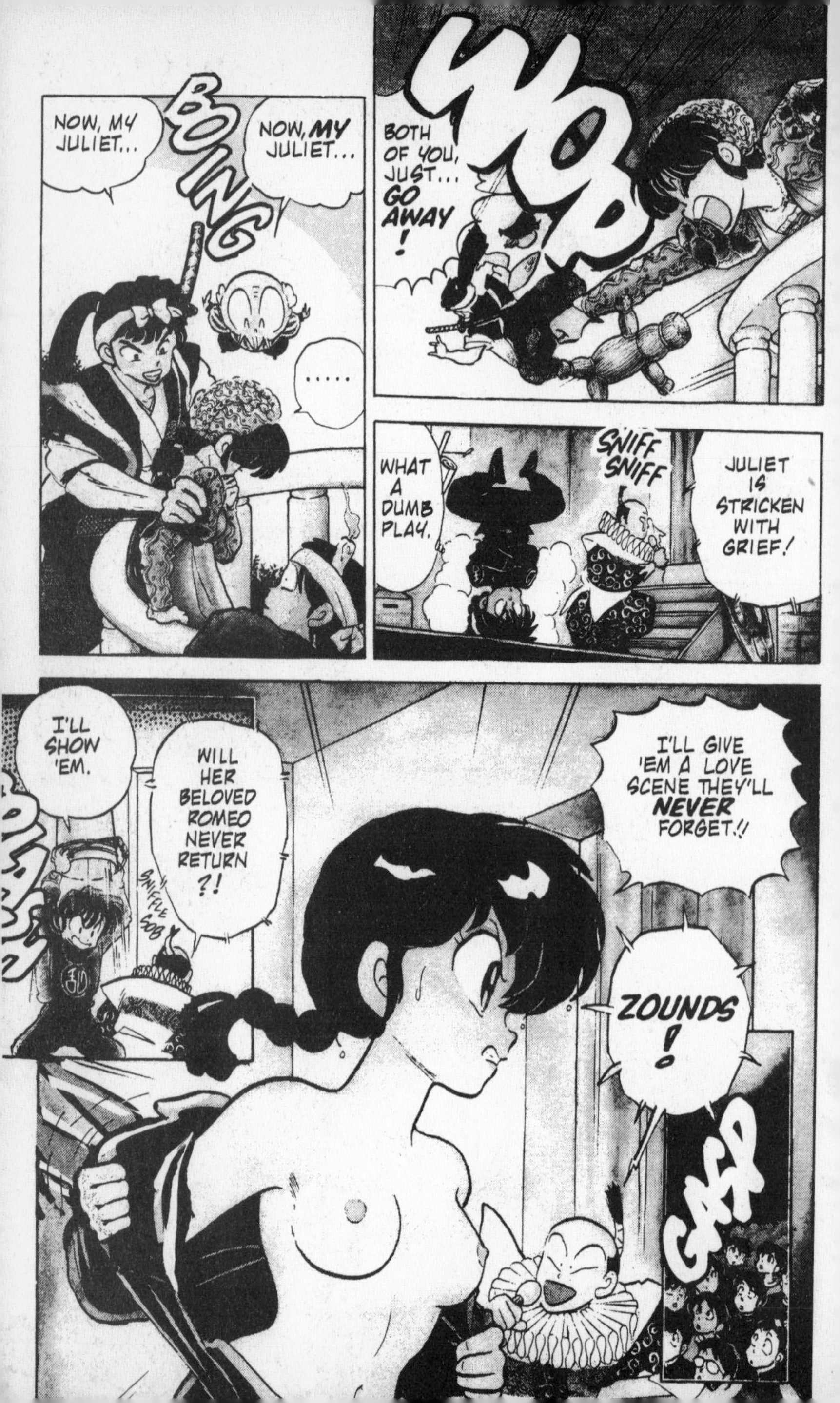
NOW, MY JULIET...
BOING
NOW, MY JULIET...
.....
WOMP
BOTH OF YOU, JUST... GO AWAY!
WHAT A DUMB PLAY.
SNIFF SNIFF
JULIET IS STRICKEN WITH GRIEF!
I'LL SHOW 'EM.
WILL HER BELOVED ROMEO NEVER RETURN?!
SNIFFLE SOB
I'LL GIVE 'EM A LOVE SCENE THEY'LL NEVER FORGET!!
ZOUNDS!
GASP

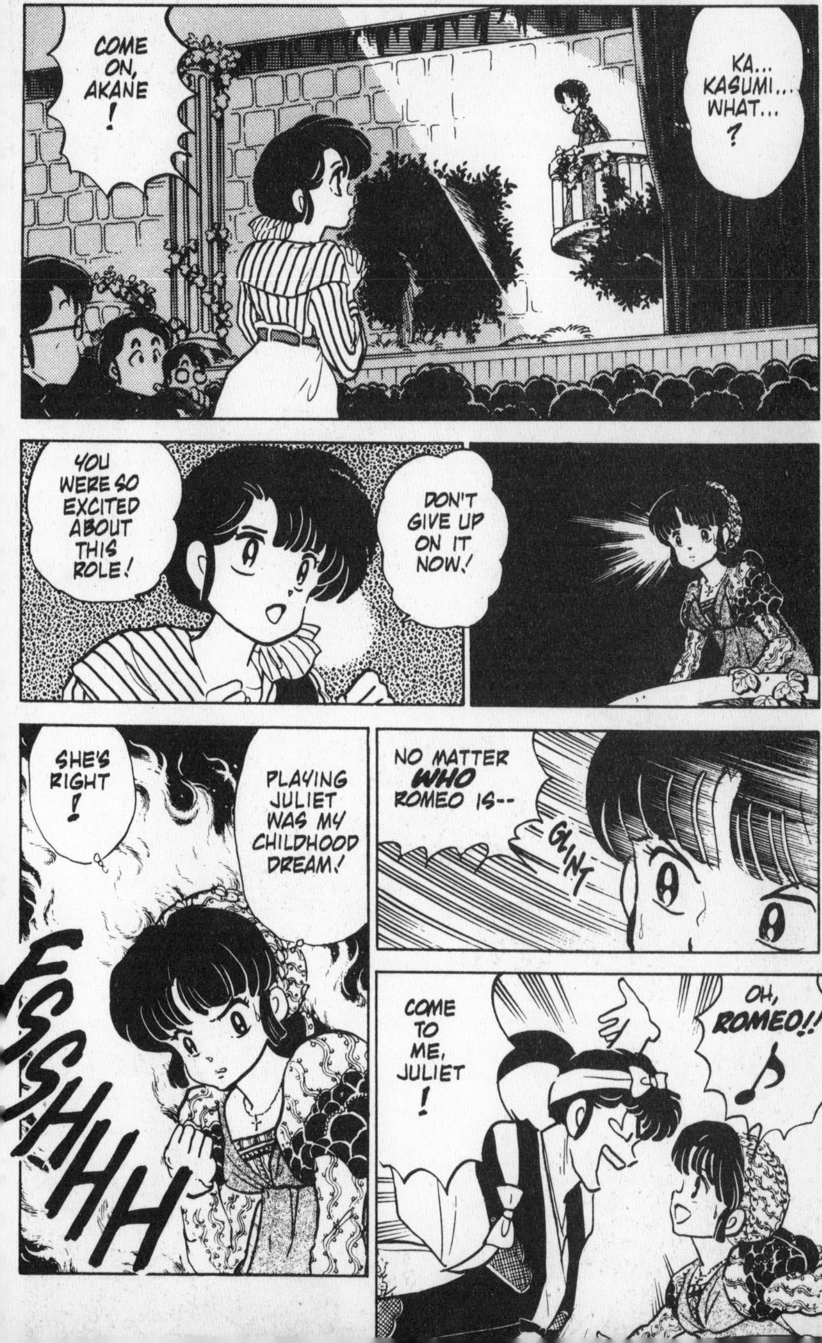
COME ON, AKANE!
KA... KASUMI... WHAT...?
YOU WERE SO EXCITED ABOUT THIS ROLE!
DON'T GIVE UP ON IT NOW!
SHE'S RIGHT!
PLAYING JULIET WAS MY CHILDHOOD DREAM!
FSSHHH
NO MATTER **WHO** ROMEO IS--
GLINT
COME TO ME, JULIET!
OH, **ROMEO!!** ♪

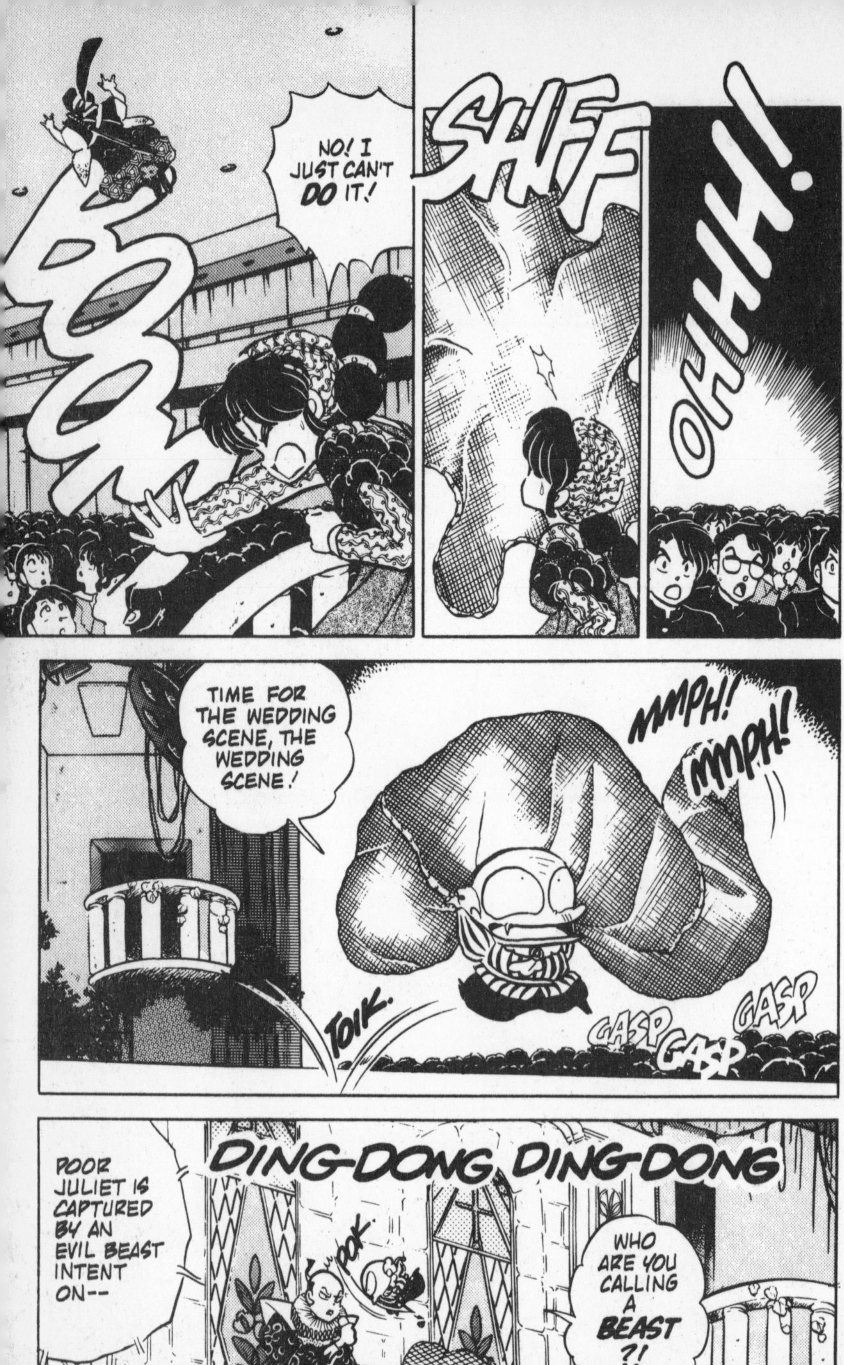
OHHH!!
SHFF
NO! I JUST CAN'T DO IT!
MMPH!
MMPH!
TIME FOR THE WEDDING SCENE, THE WEDDING SCENE!
GASP
GASP
GASP
TOIK.
DING-DONG DING-DONG
POOR JULIET IS CAPTURED BY AN EVIL BEAST INTENT ON--
POK
WHO ARE YOU CALLING A BEAST?!

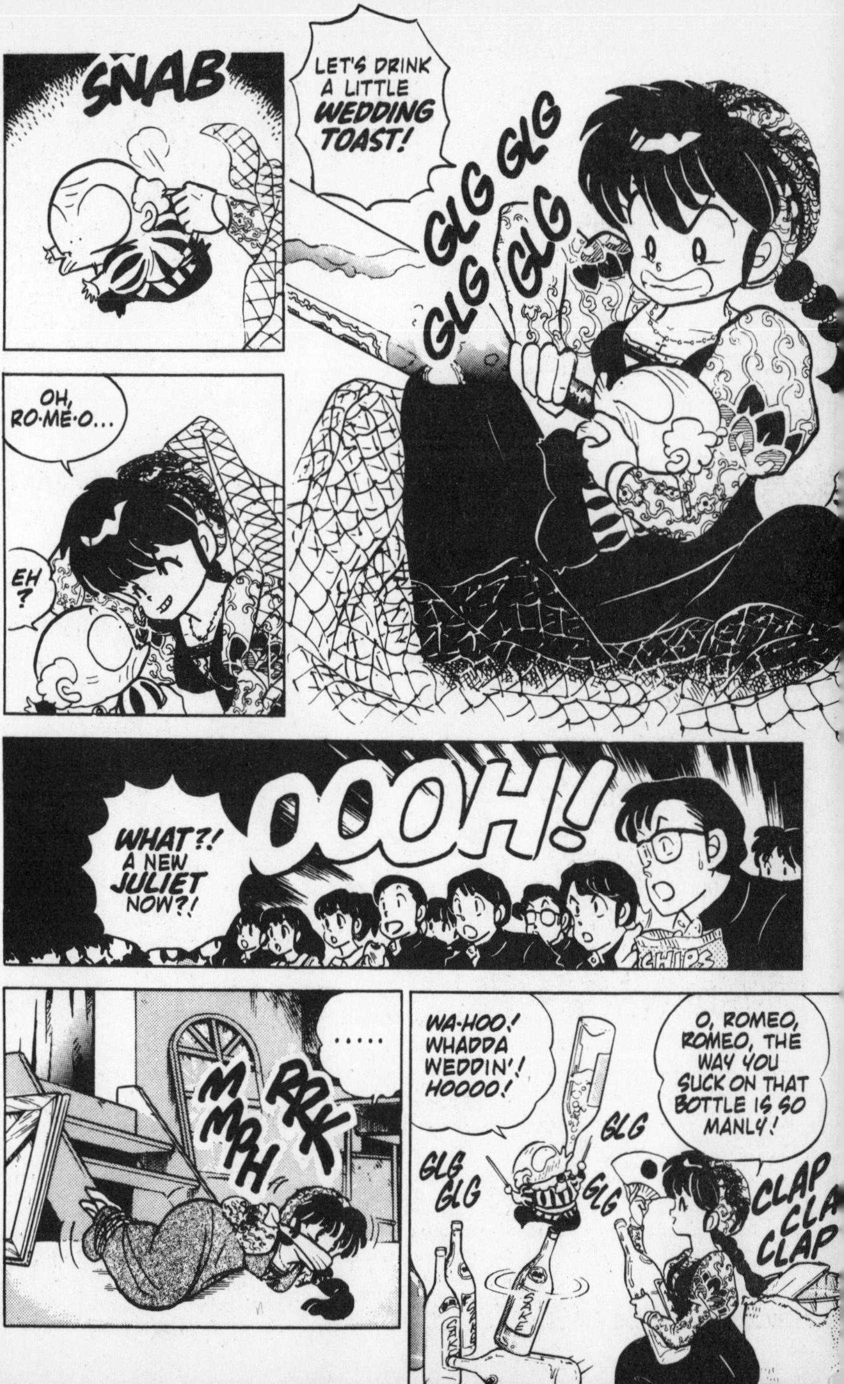
SNAB
LET'S DRINK A LITTLE WEDDING TOAST!
GLG GLG GLG GLG
OH, RO·ME·O...
EH ?
WHAT?! A NEW JULIET NOW?!
OOOH!
CHIPS
.....
MMPH
RKK
WA-HOO! WHADDA WEDDIN'! HOOOO!
GLG GLG
GLG
GLG
SAKE
O, ROMEO, ROMEO, THE WAY YOU SUCK ON THAT BOTTLE IS SO MANLY!
CLAP CLA CLAP

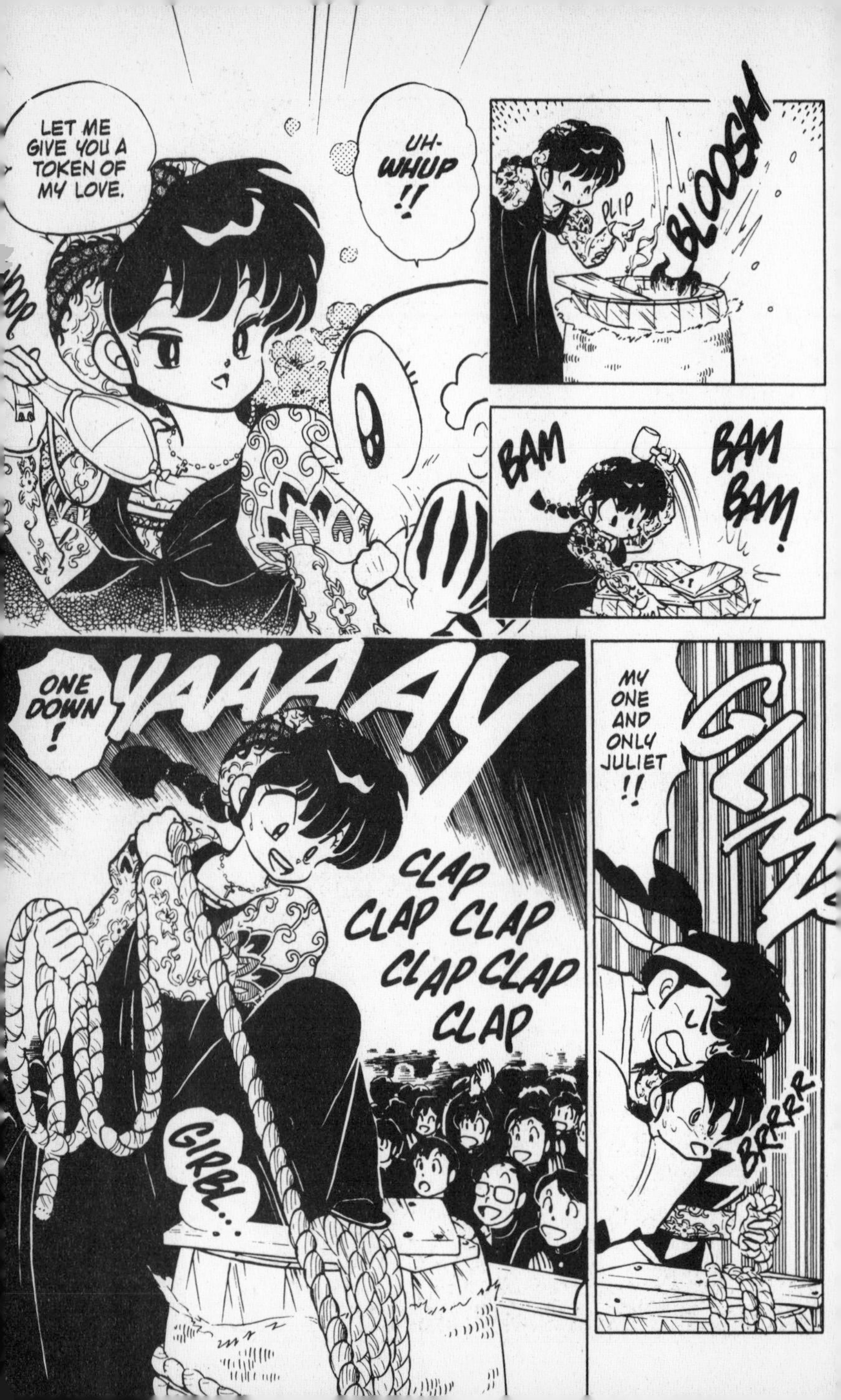
LET ME GIVE YOU A TOKEN OF MY LOVE.
UH-WHUP!!
PLIP
BLOOSH
BAM
BAM BAM!
ONE DOWN!
YAAAAY
CLAP CLAP CLAP CLAP CLAP CLAP
GIRGL...
MY ONE AND ONLY JULIET!!
BRRRR

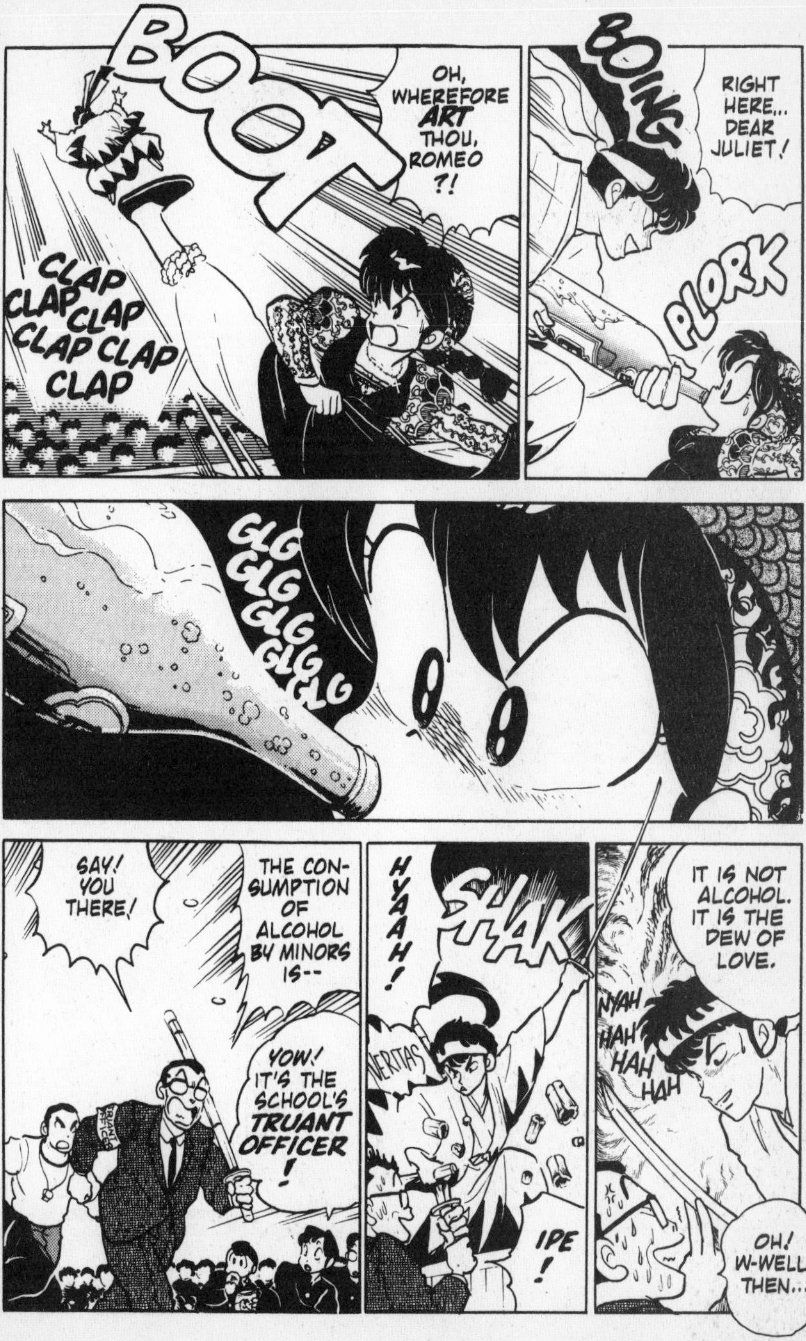
BOOT
OH, WHEREFORE ART THOU, ROMEO ?!
CLAP CLAP CLAP CLAP CLAP CLAP CLAP
BOING
RIGHT HERE... DEAR JULIET!
PLORK
GLG GLG GLG GLG GLG GLG
SAY! YOU THERE!
THE CONSUMPTION OF ALCOHOL BY MINORS IS--
YOW! IT'S THE SCHOOL'S TRUANT OFFICER!
HYAAAH!
SHAK
VERITAS
IPE!
IT IS NOT ALCOHOL. IT IS THE DEW OF LOVE.
NYAH HAH HAH HAH
OH! W-WELL, THEN...

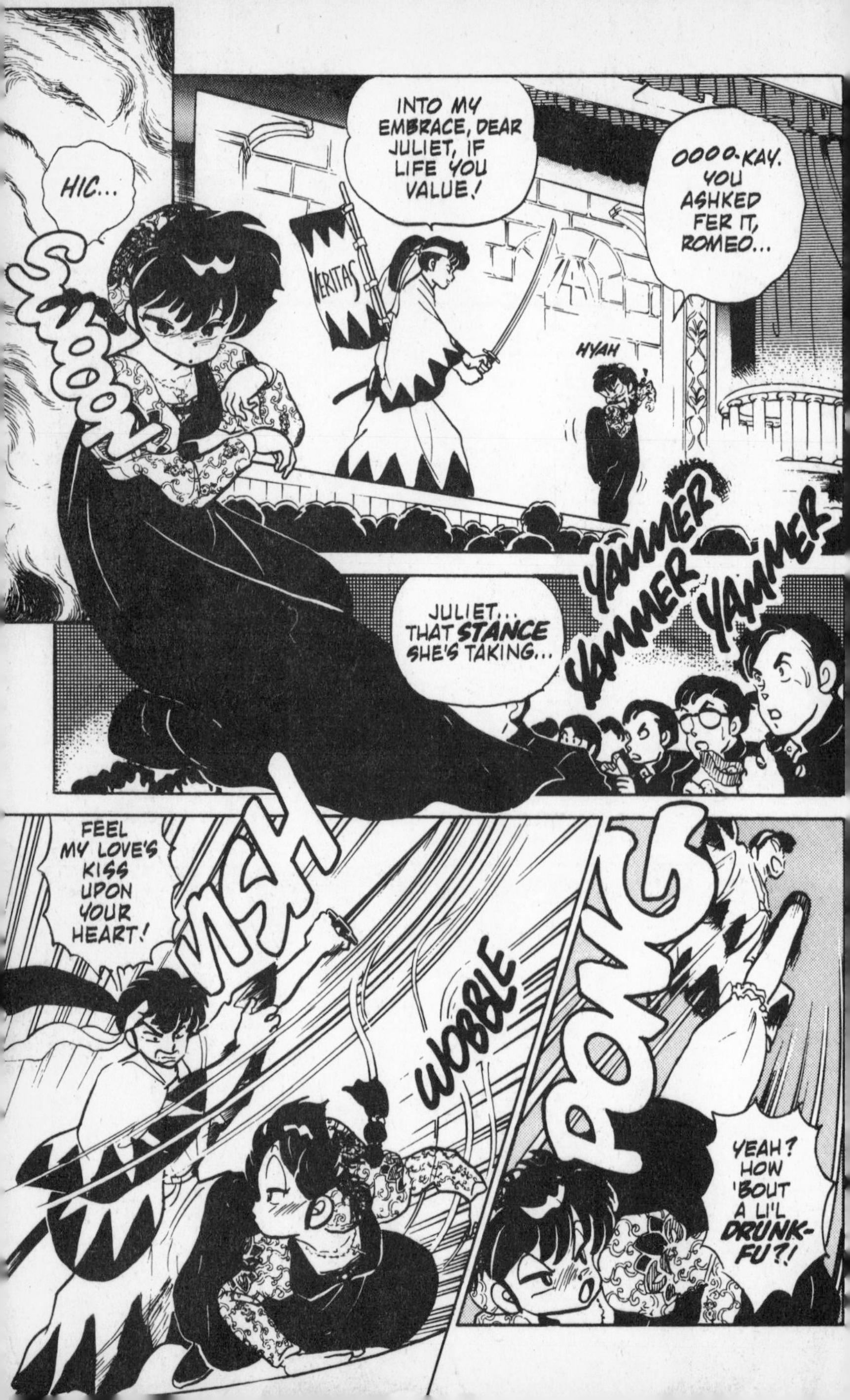
HIC...
SWOON
INTO MY EMBRACE, DEAR JULIET, IF LIFE YOU VALUE!
VERITAS
HYAH
OOOO-KAY. YOU ASHKED FER IT, ROMEO...
JULIET... THAT STANCE SHE'S TAKING...
YAMMER YAMMER YAMMER
FEEL MY LOVE'S KISS UPON YOUR HEART!
WISH
WOBBLE
POMG
YEAH? HOW 'BOUT A LI'L DRUNK-FU?!

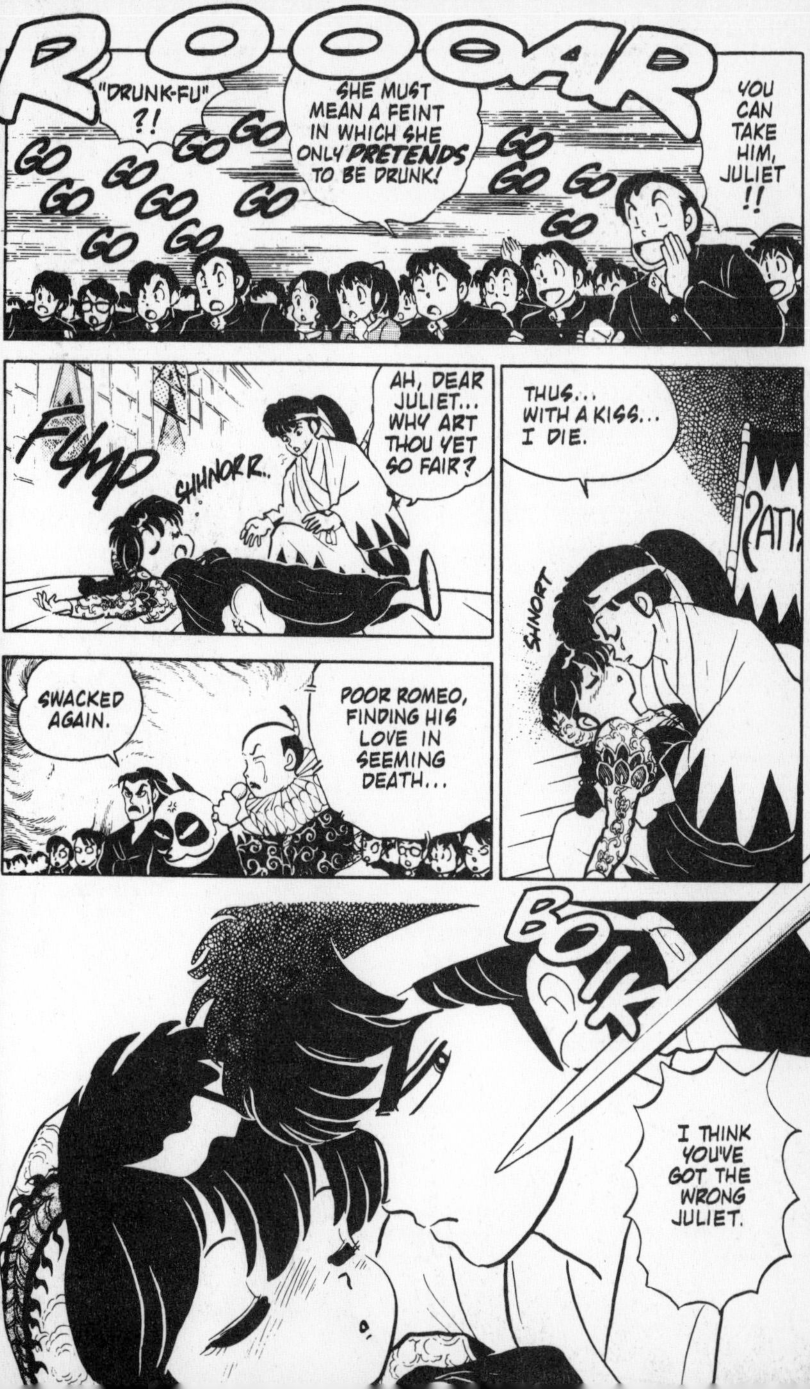
ROOOAR
"DRUNK-FU" ?!
GO GO GO GO GO GO GO GO GO GO
SHE MUST MEAN A FEINT IN WHICH SHE ONLY **PRETENDS** TO BE DRUNK!
GO GO GO GO
YOU CAN TAKE HIM, JULIET !!
FUMP
SHHNORR..
AH, DEAR JULIET... WHY ART THOU YET SO FAIR?
THUS... WITH A KISS... I DIE.
SHNORT
SWACKED AGAIN.
POOR ROMEO, FINDING HIS LOVE IN SEEMING DEATH...
BOIK
I THINK YOU'VE GOT THE WRONG JULIET.

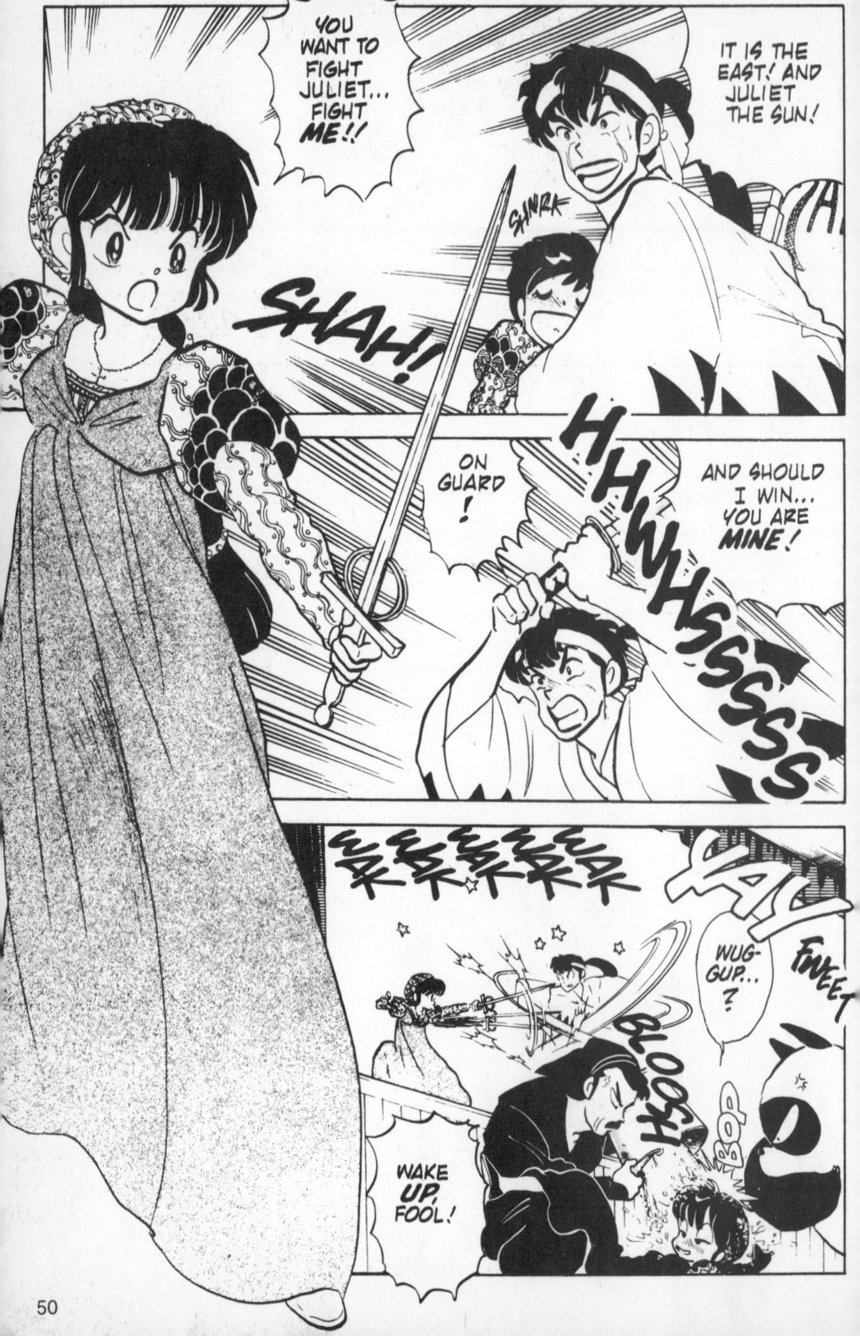
YOU WANT TO FIGHT JULIET... FIGHT ME!!
SHAH!
IT IS THE EAST! AND JULIET THE SUN!
ON GUARD!
HHWWHSSSSSS
AND SHOULD I WIN... YOU ARE MINE!
WAK WAK WAK WAK WAK
YAY
WUG-GUP...?
FWEET
BLOOSH
WAKE UP, FOOL!

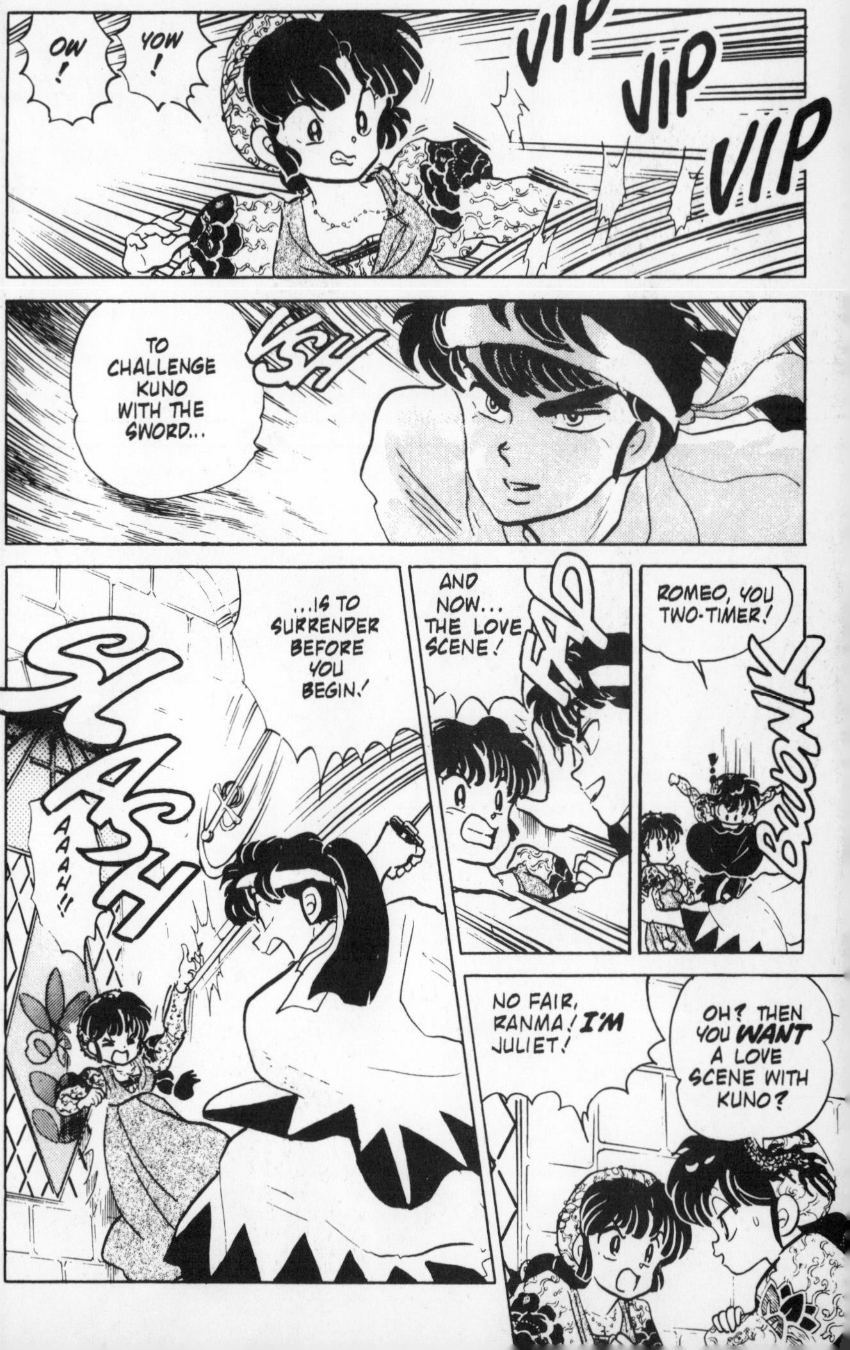
OW!
YOW!
VIP
VIP
VIP
TO CHALLENGE KUNO WITH THE SWORD...
VSH
...IS TO SURRENDER BEFORE YOU BEGIN!
CLASH
AAAAH!!
AND NOW... THE LOVE SCENE!
FAP
ROMEO, YOU TWO-TIMER!
BWOMK
NO FAIR, RANMA! I'M JULIET!
OH? THEN YOU WANT A LOVE SCENE WITH KUNO?

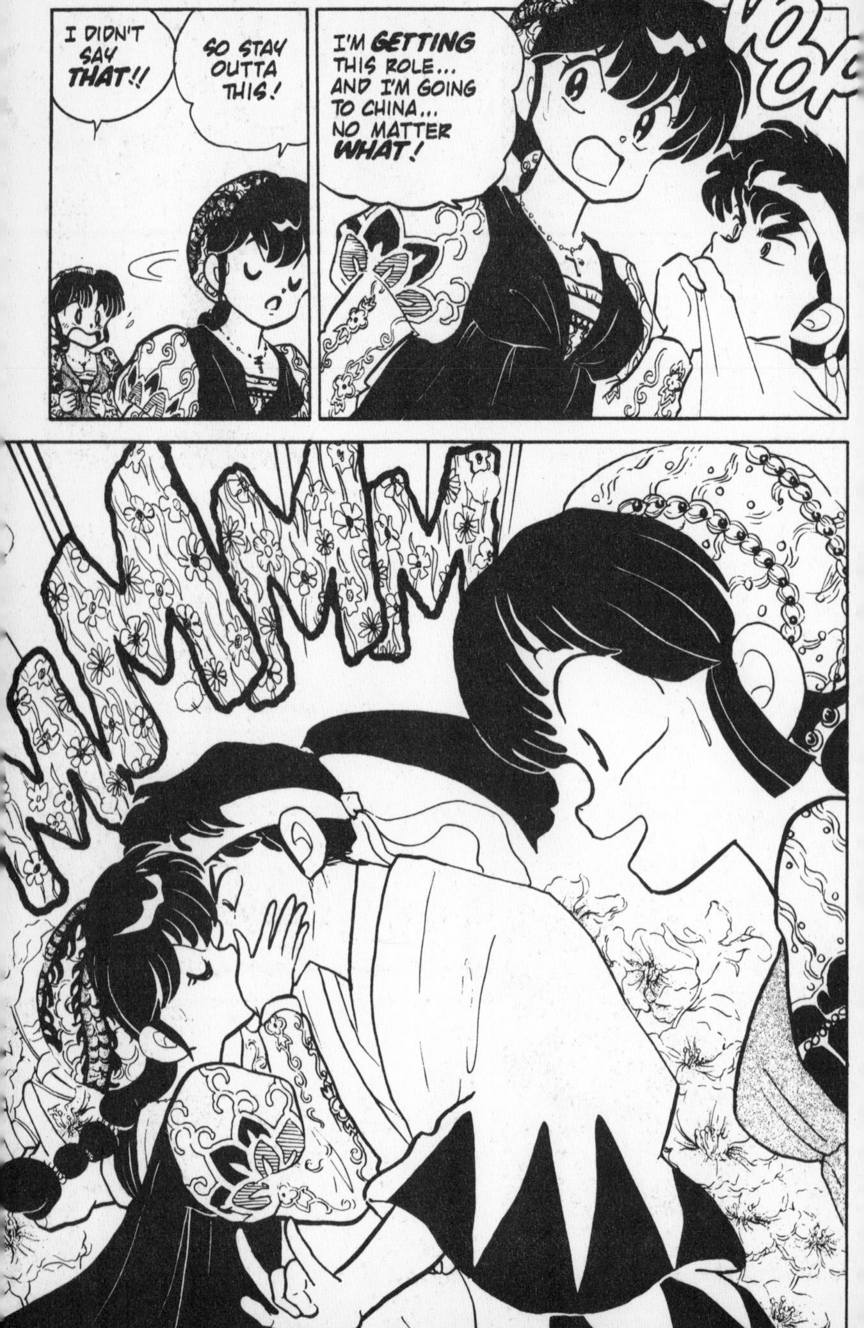
I DIDN'T SAY **THAT**!!
SO STAY OUTTA THIS!
I'M **GETTING** THIS ROLE... AND I'M GOING TO CHINA... NO MATTER **WHAT**!

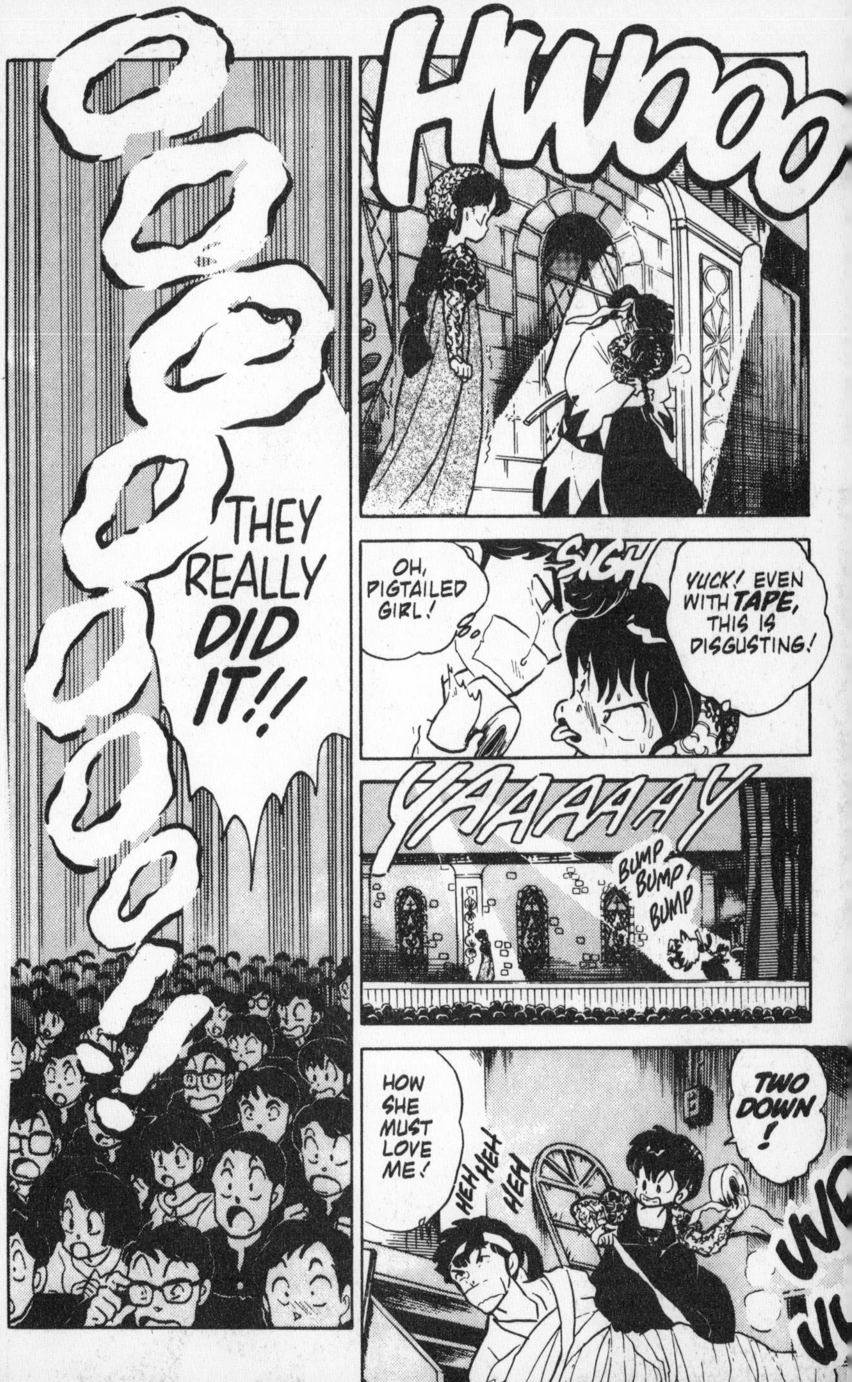
OOOOOOO!!
THEY REALLY DID IT!!
HWOOO
OH, PIGTAILED GIRL!
SIGH
YUCK! EVEN WITH TAPE, THIS IS DISGUSTING!
YAAAAAY
BUMP BUMP! BUMP
HOW SHE MUST LOVE ME!
HEH HEH HEH
TWO DOWN!

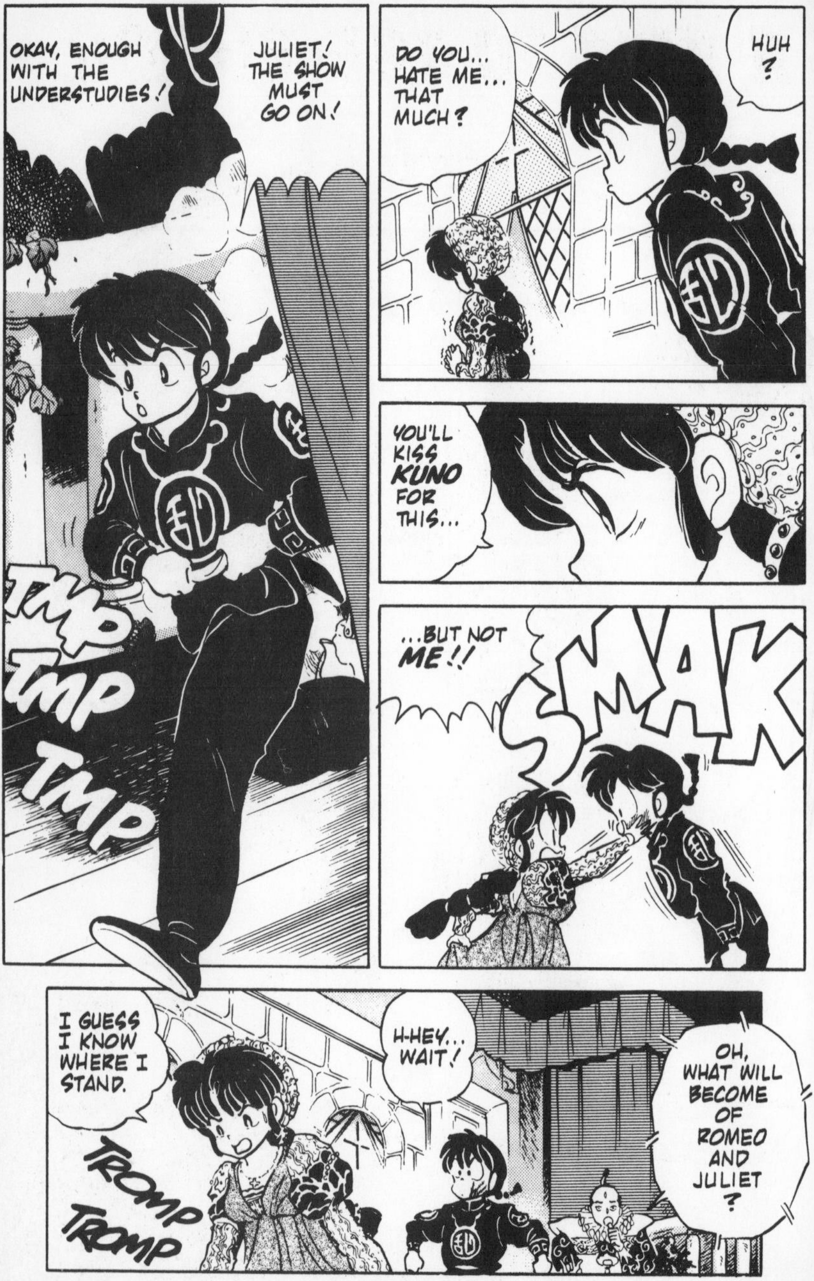
OKAY, ENOUGH WITH THE UNDERSTUDIES!
JULIET! THE SHOW MUST GO ON!
TMP TMP TMP TMP
DO YOU... HATE ME... THAT MUCH?
HUH?
YOU'LL KISS KUNO FOR THIS...
...BUT NOT ME!!
SMAK
I GUESS I KNOW WHERE I STAND.
TROMP TROMP
H-HEY... WAIT!
OH, WHAT WILL BECOME OF ROMEO AND JULIET?

Part 4

A KISS TO THE VICTOR

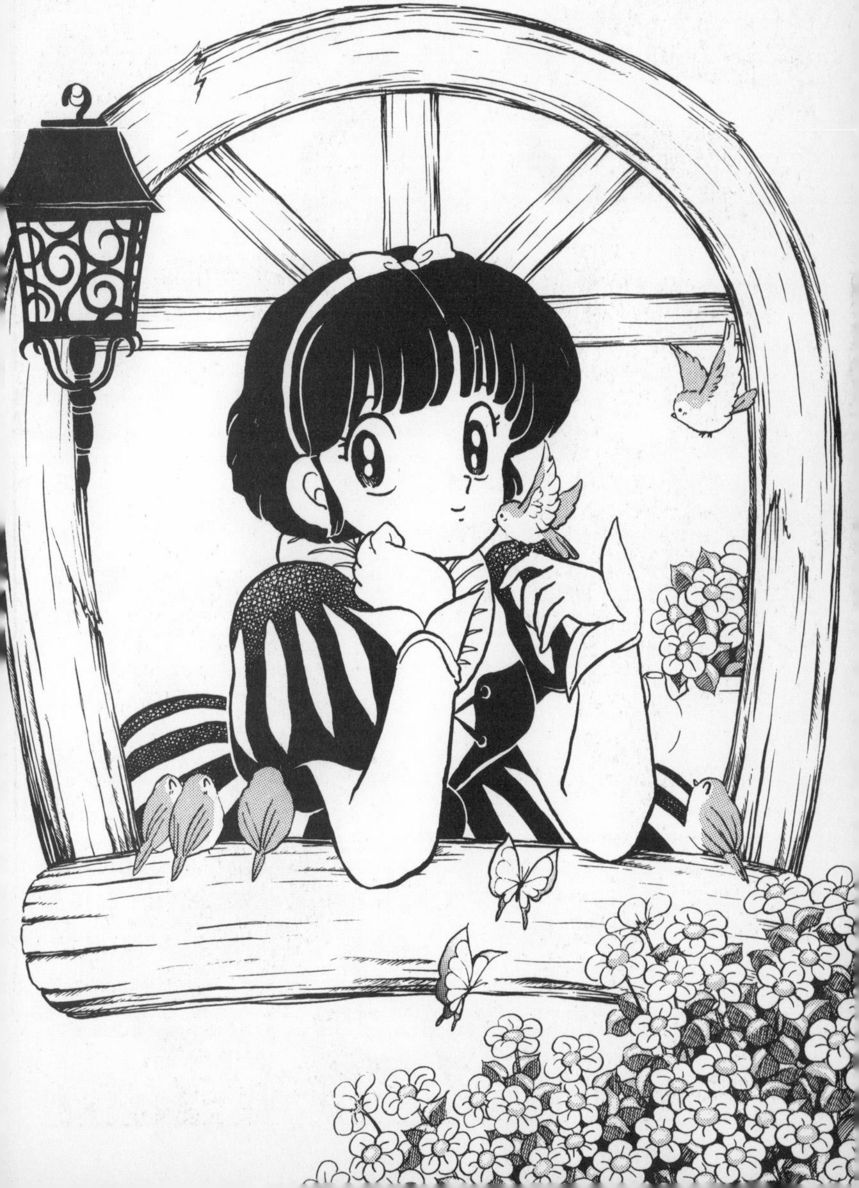

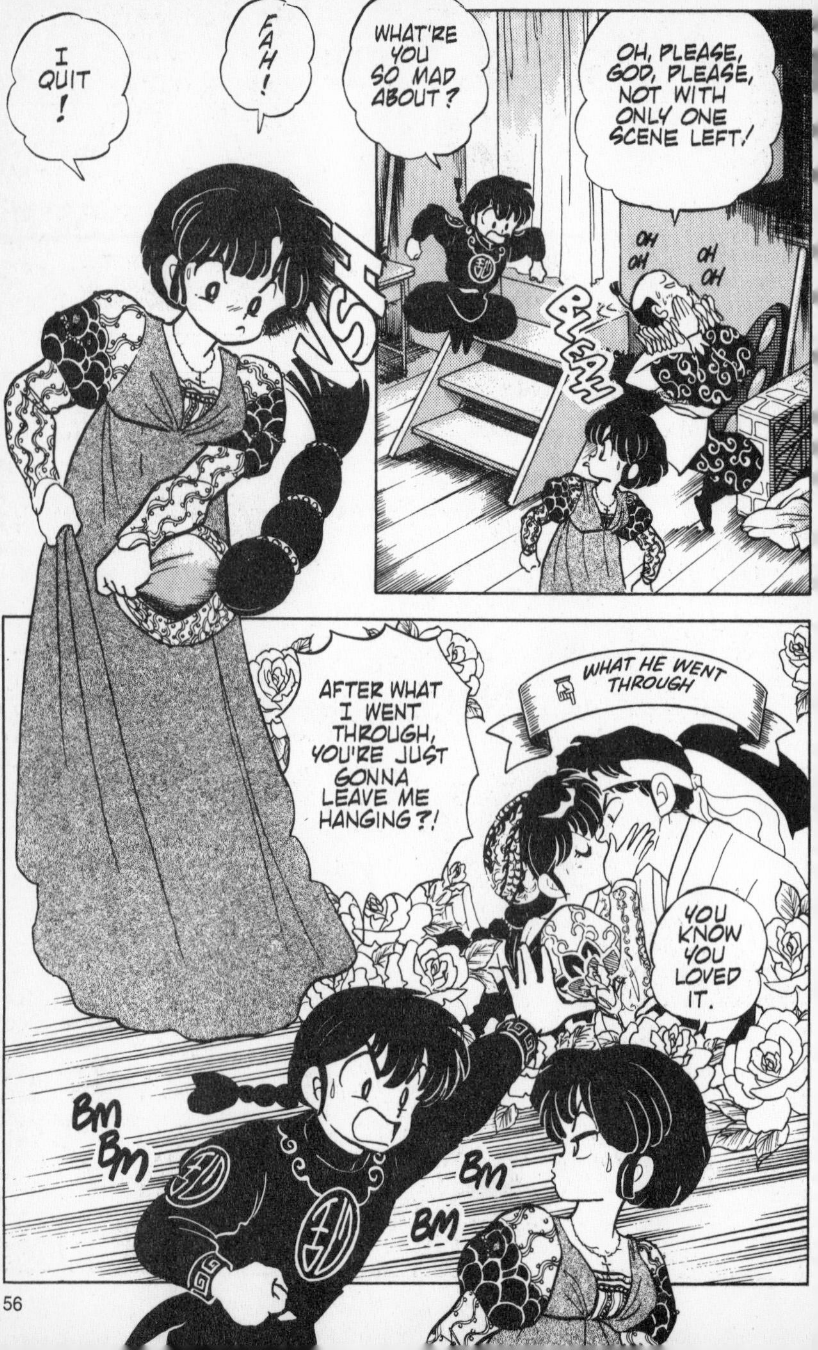
I QUIT!
FAH!
VSH
WHAT'RE YOU SO MAD ABOUT?
OH, PLEASE, GOD, PLEASE, NOT WITH ONLY ONE SCENE LEFT!
OH OH
OH OH
BLEAH
AFTER WHAT I WENT THROUGH, YOU'RE JUST GONNA LEAVE ME HANGING?!
WHAT HE WENT THROUGH
YOU KNOW YOU LOVED IT.
BM BM
BM BM

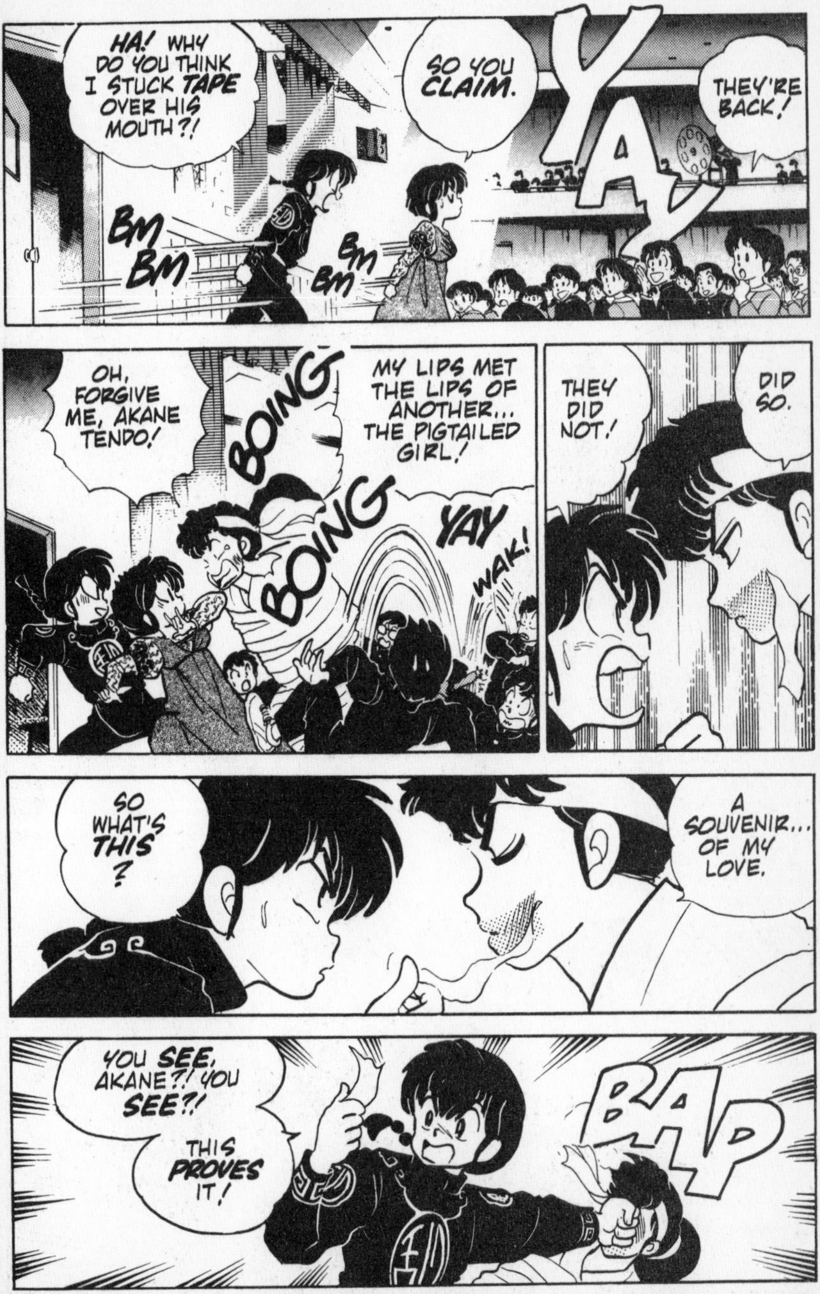
HA! WHY DO YOU THINK I STUCK TAPE OVER HIS MOUTH?!
BM BM
BM BM
SO YOU CLAIM.
YAY
THEY'RE BACK!
OH, FORGIVE ME, AKANE TENDO!
BOING
MY LIPS MET THE LIPS OF ANOTHER... THE PIGTAILED GIRL!
BOING
YAY
WAK!
THEY DID NOT!
DID SO.
SO WHAT'S THIS?
A SOUVENIR... OF MY LOVE.
YOU SEE, AKANE?! YOU SEE?!
THIS PROVES IT!
BAP

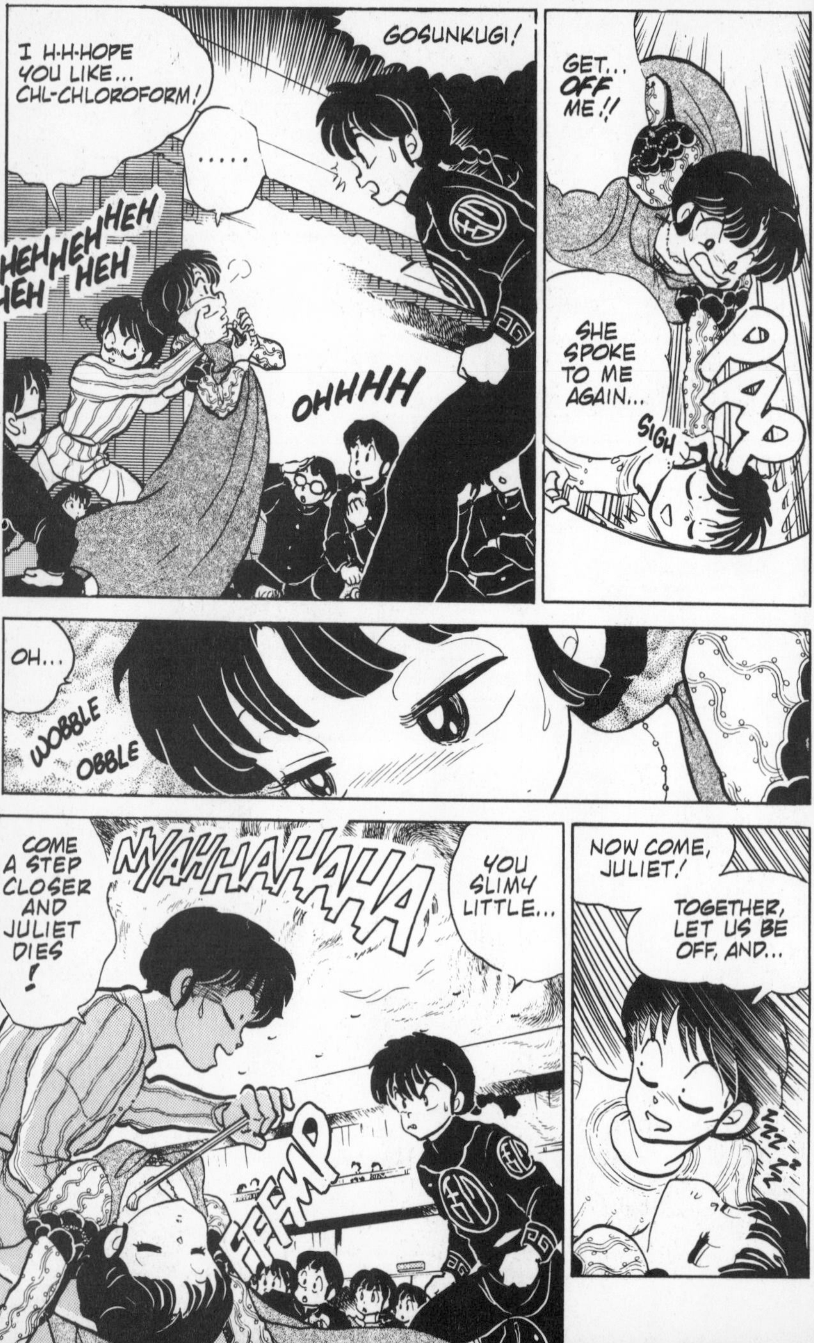
I H-H-HOPE YOU LIKE... CHL-CHLOROFORM!
......
GOSUNKUGI!
HEH HEH HEH HEH HEH
OHHHH
GET... OFF ME!!
SHE SPOKE TO ME AGAIN...
SIGH
PAP
OH...
WOBBLE
OBBLE
COME A STEP CLOSER AND JULIET DIES!
NYAHAHAHAHA
YOU SLIMY LITTLE...
FFFMP
NOW COME, JULIET!
TOGETHER, LET US BE OFF, AND...

UNGH... T-TOO...! HEAVY...!

SHMP SHMP .....

ZIP ZIP

BZZ BZZ BZZ BZZ

JULIET!!

POW

USH

NOW THAT I HAVE KISSED THE PIGTAILED GIRL, IT IS ONLY HONORABLE... THAT I DO THE SAME FOR YOU!

IT WASN'T FOR REAL, I SAID!!

SPLAT

SOBB

ZZZ ZZZ ZZZ

WAKE UP, STUPID! WE GOT A PLAY TO FINISH!

ZZ ZZ

WAAH!

YET FOR ALL ROMEO'S LOVING ENTREATIES... JULIET DOES NOT AWAKEN!

ALAS!

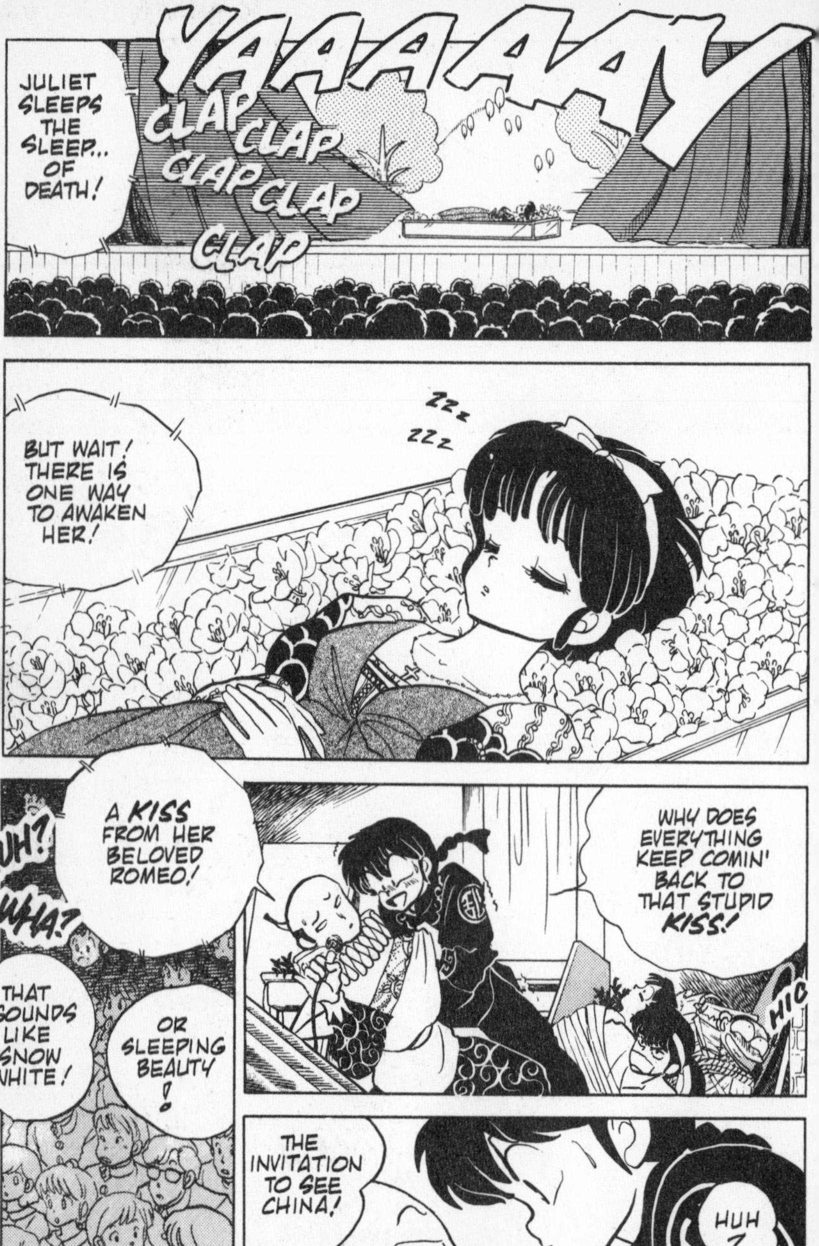
YAAAAAY
JULIET SLEEPS THE SLEEP... OF DEATH!
CLAP CLAP CLAP CLAP CLAP
ZZZ ZZZ
BUT WAIT! THERE IS ONE WAY TO AWAKEN HER!
HUH?
UHA?
A KISS FROM HER BELOVED ROMEO!
THAT SOUNDS LIKE SNOW WHITE!
OR SLEEPING BEAUTY!
WHY DOES EVERYTHING KEEP COMIN' BACK TO THAT STUPID KISS!
HIC
THE INVITATION TO SEE CHINA!
HUH?

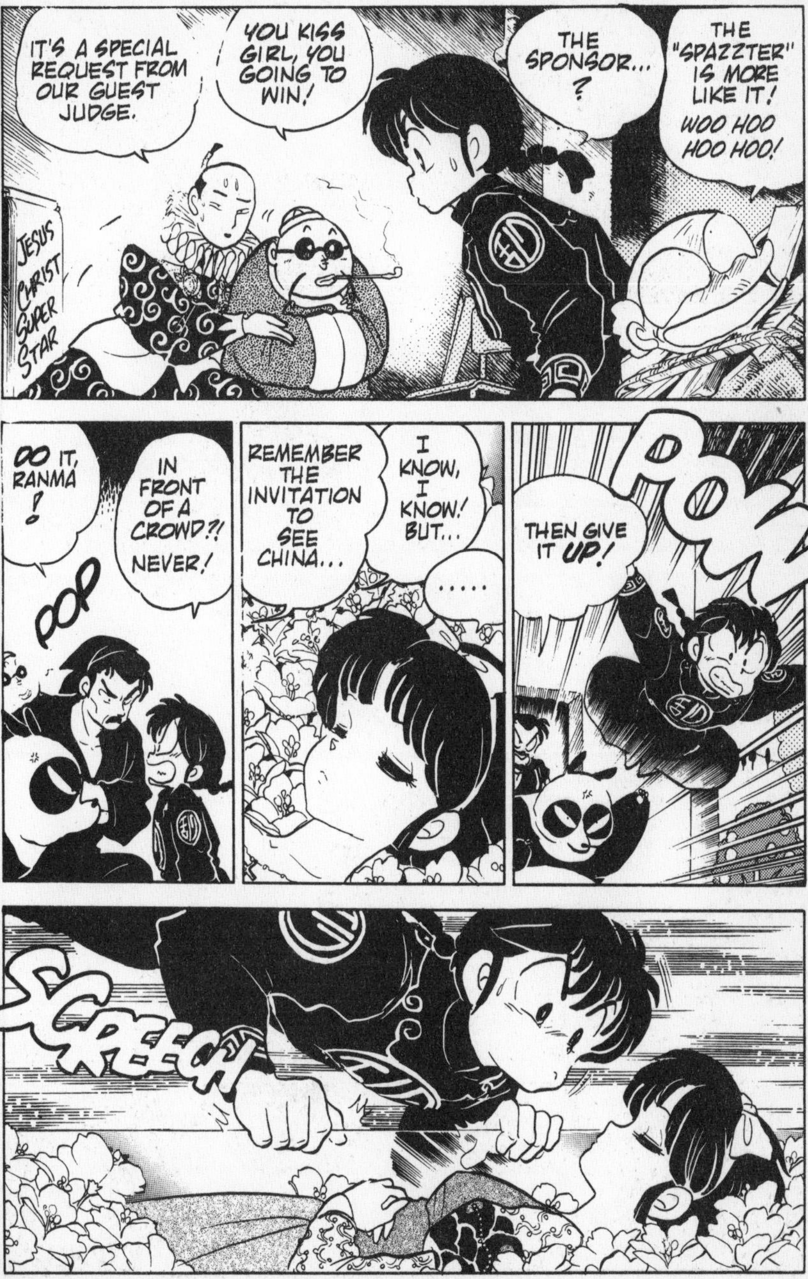
IT'S A SPECIAL REQUEST FROM OUR GUEST JUDGE.
YOU KISS GIRL, YOU GOING TO WIN!
JESUS CHRIST SUPER STAR
THE SPONSOR... ?
THE "SPAZZTER" IS MORE LIKE IT! WOO HOO HOO HOO!
DO IT, RANMA!
IN FRONT OF A CROWD?! NEVER!
POP
REMEMBER THE INVITATION TO SEE CHINA...
I KNOW, I KNOW! BUT...
.....
POW
THEN GIVE IT UP!
SCREECH

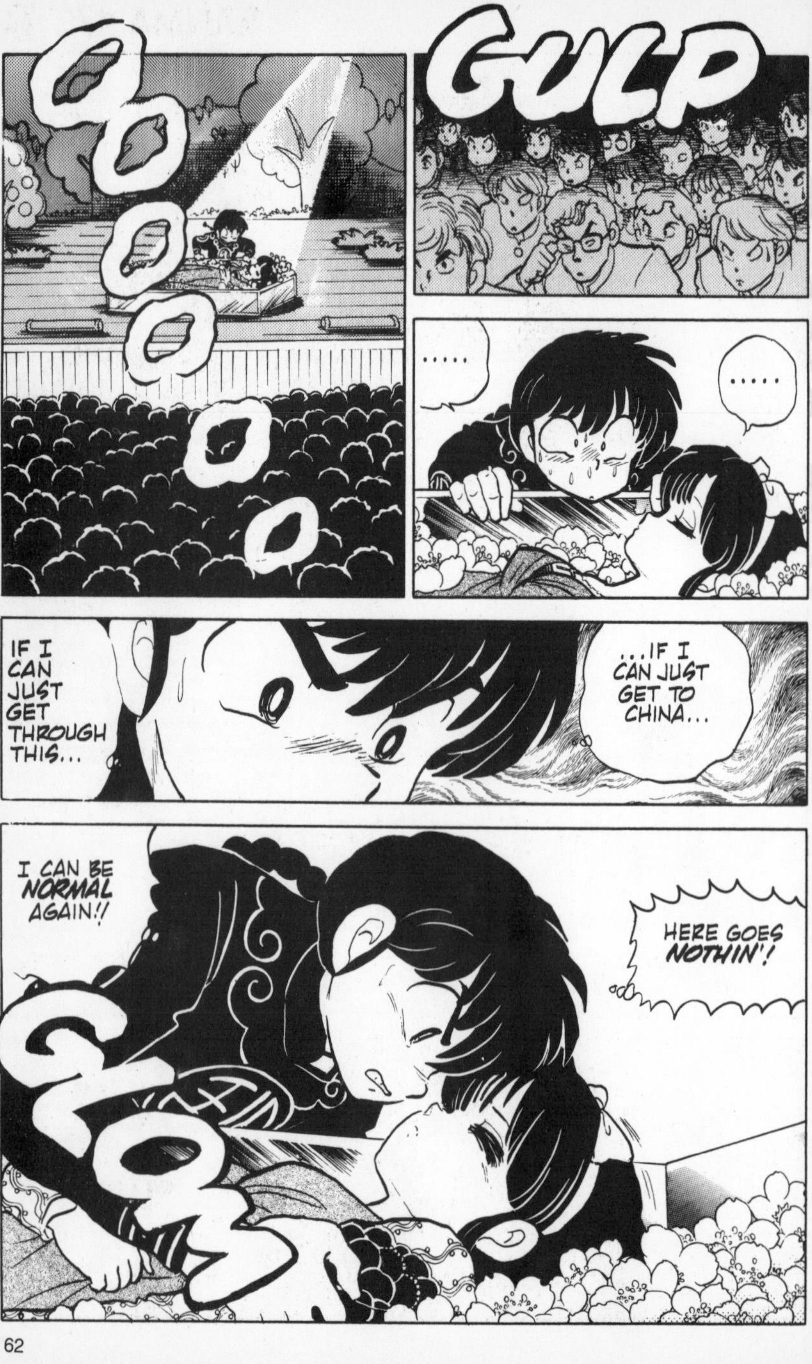
GULP
.....
.....
IF I CAN JUST GET THROUGH THIS...
...IF I CAN JUST GET TO CHINA...
I CAN BE NORMAL AGAIN!!
HERE GOES NOTHIN'!
GLOM

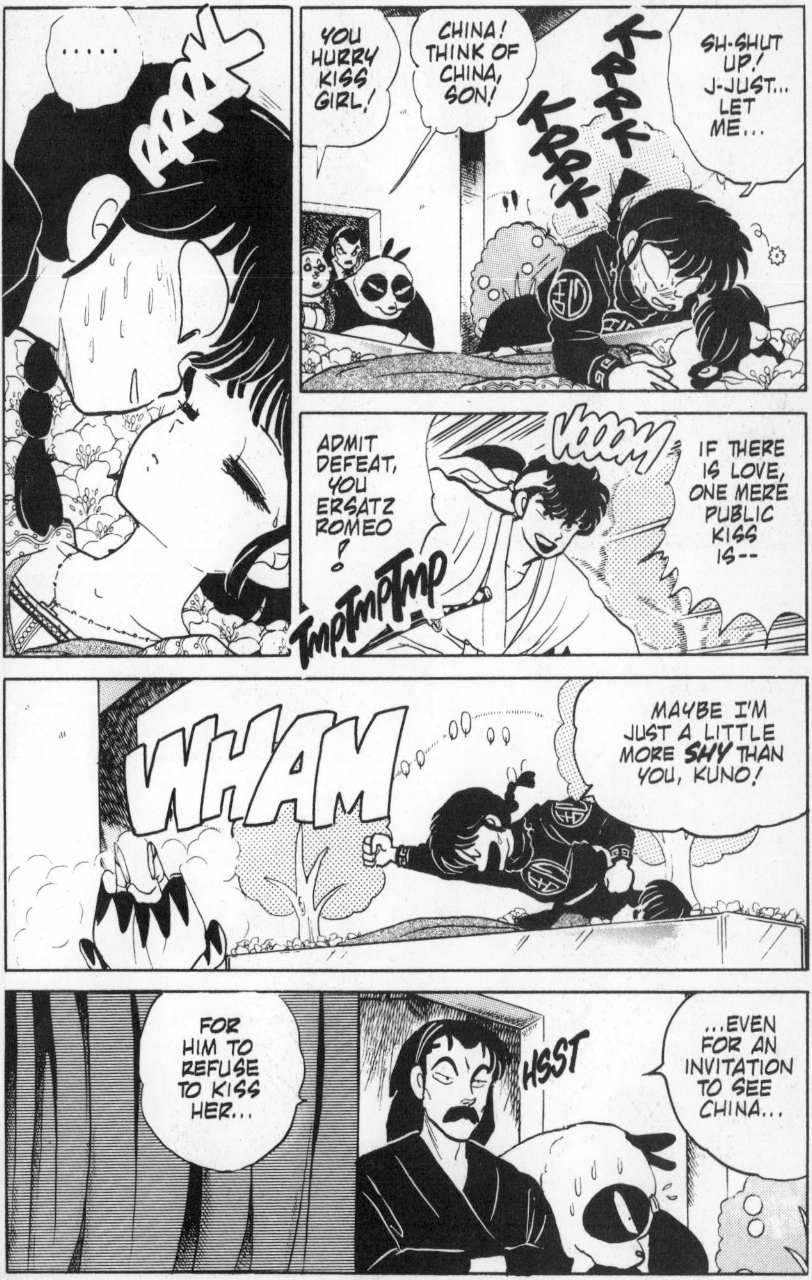
.....
YOU HURRY KISS GIRL!
CHINA! THINK OF CHINA, SON!
KRRK KRRK
SH-SHUT UP! J-JUST... LET ME...
ADMIT DEFEAT, YOU ERSATZ ROMEO!
IF THERE IS LOVE, ONE MERE PUBLIC KISS IS--
TMPTMPTMP
WHAM
MAYBE I'M JUST A LITTLE MORE SHY THAN YOU, KUNO!
FOR HIM TO REFUSE TO KISS HER...
HSST
...EVEN FOR AN INVITATION TO SEE CHINA...

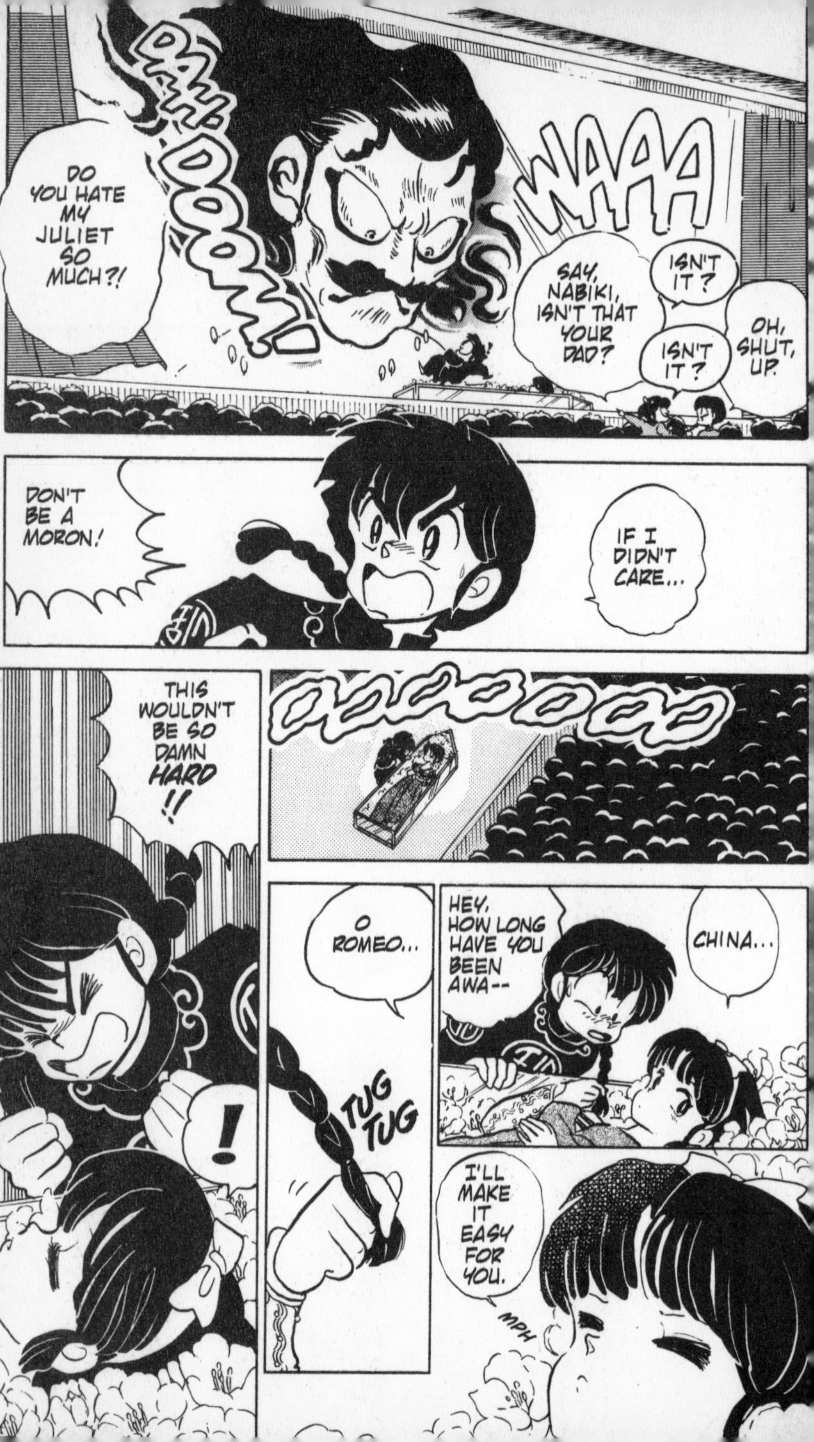
DO YOU HATE MY JULIET SO MUCH?!
BAH-DOOOM!
WAAA
SAY, NABIKI, ISN'T THAT YOUR DAD?
ISN'T IT?
ISN'T IT?
OH, SHUT UP.
DON'T BE A MORON!
IF I DIDN'T CARE...
THIS WOULDN'T BE SO DAMN **HARD**!!
!
OOOOOOOO
O ROMEO...
TUG TUG
HEY, HOW LONG HAVE YOU BEEN AWA--
CHINA...
I'LL MAKE IT EASY FOR YOU.
MPH

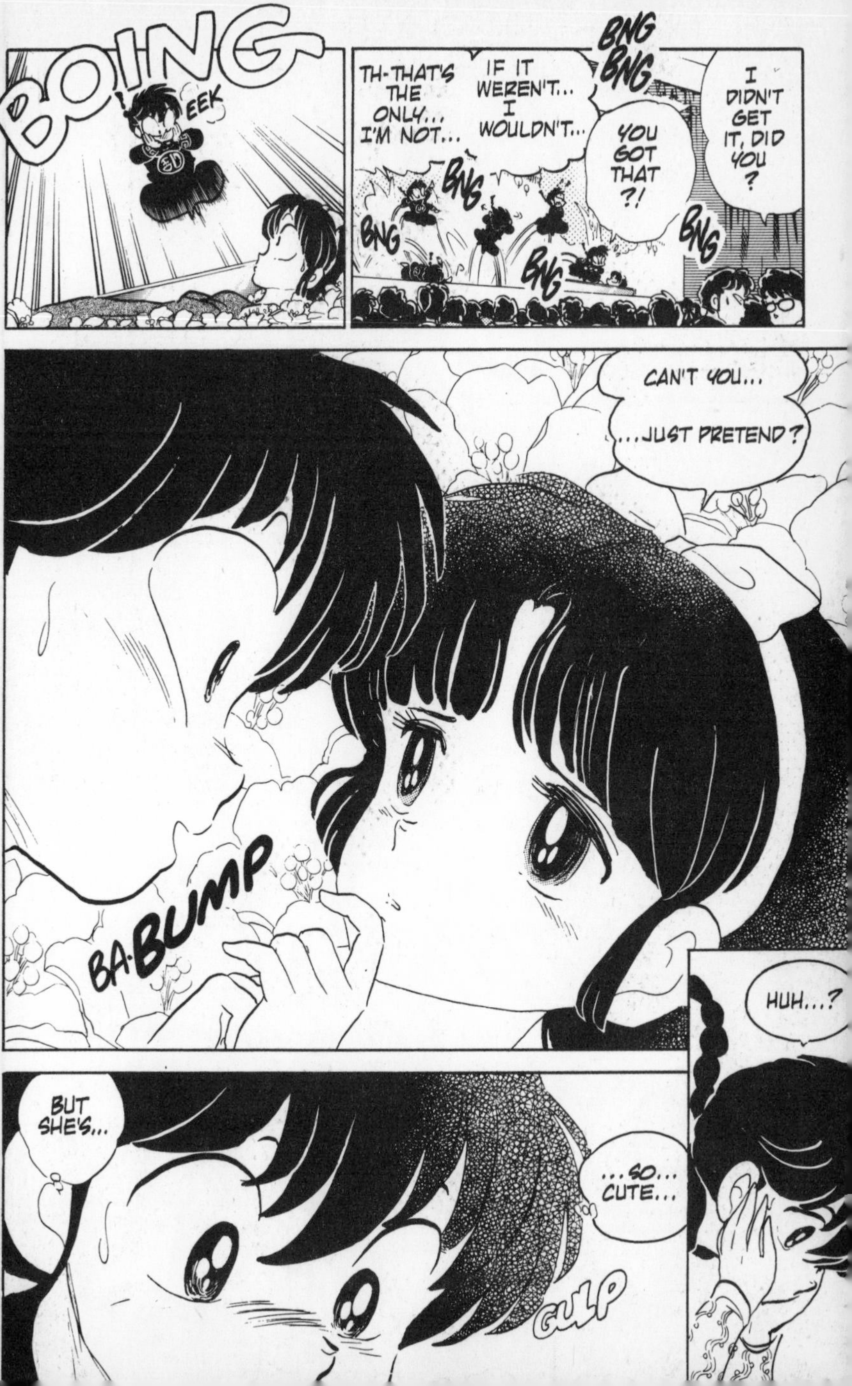
BOING
EEK
TH-THAT'S THE ONLY... I'M NOT...
IF IT WEREN'T... I WOULDN'T...
BNG BNG
YOU GOT THAT?!
I DIDN'T GET IT, DID YOU?
BNG
BNG
BNG
BNG
CAN'T YOU...
...JUST PRETEND?
BA-BUMP
BUT SHE'S...
...SO... CUTE...
GULP
HUH...?

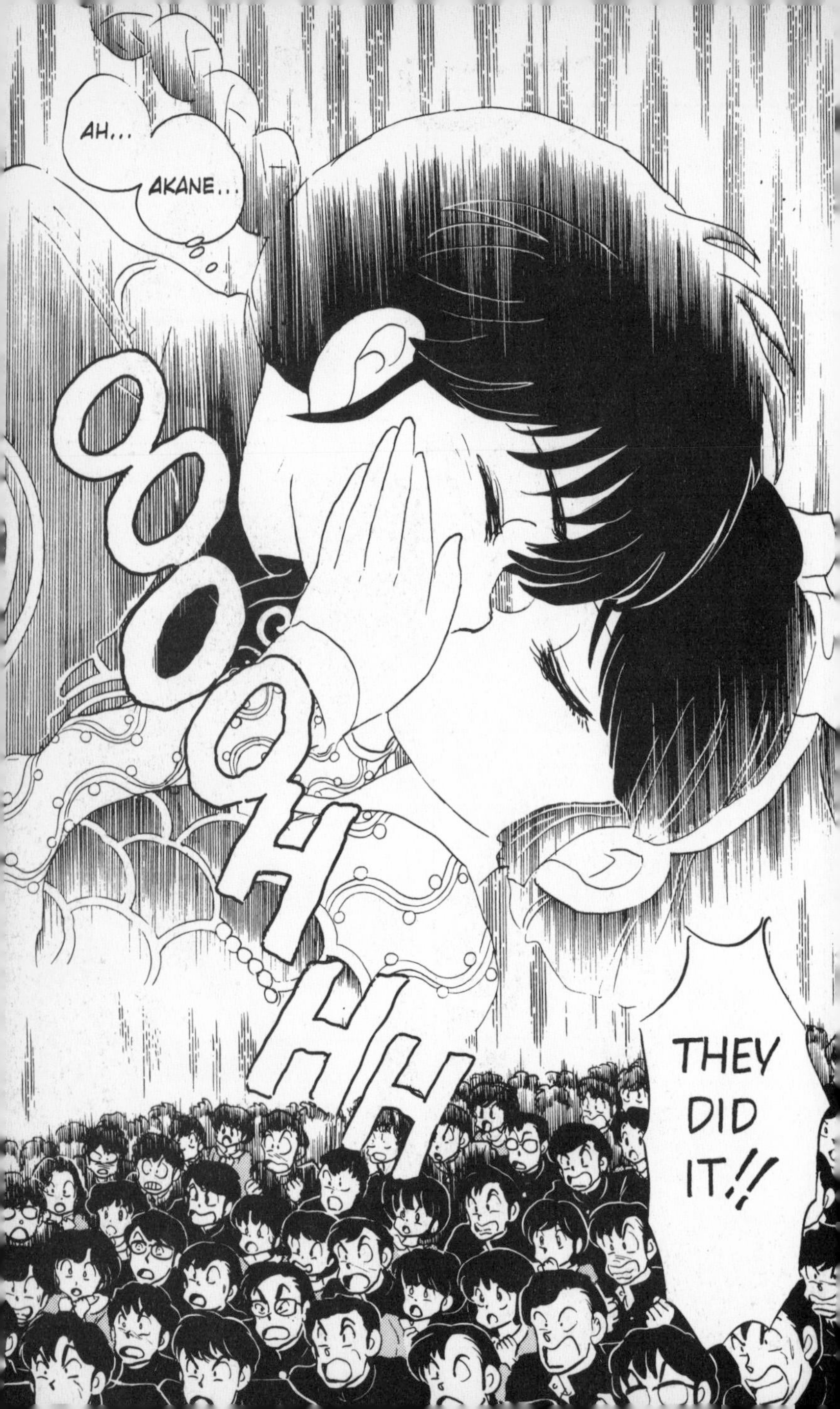
AH...
AKANE...
OOOOHHH
THEY DID IT!!

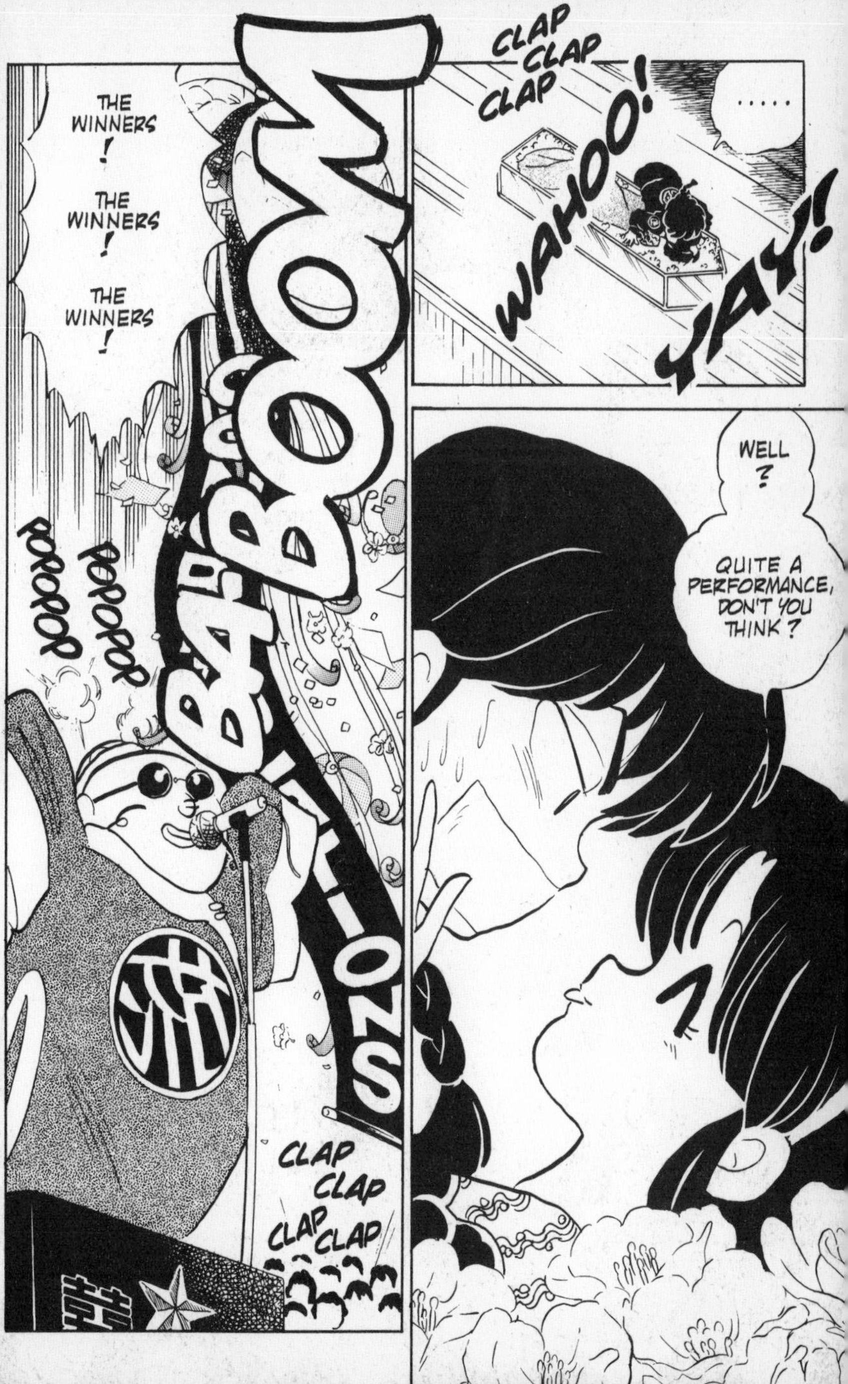
THE WINNERS!
THE WINNERS!
THE WINNERS!
BADABOOM
POPOPOPOP
POPOPOPOP
CLAP CLAP CLAP CLAP
CLAP CLAP CLAP
WAHOO!
......
YAY!
WELL?
QUITE A PERFORMANCE, DON'T YOU THINK?

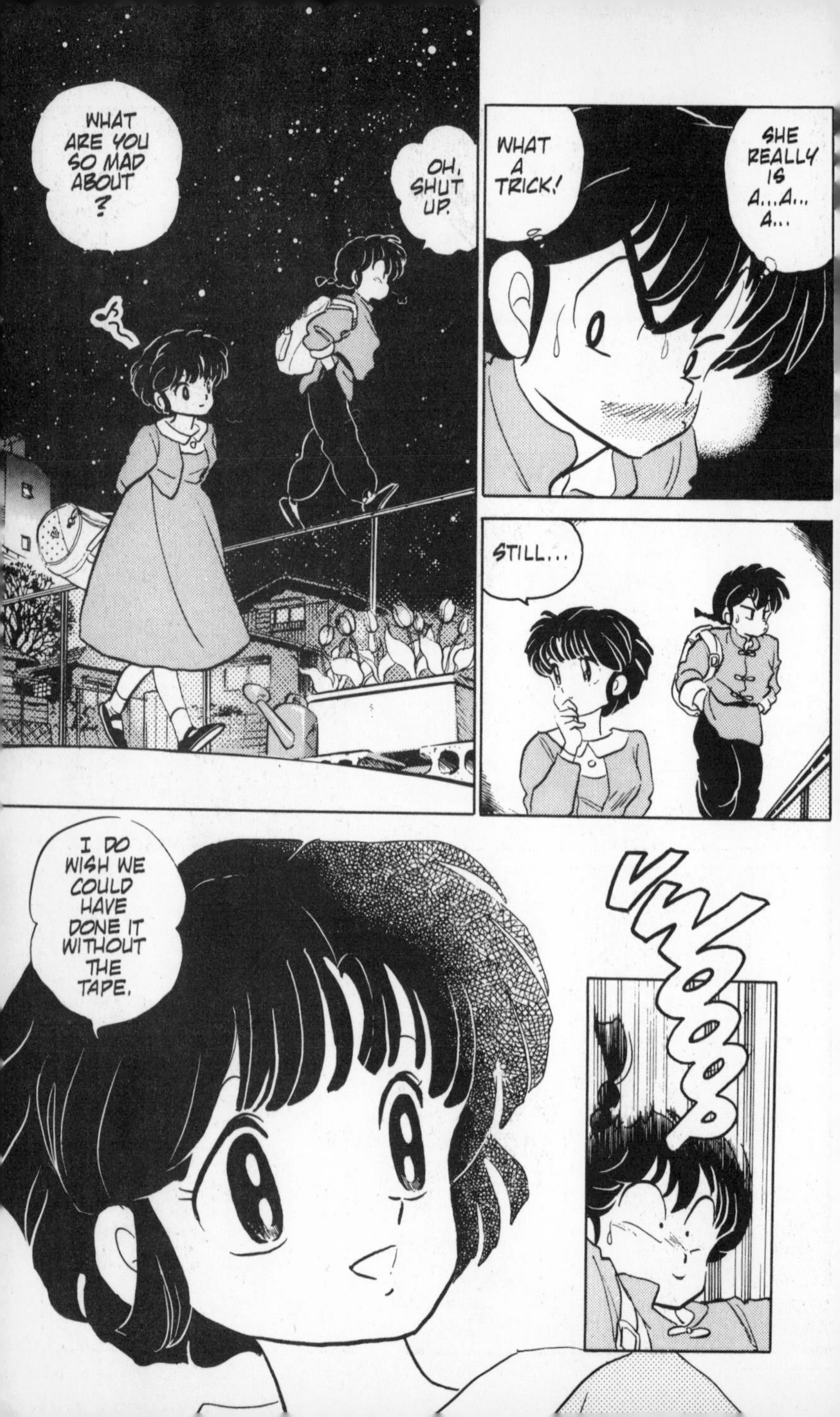
WHAT ARE YOU SO MAD ABOUT?
OH, SHUT UP.
WHAT A TRICK!
SHE REALLY IS A...A... A...
STILL...
I DO WISH WE COULD HAVE DONE IT WITHOUT THE TAPE.
VWOOOOP

IT WAS JUST A JOKE!
OH, RANMA, YOU'RE SUCH A DOPE!
AND YOU'RE SO...SO... SO... NON-CUTE!
KWNNN
YOU SHOULD THANK ME, YOU KNOW.
YOU'D NEVER GET TO CHINA WITHOUT ME.
I KNOW, I KNOW. YOU CAN DROP IT NOW.
WA HA HA HA HA HA
BADA-BOOM BADA-BOOM
TENDO TRAINING HALL
YOU TWO ARE LATE!
YEAH, EVERYBODY ELSE IS ALREADY SEEING CHINA!
HUH...?
ALREADY...?
BUM BUM BA BUM
MINO

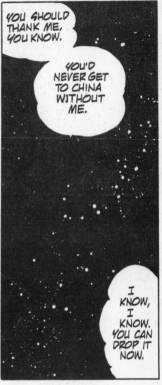

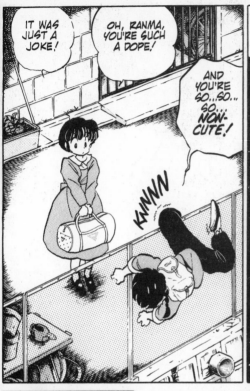

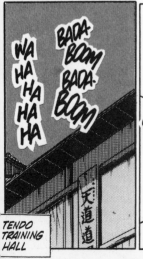

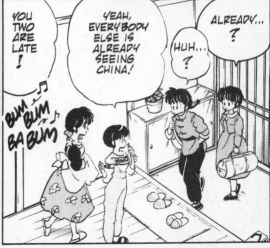

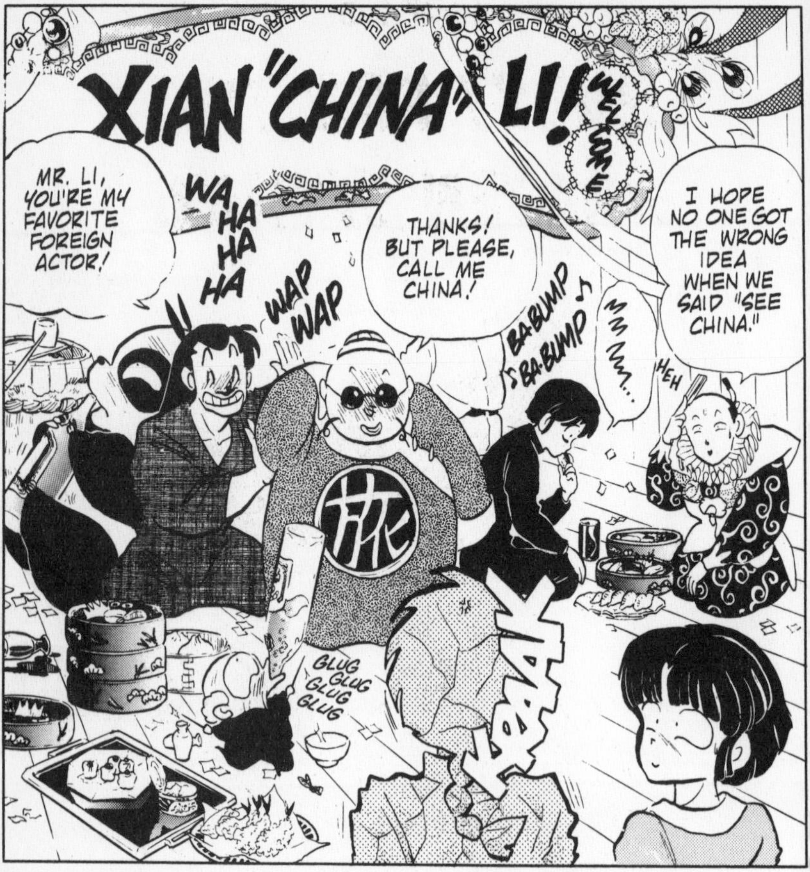
XIAN "CHINA" LI!
WELCOME
MR. LI, YOU'RE MY FAVORITE FOREIGN ACTOR!
WA HA HA HA
WAP WAP
THANKS! BUT PLEASE, CALL ME CHINA!
BA-BUMP BA-BUMP
MMMM...
I HOPE NO ONE GOT THE WRONG IDEA WHEN WE SAID "SEE CHINA."
HEH
GLUG GLUG GLUG GLUG
KRAAK

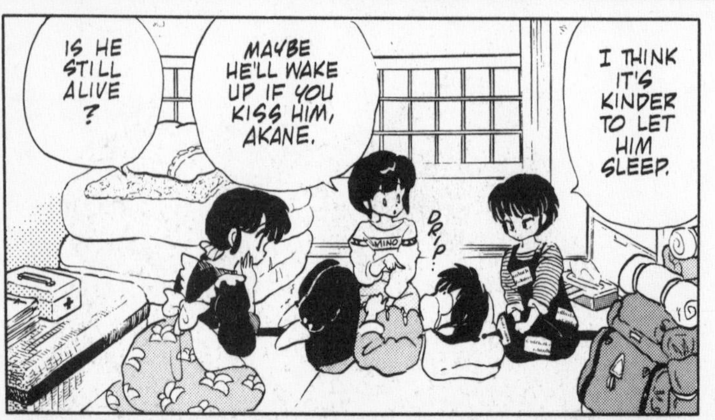
IS HE STILL ALIVE?
MAYBE HE'LL WAKE UP IF YOU KISS HIM, AKANE.
DRIP...
I THINK IT'S KINDER TO LET HIM SLEEP.

Part 5

QUEST FOR THE HIDDEN SPRING

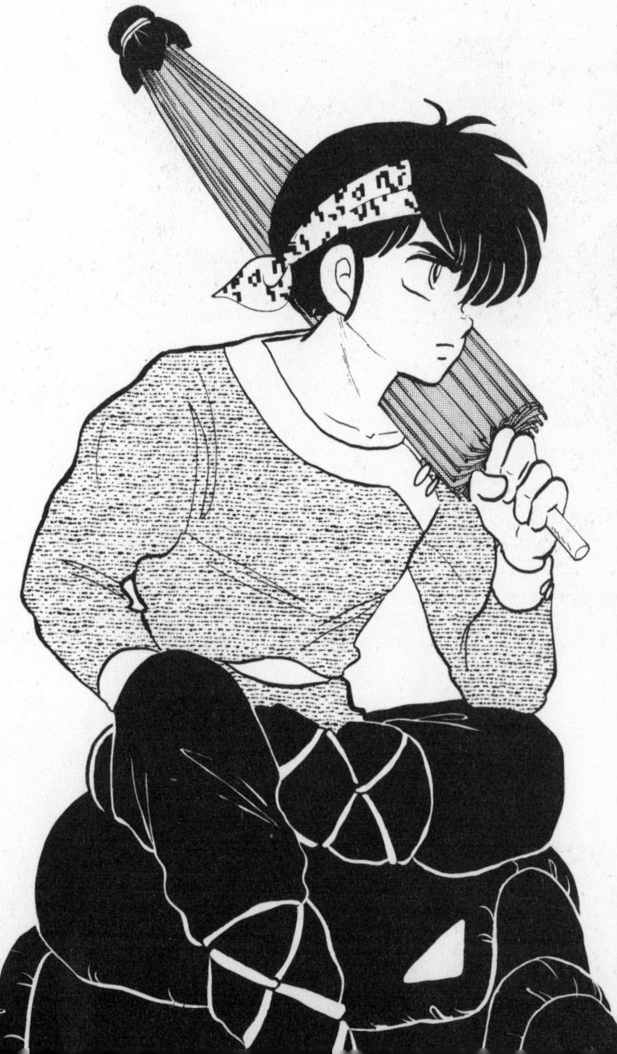

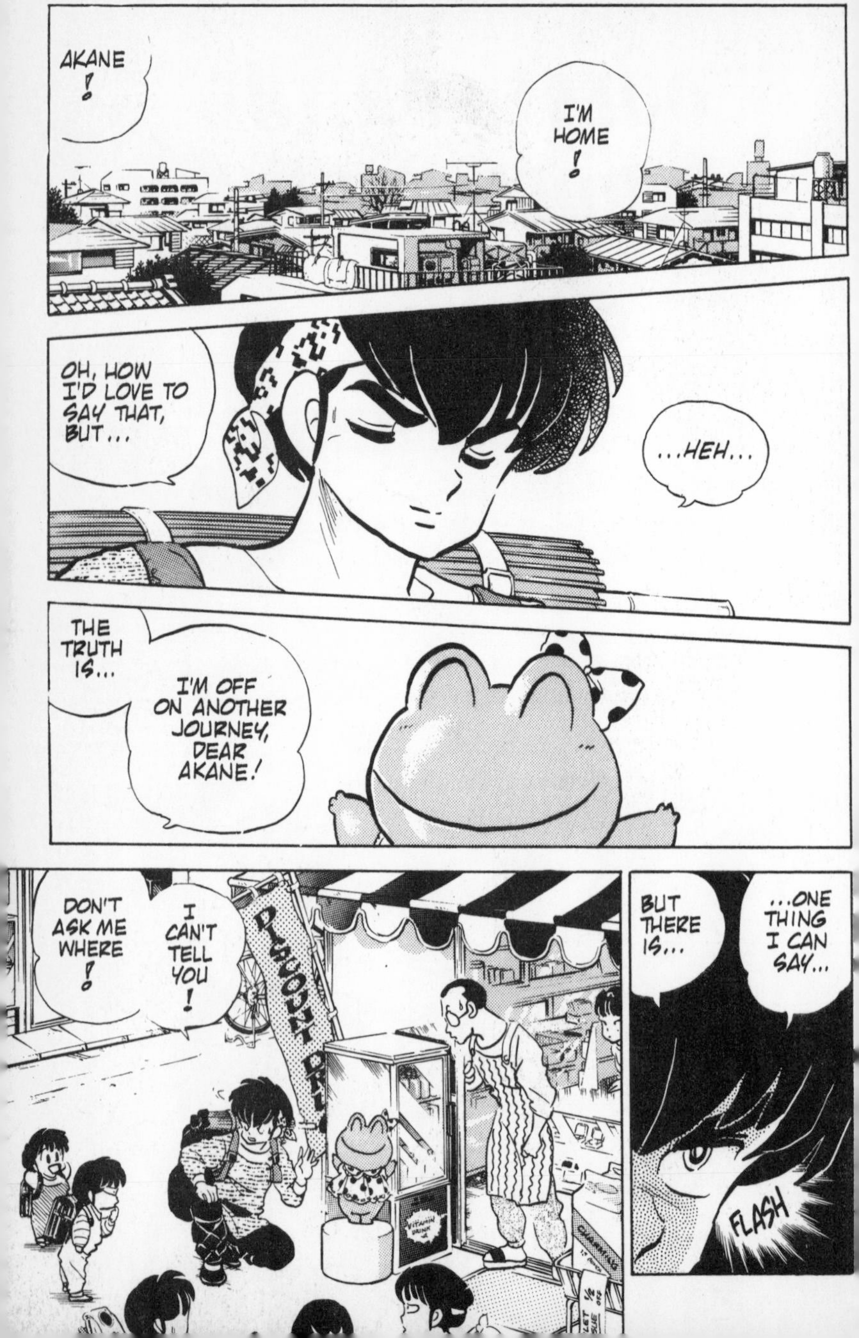
AKANE!
I'M HOME!
OH, HOW I'D LOVE TO SAY THAT, BUT...
...HEH...
THE TRUTH IS...
I'M OFF ON ANOTHER JOURNEY, DEAR AKANE!
DON'T ASK ME WHERE!
I CAN'T TELL YOU!
DISCOUNT
VITAMIN DRINK
BUT THERE IS...
...ONE THING I CAN SAY...
FLASH

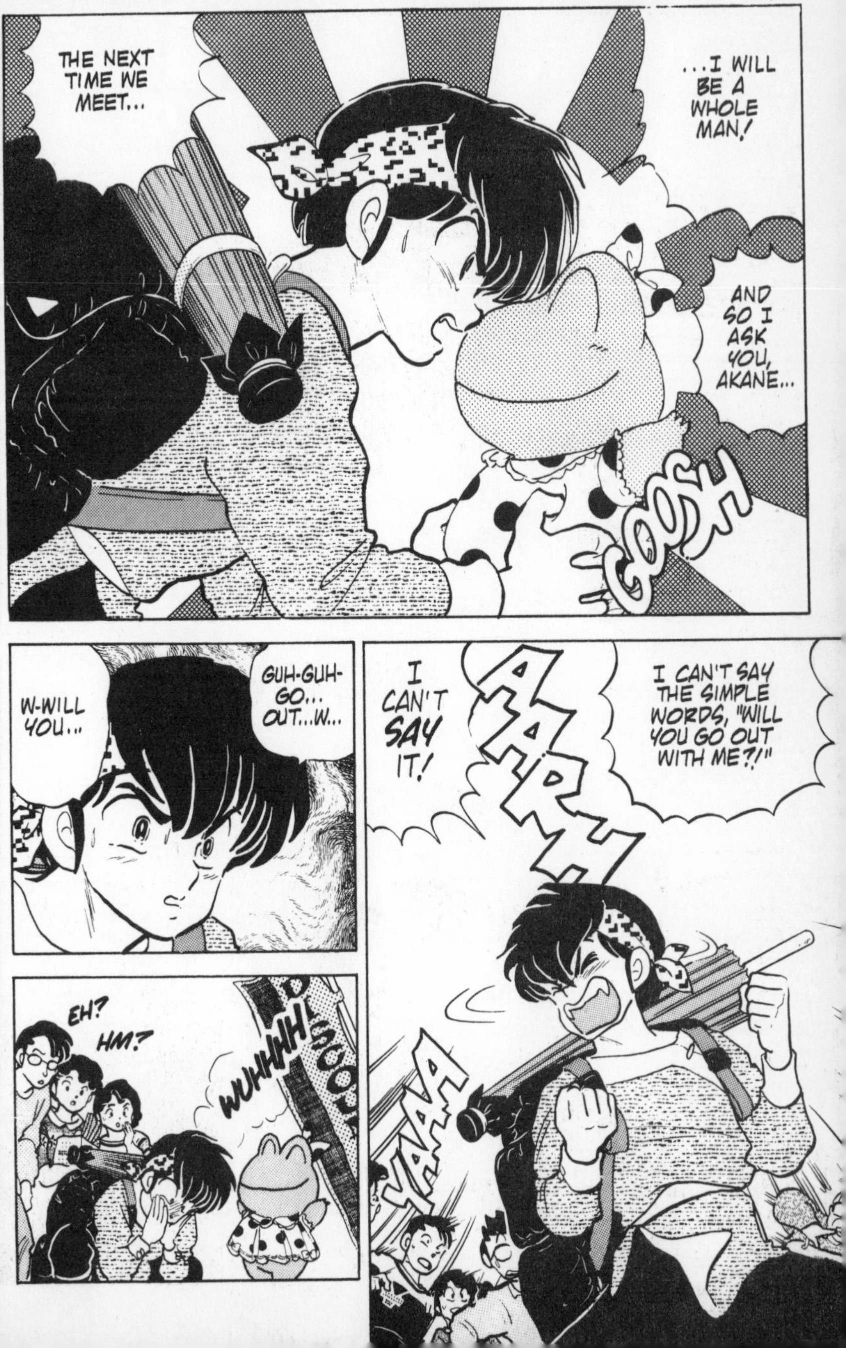
THE NEXT TIME WE MEET...
...I WILL BE A WHOLE MAN!
AND SO I ASK YOU, AKANE...
GOOSH
W-WILL YOU...
GUH-GUH-GO... OUT...W...
EH?
HM?
WUHHHH
I CAN'T SAY IT!
I CAN'T SAY THE SIMPLE WORDS, "WILL YOU GO OUT WITH ME?!"

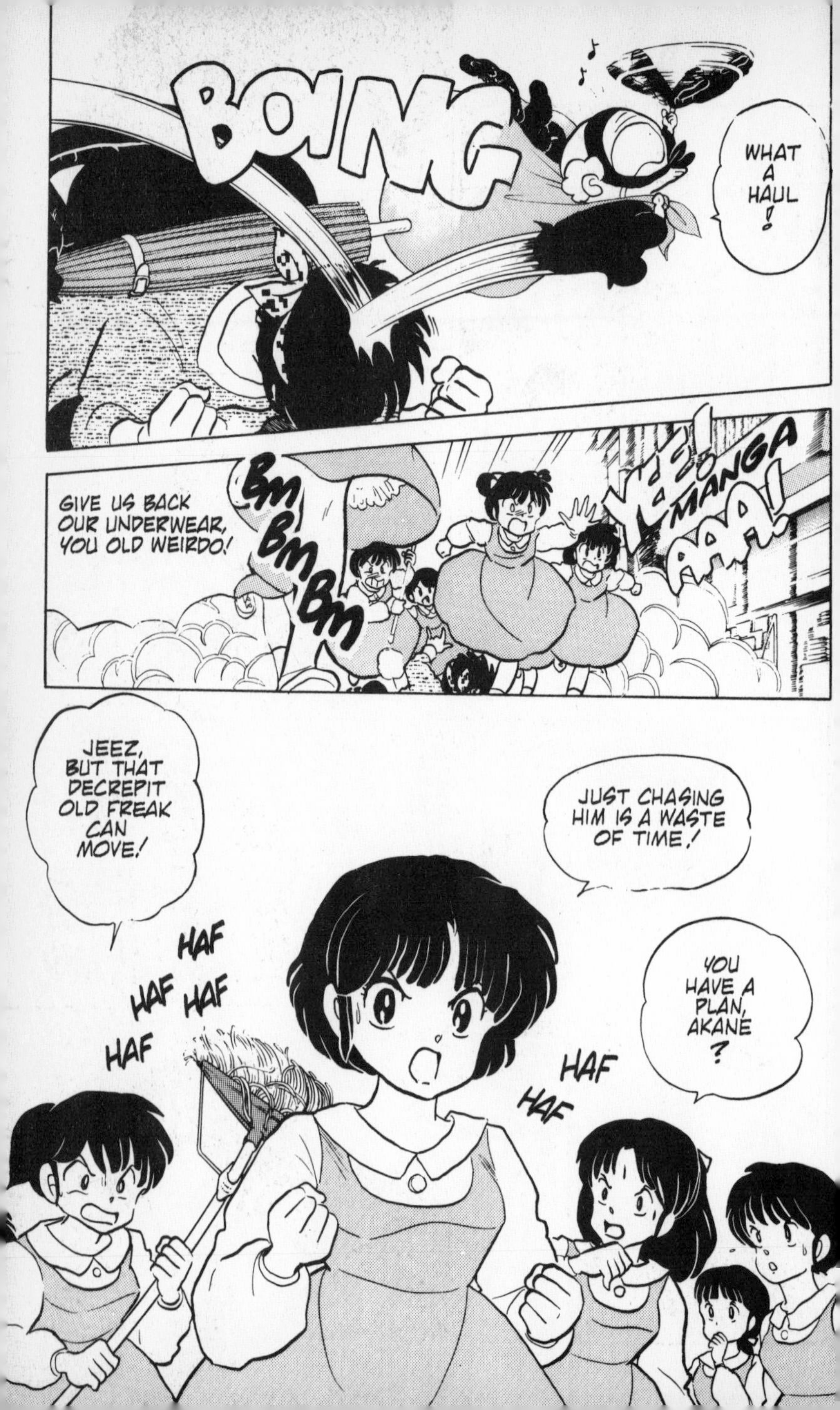
BOING
WHAT A HAUL!
GIVE US BACK OUR UNDERWEAR, YOU OLD WEIRDO!
Bm Bm Bm Bm
MANGA
AAA!
JEEZ, BUT THAT DECREPIT OLD FREAK CAN MOVE!
JUST CHASING HIM IS A WASTE OF TIME!
HAF HAF HAF HAF
HAF HAF
YOU HAVE A PLAN, AKANE?

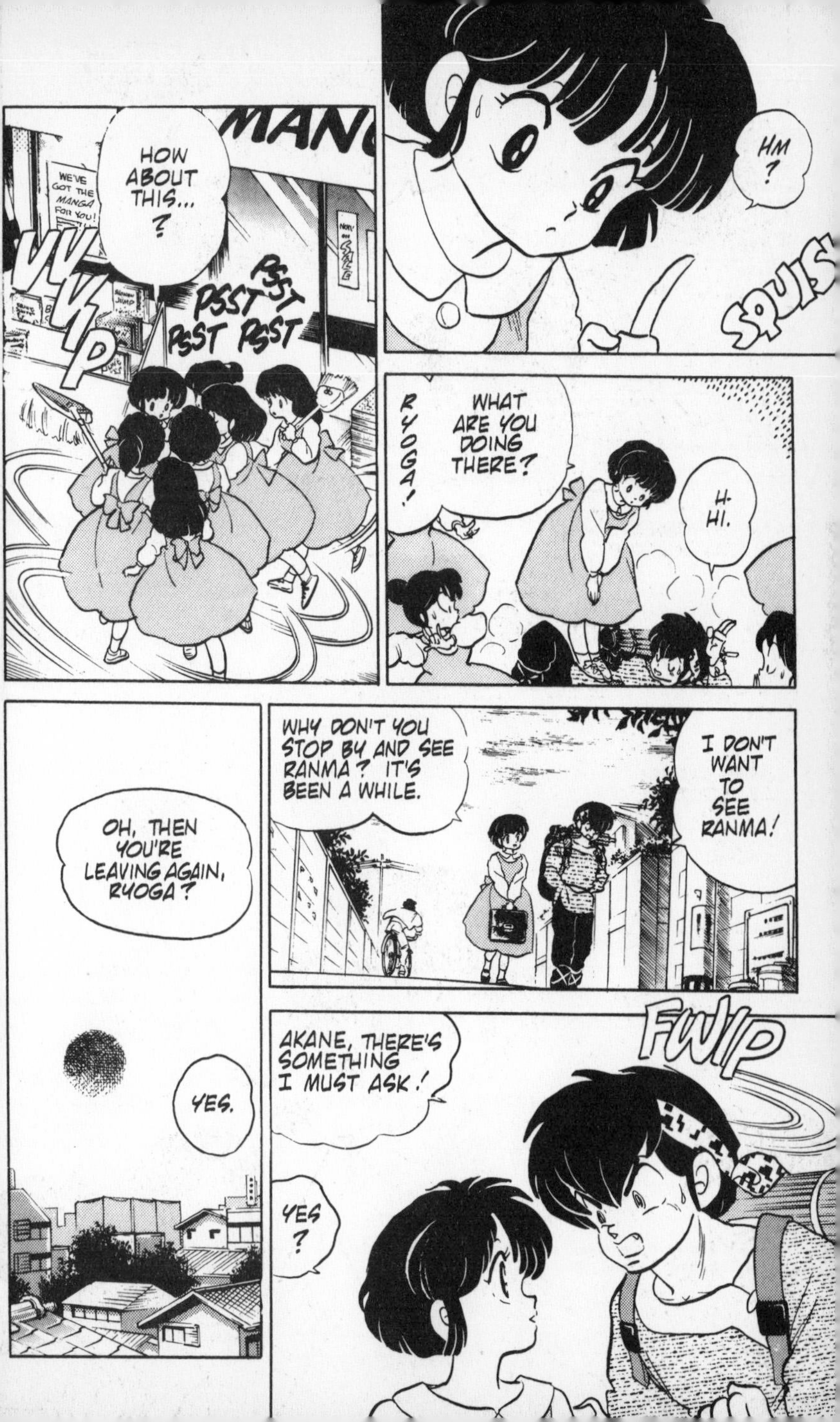
MANG
WE'VE GOT THE MANGA FOR YOU!
VVVIP
HOW ABOUT THIS...?
PSST PSST PSST PSST
HM?
SQUISH
RYOGA!
WHAT ARE YOU DOING THERE?
H-HI.
OH, THEN YOU'RE LEAVING AGAIN, RYOGA?
YES.
WHY DON'T YOU STOP BY AND SEE RANMA? IT'S BEEN A WHILE.
I DON'T WANT TO SEE RANMA!
FWIP
AKANE, THERE'S SOMETHING I MUST ASK!
YES?

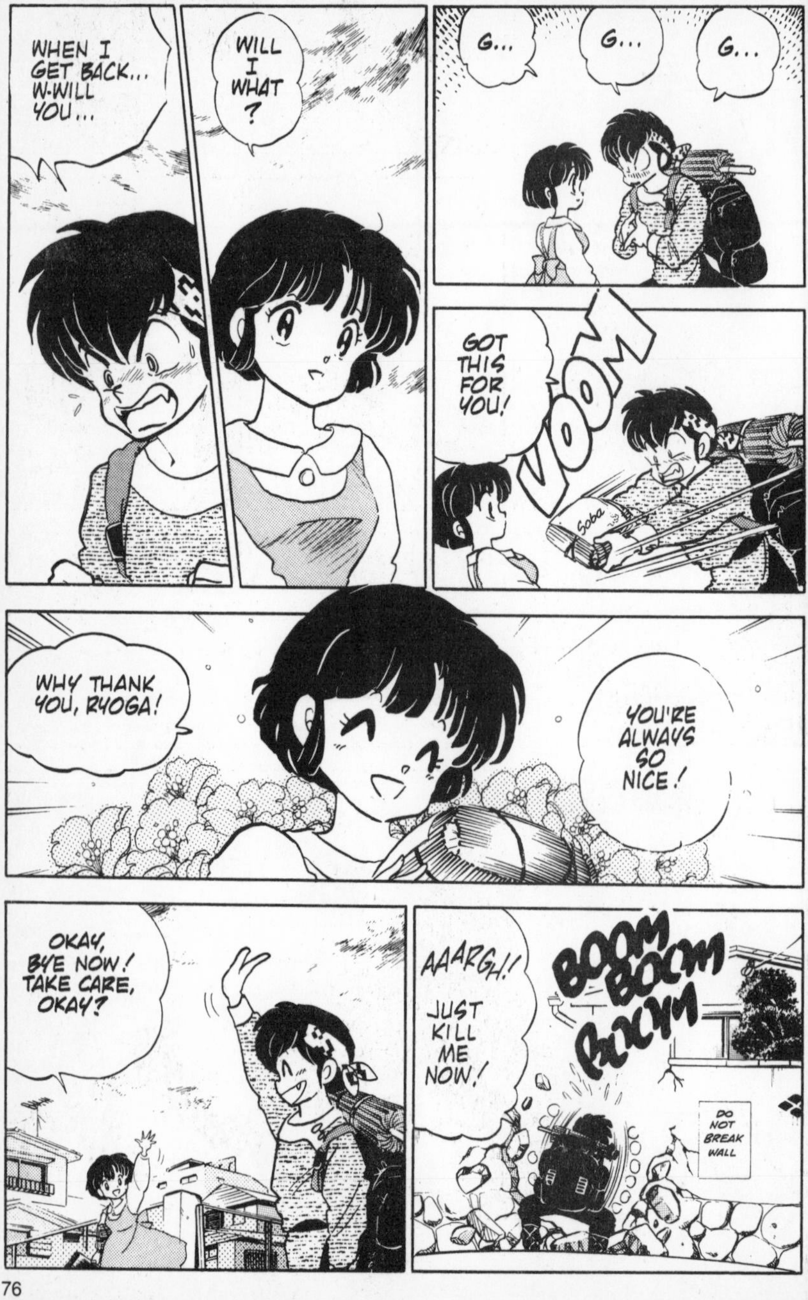
WHEN I GET BACK... W-WILL YOU...
WILL I WHAT?
G...
G...
G...
GOT THIS FOR YOU!
VOOM
Soba
WHY THANK YOU, RYOGA!
YOU'RE ALWAYS SO NICE!
OKAY, BYE NOW! TAKE CARE, OKAY?
AAARGH!! JUST KILL ME NOW!
BOOM
BOOM
DO NOT BREAK WALL

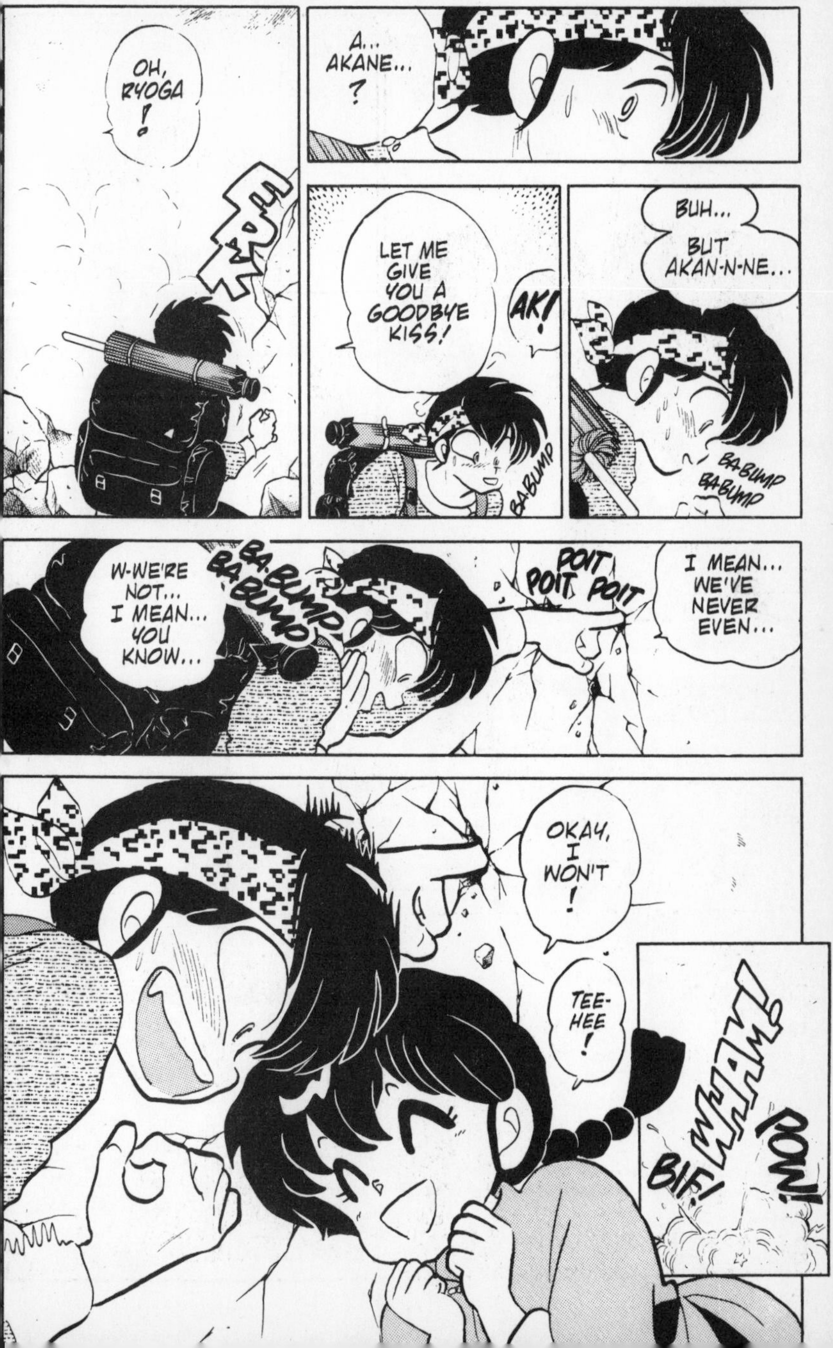
OH, RYOGA!
A... AKANE...?
LET ME GIVE YOU A GOODBYE KISS!
AK!
BA-BUMP
BUH... BUT AKAN-N-NE...
BA-BUMP BA-BUMP
W-WE'RE NOT... I MEAN... YOU KNOW...
BA-BUMP BA-BUMP
POIT POIT POIT
I MEAN... WE'VE NEVER EVEN...
OKAY, I WON'T!
TEE-HEE!
BIF! WHAM! POW!

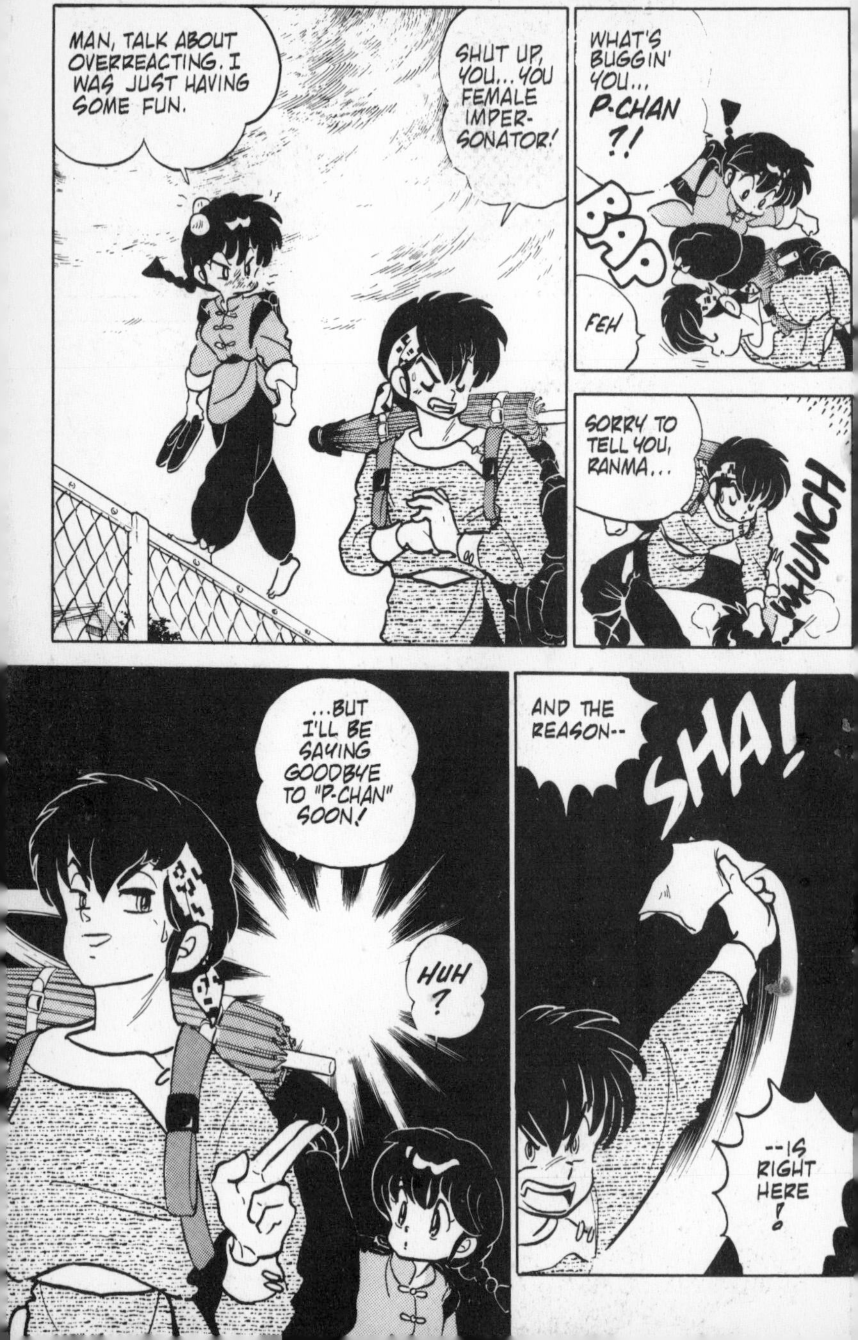
MAN, TALK ABOUT OVERREACTING. I WAS JUST HAVING SOME FUN.
SHUT UP, YOU... YOU FEMALE IMPER-SONATOR!
WHAT'S BUGGIN' YOU... P-CHAN ?!
BAP
FEH
SORRY TO TELL YOU, RANMA...
WHUNCH
...BUT I'LL BE SAYING GOODBYE TO "P-CHAN" SOON!
HUH ?
AND THE REASON--
SHA!
--IS RIGHT HERE!

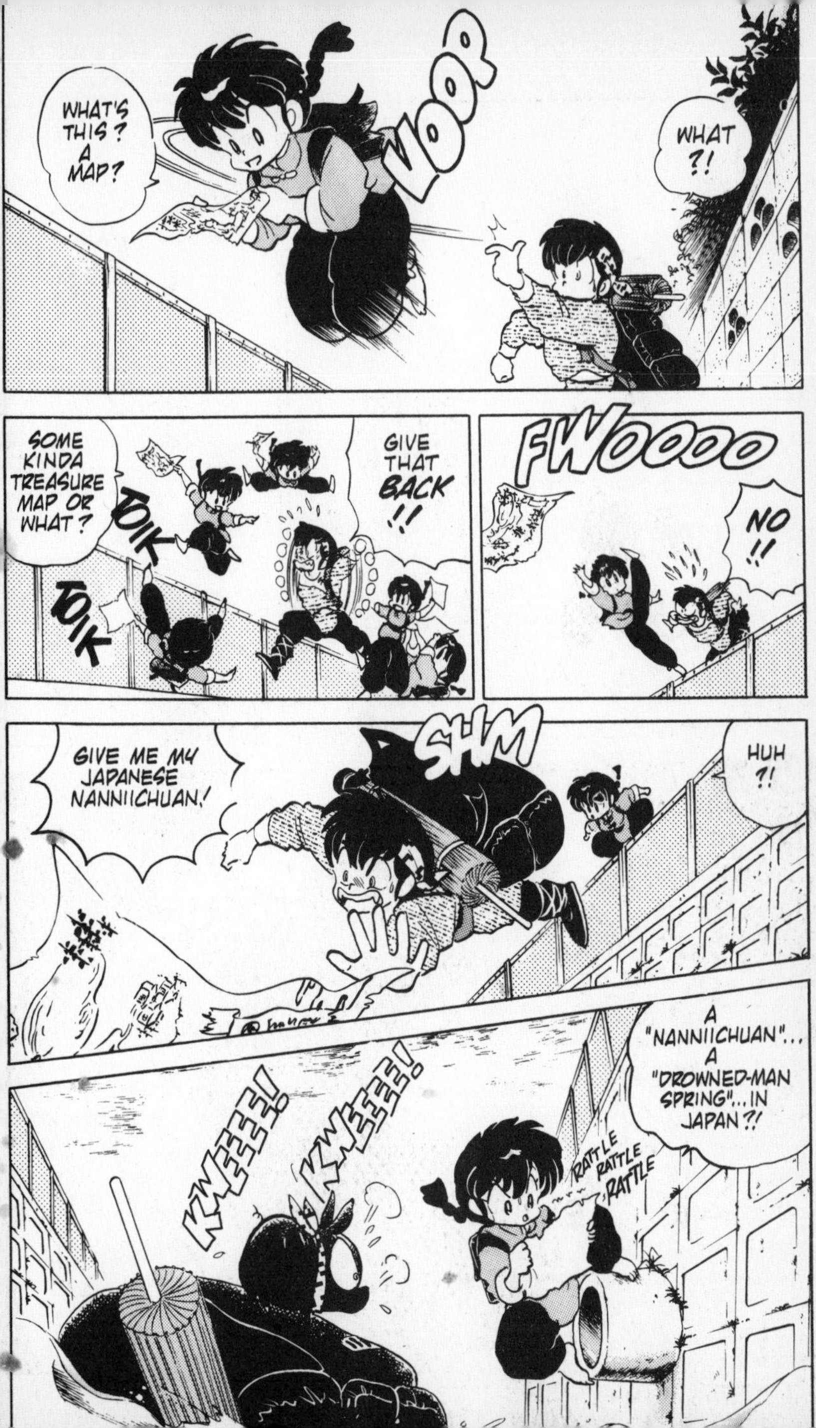
WHAT'S THIS? A MAP?
VOOP
WHAT ?!
SOME KINDA TREASURE MAP OR WHAT?
TOIK
TOIK
GIVE THAT BACK !!
FWOOOO
NO !!
GIVE ME MY JAPANESE NANNIICHUAN!
SHM
HUH ?!
KWEEEE!
KWEEEE!
RATTLE RATTLE RATTLE
A "NANNIICHUAN"... A "DROWNED-MAN SPRING"... IN JAPAN?!

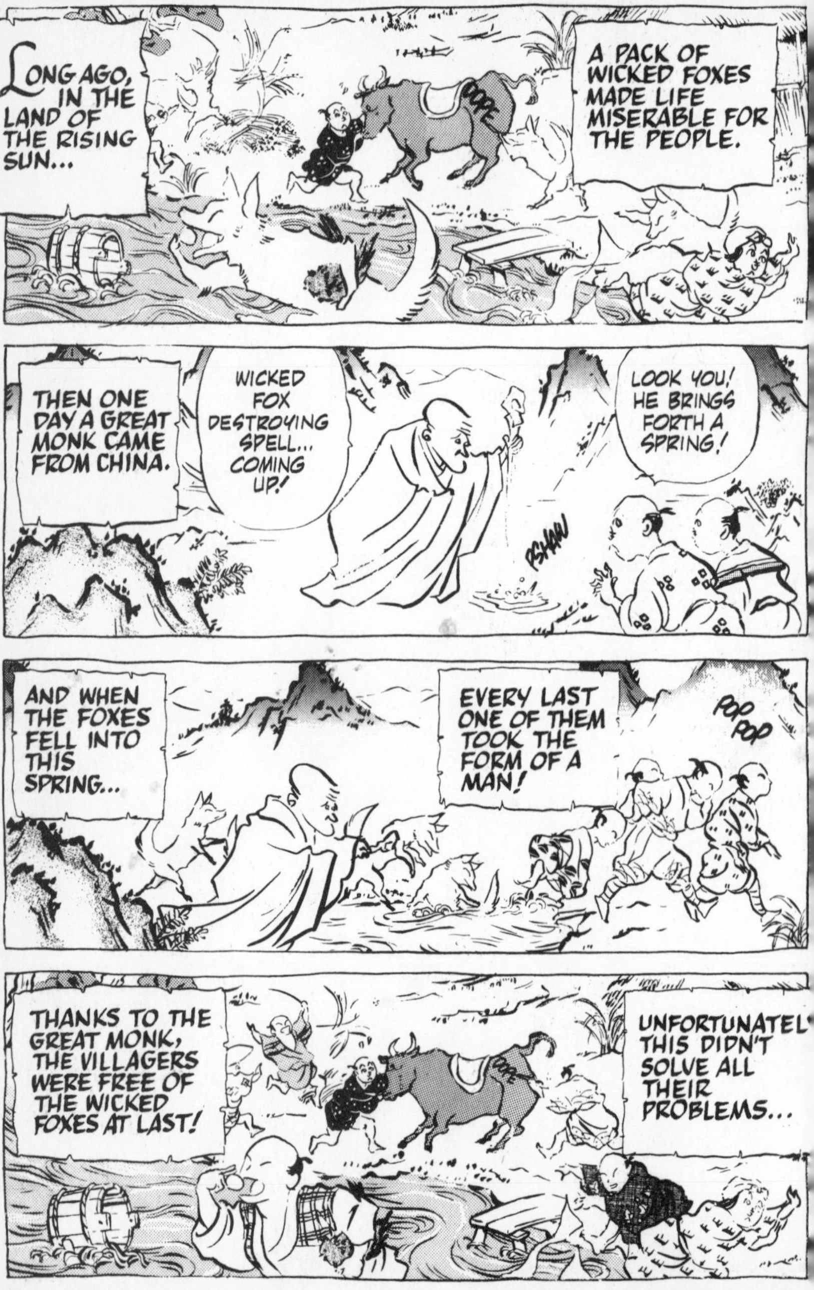
LONG AGO, IN THE LAND OF THE RISING SUN...
A PACK OF WICKED FOXES MADE LIFE MISERABLE FOR THE PEOPLE.
THEN ONE DAY A GREAT MONK CAME FROM CHINA.
WICKED FOX DESTROYING SPELL... COMING UP!
PSHAW
LOOK YOU! HE BRINGS FORTH A SPRING!
AND WHEN THE FOXES FELL INTO THIS SPRING...
EVERY LAST ONE OF THEM TOOK THE FORM OF A MAN!
POP POP
THANKS TO THE GREAT MONK, THE VILLAGERS WERE FREE OF THE WICKED FOXES AT LAST!
UNFORTUNATEL THIS DIDN'T SOLVE ALL THEIR PROBLEMS...

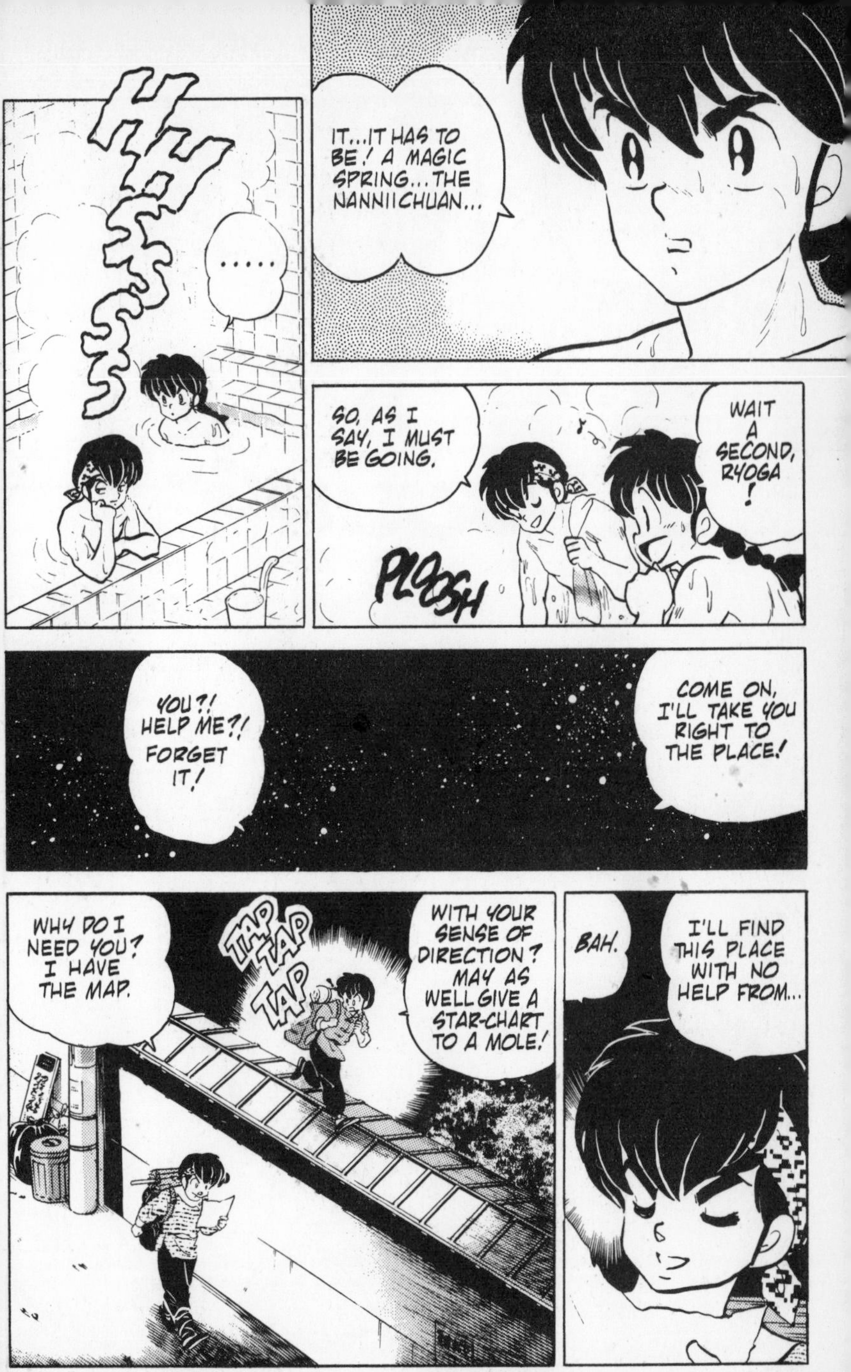

HUFF
.....
IT...IT HAS TO BE! A MAGIC SPRING...THE NANNIICHUAN...
SO, AS I SAY, I MUST BE GOING.
PLOOSH
WAIT A SECOND, RYOGA!
YOU?! HELP ME?! FORGET IT!
COME ON, I'LL TAKE YOU RIGHT TO THE PLACE!
WHY DO I NEED YOU? I HAVE THE MAP.
TAP TAP TAP
WITH YOUR SENSE OF DIRECTION? MAY AS WELL GIVE A STAR-CHART TO A MOLE!
BAH.
I'LL FIND THIS PLACE WITH NO HELP FROM...

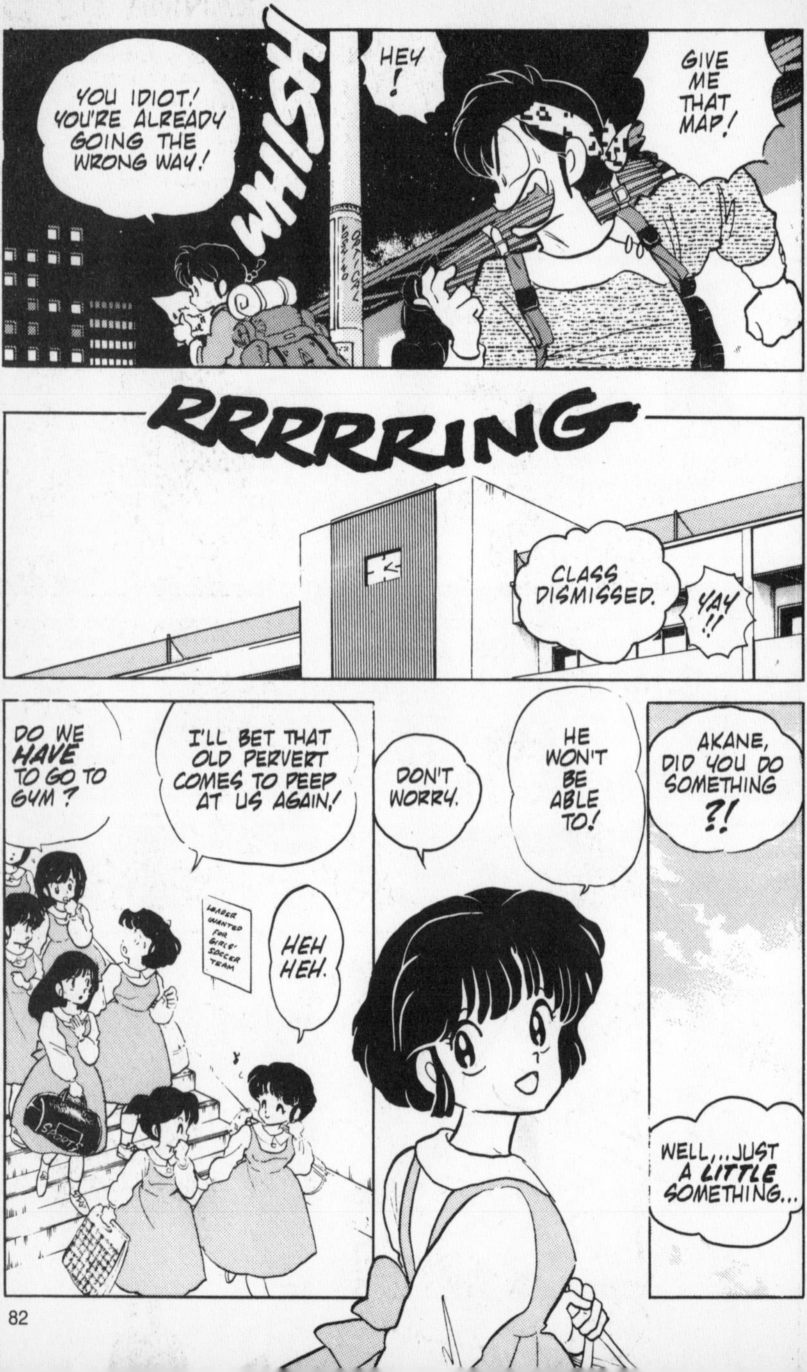

YOU IDIOT! YOU'RE ALREADY GOING THE WRONG WAY!
WHISH
HEY!
GIVE ME THAT MAP!
RRRRRING
CLASS DISMISSED.
YAY!!
DO WE HAVE TO GO TO GYM?
I'LL BET THAT OLD PERVERT COMES TO PEEP AT US AGAIN!
LEADER WANTED FOR GIRLS' SOCCER TEAM
HEH HEH.
DON'T WORRY.
HE WON'T BE ABLE TO!
AKANE, DID YOU DO SOMETHING?!
WELL,..JUST A LITTLE SOMETHING...

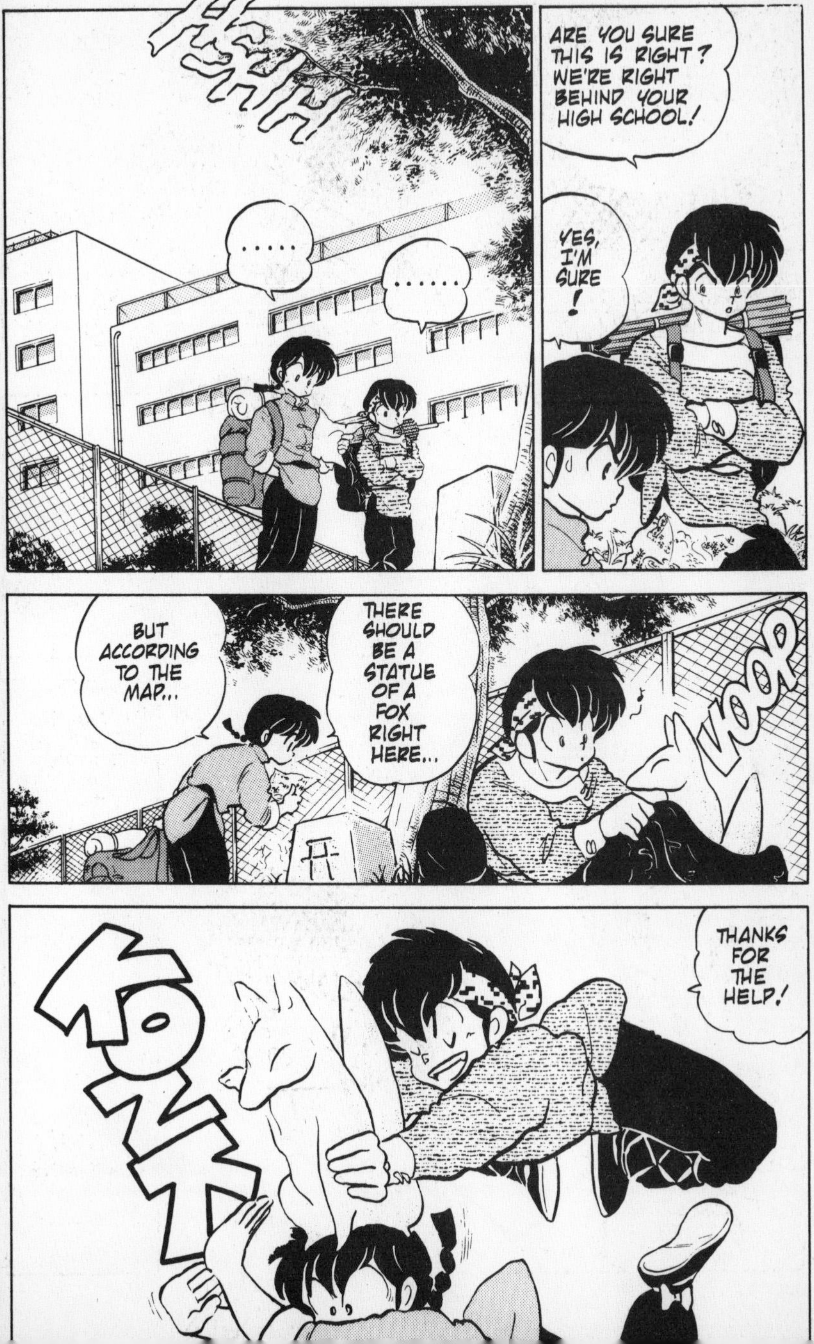
HSSH!
......
......
ARE YOU SURE THIS IS RIGHT? WE'RE RIGHT BEHIND YOUR HIGH SCHOOL!
YES, I'M SURE!
BUT ACCORDING TO THE MAP...
THERE SHOULD BE A STATUE OF A FOX RIGHT HERE...
VOOP
KONK
THANKS FOR THE HELP!

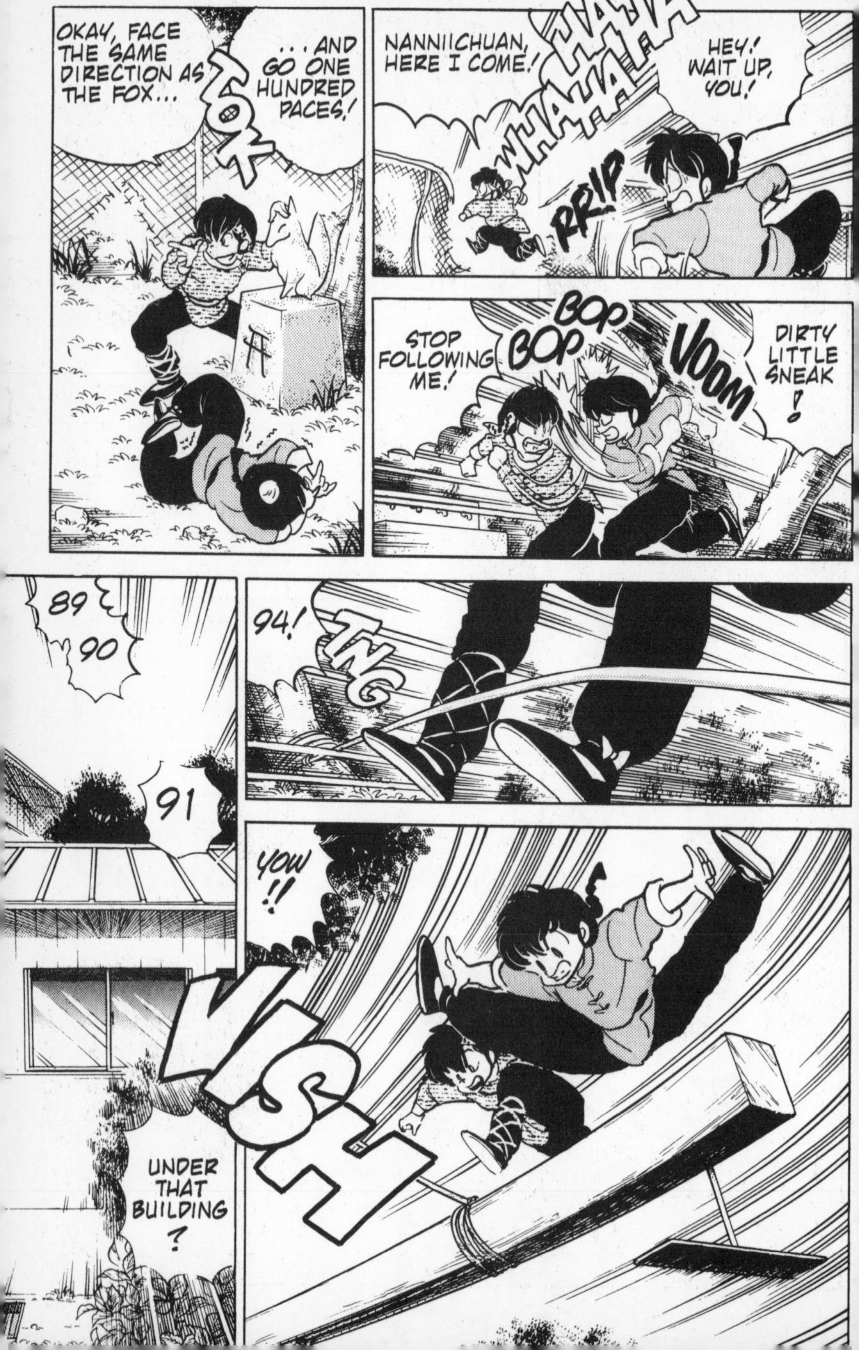
OKAY, FACE THE SAME DIRECTION AS THE FOX...
TOK
...AND GO ONE HUNDRED PACES!
NANNIICHUAN, HERE I COME!
WHAHAHAHAHA
HEY! WAIT UP, YOU!
RRIP
STOP FOLLOWING ME!
BOP BOP
VOOM
DIRTY LITTLE SNEAK!
89
90
91
94!
TNG
YOW!!
VISH
UNDER THAT BUILDING?

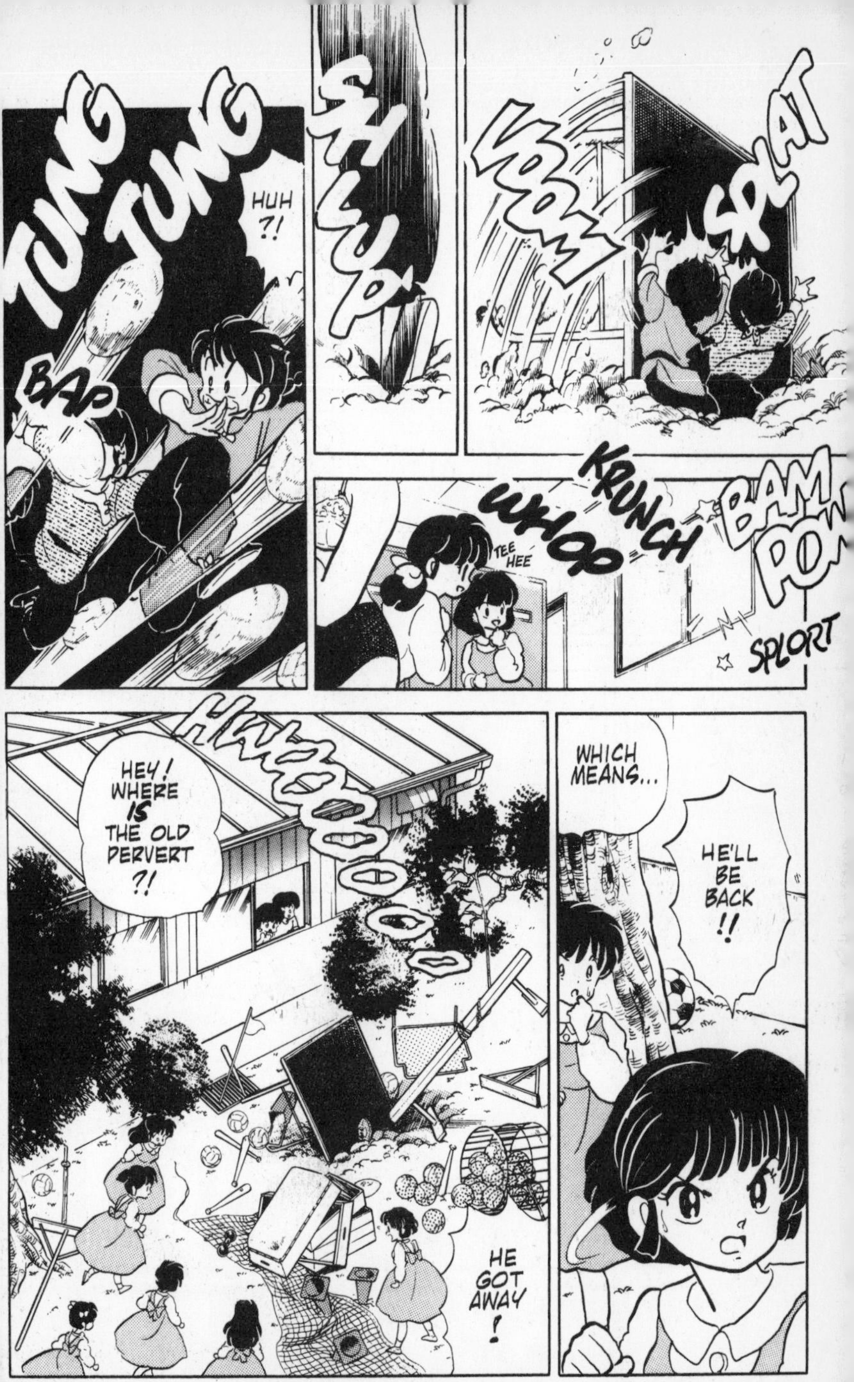
TUNG TUNG
HUH ?!
BAP
SHLUP
VOOM
SPLAT
KRUNCH
WHOP
TEE HEE
BAM POW
SPLORT
HWOOOOOO
HEY! WHERE IS THE OLD PERVERT ?!
HE GOT AWAY !
WHICH MEANS...
HE'LL BE BACK !!

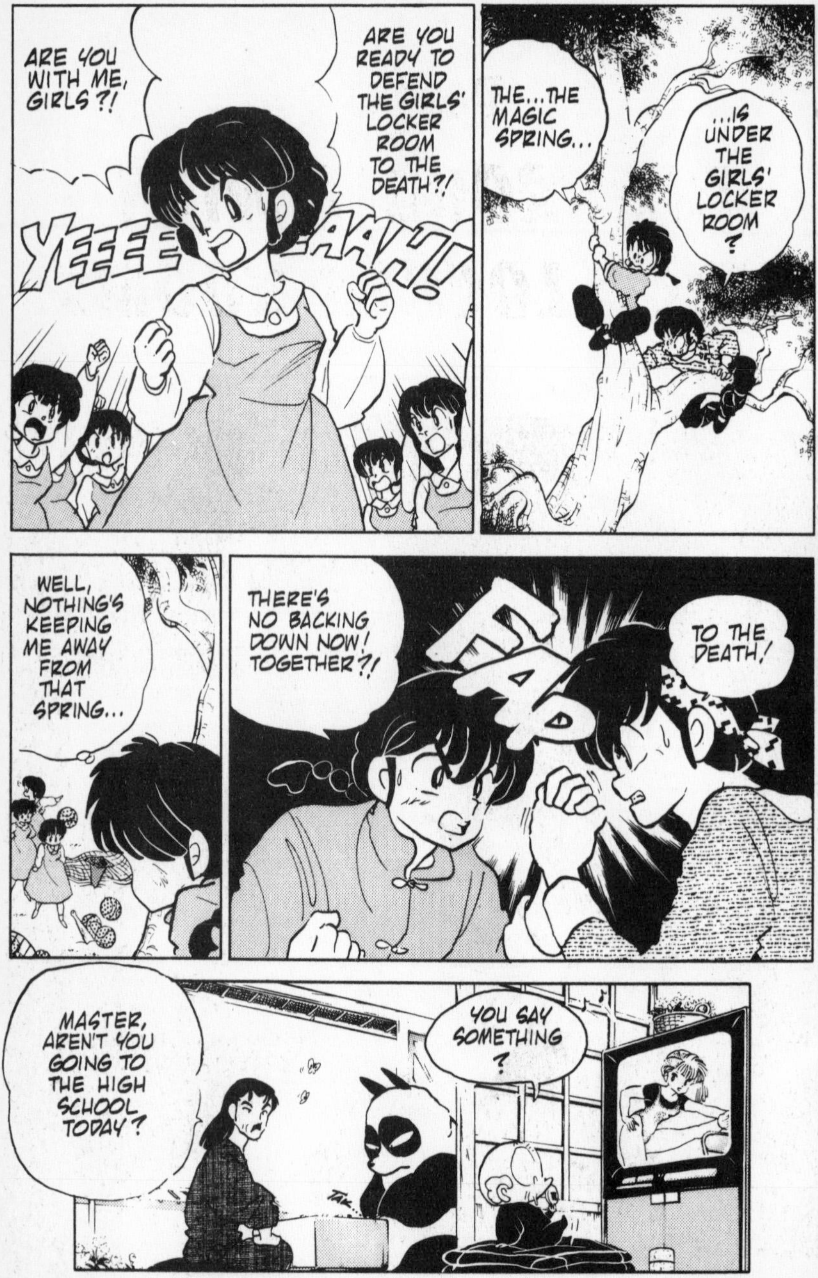
ARE YOU WITH ME, GIRLS ?!
ARE YOU READY TO DEFEND THE GIRLS' LOCKER ROOM TO THE DEATH ?!
YEEEEEAAAH!
THE...THE MAGIC SPRING...
...IS UNDER THE GIRLS' LOCKER ROOM ?
WELL, NOTHING'S KEEPING ME AWAY FROM THAT SPRING...
THERE'S NO BACKING DOWN NOW! TOGETHER ?!
FAP
TO THE DEATH!
MASTER, AREN'T YOU GOING TO THE HIGH SCHOOL TODAY ?
YOU SAY SOMETHING ?
TAK

Part 6
THE TROUBLE WITH GIRLS' LOCKER ROOMS

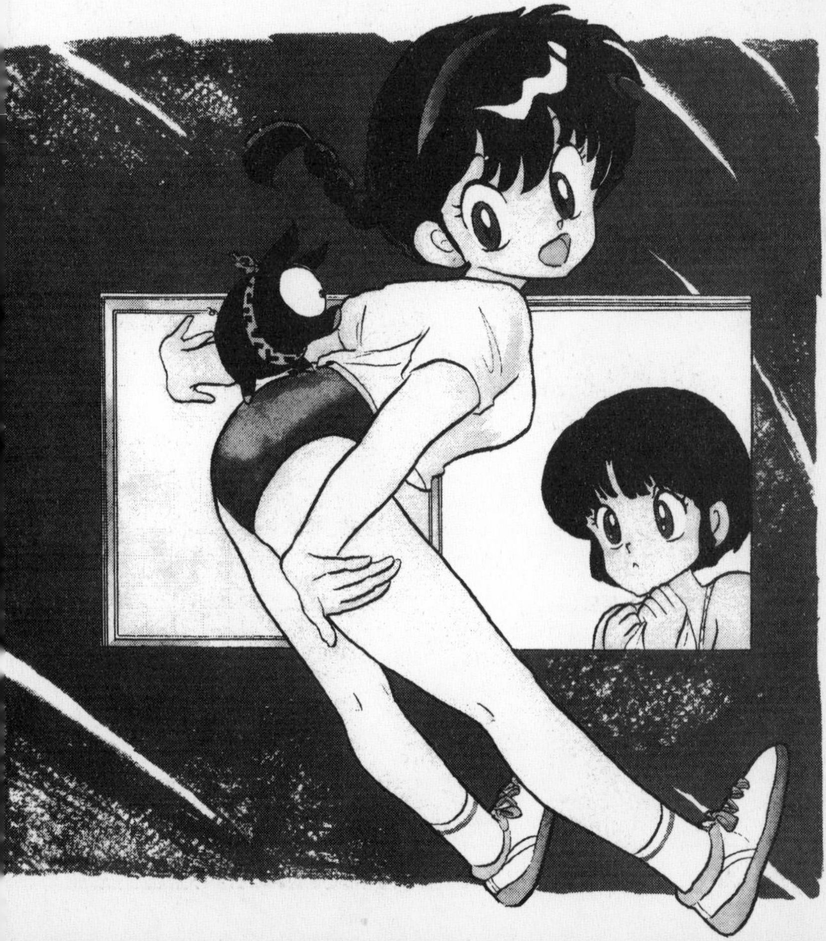

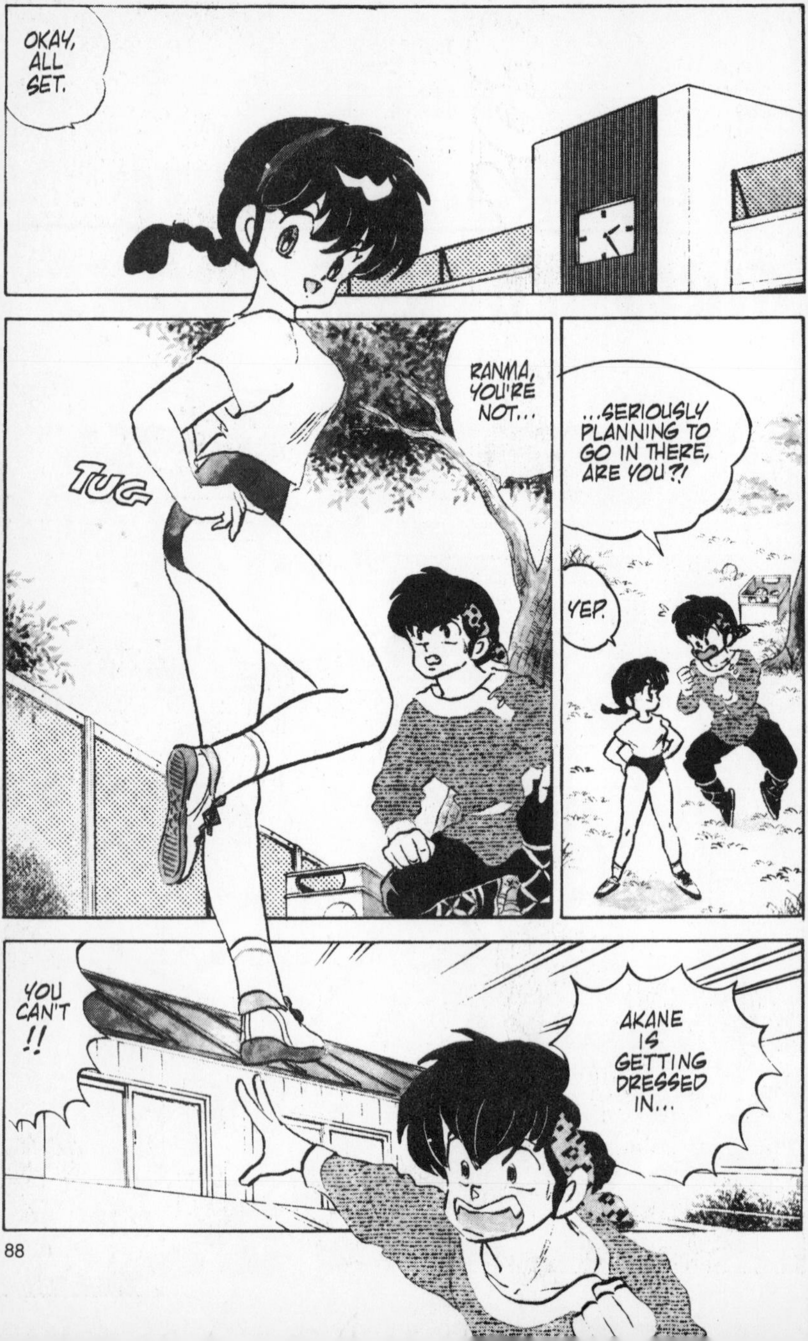
OKAY, ALL SET.
TUG
RANMA, YOU'RE NOT...
...SERIOUSLY PLANNING TO GO IN THERE, ARE YOU?!
YEP.
YOU CAN'T!!
AKANE IS GETTING DRESSED IN...

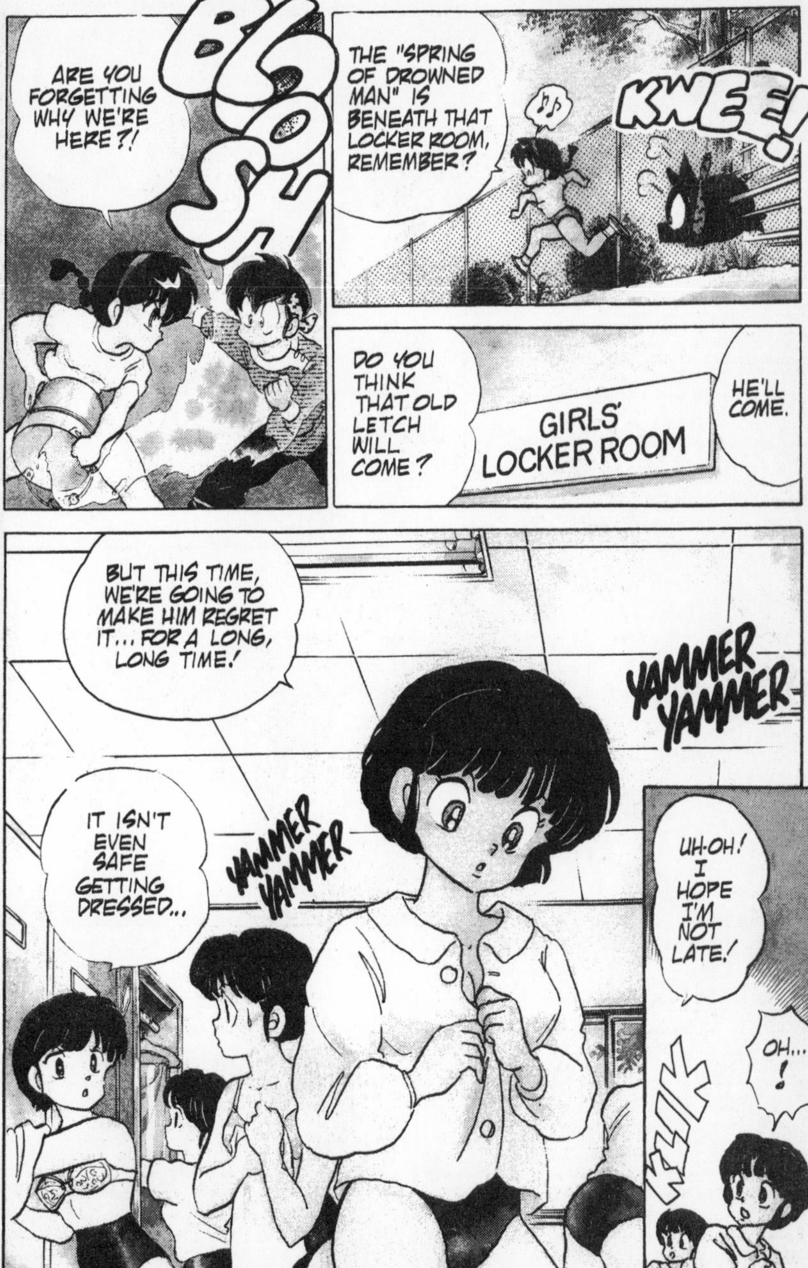
ARE YOU FORGETTING WHY WE'RE HERE?!
BLOSH
THE "SPRING OF DROWNED MAN" IS BENEATH THAT LOCKER ROOM, REMEMBER?
KWEE!
DO YOU THINK THAT OLD LETCH WILL COME?
GIRLS' LOCKER ROOM
HE'LL COME.
BUT THIS TIME, WE'RE GOING TO MAKE HIM REGRET IT... FOR A LONG, LONG TIME!
YAMMER YAMMER
IT ISN'T EVEN SAFE GETTING DRESSED...
YAMMER YAMMER
UH-OH! I HOPE I'M NOT LATE!
KLIK
OH...!

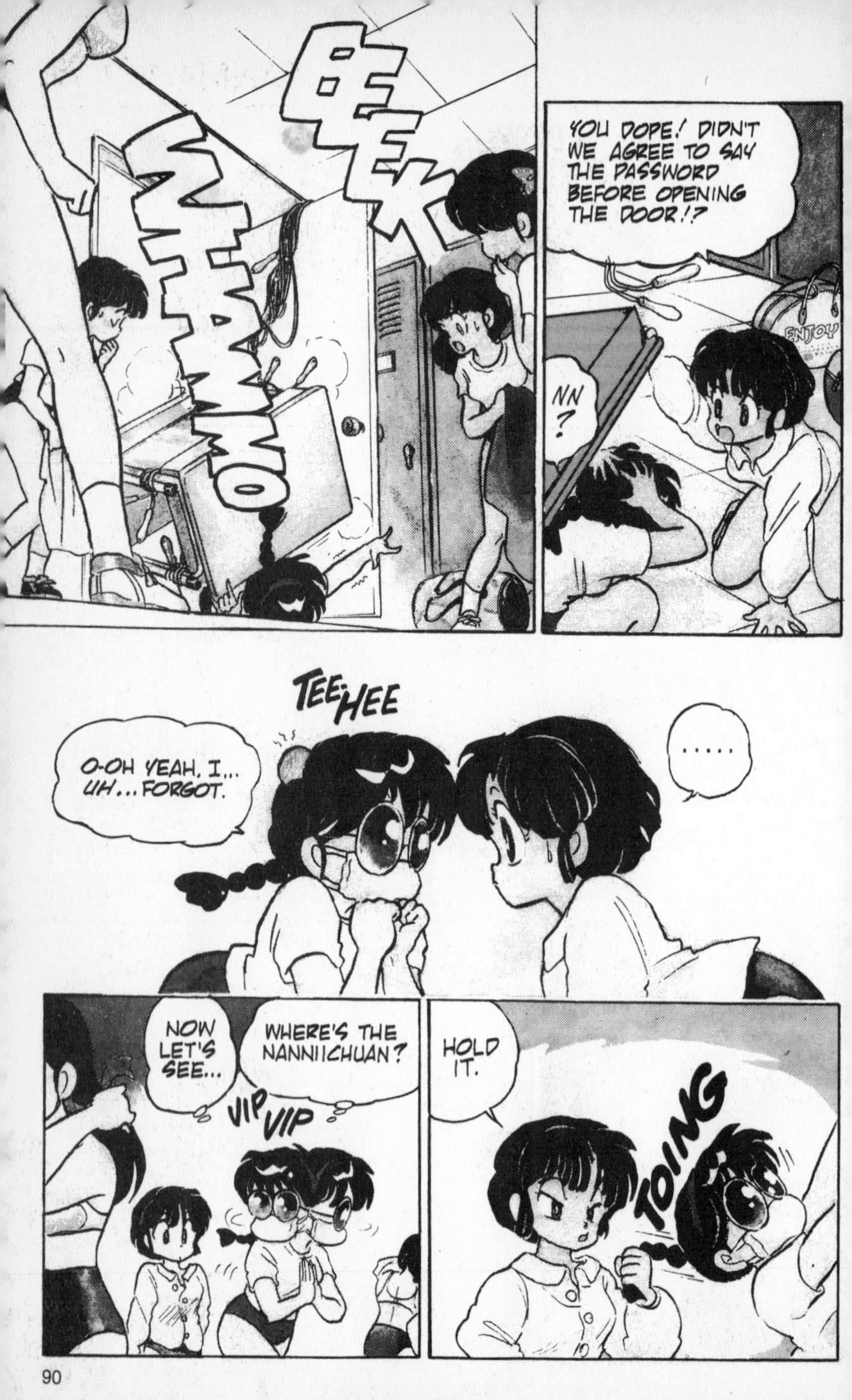
WHAMMO
YOU DOPE! DIDN'T WE AGREE TO SAY THE PASSWORD BEFORE OPENING THE DOOR!?
NN?
ENJOY
TEE-HEE
O-OH YEAH. I... UH... FORGOT.
.....
NOW LET'S SEE...
WHERE'S THE NANNIICHUAN?
VIP VIP
HOLD IT.
TOING

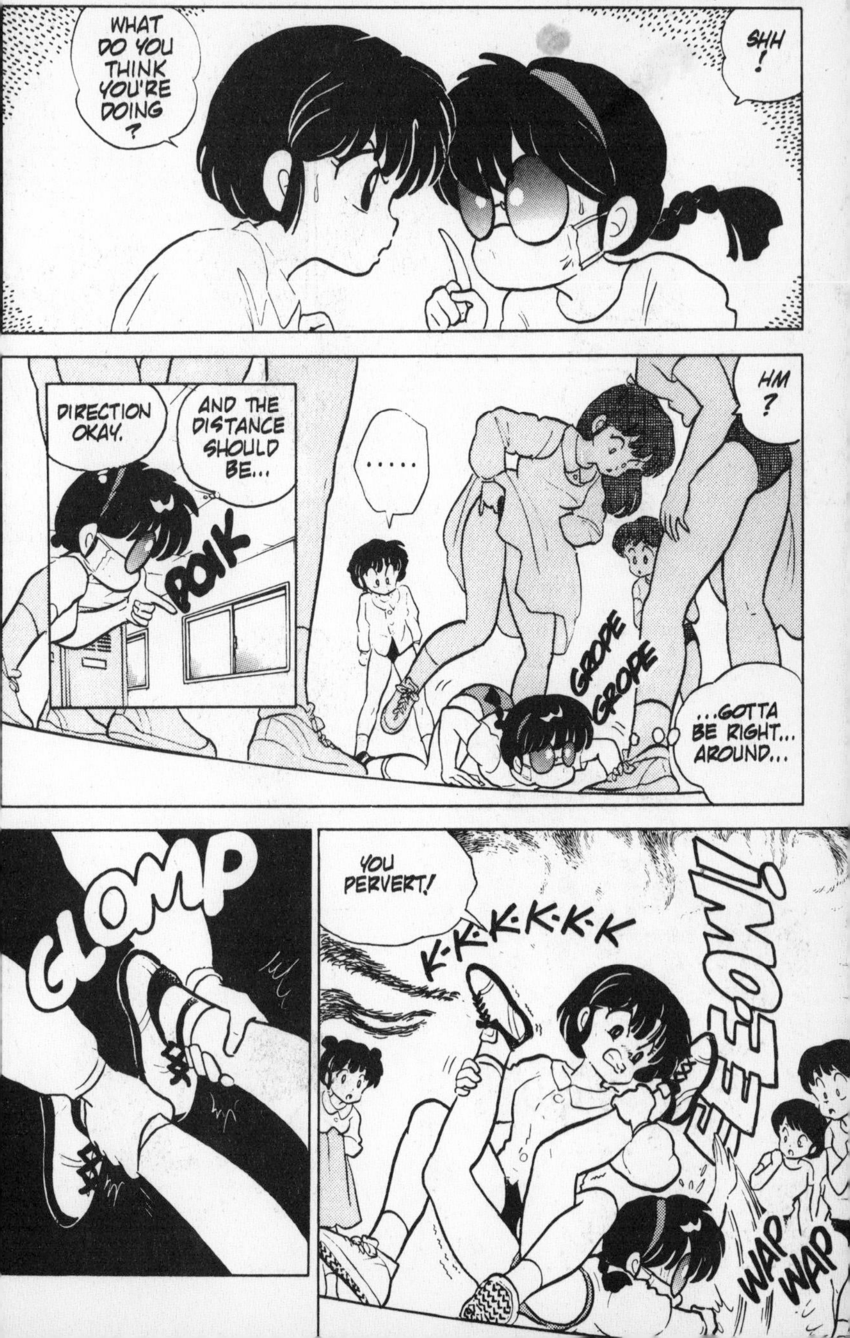
WHAT DO YOU THINK YOU'RE DOING?
SHH!
DIRECTION OKAY.
AND THE DISTANCE SHOULD BE...
POIK
.....
HM?
GROPE GROPE
...GOTTA BE RIGHT... AROUND...
GLOMP
YOU PERVERT!
K-K-K-K-K-K
EEE-OW!!
WAP WAP

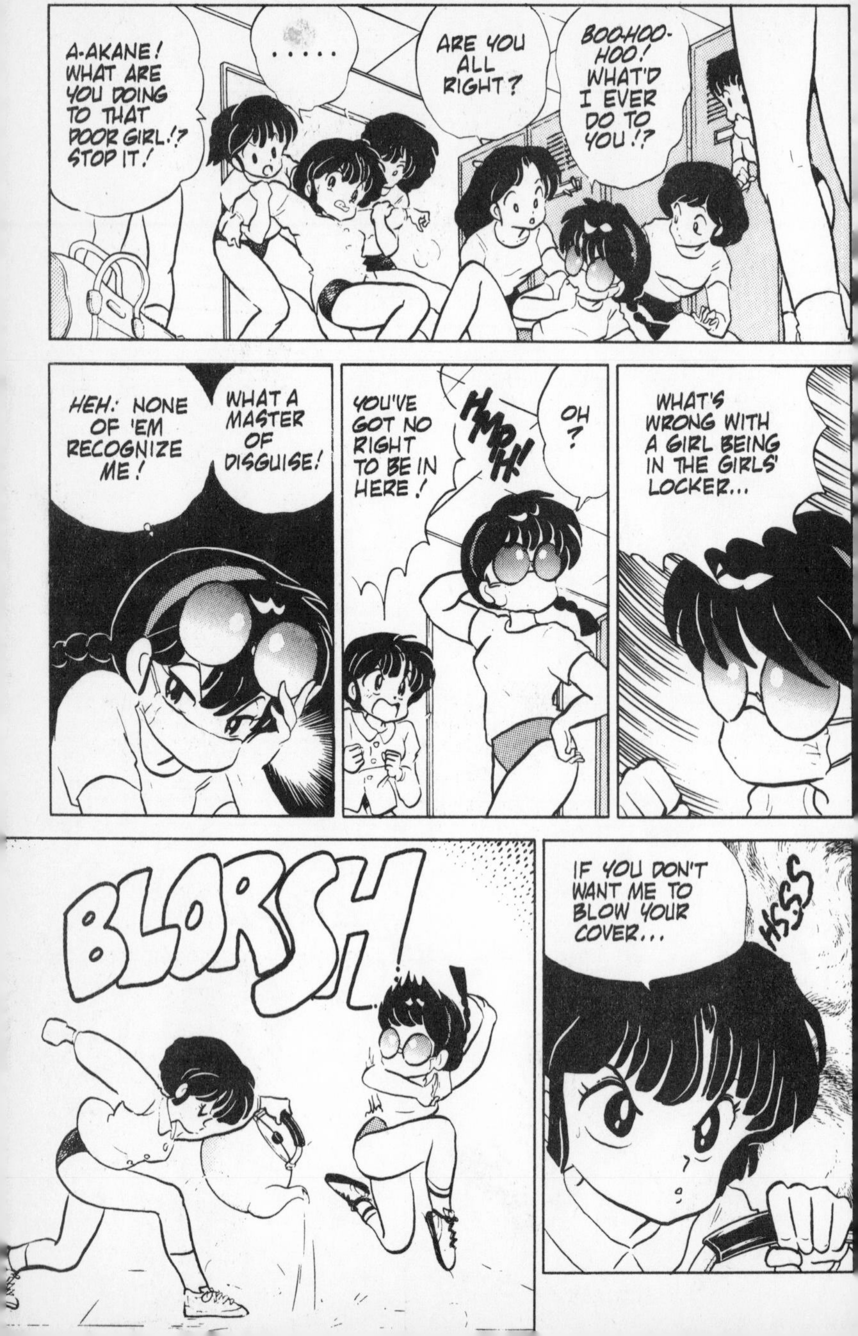
A-AKANE! WHAT ARE YOU DOING TO THAT POOR GIRL!? STOP IT!
.....
ARE YOU ALL RIGHT?
BOO-HOO-HOO! WHAT'D I EVER DO TO YOU!?
HEH: NONE OF 'EM RECOGNIZE ME!
WHAT A MASTER OF DISGUISE!
YOU'VE GOT NO RIGHT TO BE IN HERE!
HMPH!
OH?
WHAT'S WRONG WITH A GIRL BEING IN THE GIRLS' LOCKER...
BLORSH
IF YOU DON'T WANT ME TO BLOW YOUR COVER...
HSSS

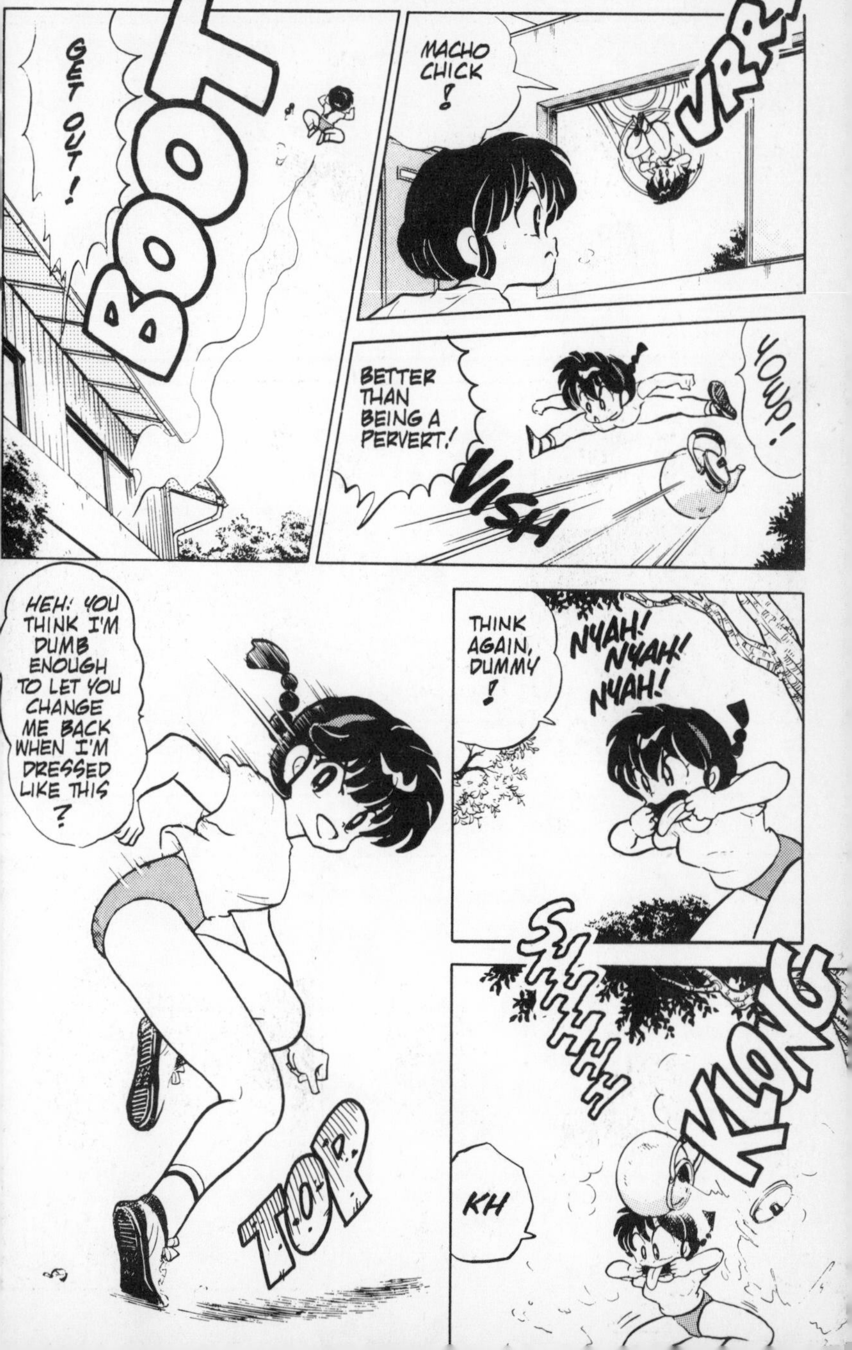
GET OUT!
BOOT
MACHO CHICK!
VRRR
BETTER THAN BEING A PERVERT!
VISH
YOWP!
HEH: YOU THINK I'M DUMB ENOUGH TO LET YOU CHANGE ME BACK WHEN I'M DRESSED LIKE THIS?
TOP
THINK AGAIN, DUMMY!
NYAH! NYAH! NYAH!
SHHHHH
KLONG
KH

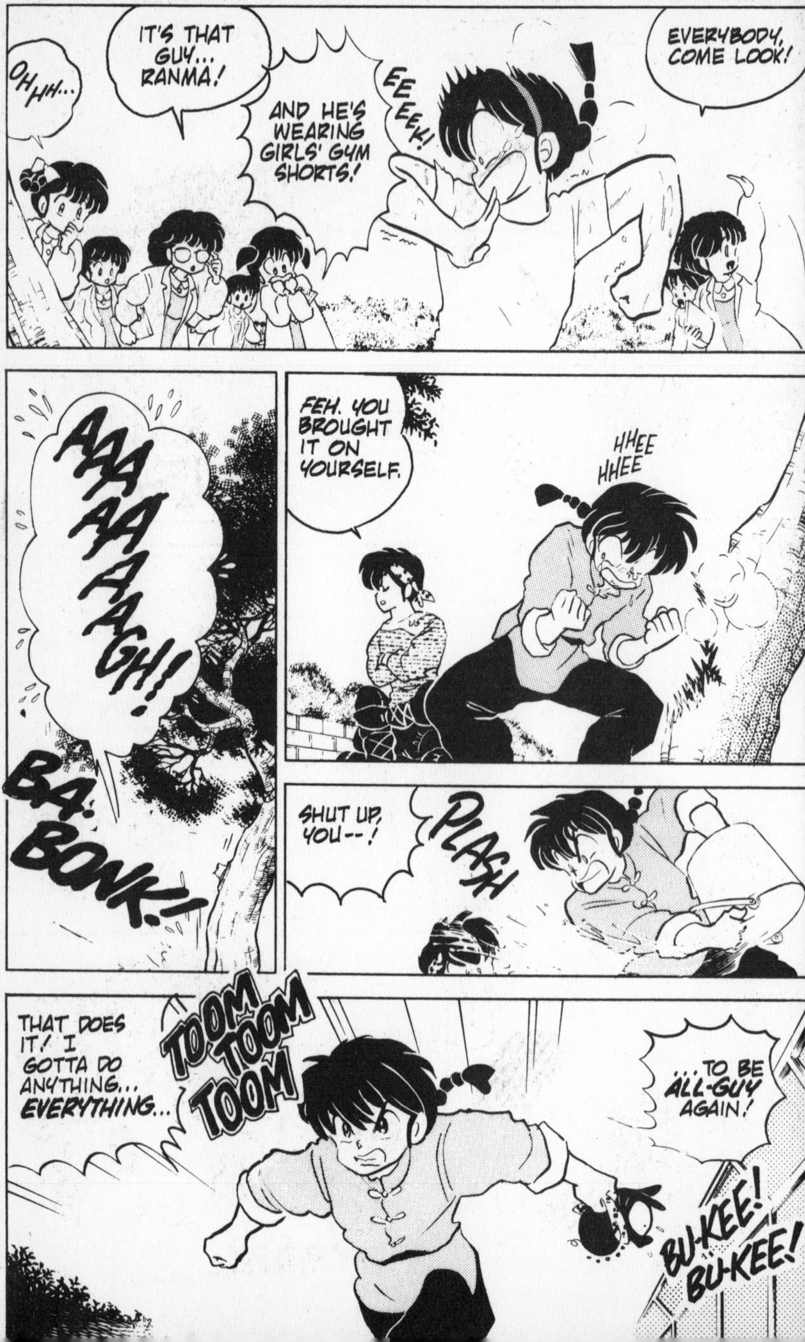
OHHH...
IT'S THAT GUY... RANMA!
AND HE'S WEARING GIRLS' GYM SHORTS!
EEEEK!
EVERYBODY, COME LOOK!
AAAAAAAAGH!!
BA-BONK!!
FEH. YOU BROUGHT IT ON YOURSELF.
HHEE HHEE
SHUT UP, YOU--!
PLASH
THAT DOES IT! I GOTTA DO ANYTHING... EVERYTHING...
TOOM TOOM TOOM
...TO BE ALL-GUY AGAIN!
BU-KEE! BU-KEE!

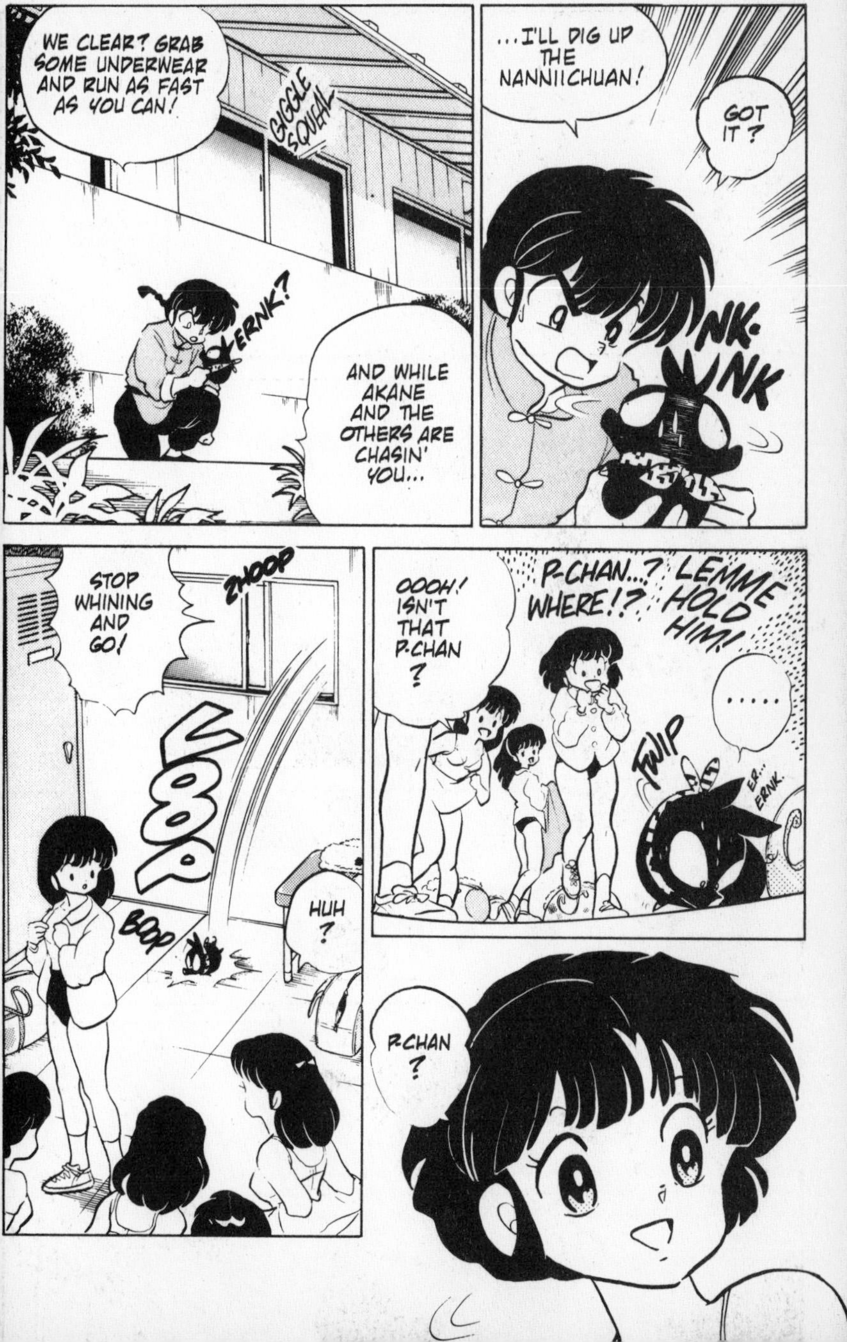
WE CLEAR? GRAB SOME UNDERWEAR AND RUN AS FAST AS YOU CAN!
GIGGLE SQUEAL
ERNK?
AND WHILE AKANE AND THE OTHERS ARE CHASIN' YOU...
...I'LL DIG UP THE NANNIICHUAN!
GOT IT?
NK-NK
STOP WHINING AND GO!
ZHOOP
VOOOP
BOOP
HUH?
OOOH! ISN'T THAT P-CHAN?
P-CHAN...? WHERE!?
LEMME HOLD HIM!
.....
FWIP
ER... ERNK.
P-CHAN?

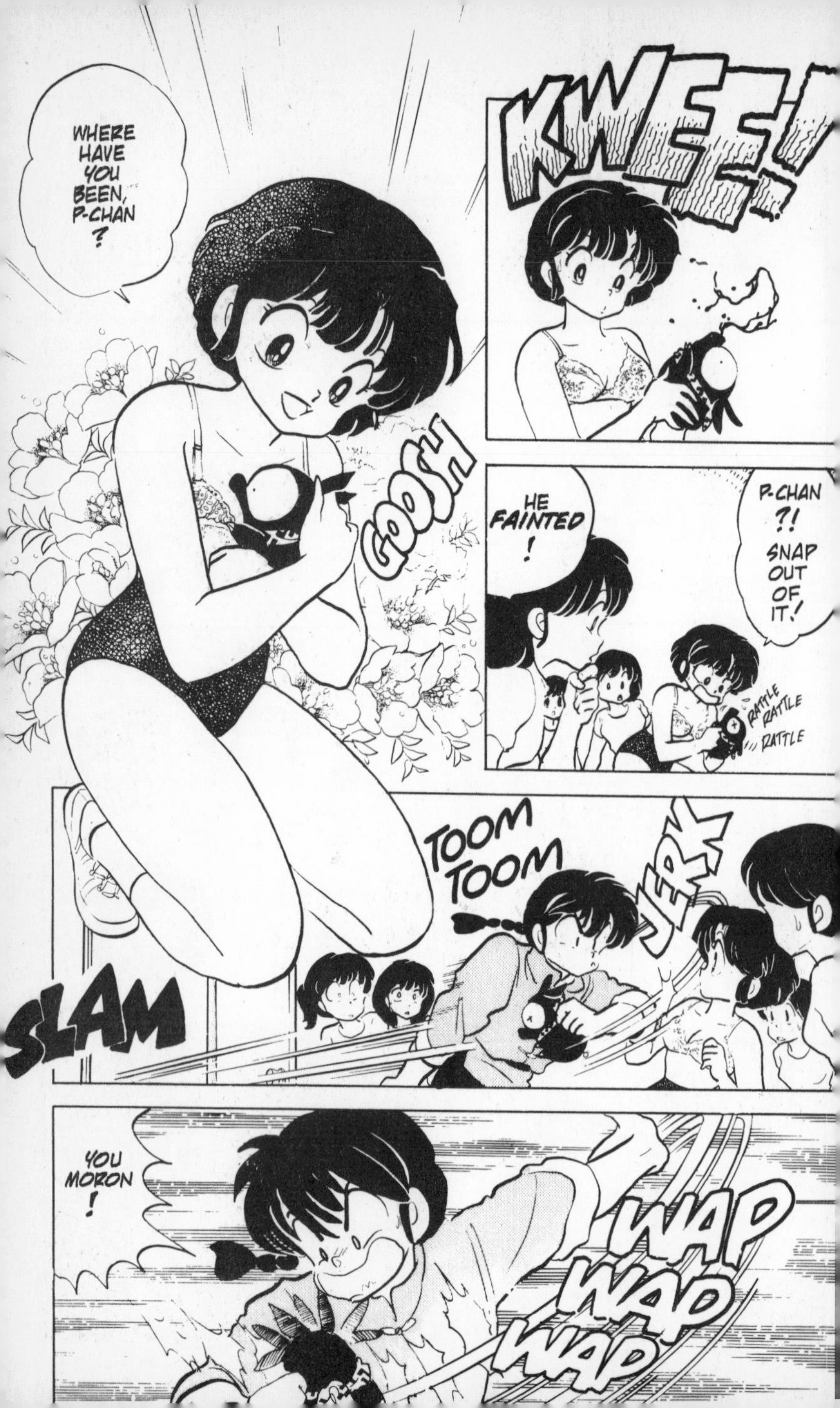
WHERE HAVE YOU BEEN, P-CHAN?
GOOSH
KWEE!?!
HE FAINTED!
P-CHAN?! SNAP OUT OF IT!
RATTLE RATTLE RATTLE
SLAM
TOOM TOOM
JERK
YOU MORON!
WAP WAP WAP

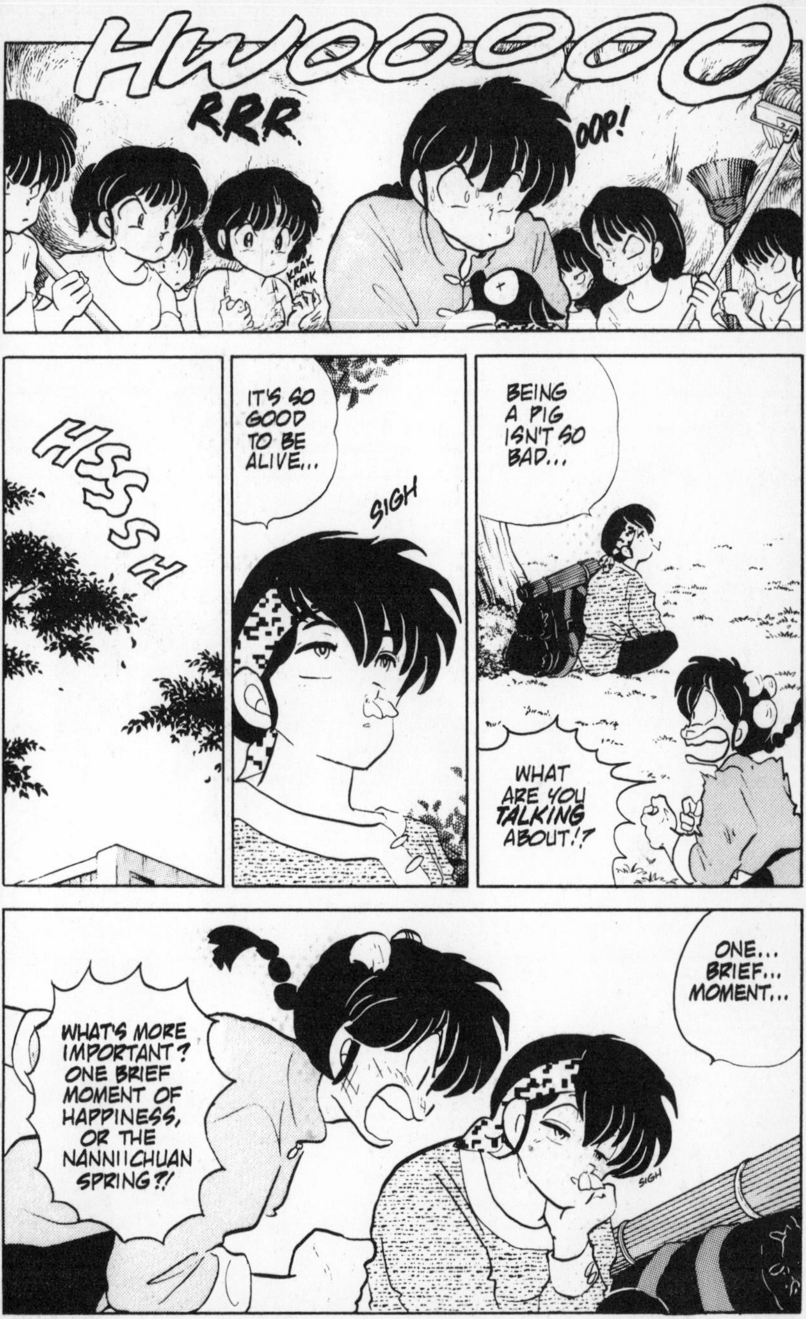
HWOOOOOO
RRR
KRAK KRAK
OOP!
HISSSH
IT'S SO GOOD TO BE ALIVE...
SIGH
BEING A PIG ISN'T SO BAD...
WHAT ARE YOU TALKING ABOUT!?
WHAT'S MORE IMPORTANT? ONE BRIEF MOMENT OF HAPPINESS, OR THE NANNIICHUAN SPRING?!
ONE... BRIEF... MOMENT...
SIGH

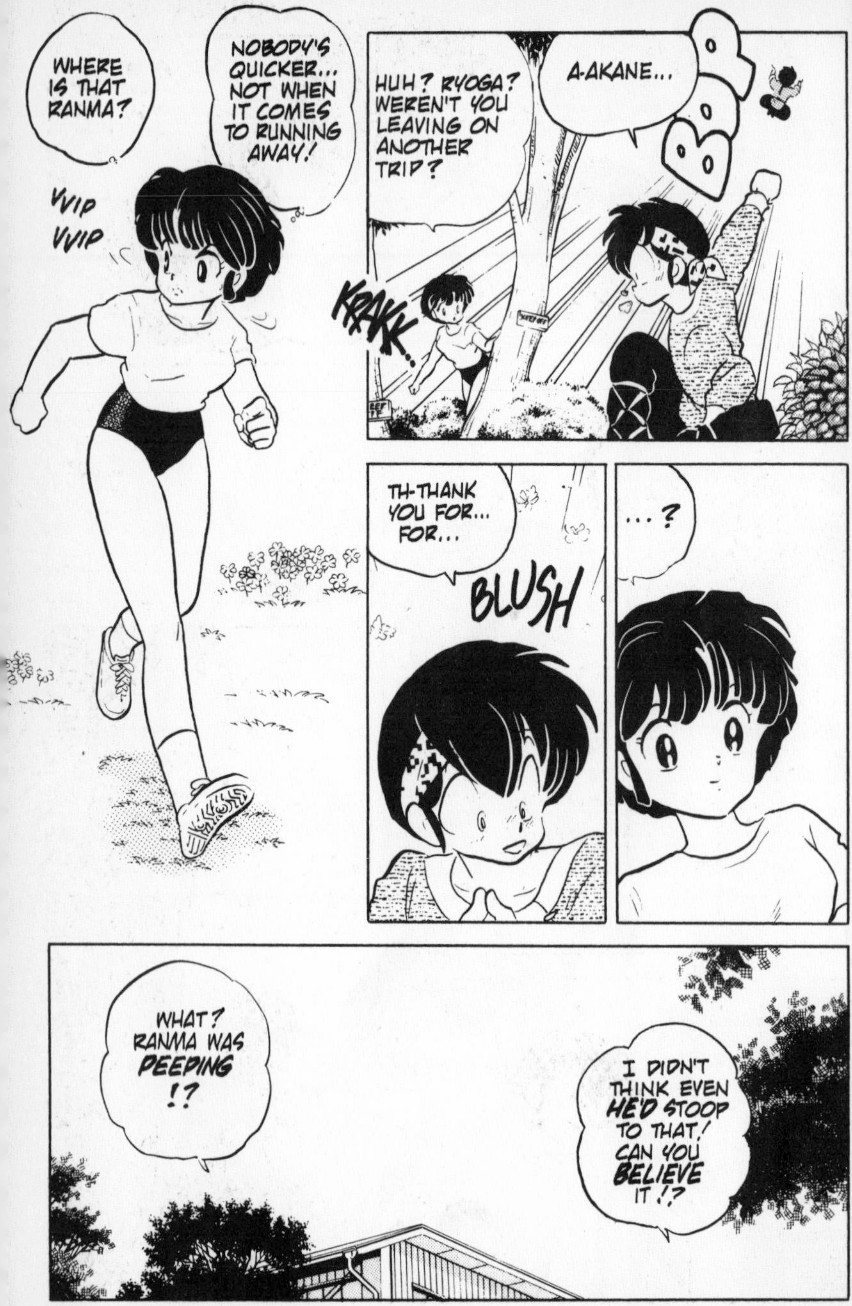
WHERE IS THAT RANMA?
NOBODY'S QUICKER... NOT WHEN IT COMES TO RUNNING AWAY!
VVIP VVIP
HUH? RYOGA? WEREN'T YOU LEAVING ON ANOTHER TRIP?
A-AKANE...
BOOP
KRAKK...
TH-THANK YOU FOR... FOR...
BLUSH
...?
WHAT? RANMA WAS PEEPING!?
I DIDN'T THINK EVEN HE'D STOOP TO THAT! CAN YOU BELIEVE IT!?

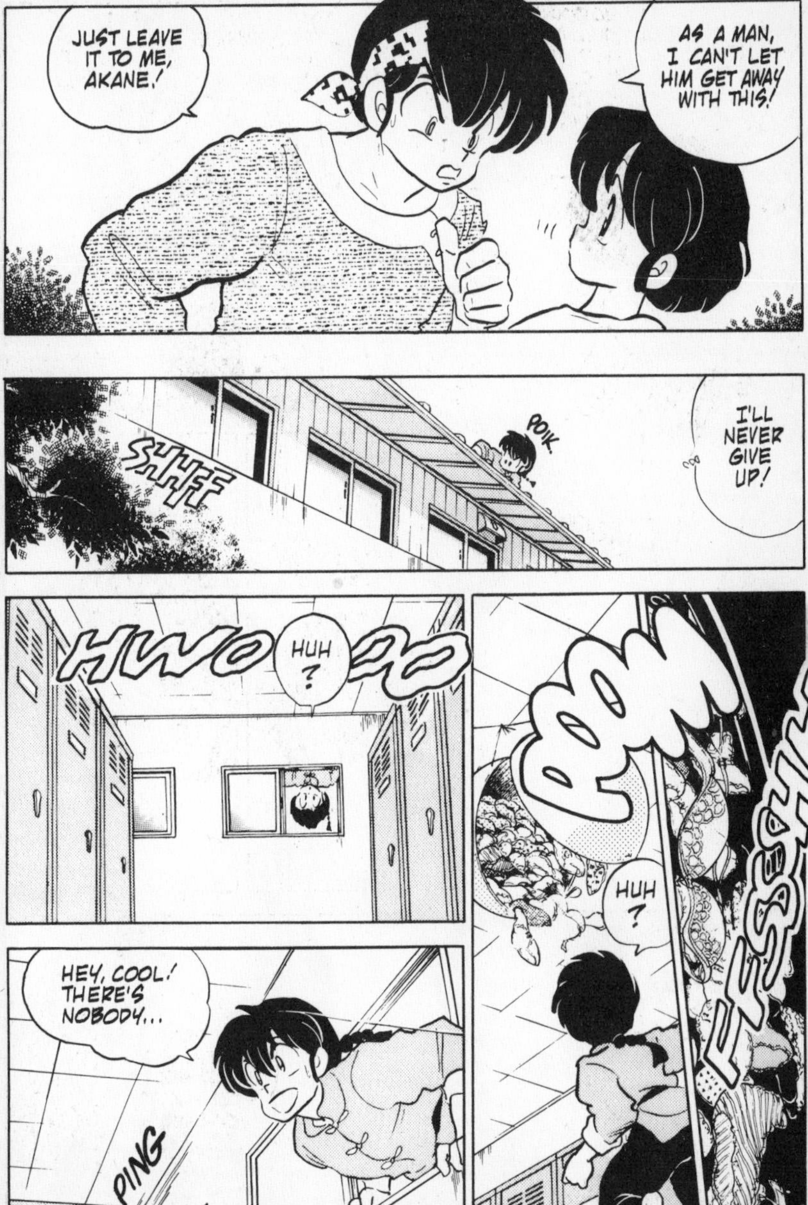
JUST LEAVE IT TO ME, AKANE!
AS A MAN, I CAN'T LET HIM GET AWAY WITH THIS!
SHFF
POIK
I'LL NEVER GIVE UP!
HWOOOO
HUH ?
HEY, COOL! THERE'S NOBODY...
PING
BOOM
HUH ?
FSSSHH

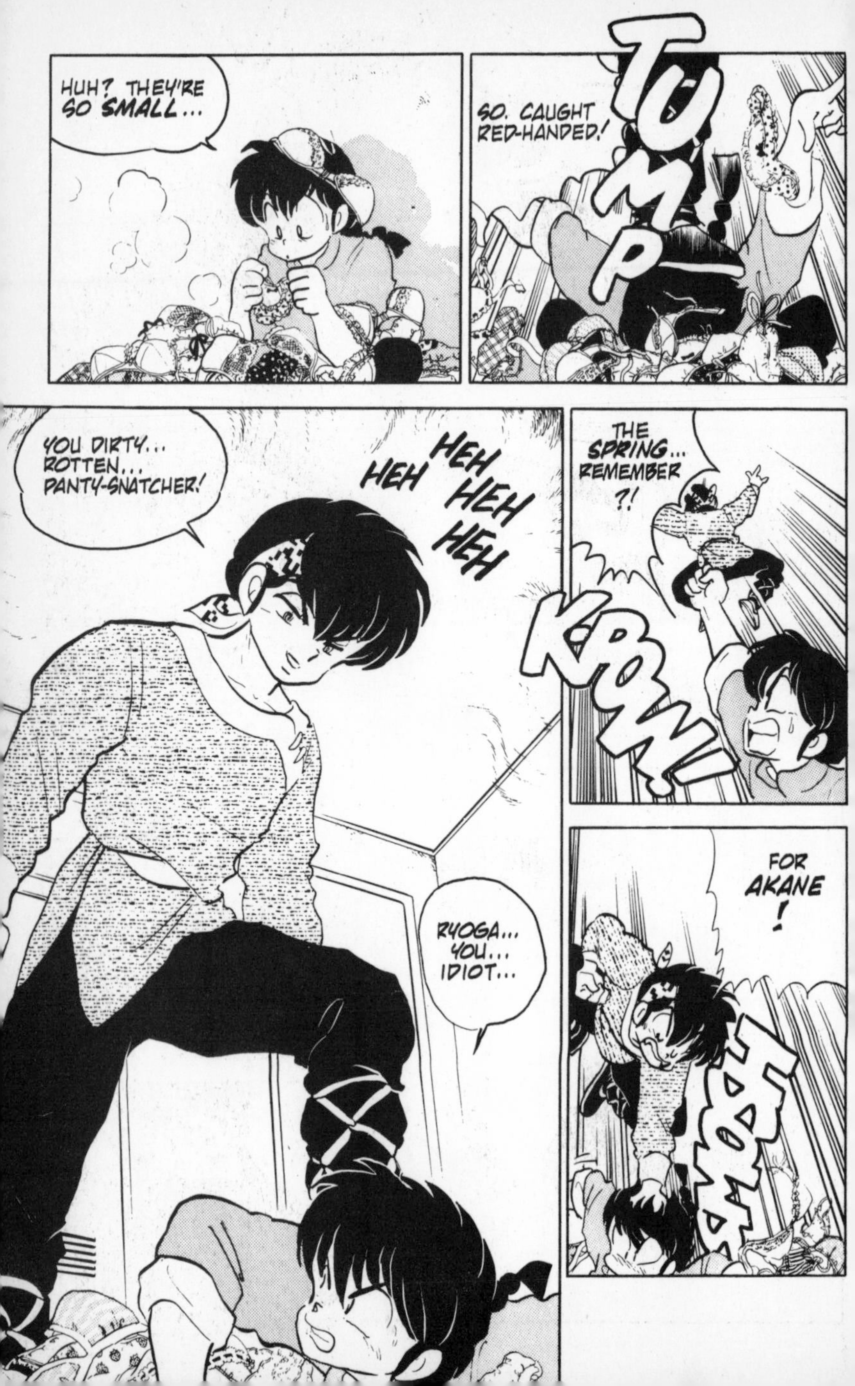
HUH? THEY'RE SO SMALL...
SO. CAUGHT RED-HANDED!
TOMP
YOU DIRTY... ROTTEN... PANTY-SNATCHER!
HEH HEH HEH HEH HEH
RYOGA... YOU... IDIOT...
THE SPRING... REMEMBER ?!
KBOW!
FOR AKANE!
THOMP

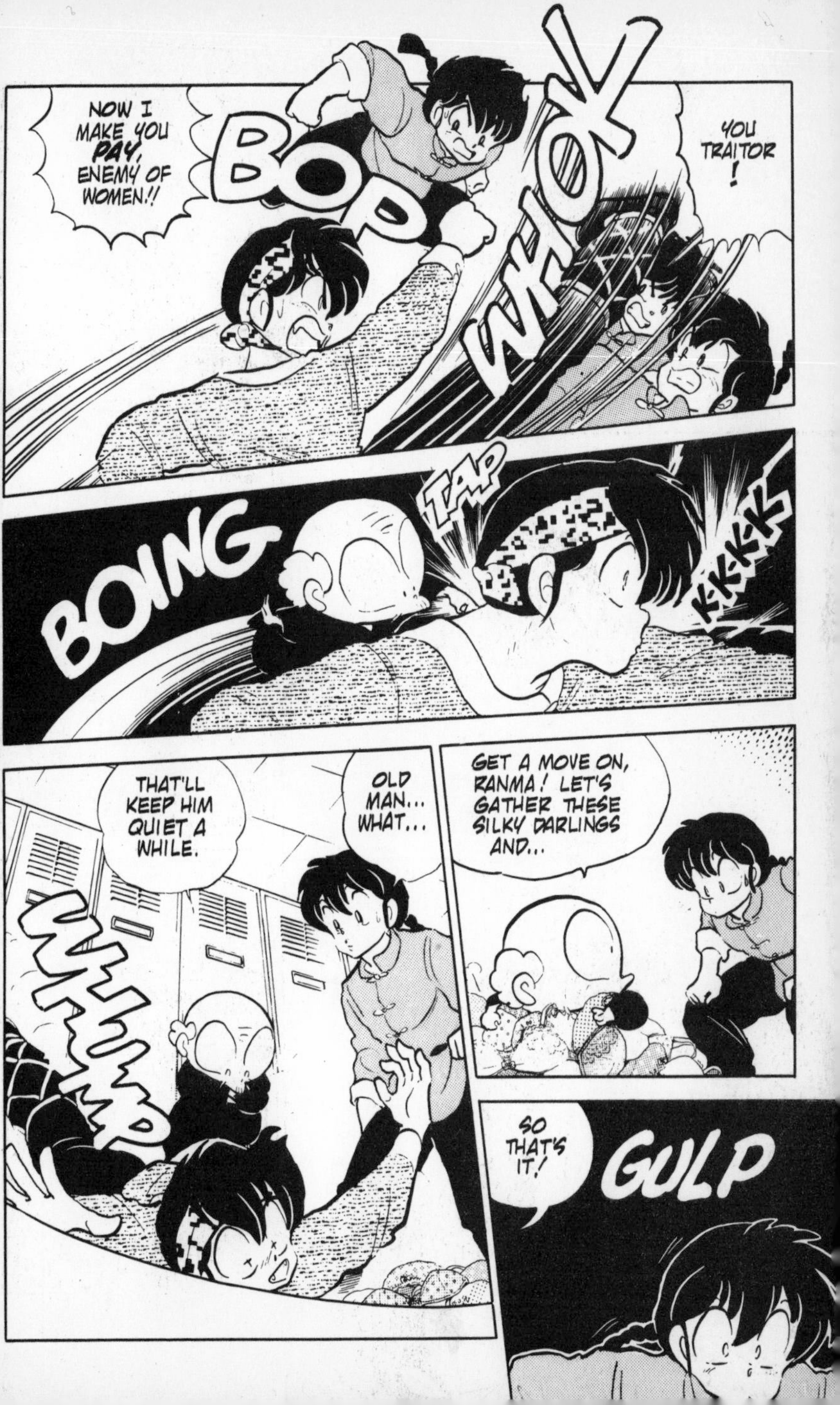

NOW I MAKE YOU PAY, ENEMY OF WOMEN!!
BOP
WHOK
YOU TRAITOR!
BOING
TAP
K-K-K-K
THAT'LL KEEP HIM QUIET A WHILE.
WHUMP
OLD MAN... WHAT...
GET A MOVE ON, RANMA! LET'S GATHER THESE SILKY DARLINGS AND...
SO THAT'S IT!
GULP

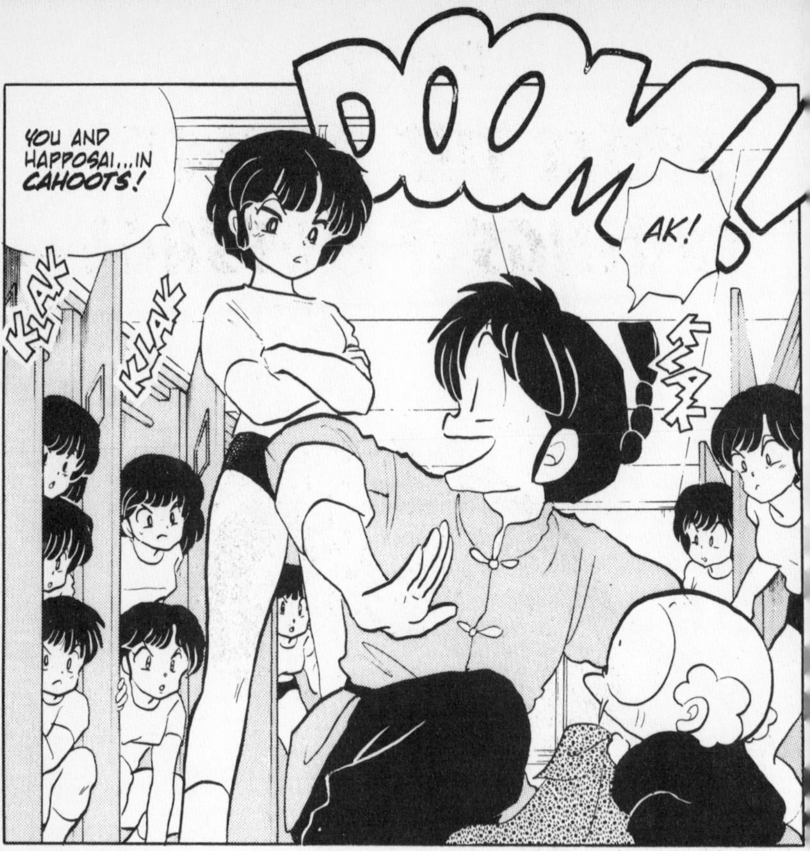
DOOM!
YOU AND HAPPOSAI...IN CAHOOTS!
AK!
KLAK
KLAK
KLAK
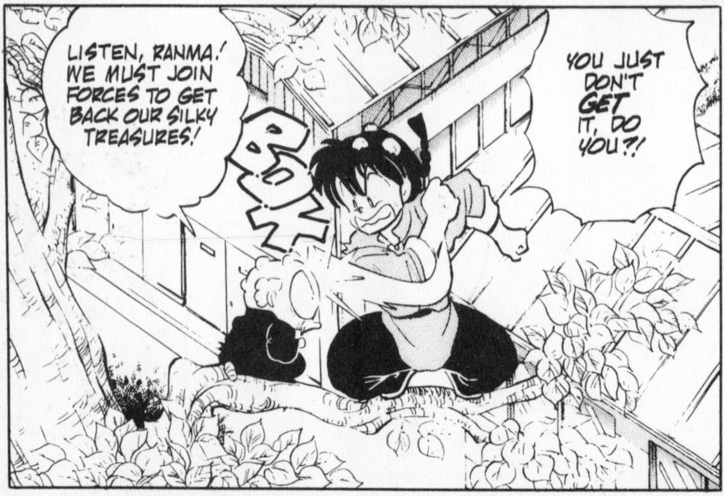
LISTEN, RANMA! WE MUST JOIN FORCES TO GET BACK OUR SILKY TREASURES!
POW
YOU JUST DON'T GET IT, DO YOU?!

Part 7

FROM THE SPRING, SPRINGS A MESSAGE

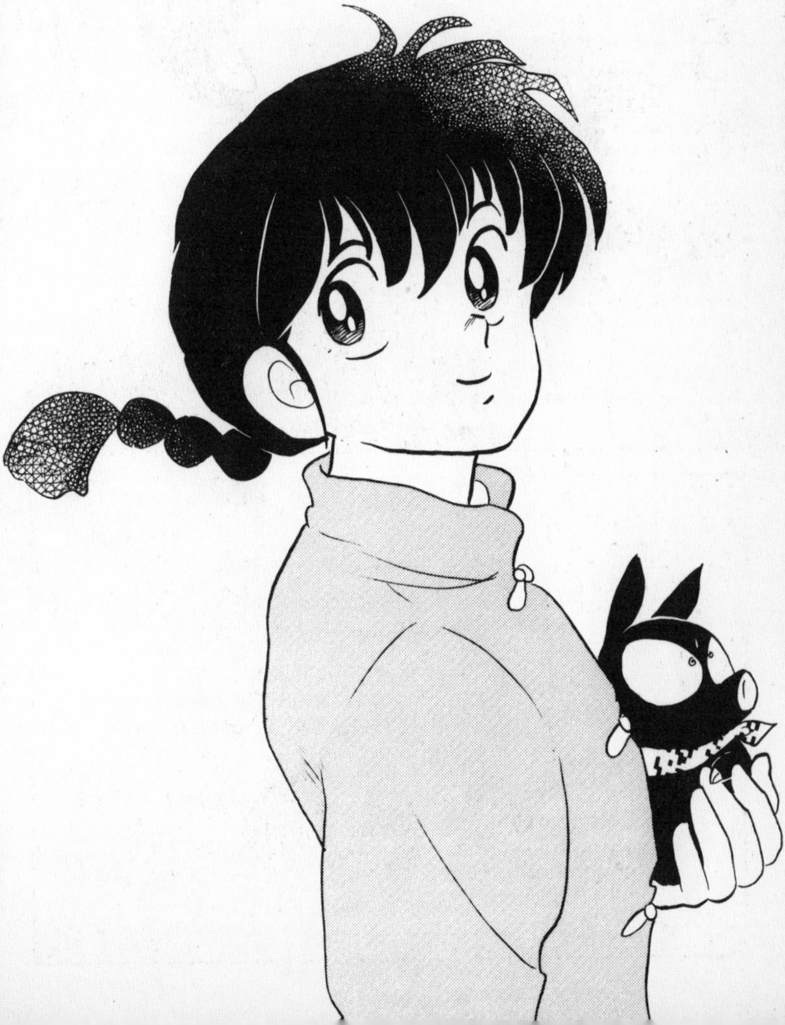

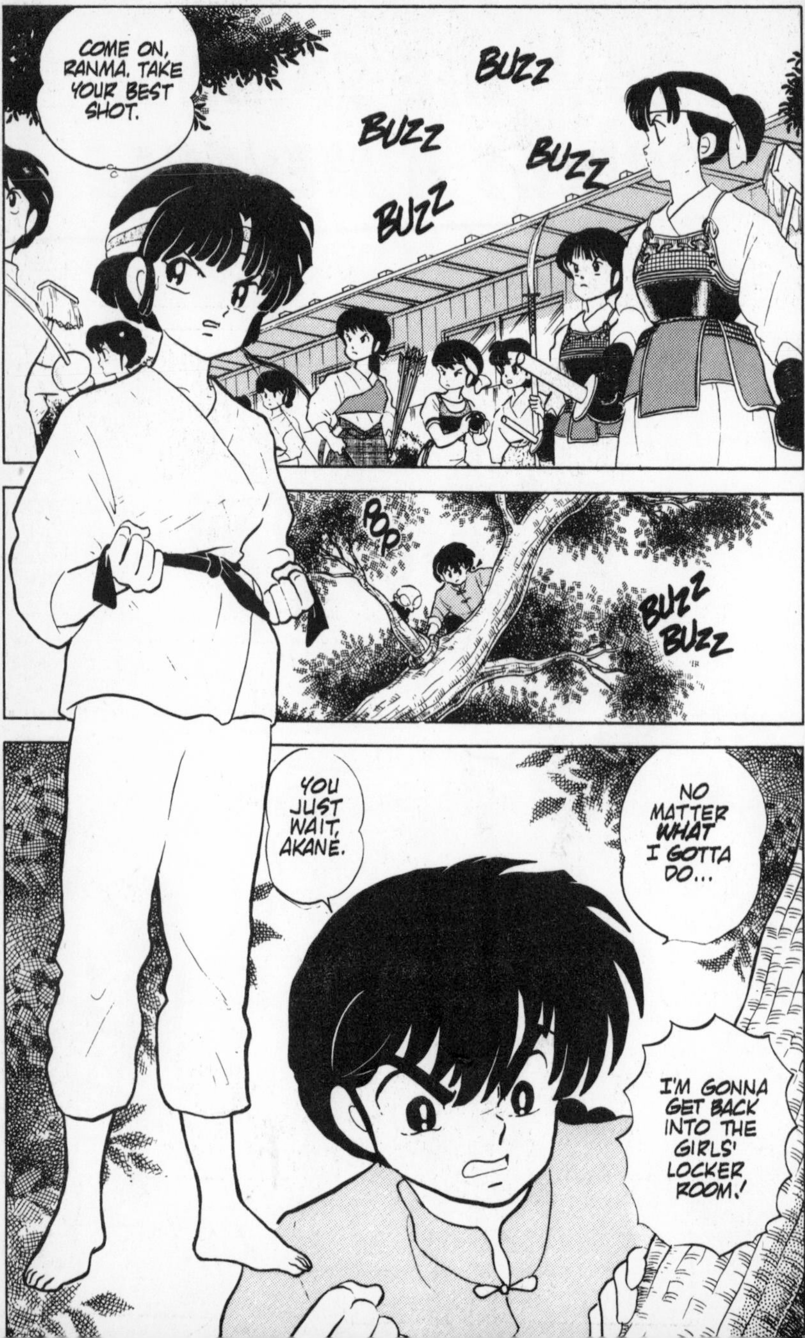
COME ON, RANMA. TAKE YOUR BEST SHOT.
BUZZ
BUZZ
BUZZ
BUZZ
POP
BUZZ BUZZ
YOU JUST WAIT, AKANE.
NO MATTER WHAT I GOTTA DO...
I'M GONNA GET BACK INTO THE GIRLS' LOCKER ROOM!

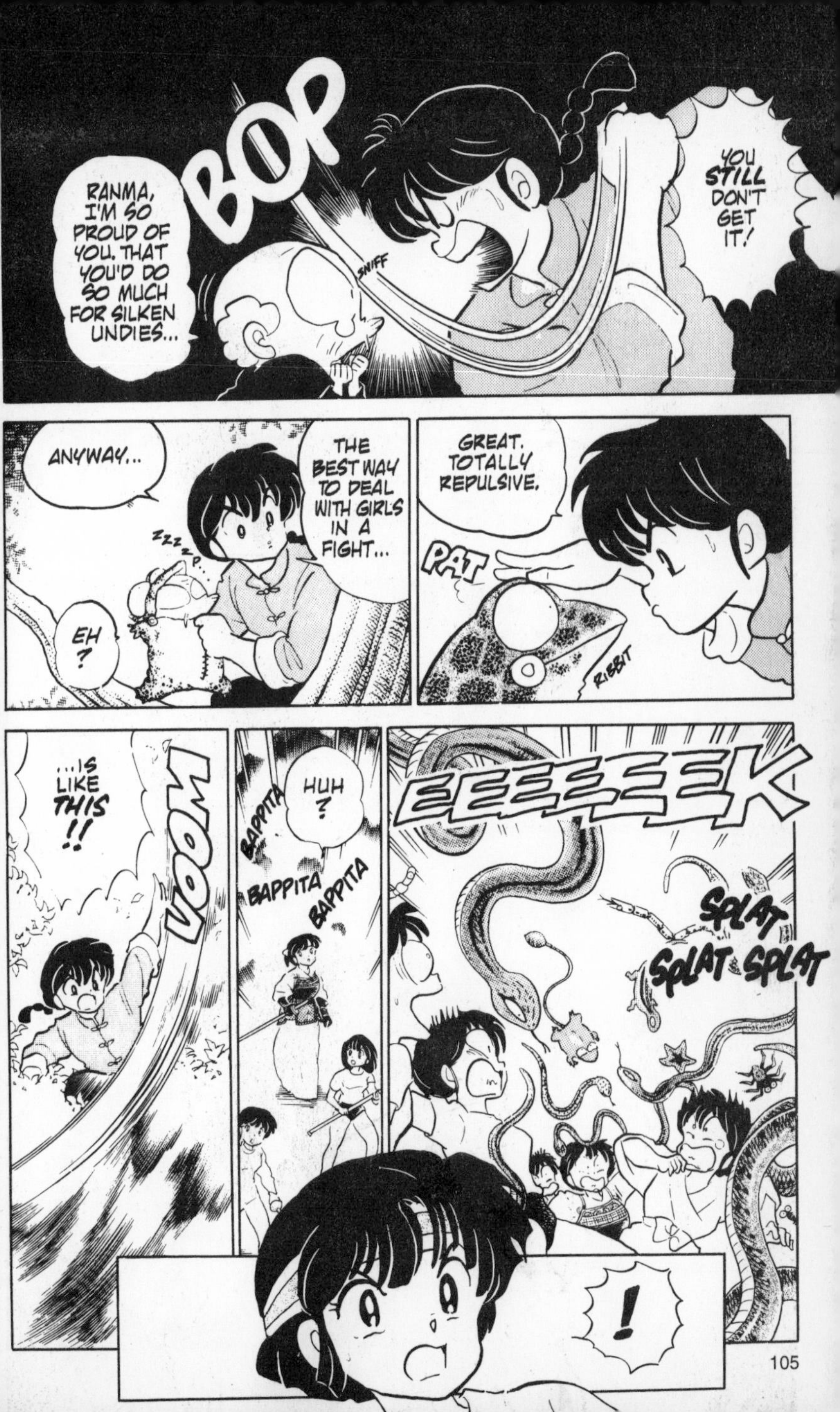

RANMA, I'M SO PROUD OF YOU. THAT YOU'D DO SO MUCH FOR SILKEN UNDIES...
SNIFF
BOP
YOU STILL DON'T GET IT!
ANYWAY...
EH?
ZZZZP...
THE BEST WAY TO DEAL WITH GIRLS IN A FIGHT...
GREAT. TOTALLY REPULSIVE.
PAT
RIBBIT
...IS LIKE THIS!!
VOOOM
HUH?
BAPPITA
BAPPITA
BAPPITA
EEEEEEK
SPLAT
SPLAT SPLAT
!

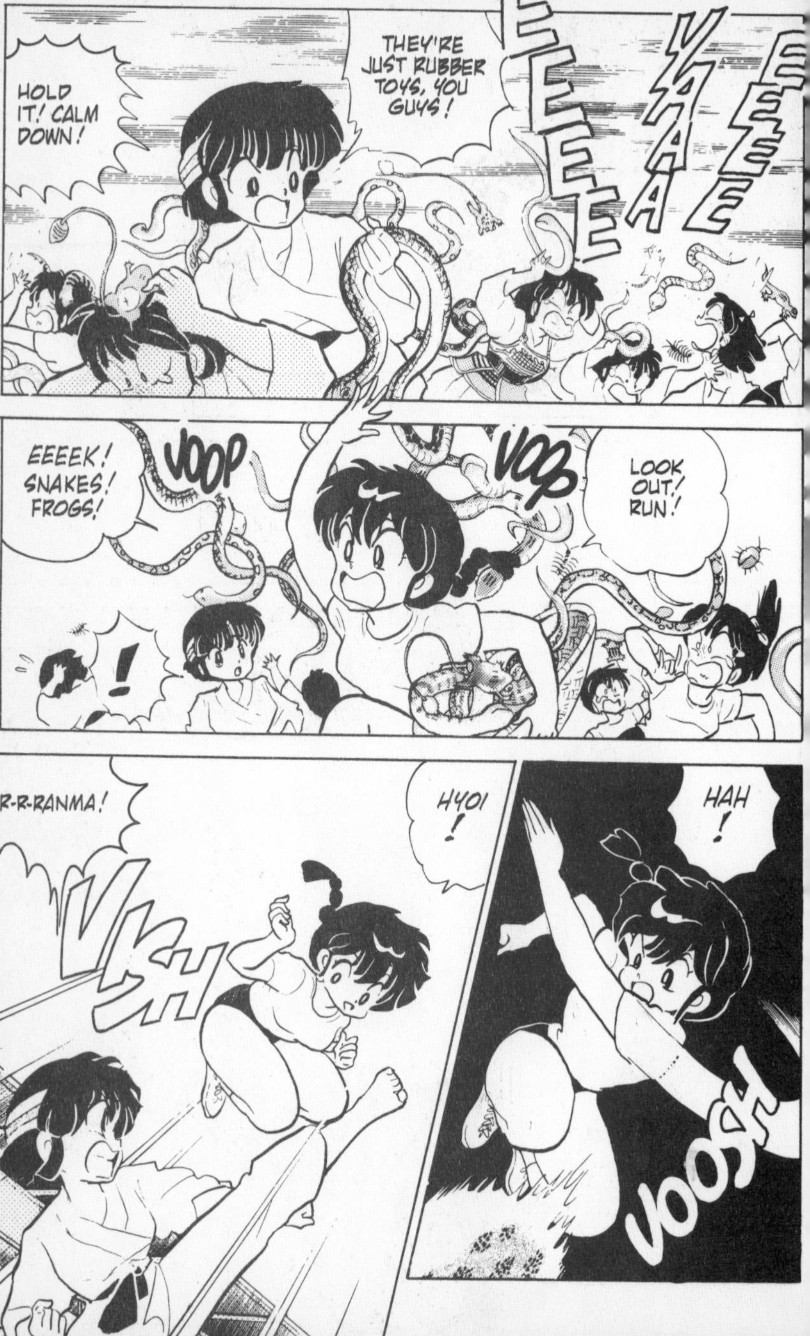
HOLD IT! CALM DOWN!
THEY'RE JUST RUBBER TOYS, YOU GUYS!
EEEEE
YAAAA
EEEEE
EEEEK! SNAKES! FROGS!
VOOP
!
VOOP
LOOK OUT! RUN!
R-R-RANMA!
HYOI!
HAH!
VOOSH

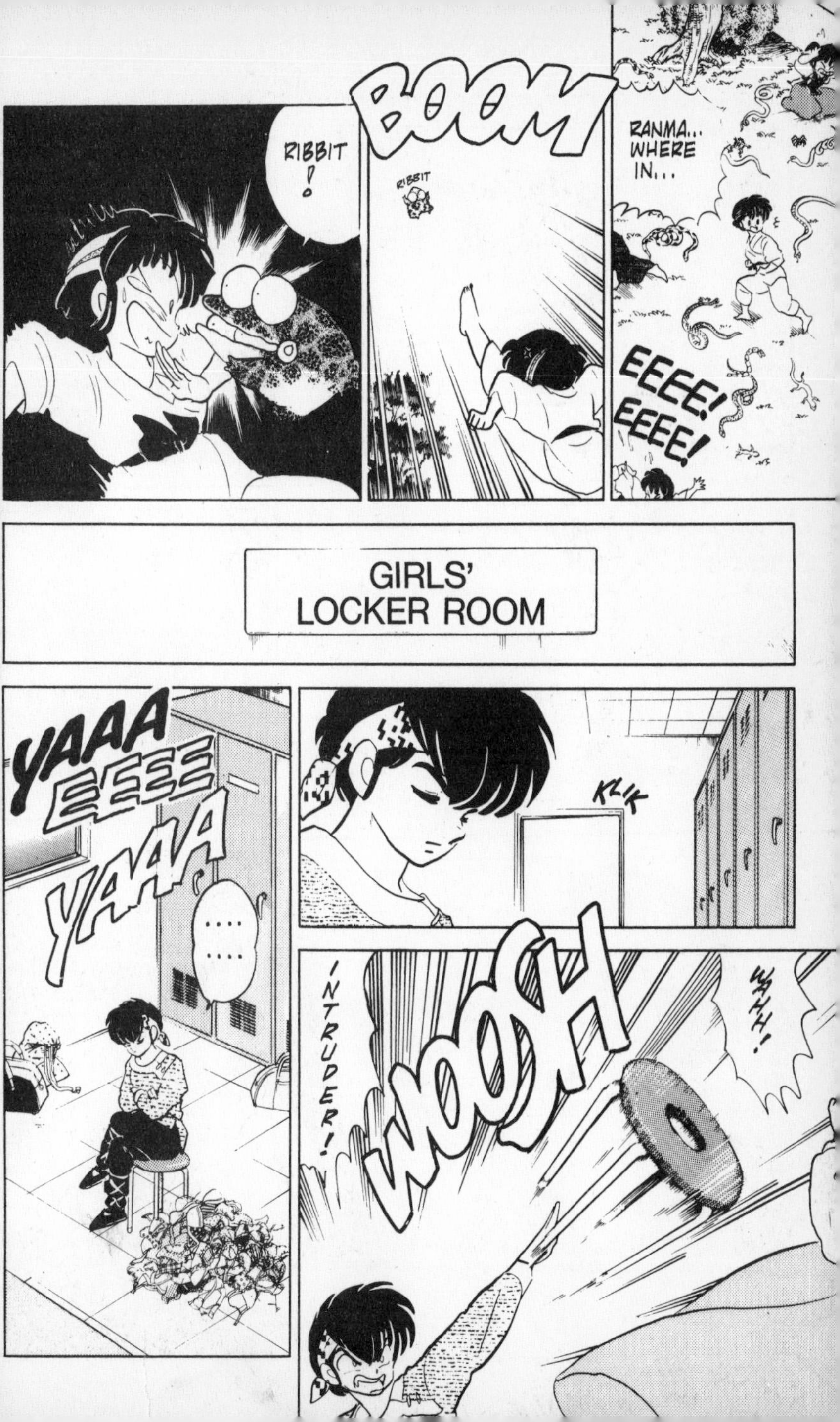
RIBBIT!
BOOM
RIBBIT
RANMA... WHERE IN...
EEEE! EEEE!
GIRLS' LOCKER ROOM
YAAA EEEE YAAA
....
....
KLIK
INTRUDER!
WOOSH
WAHH!

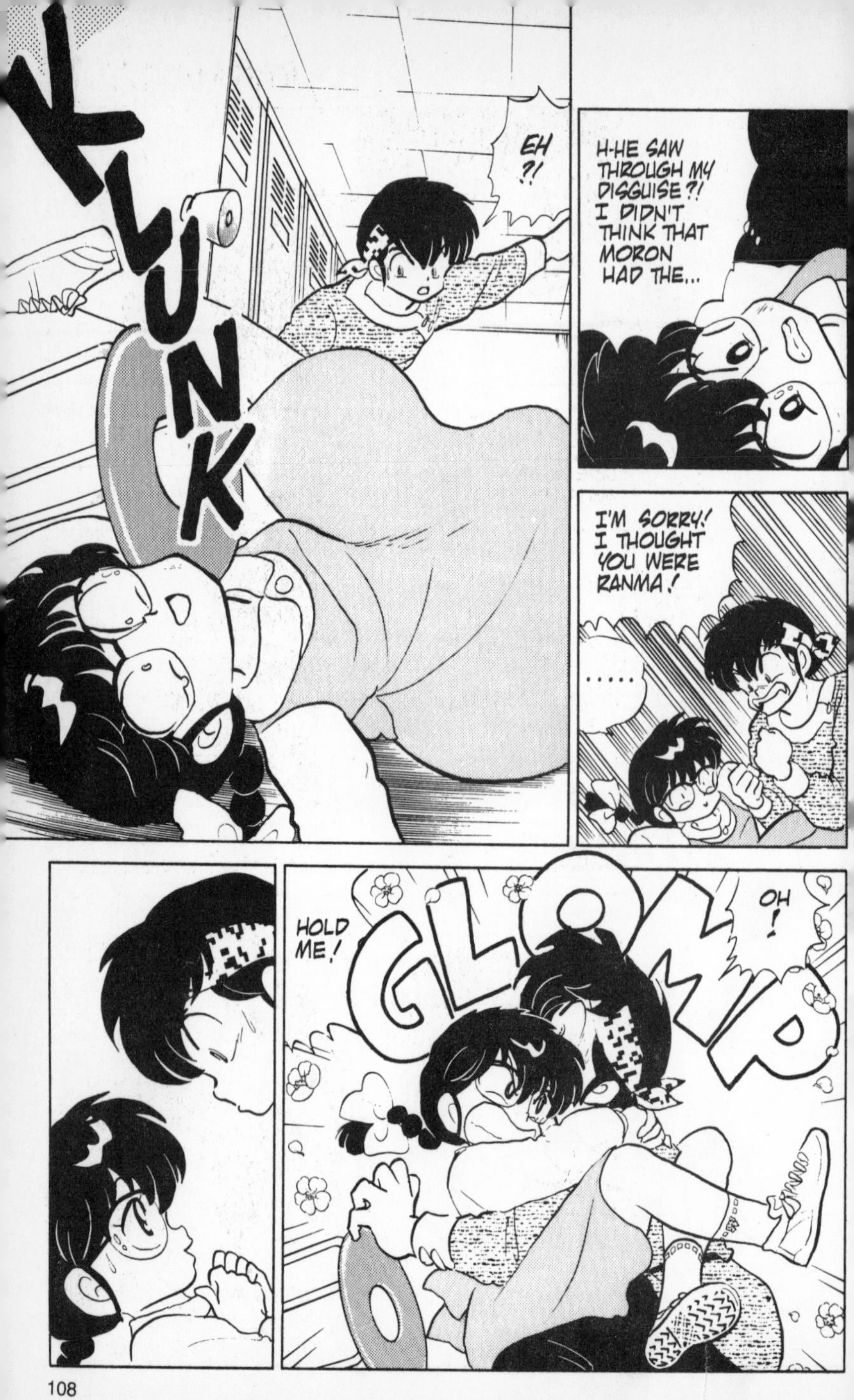
KLUNK
EH ?!
H-HE SAW THROUGH MY DISGUISE ?! I DIDN'T THINK THAT MORON HAD THE...
I'M SORRY! I THOUGHT YOU WERE RANMA!
.....
HOLD ME!
GLOMP
OH!

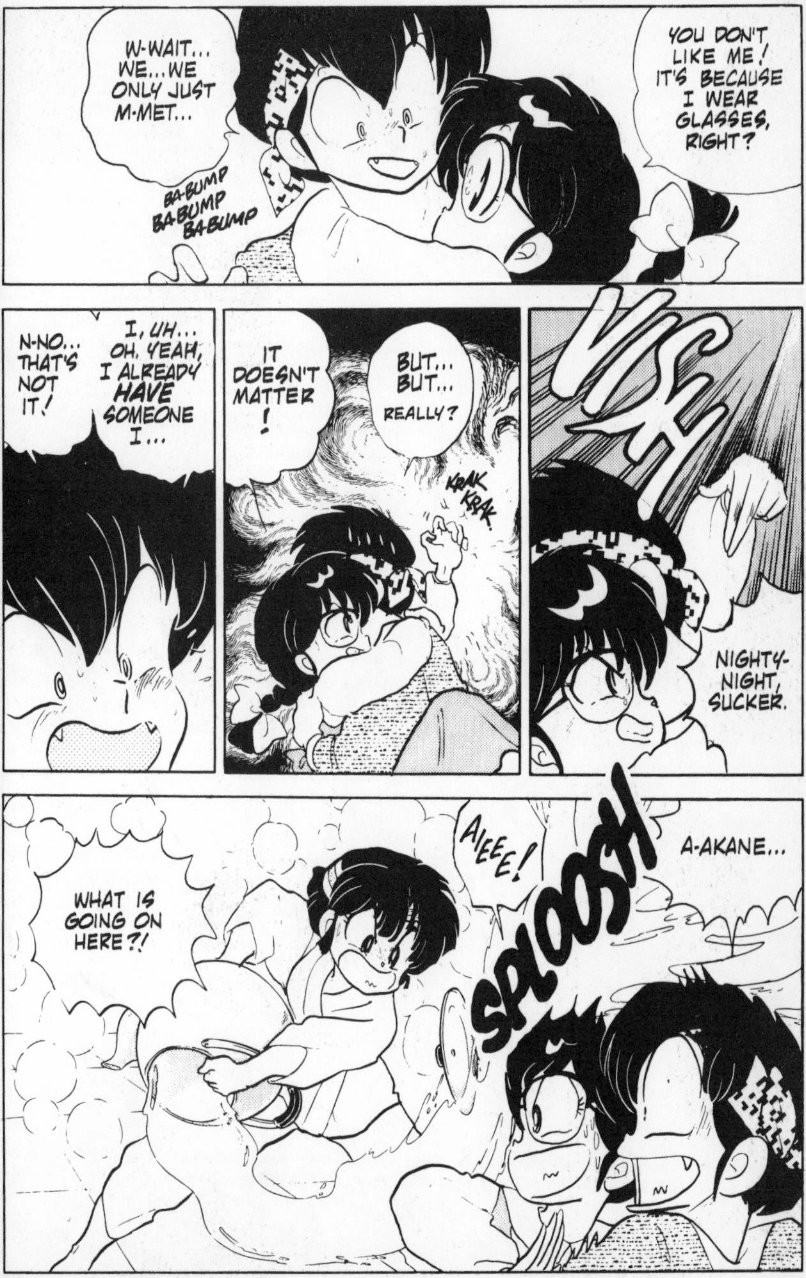
W-WAIT... WE...WE ONLY JUST M-MET...
BA-BUMP BA-BUMP BA-BUMP
YOU DON'T LIKE ME! IT'S BECAUSE I WEAR GLASSES, RIGHT?
N-NO... THAT'S NOT IT!
I, UH... OH, YEAH, I ALREADY **HAVE** SOMEONE I...
IT DOESN'T MATTER!
BUT... BUT... REALLY?
KRAK KRAK
VISH
NIGHTY-NIGHT, SUCKER.
WHAT IS GOING ON HERE?!
AIEEE!
SPLOOSH
A-AKANE...

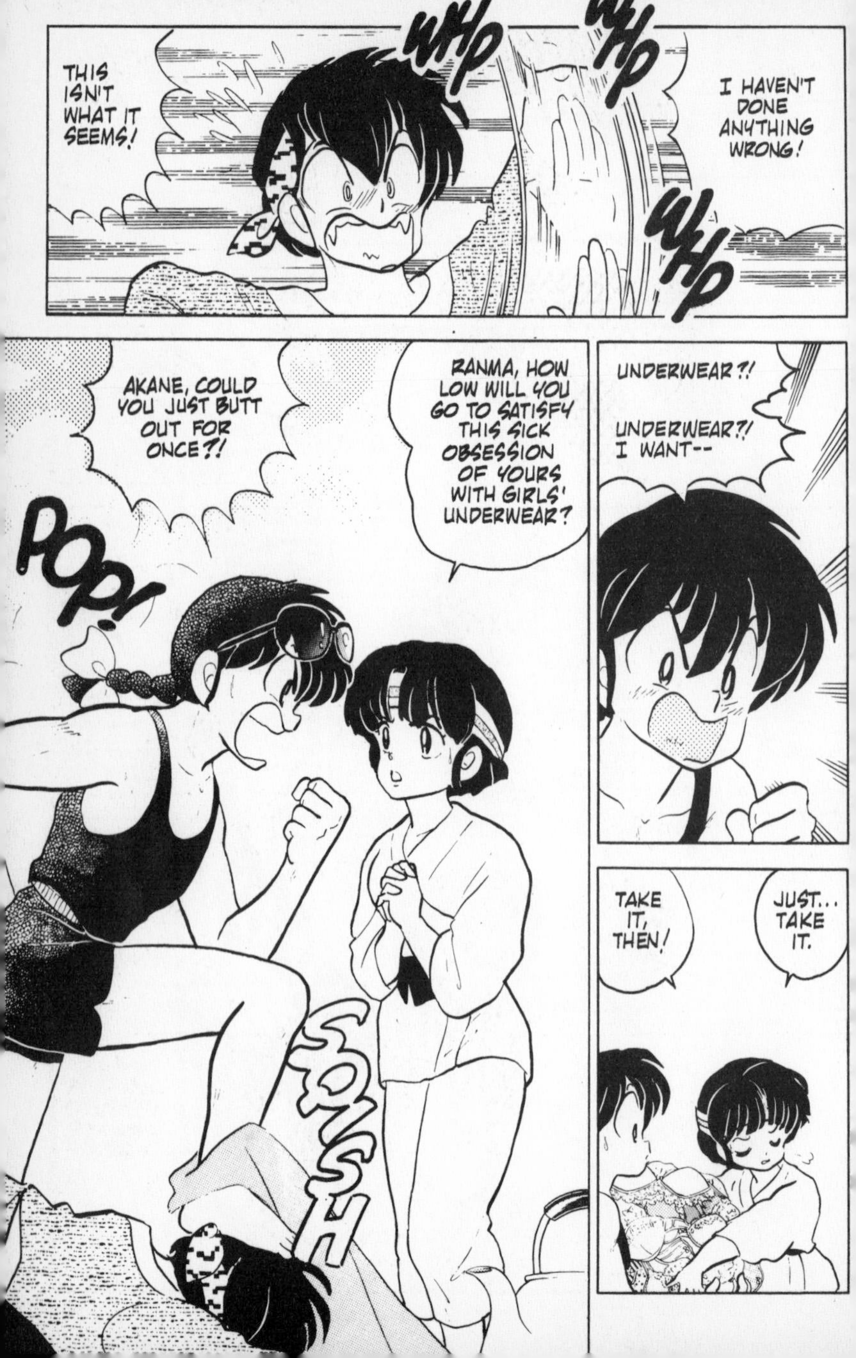
THIS ISN'T WHAT IT SEEMS!
WHP
WHP
I HAVEN'T DONE ANYTHING WRONG!
WHP
AKANE, COULD YOU JUST BUTT OUT FOR ONCE?!
RANMA, HOW LOW WILL YOU GO TO SATISFY THIS SICK OBSESSION OF YOURS WITH GIRLS' UNDERWEAR?
POP!
SQUISH
UNDERWEAR?!
UNDERWEAR?! I WANT--
TAKE IT, THEN!
JUST... TAKE IT.

HEY... LISTEN...

I WON'T STOP YOU... JUST...PLEASE, RANMA... FIND HELP!

AND I USED TO THINK ONLY YOUR *BODY* WAS SICK AND TWISTED...

Sniff.

GOODBYE, RANMA!

SOB

WAIT!

LISTEN TO ME!

I'M ONLY IN HERE TO FIND THE NANNIICHUAN!

NANNIICHUAN...?

Y'MEAN... BENEATH THE FLOOR OF THE GIRLS' LOCKER ROOM...

...IS A JAPANESE "SPRING OF DROWNED MAN"?

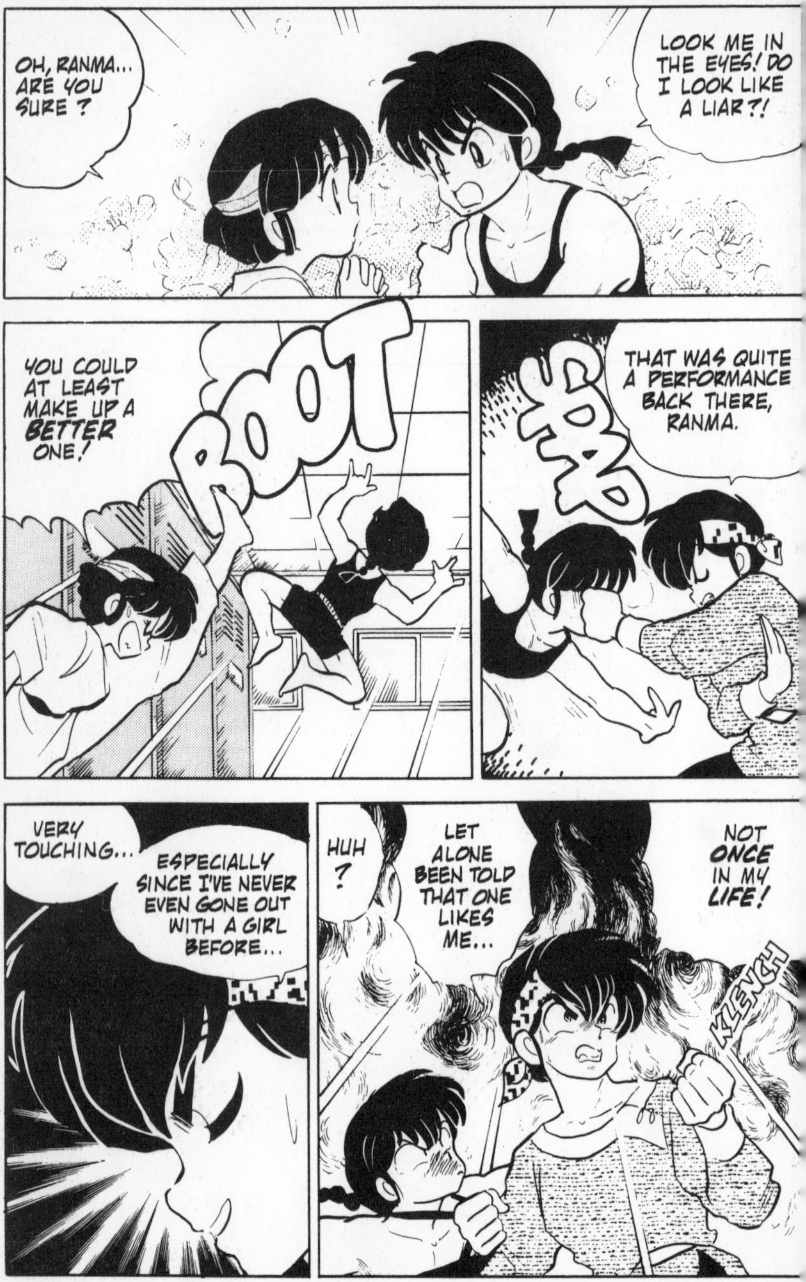
OH, RANMA... ARE YOU SURE ?
LOOK ME IN THE EYES! DO I LOOK LIKE A LIAR?!
YOU COULD AT LEAST MAKE UP A BETTER ONE!
BOOT
SNAP
THAT WAS QUITE A PERFORMANCE BACK THERE, RANMA.
VERY TOUCHING...
ESPECIALLY SINCE I'VE NEVER EVEN GONE OUT WITH A GIRL BEFORE...
HUH ?
LET ALONE BEEN TOLD THAT ONE LIKES ME...
NOT ONCE IN MY LIFE!
KLENCH

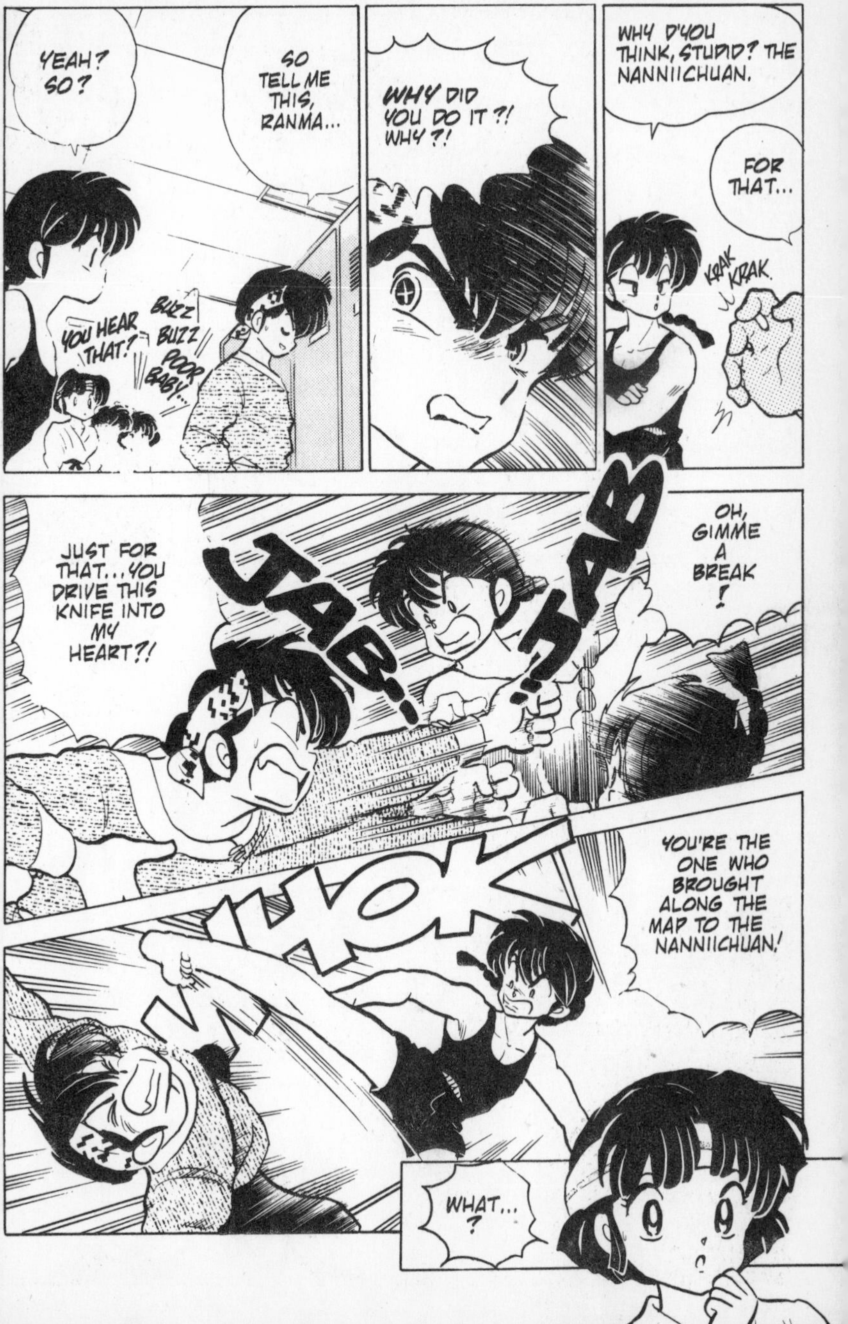
YEAH? SO?
SO TELL ME THIS, RANMA...
YOU HEAR THAT?
BUZZ BUZZ POOR BABY...
WHY DID YOU DO IT?! WHY?!
WHY D'YOU THINK, STUPID? THE NANNIICHUAN.
FOR THAT...
KRAK KRAK.
JUST FOR THAT...YOU DRIVE THIS KNIFE INTO MY HEART?!
JAB!!
JAB!!
OH, GIMME A BREAK!
WHOK
YOU'RE THE ONE WHO BROUGHT ALONG THE MAP TO THE NANNIICHUAN!
WHAT...?

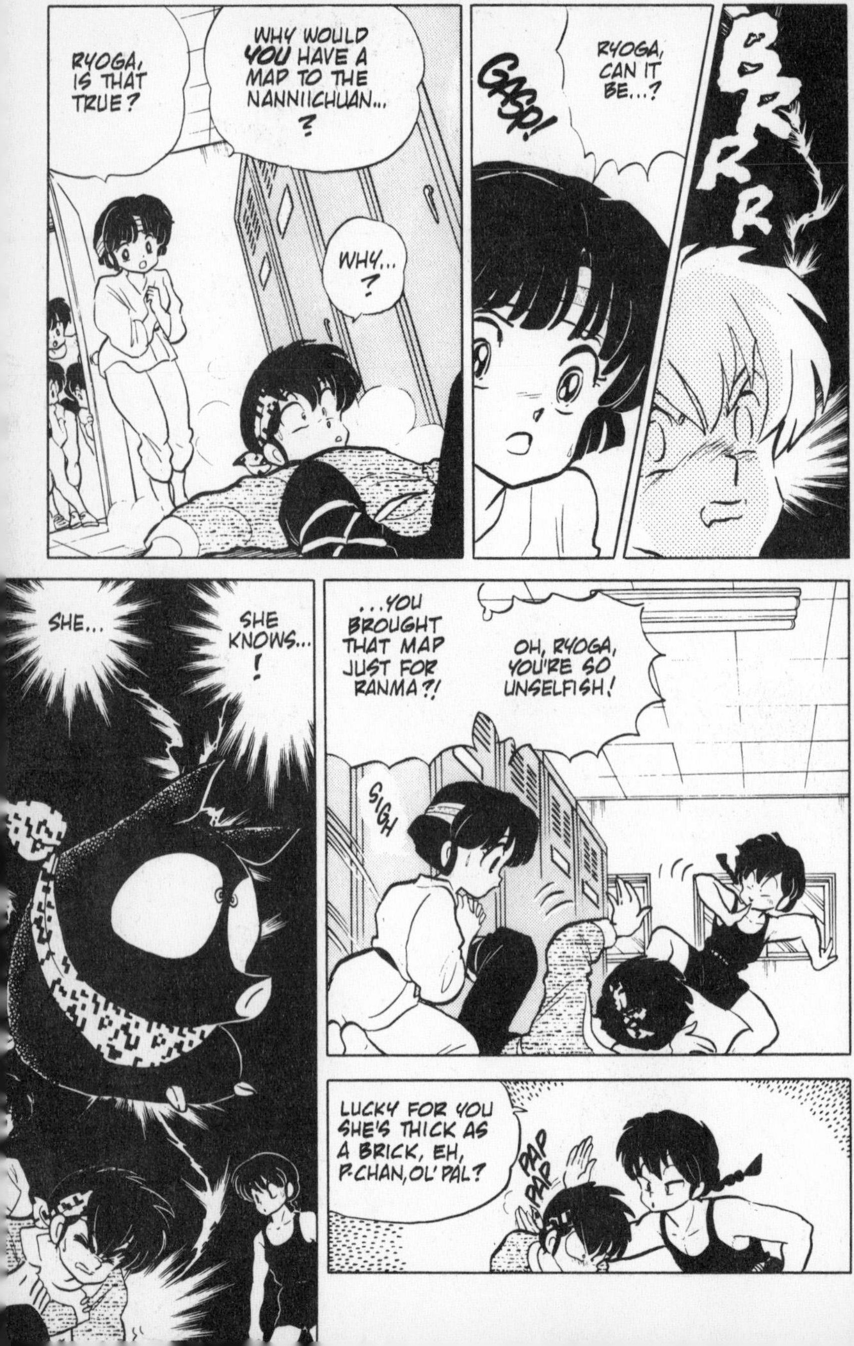
RYOGA, IS THAT TRUE?
WHY WOULD YOU HAVE A MAP TO THE NANNIICHUAN...?
WHY...?
GASP!
RYOGA, CAN IT BE...?
GRRR
SHE...
SHE KNOWS...!
...YOU BROUGHT THAT MAP JUST FOR RANMA?!
OH, RYOGA, YOU'RE SO UNSELFISH!
SIGH
LUCKY FOR YOU SHE'S THICK AS A BRICK, EH, P-CHAN, OL' PAL?
PAP PAP

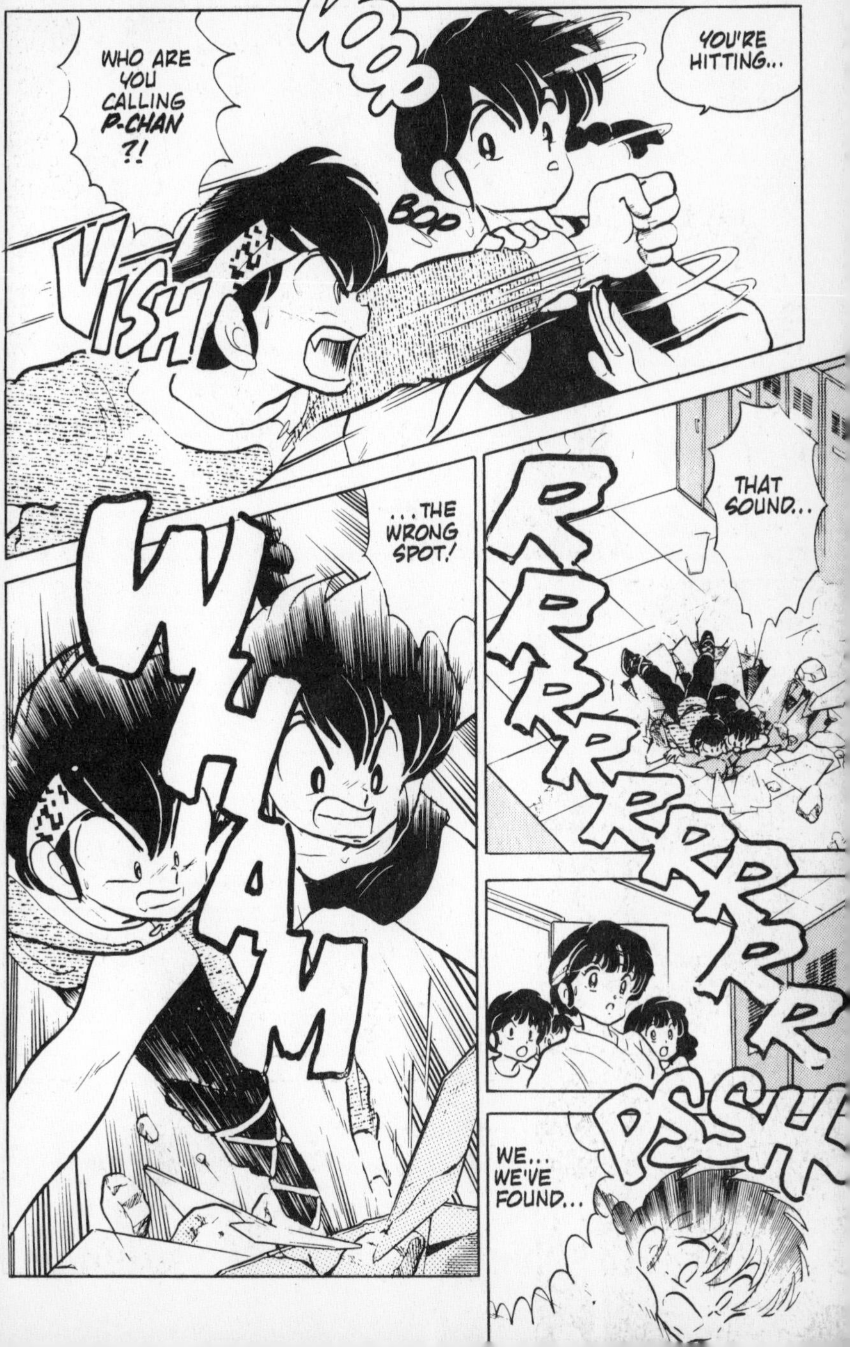
WHO ARE YOU CALLING P-CHAN ?!
VOOP
YOU'RE HITTING...
BOP
VISH!
...THE WRONG SPOT!
WHAM
THAT SOUND...
RRRRRRRRR
PSSH
WE... WE'VE FOUND...

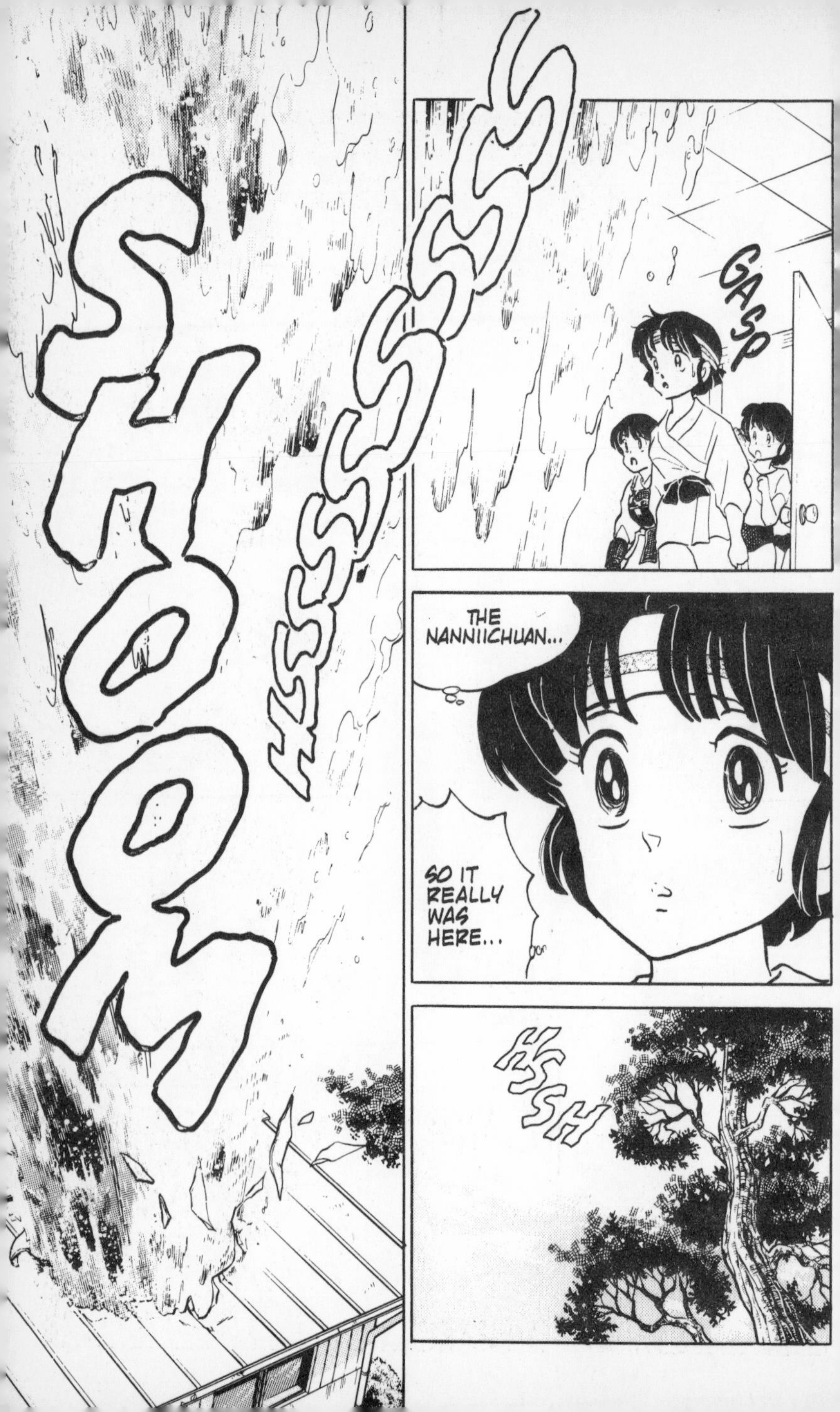
HSSSSSSS
GASP
THE NANNIICHUAN...
SO IT REALLY WAS HERE...
HSSH

ARE YOU SURE THAT WAS A MAP TO THE SPRING OF DROWNED MAN!?

TREMBLE

HEY...

.....

THEN WHY AREN'T WE BACK TO NORMAL?

BONK BONK

ANSWER ME, PIG!

BWKEE!

WH-WHAT'S THIS...?

WHRRR

WHONK

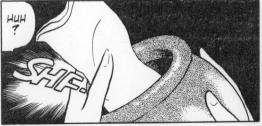

HUH?

SHF

117

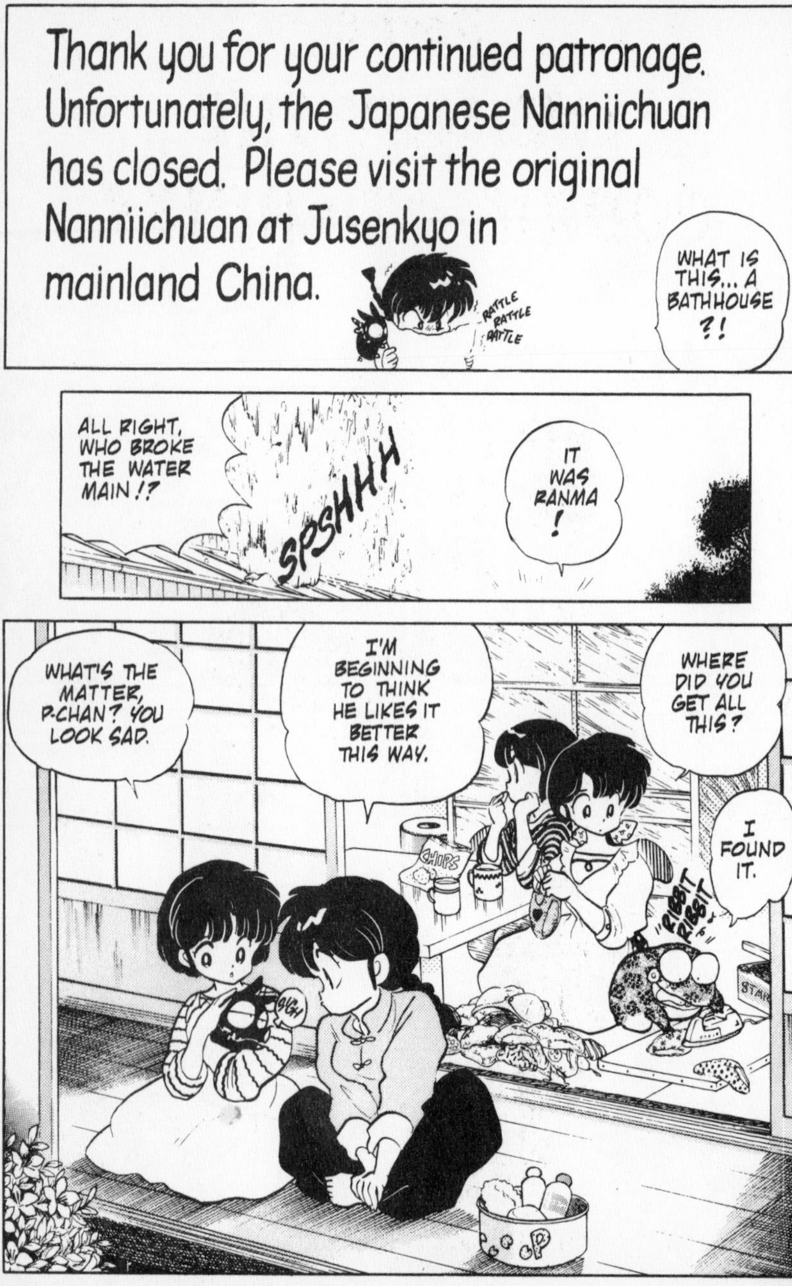
Thank you for your continued patronage. Unfortunately, the Japanese Nanniichuan has closed. Please visit the original Nanniichuan at Jusenkyo in mainland China.
RATTLE RATTLE RATTLE
WHAT IS THIS... A BATHHOUSE ?!
ALL RIGHT, WHO BROKE THE WATER MAIN!?
SPSHHH
IT WAS RANMA!
WHAT'S THE MATTER, P-CHAN? YOU LOOK SAD.
SIGH
I'M BEGINNING TO THINK HE LIKES IT BETTER THIS WAY.
CHIPS
WHERE DID YOU GET ALL THIS?
I FOUND IT.
RIBBIT RIBBIT

Part 8

THE WAY THE COOKIE CRUMBLES

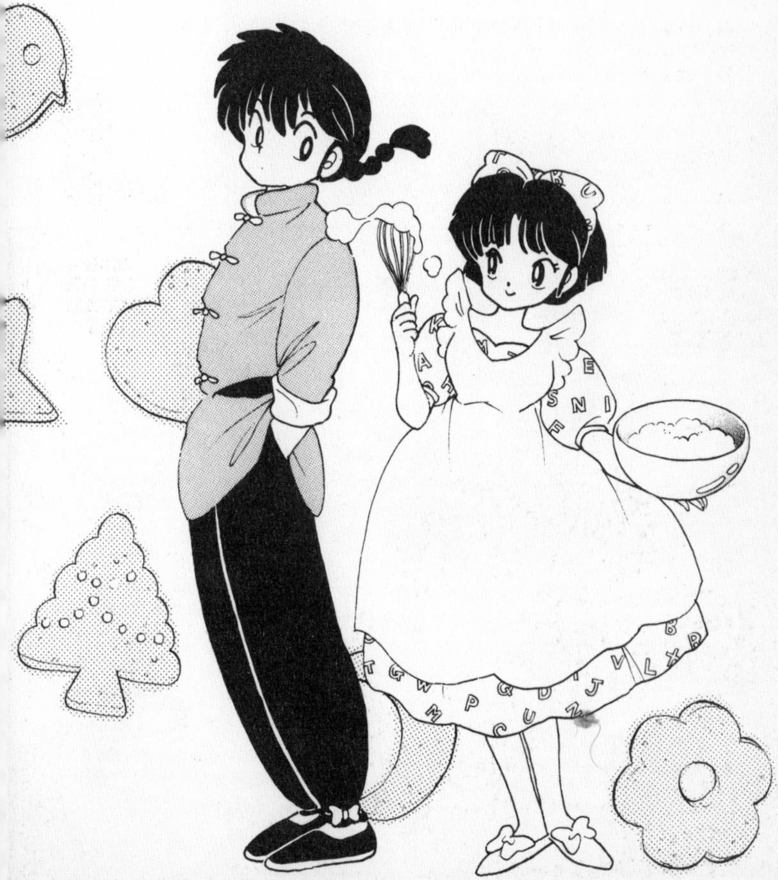

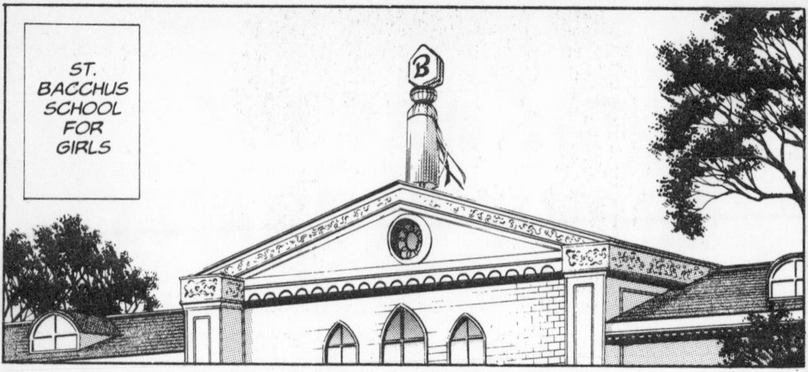
ST. BACCHUS SCHOOL FOR GIRLS

HOME ECONOMICS

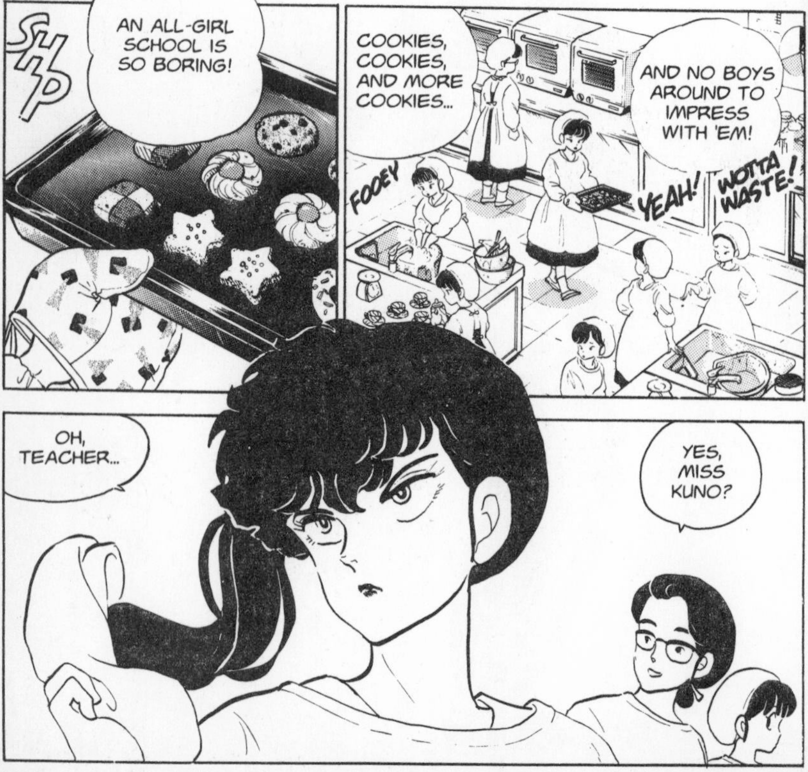
SHP
AN ALL-GIRL SCHOOL IS SO BORING!
COOKIES, COOKIES, AND MORE COOKIES...
AND NO BOYS AROUND TO IMPRESS WITH 'EM!
FOOEY
YEAH!
WOTTA WASTE!
OH, TEACHER...
YES, MISS KUNO?

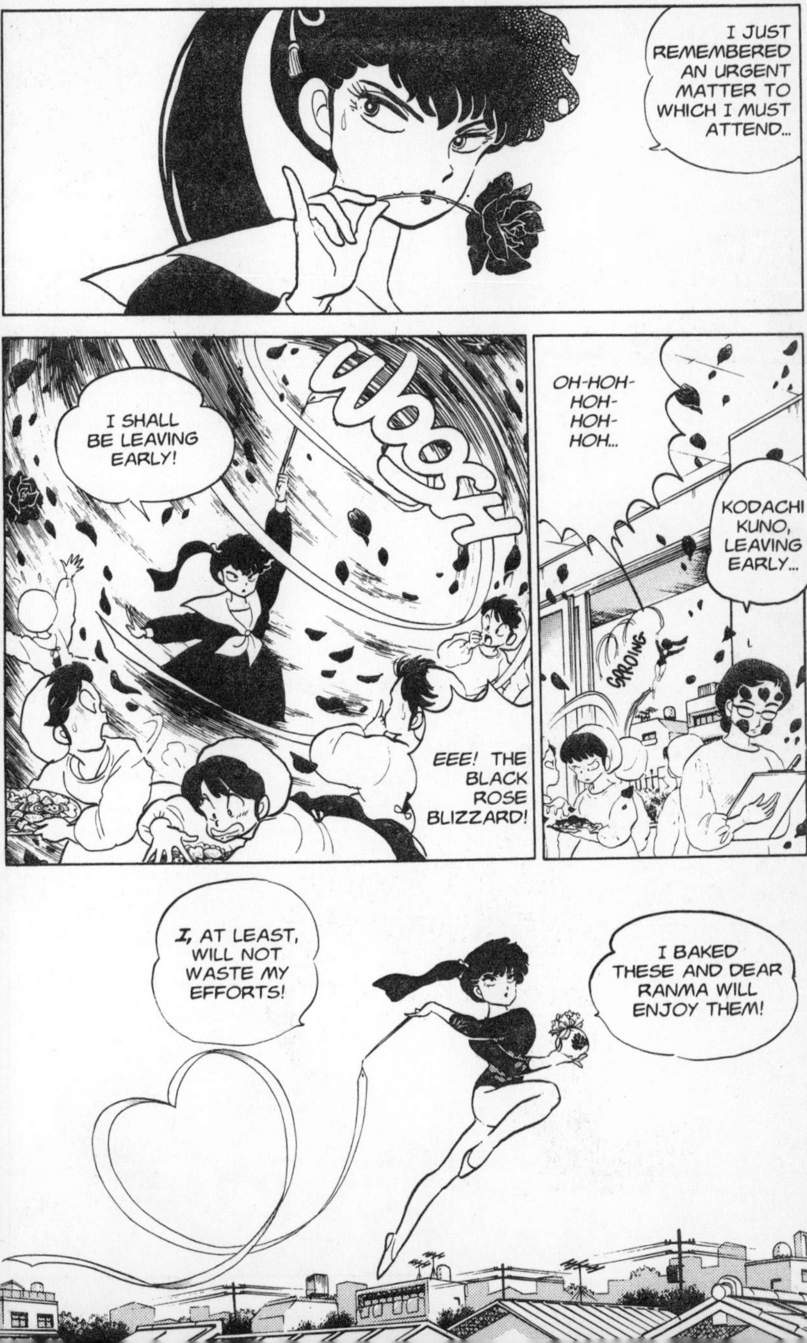
I JUST REMEMBERED AN URGENT MATTER TO WHICH I MUST ATTEND...
I SHALL BE LEAVING EARLY!
WOOSH
EEE! THE BLACK ROSE BLIZZARD!
OH-HOH-HOH-HOH-HOH...
KODACHI KUNO, LEAVING EARLY...
GROING
I, AT LEAST, WILL NOT WASTE MY EFFORTS!
I BAKED THESE AND DEAR RANMA WILL ENJOY THEM!

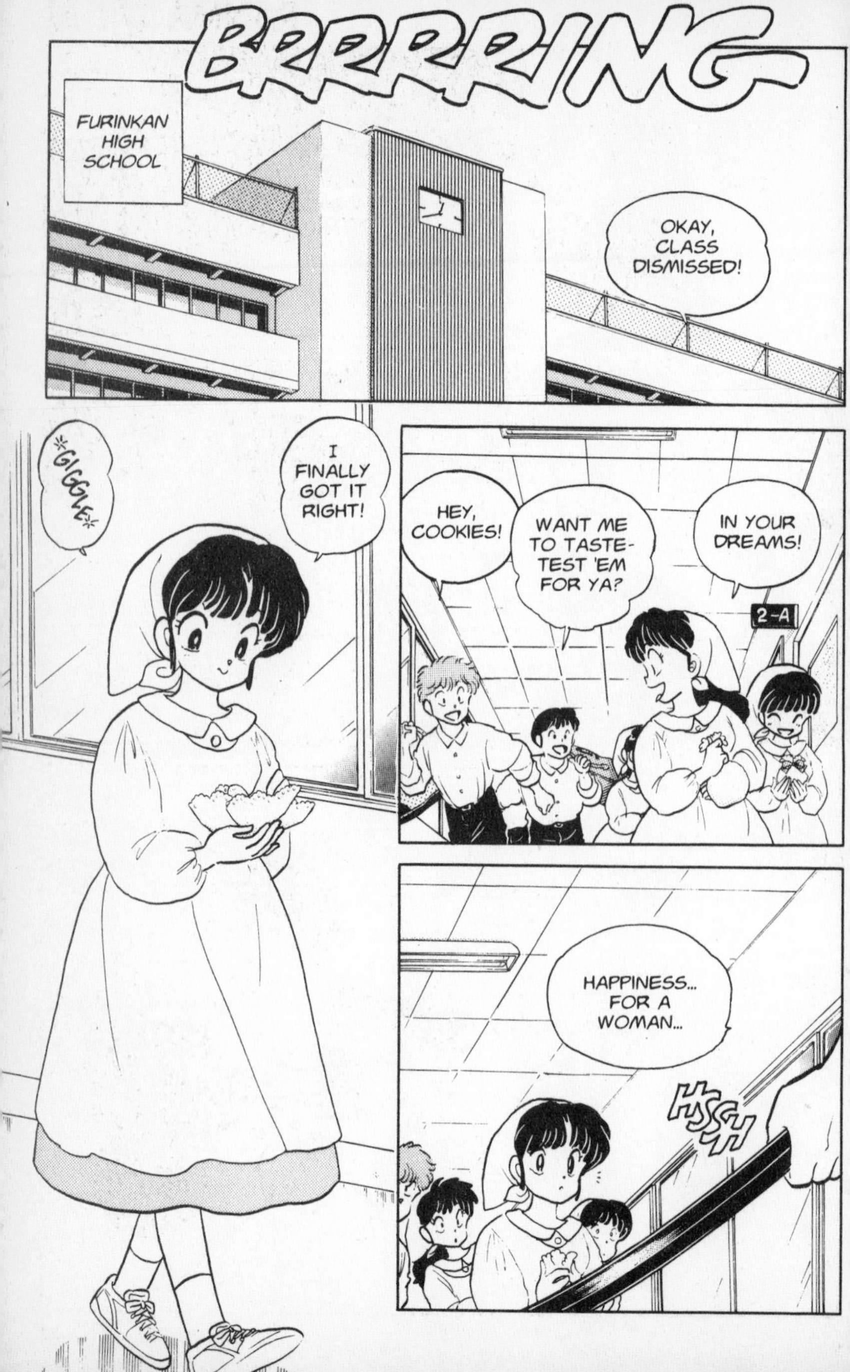
BRRRRING
FURINKAN HIGH SCHOOL
OKAY, CLASS DISMISSED!
GIGGLE
I FINALLY GOT IT RIGHT!
HEY, COOKIES!
WANT ME TO TASTE-TEST 'EM FOR YA?
IN YOUR DREAMS!
2-A
HAPPINESS... FOR A WOMAN...
HSSH

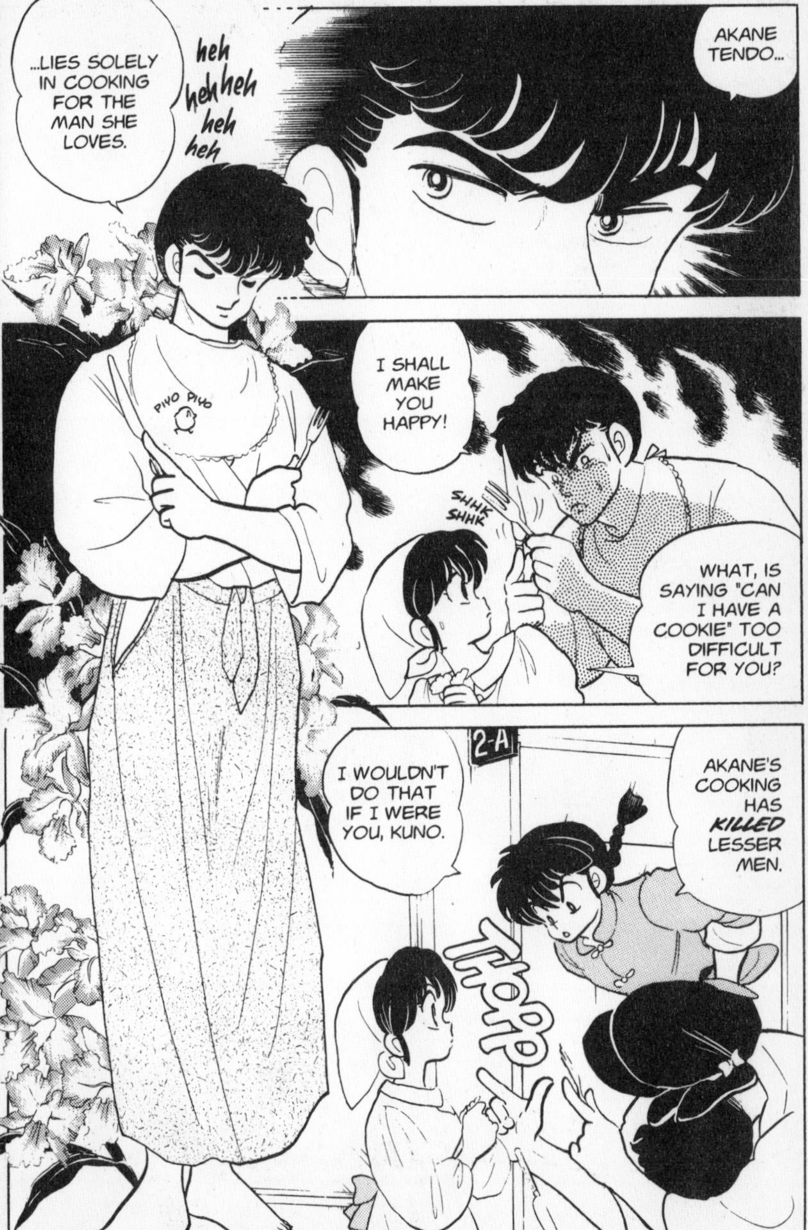
...LIES SOLELY IN COOKING FOR THE MAN SHE LOVES.
heh heh heh heh heh
AKANE TENDO...
PIYO PIYO
I SHALL MAKE YOU HAPPY!
SHHK SHHK
WHAT, IS SAYING "CAN I HAVE A COOKIE" TOO DIFFICULT FOR YOU?
2-A
I WOULDN'T DO THAT IF I WERE YOU, KUNO.
AKANE'S COOKING HAS *KILLED* LESSER MEN.
THOP

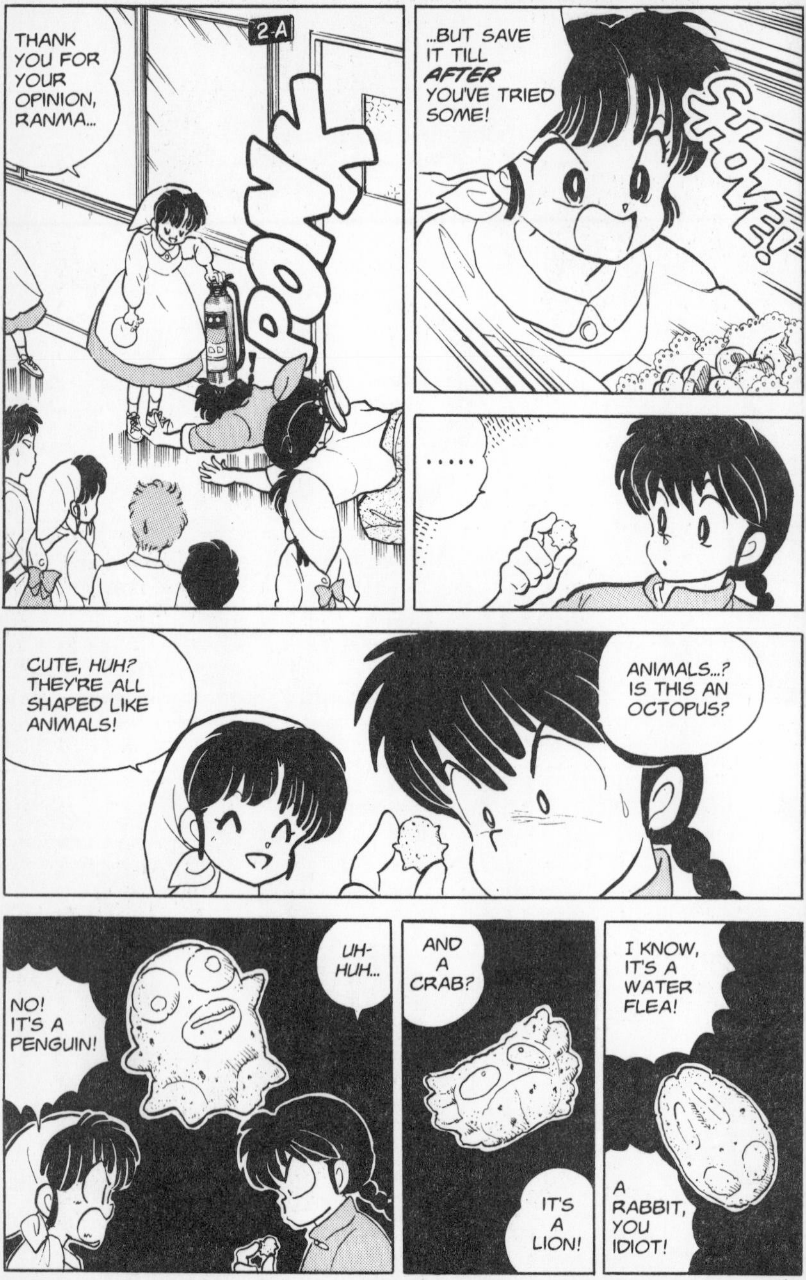
THANK YOU FOR YOUR OPINION, RANMA...
2-A
POKK
!
...BUT SAVE IT TILL *AFTER* YOU'VE TRIED SOME!
SHOVE!
.....
CUTE, HUH? THEY'RE ALL SHAPED LIKE ANIMALS!
ANIMALS...? IS THIS AN OCTOPUS?
NO! IT'S A PENGUIN!
UH-HUH...
AND A CRAB?
IT'S A LION!
I KNOW, IT'S A WATER FLEA!
A RABBIT, YOU IDIOT!

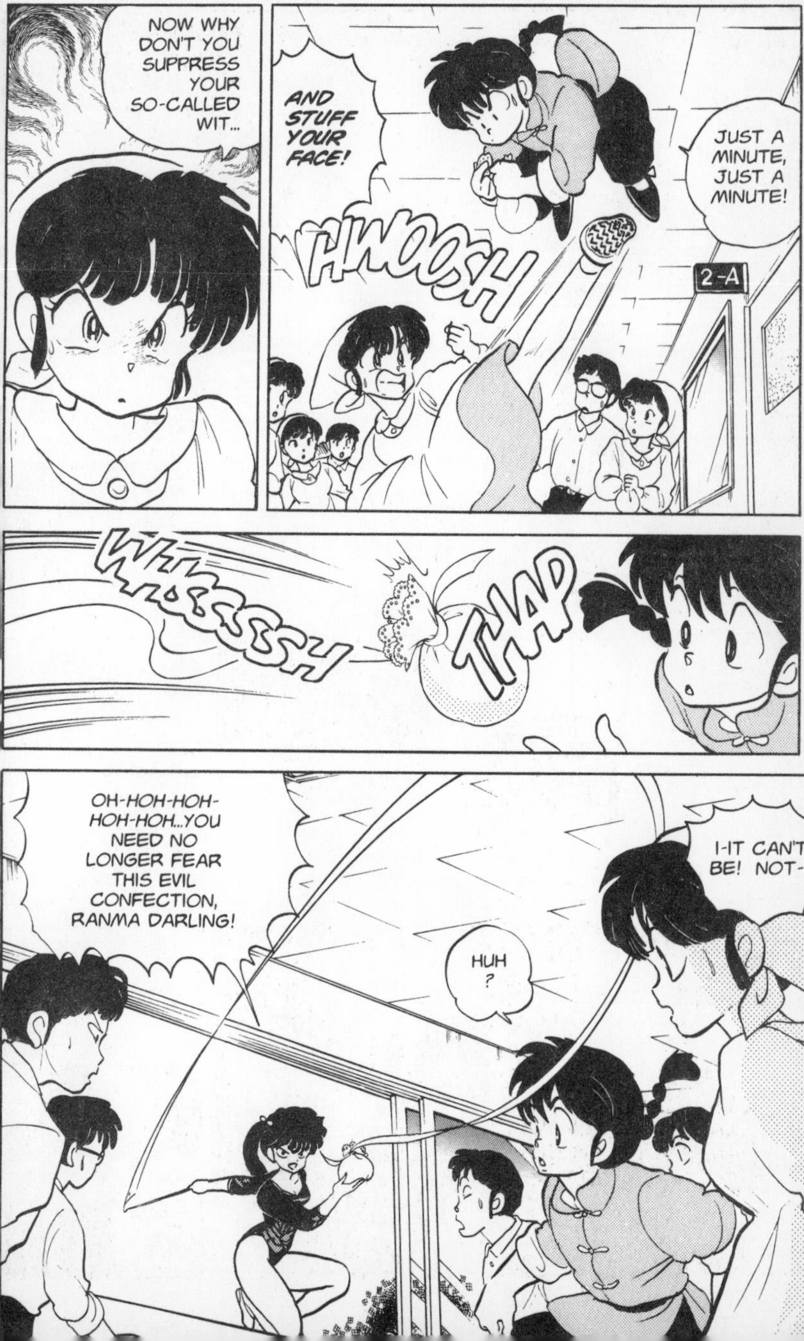
NOW WHY DON'T YOU SUPPRESS YOUR SO-CALLED WIT...
AND STUFF YOUR FACE!
JUST A MINUTE, JUST A MINUTE!
HWOOSH
2-A
WHISSSSH
THAP
OH-HOH-HOH-HOH-HOH...YOU NEED NO LONGER FEAR THIS EVIL CONFECTION, RANMA DARLING!
HUH?
I-IT CAN'T BE! NOT--

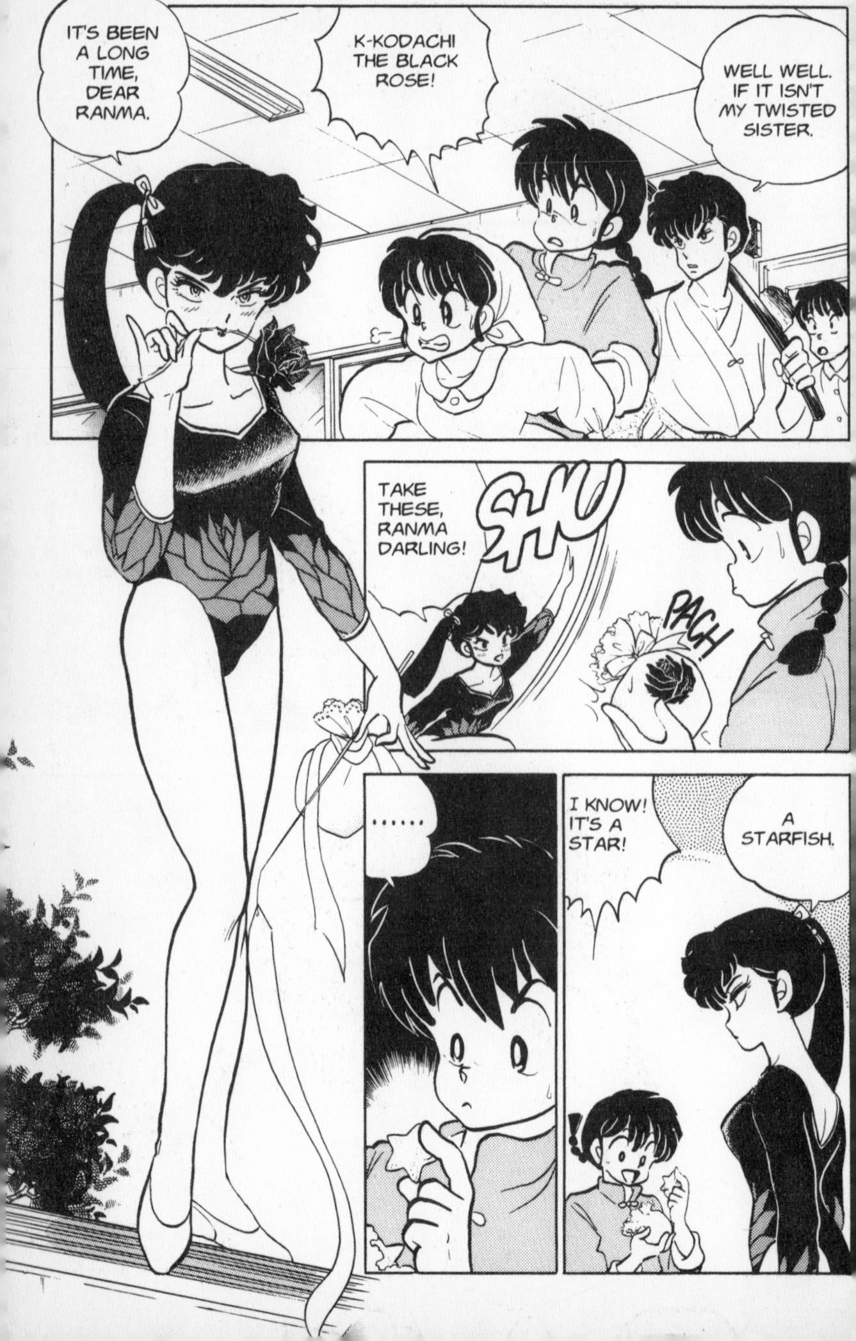
IT'S BEEN A LONG TIME, DEAR RANMA.
K-KODACHI THE BLACK ROSE!
WELL WELL. IF IT ISN'T MY TWISTED SISTER.
TAKE THESE, RANMA DARLING!
SHU
PACH!
......
I KNOW! IT'S A STAR!
A STARFISH.

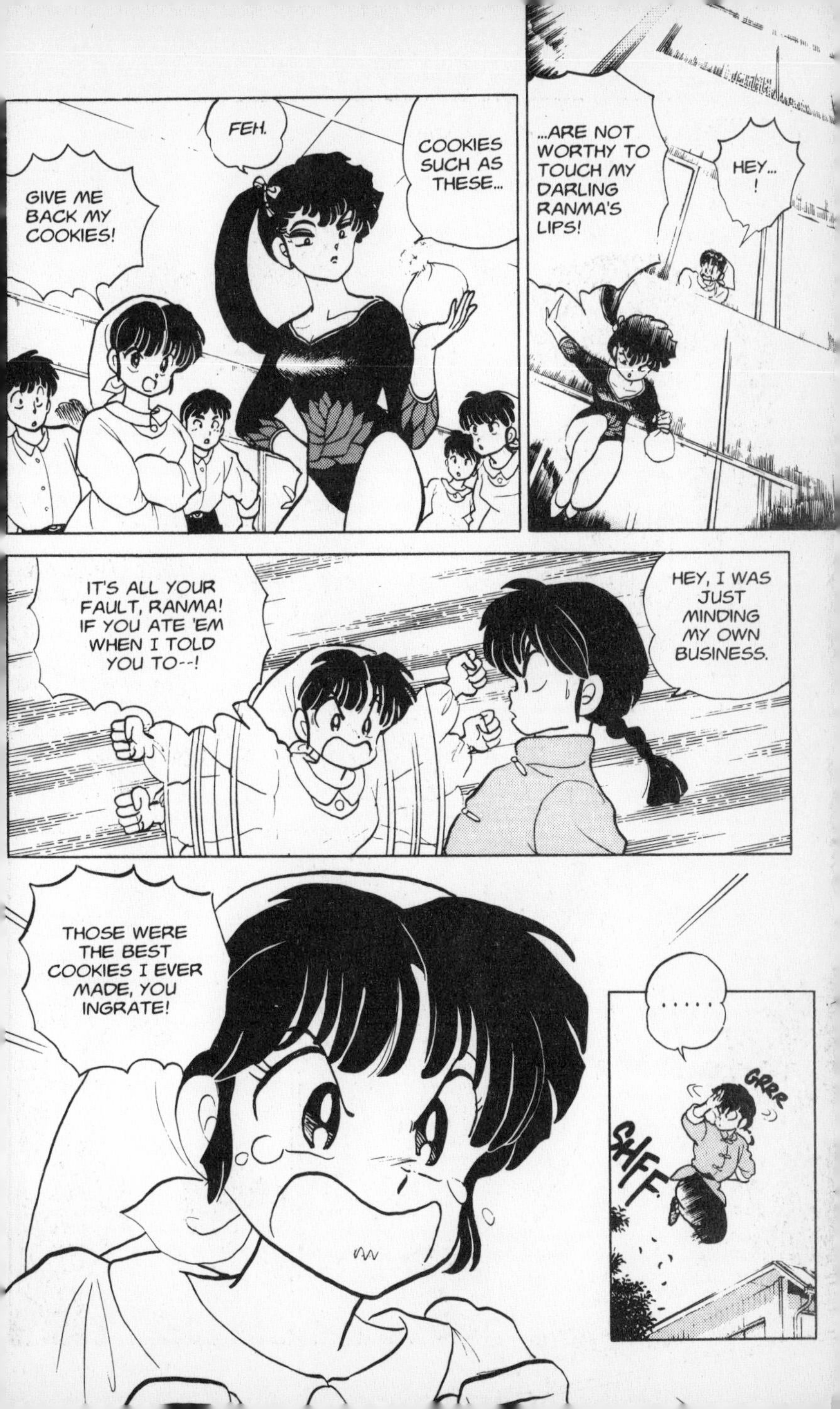
GIVE ME BACK MY COOKIES!
FEH.
COOKIES SUCH AS THESE...
...ARE NOT WORTHY TO TOUCH MY DARLING RANMA'S LIPS!
HEY... !
IT'S ALL YOUR FAULT, RANMA! IF YOU ATE 'EM WHEN I TOLD YOU TO--!
HEY, I WAS JUST MINDING MY OWN BUSINESS.
THOSE WERE THE BEST COOKIES I EVER MADE, YOU INGRATE!
.....
GRRR
SHFF

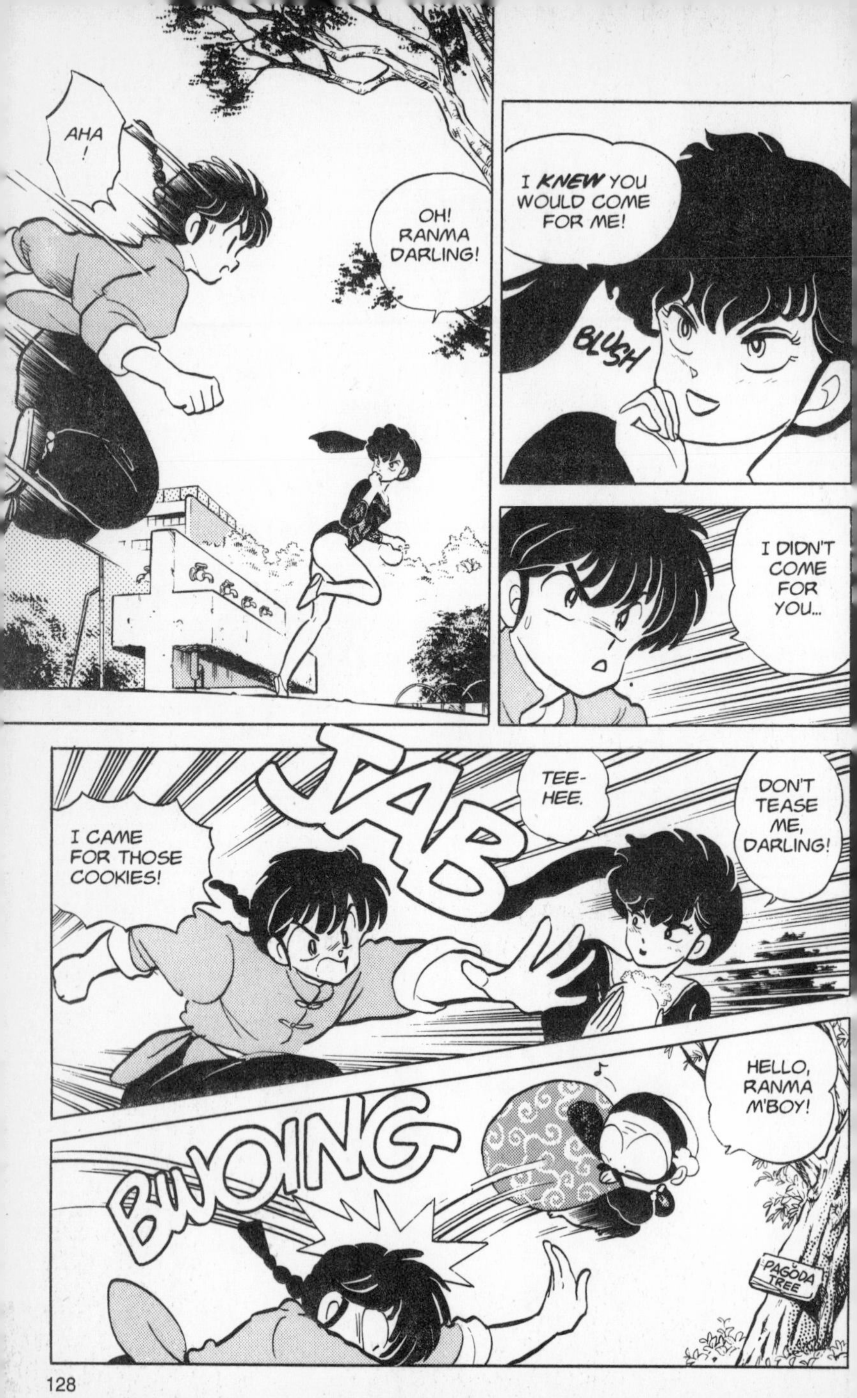
AHA!
OH! RANMA DARLING!
I KNEW YOU WOULD COME FOR ME!
BLUSH
I DIDN'T COME FOR YOU...
I CAME FOR THOSE COOKIES!
JAB
TEE-HEE.
DON'T TEASE ME, DARLING!
BWOING
HELLO, RANMA M'BOY!
PAGODA TREE

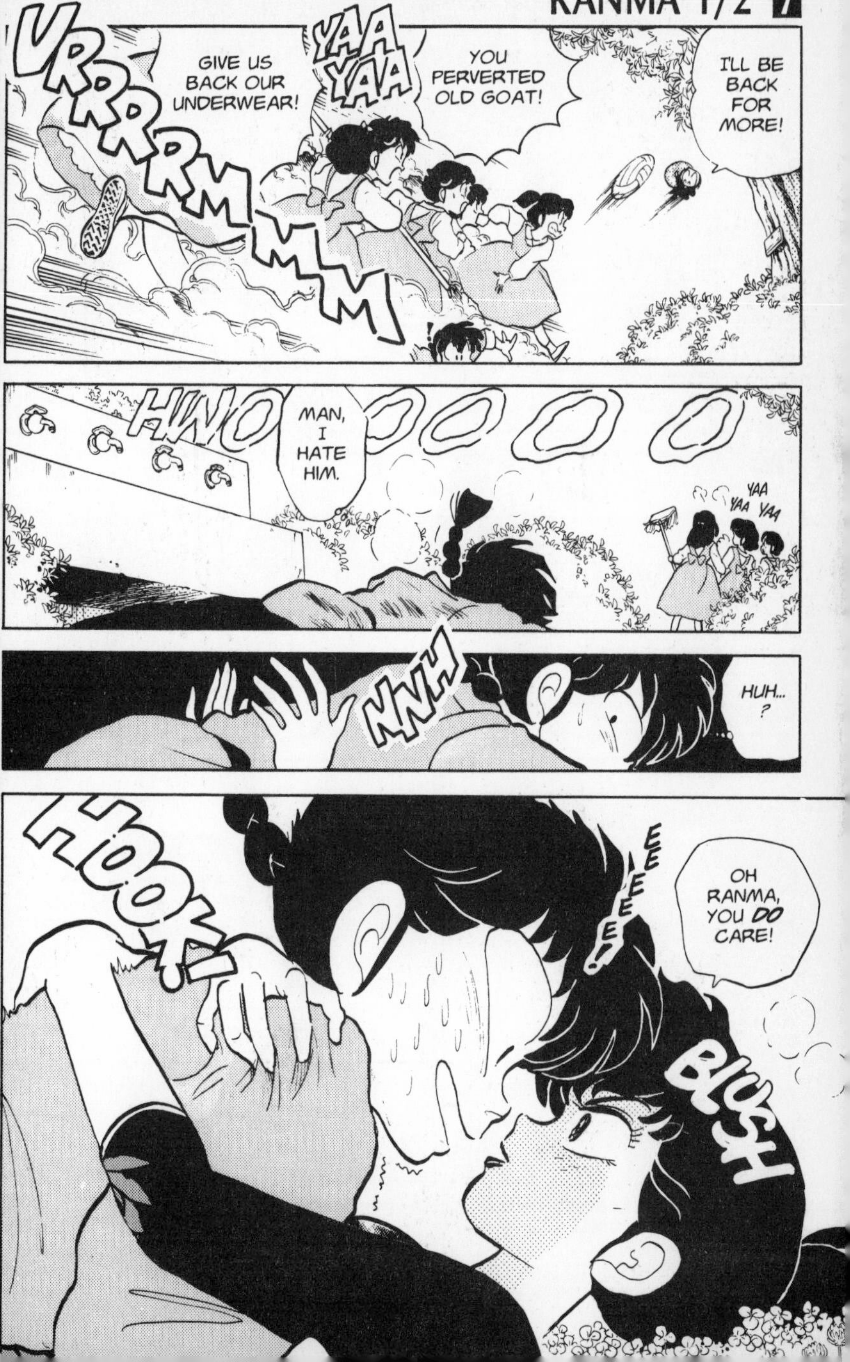
VRRRRRMMMMMM
GIVE US BACK OUR UNDERWEAR!
YAA YAA
YOU PERVERTED OLD GOAT!
I'LL BE BACK FOR MORE!
HWOOOOOO
MAN, I HATE HIM.
YAA YAA YAA
NNH
HUH... ?
HOOK!
EEEEE!
OH RANMA, YOU *DO* CARE!
BLUSH

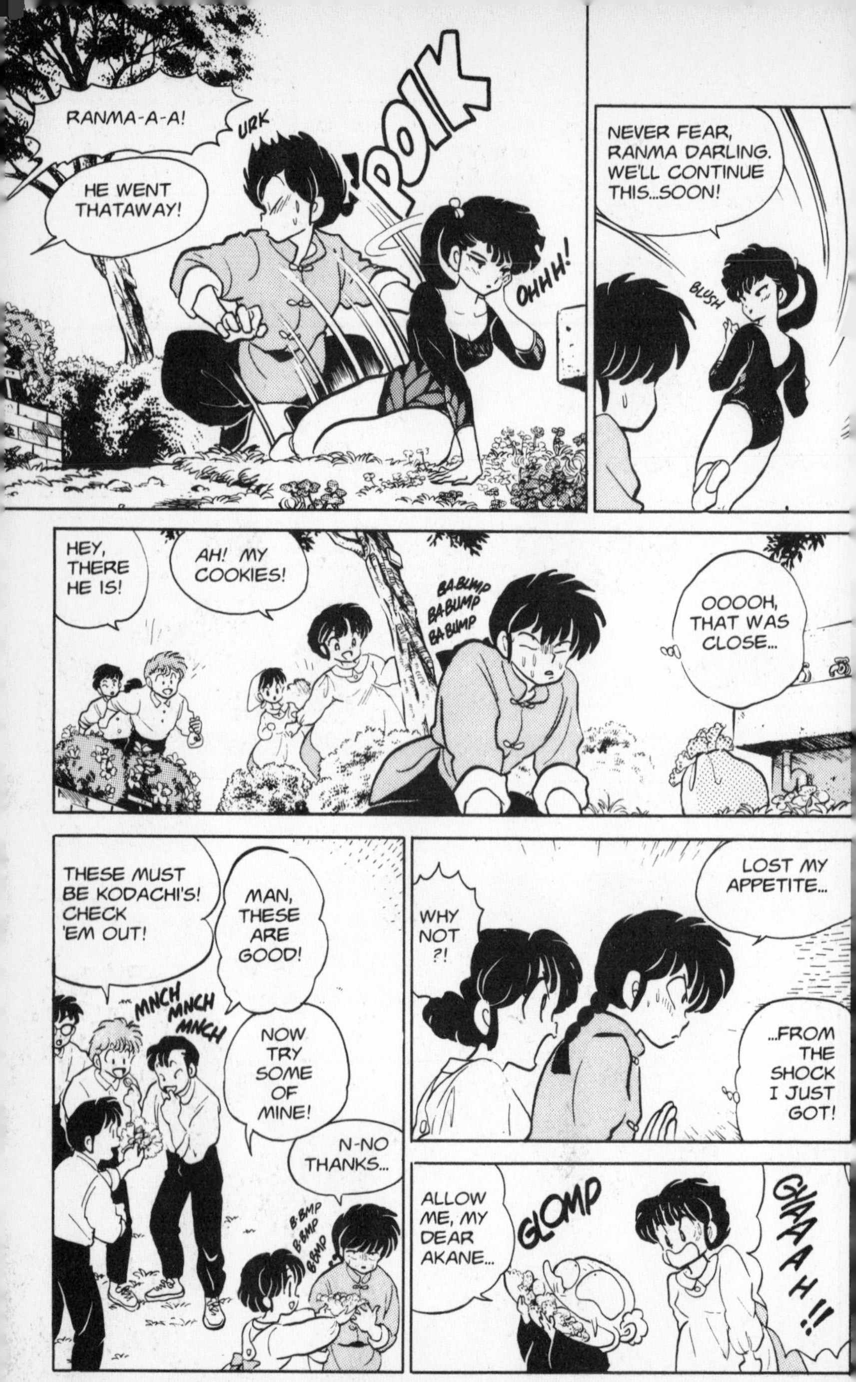
RANMA-A-A!
HE WENT THATAWAY!
URK
POIK
OHHH!
NEVER FEAR, RANMA DARLING. WE'LL CONTINUE THIS...SOON!
BLUSH
HEY, THERE HE IS!
AH! MY COOKIES!
BA-BUMP BA-BUMP BA-BUMP
OOOOH, THAT WAS CLOSE...
THESE MUST BE KODACHI'S! CHECK 'EM OUT!
MAN, THESE ARE GOOD!
MNCH MNCH MNCH
NOW TRY SOME OF MINE!
N-NO THANKS...
B-BMP B-BMP B-BMP
WHY NOT ?!
LOST MY APPETITE...
...FROM THE SHOCK I JUST GOT!
ALLOW ME, MY DEAR AKANE...
GLOMP
GHAAAH!!

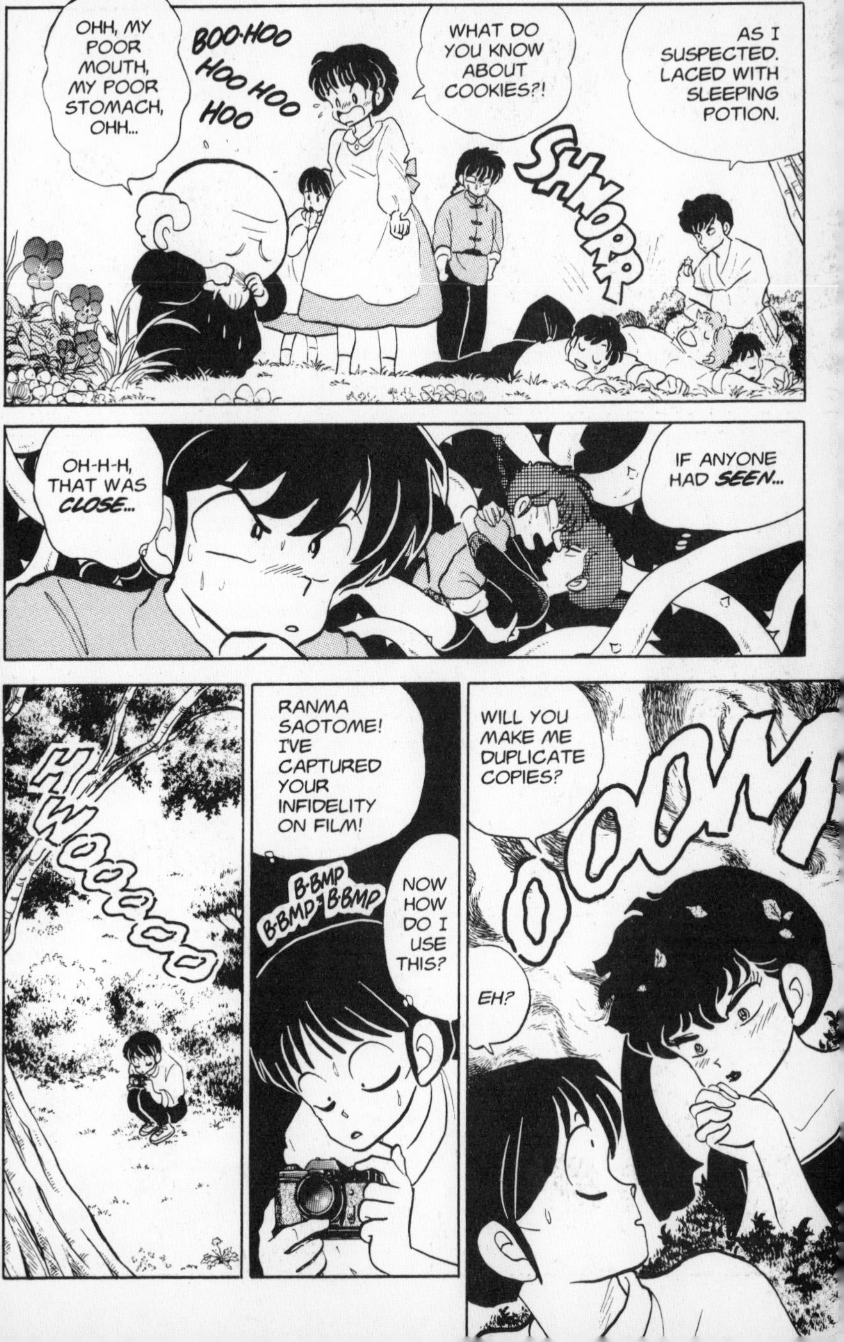
OHH, MY POOR MOUTH, MY POOR STOMACH, OHH...
BOO-HOO HOO HOO HOO
WHAT DO YOU KNOW ABOUT COOKIES?!
SHNORR
AS I SUSPECTED. LACED WITH SLEEPING POTION.
OH-H-H, THAT WAS CLOSE...
IF ANYONE HAD SEEN...
HWOOOOOO
RANMA SAOTOME! I'VE CAPTURED YOUR INFIDELITY ON FILM!
B-BMP B-BMP B-BMP
NOW HOW DO I USE THIS?
WILL YOU MAKE ME DUPLICATE COPIES?
OOOM
EH?

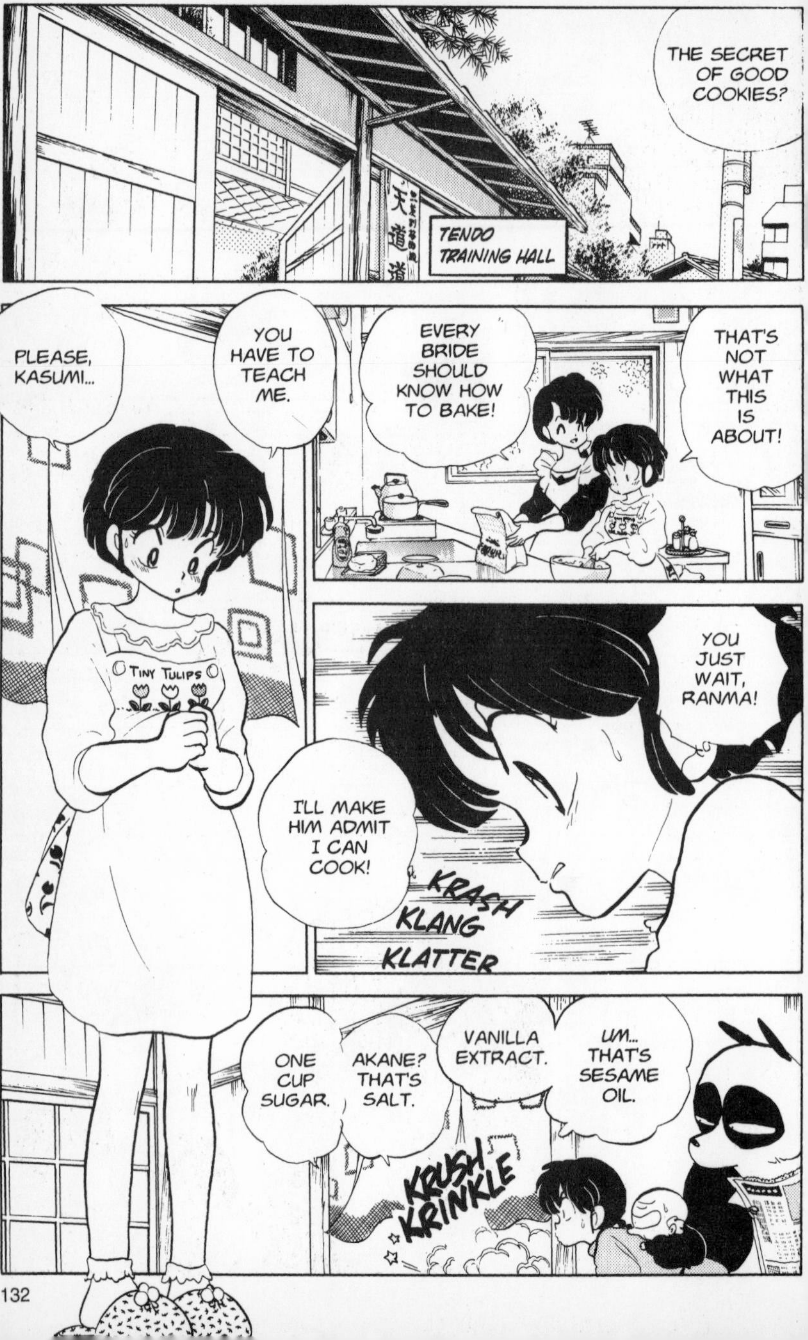
THE SECRET OF GOOD COOKIES?
TENDO TRAINING HALL
PLEASE, KASUMI...
YOU HAVE TO TEACH ME.
TINY TULIPS
EVERY BRIDE SHOULD KNOW HOW TO BAKE!
THAT'S NOT WHAT THIS IS ABOUT!
YOU JUST WAIT, RANMA!
I'LL MAKE HIM ADMIT I CAN COOK!
KRASH
KLANG
KLATTER
ONE CUP SUGAR.
AKANE? THAT'S SALT.
VANILLA EXTRACT.
UM... THAT'S SESAME OIL.
KRUSH
KRINKLE

THEY'RE DONE!

WELL? GO AHEAD!

SHOW YOUR GRATITUDE, BOY.

. . . . .

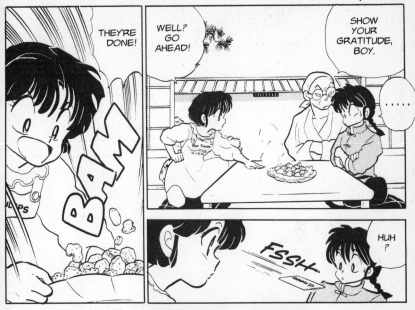

HUH?

FSSH.

A BLACK ROSE EMBLEM...

FROM KODACHI?

I've prepared you a feast. Come to me. You won't be sorry.

A "FEAST," HUH? SHE DOESN'T GIVE UP, DOES SHE?

WHO'RE *YOU* TO TALK?

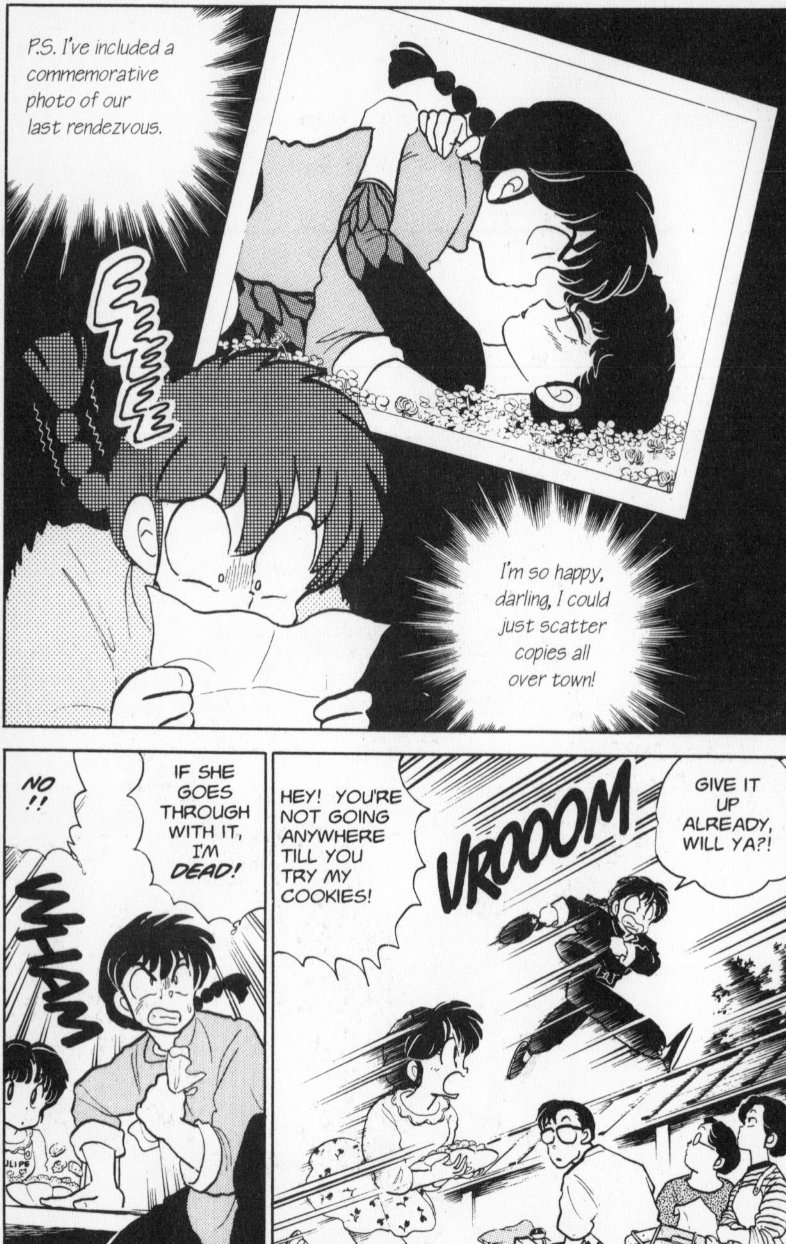
P.S. I've included a commemorative photo of our last rendezvous.
EEEEEE
I'm so happy, darling, I could just scatter copies all over town!
NO !!
IF SHE GOES THROUGH WITH IT, I'M DEAD!
WHAM
HEY! YOU'RE NOT GOING ANYWHERE TILL YOU TRY MY COOKIES!
VROOOM
GIVE IT UP ALREADY, WILL YA?!

Part 9

NEGATIVE FEELINGS

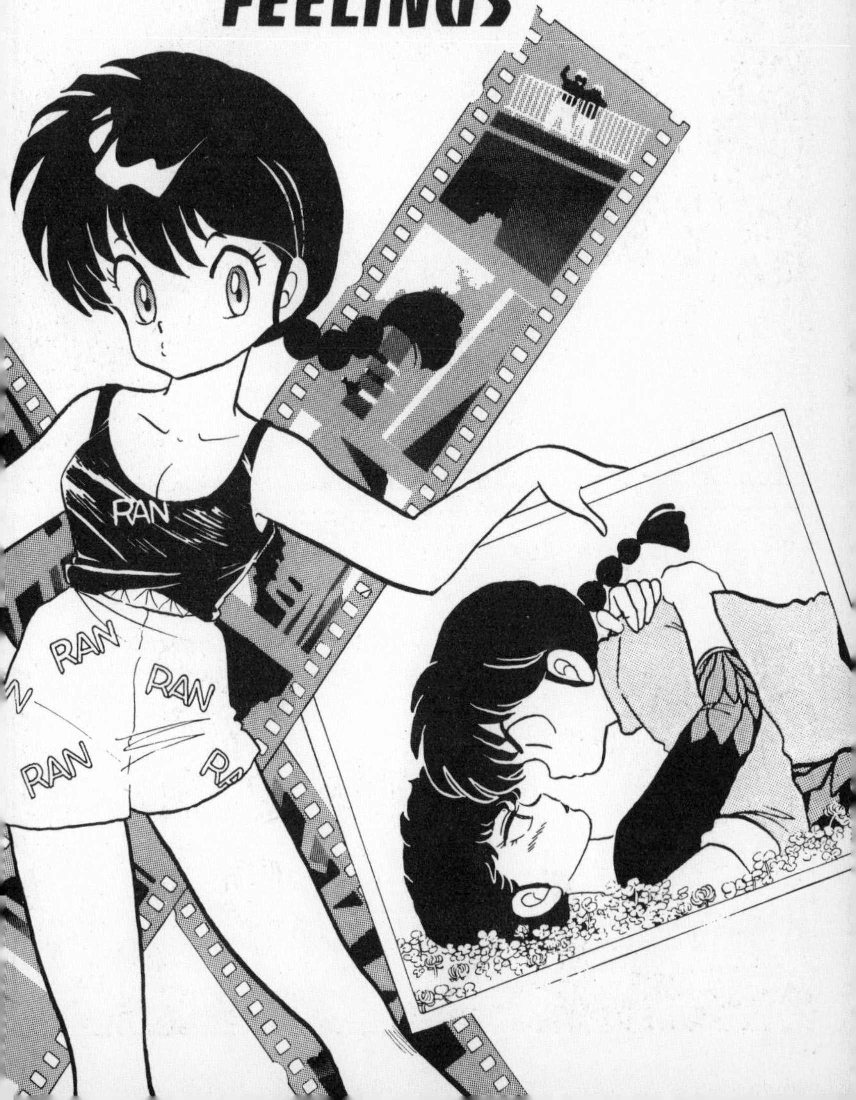
RAN
RAN
RAN
RAN

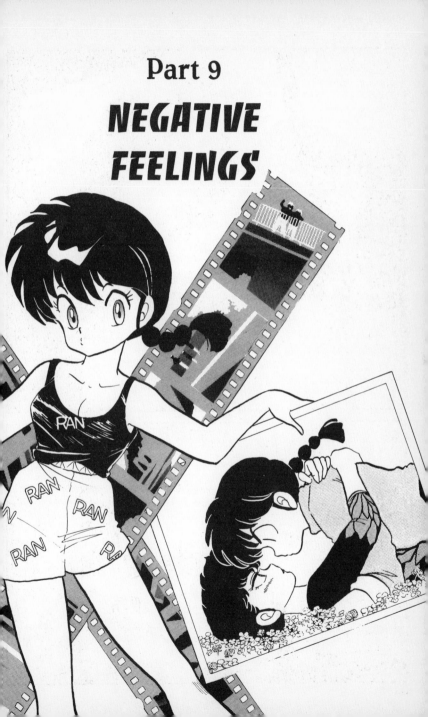

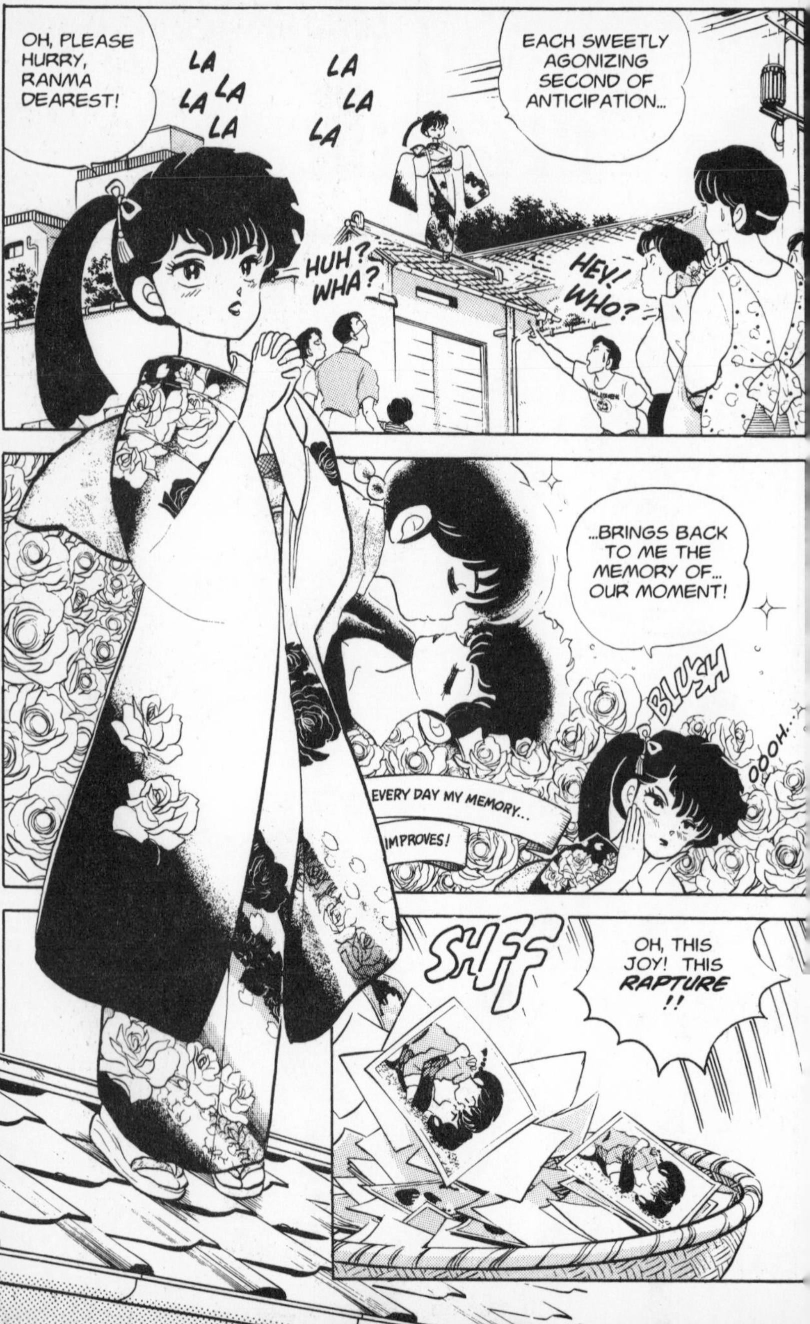

OH, PLEASE HURRY, RANMA DEAREST!
LA LA LA LA
LA LA LA
EACH SWEETLY AGONIZING SECOND OF ANTICIPATION...
HUH? WHA?
HEY! WHO?
...BRINGS BACK TO ME THE MEMORY OF... OUR MOMENT!
BLUSH
OOOH...
EVERY DAY MY MEMORY...
IMPROVES!
SHFF
OH, THIS JOY! THIS RAPTURE!!

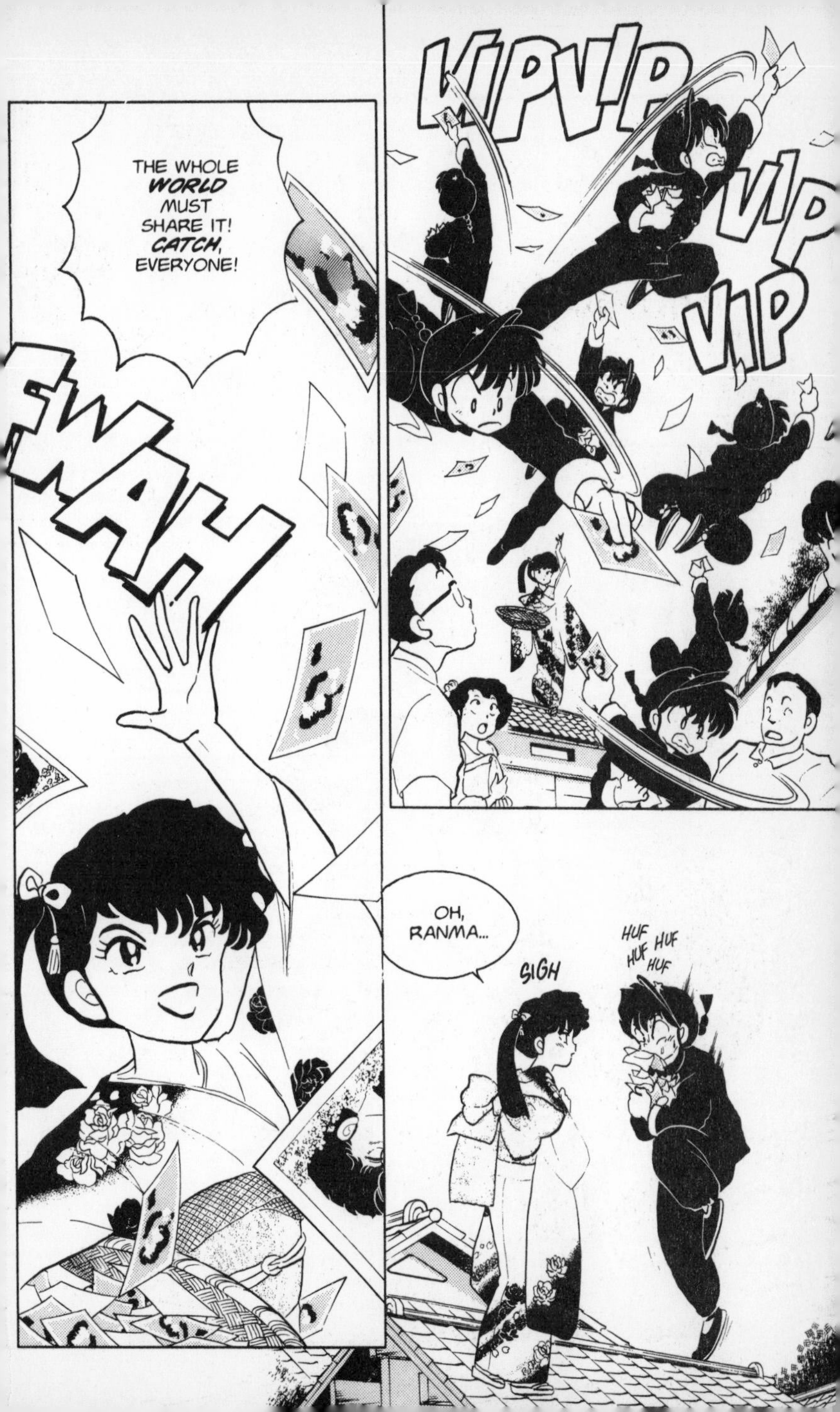
THE WHOLE WORLD MUST SHARE IT! CATCH, EVERYONE!
WAH
VIPVIP
VIP
VIP
OH, RANMA...
HUF HUF HUF HUF HUF
SIGH

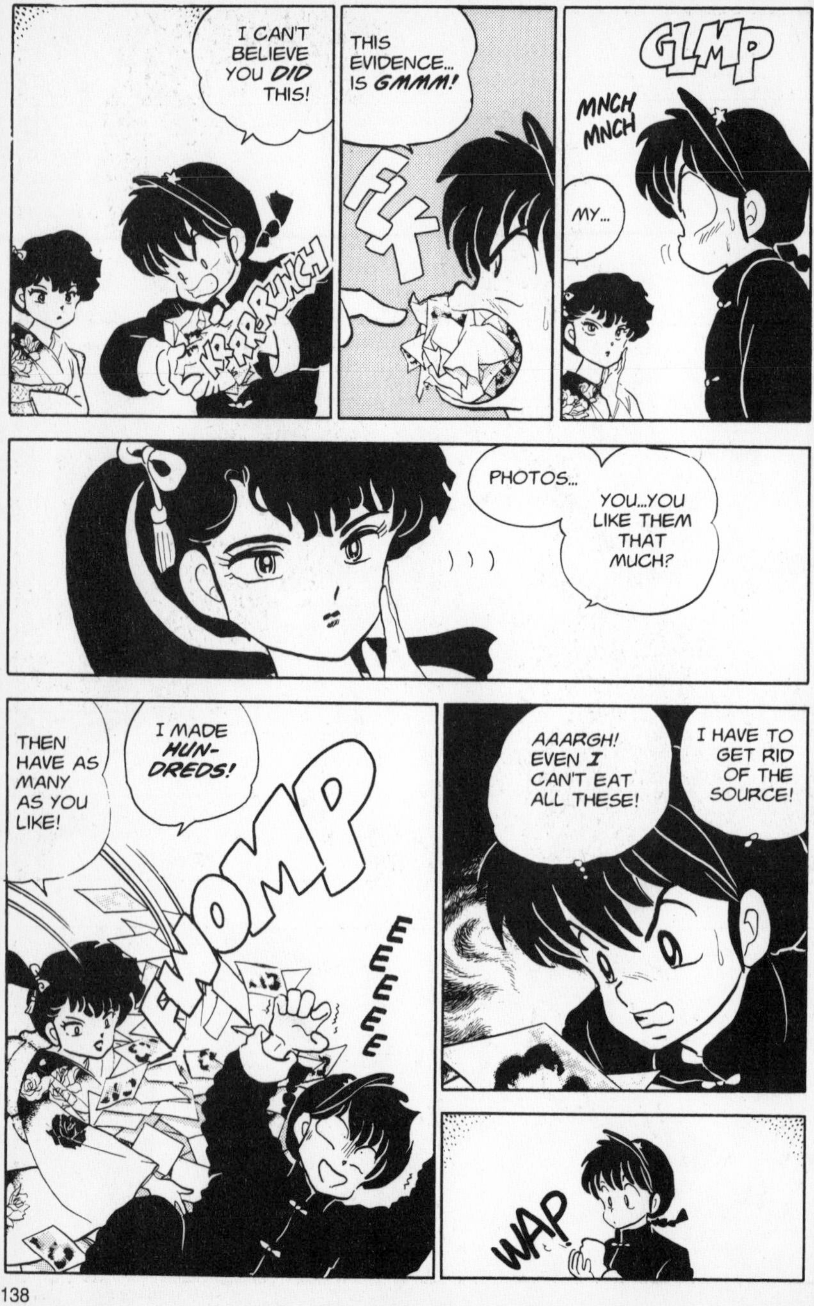
I CAN'T BELIEVE YOU *DID* THIS!
SKRRRUNCH
THIS EVIDENCE... IS *GMMM!*
FLK
GLMP
MNCH MNCH
MY...
PHOTOS...
YOU...YOU LIKE THEM THAT MUCH?
THEN HAVE AS MANY AS YOU LIKE!
I MADE *HUN-DREDS!*
FWOMP
EEEEEE
AAARGH! EVEN *I* CAN'T EAT ALL THESE!
I HAVE TO GET RID OF THE SOURCE!
WAP

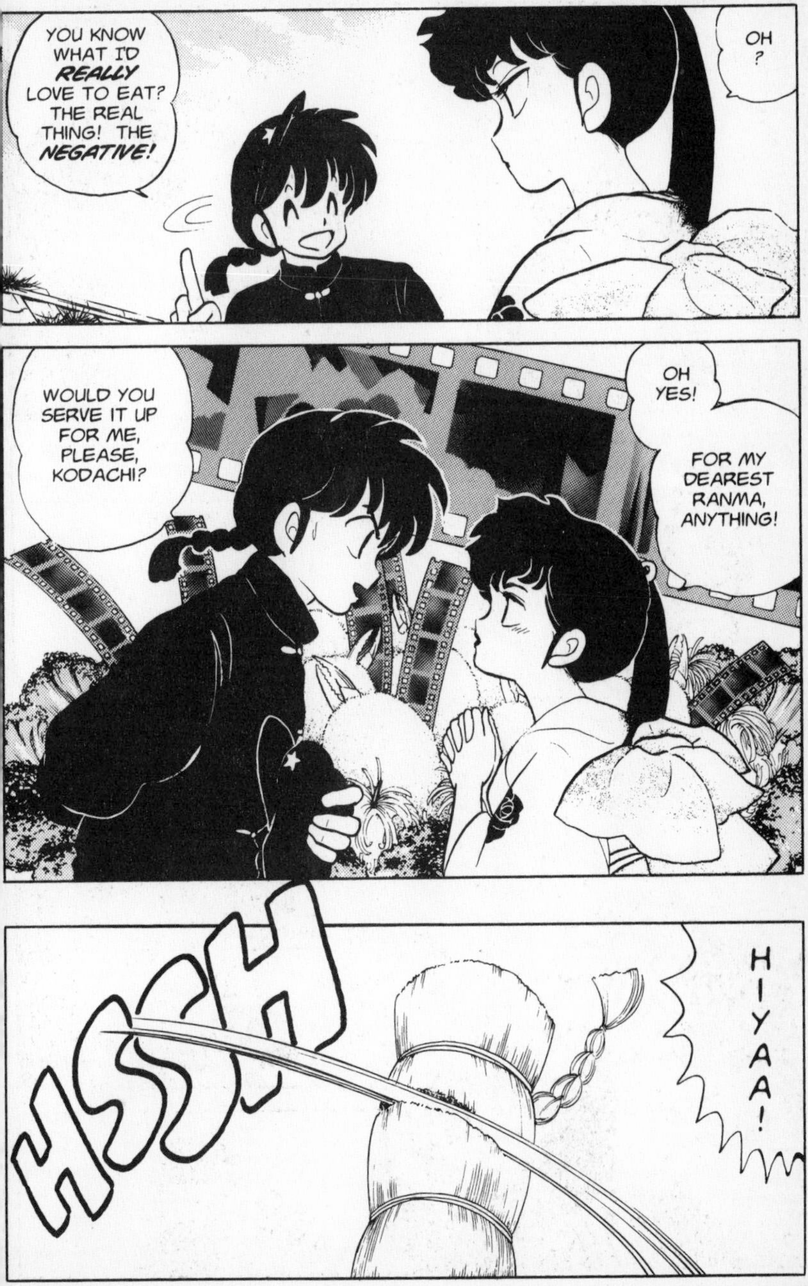
YOU KNOW WHAT I'D REALLY LOVE TO EAT? THE REAL THING! THE NEGATIVE!
OH ?
WOULD YOU SERVE IT UP FOR ME, PLEASE, KODACHI?
OH YES!
FOR MY DEAREST RANMA, ANYTHING!
HISSH
HIYAAA!

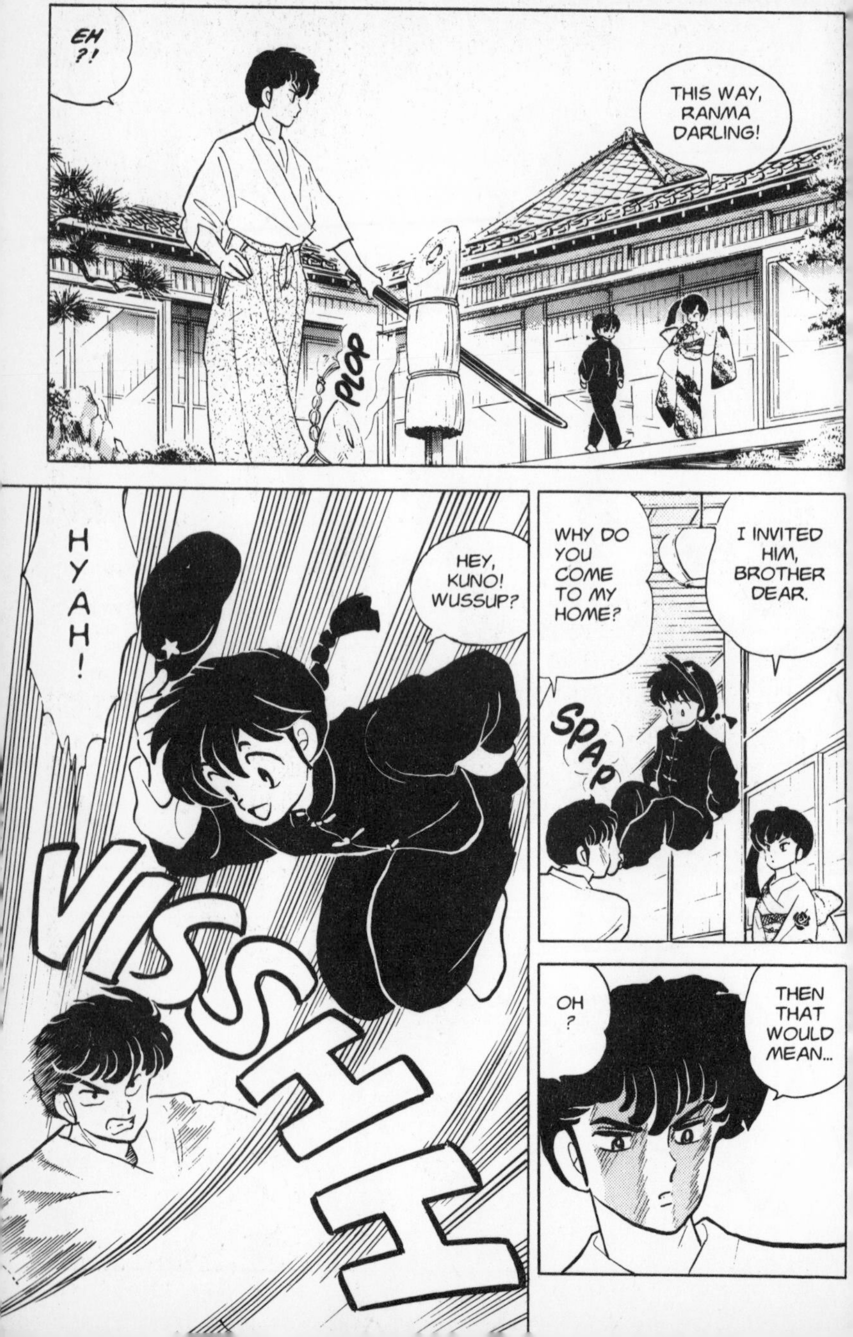
EH ?!
THIS WAY, RANMA DARLING!
PLOP
HYAH!
HEY, KUNO! WUSSUP?
VISSHH
WHY DO YOU COME TO MY HOME?
I INVITED HIM, BROTHER DEAR.
SPAP
OH ?
THEN THAT WOULD MEAN...

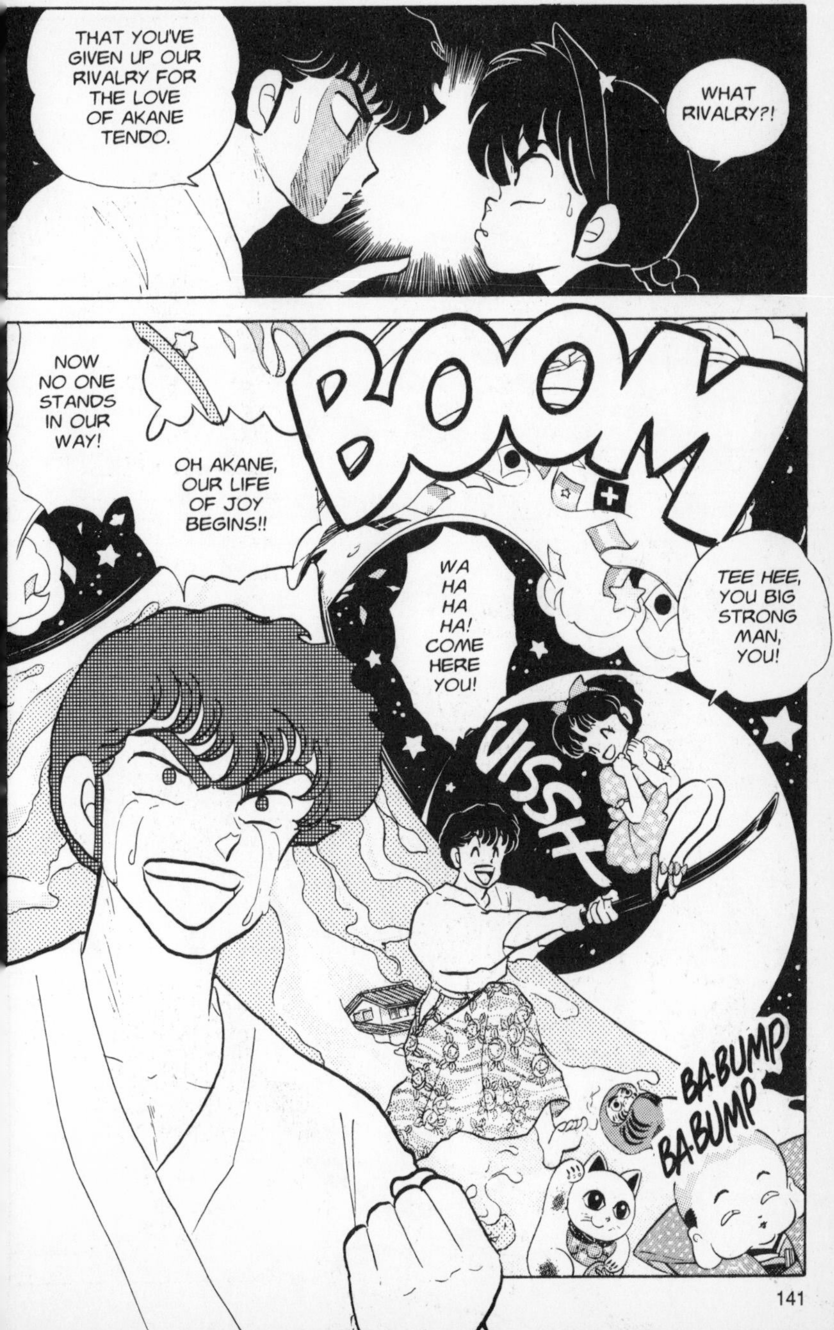
THAT YOU'VE GIVEN UP OUR RIVALRY FOR THE LOVE OF AKANE TENDO.
WHAT RIVALRY?!
NOW NO ONE STANDS IN OUR WAY!
OH AKANE, OUR LIFE OF JOY BEGINS!!
BOOM
WA HA HA HA! COME HERE YOU!
TEE HEE, YOU BIG STRONG MAN, YOU!
VISSH
BA-BUMP BA-BUMP

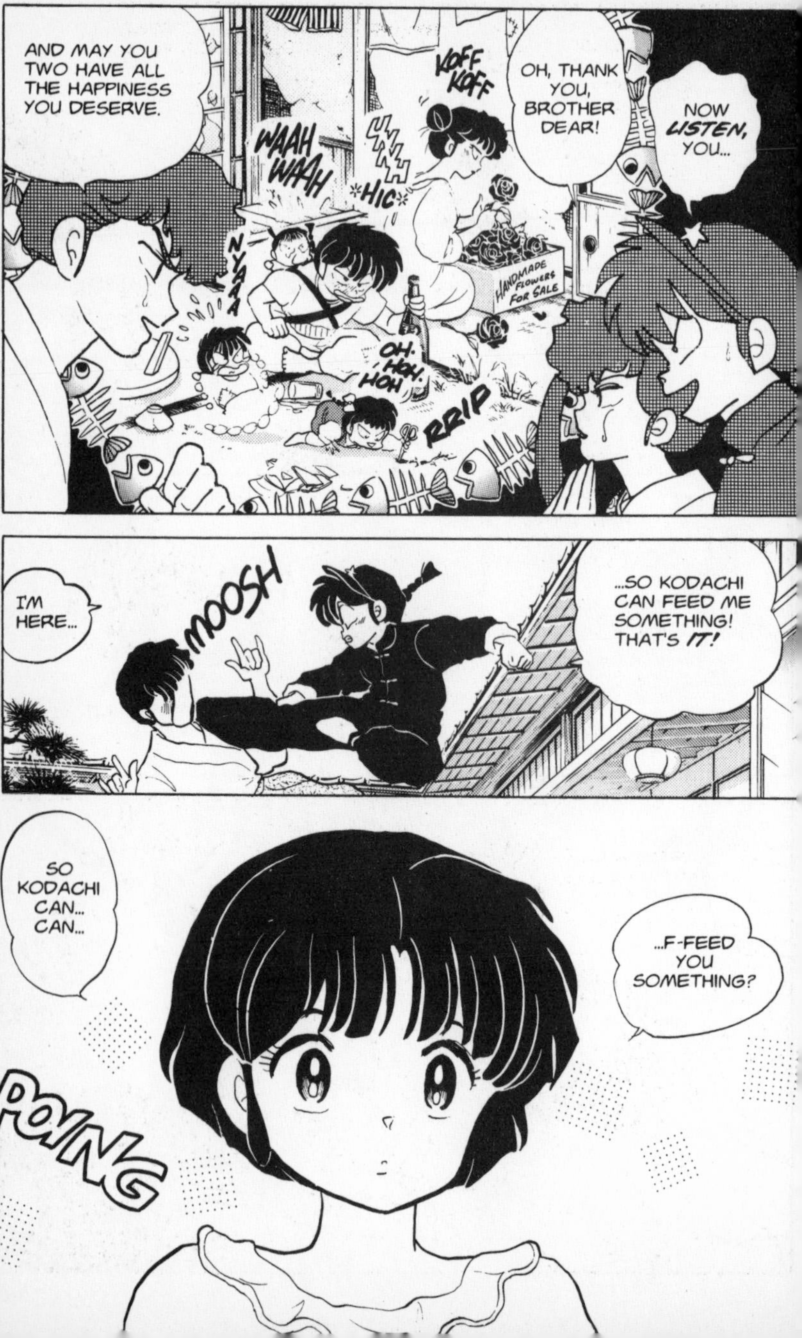
AND MAY YOU TWO HAVE ALL THE HAPPINESS YOU DESERVE.
WAAH WAAH
NYAAA
UNNH
HIC
KOFF KOFF
OH, THANK YOU, BROTHER DEAR!
HANDMADE FLOWERS FOR SALE
OH. HOH. HOH.
RRIP
NOW *LISTEN,* YOU...
I'M HERE...
MOOSH
...SO KODACHI CAN FEED ME SOMETHING! THAT'S *IT!*
SO KODACHI CAN... CAN...
POING
...F-FEED YOU SOMETHING?

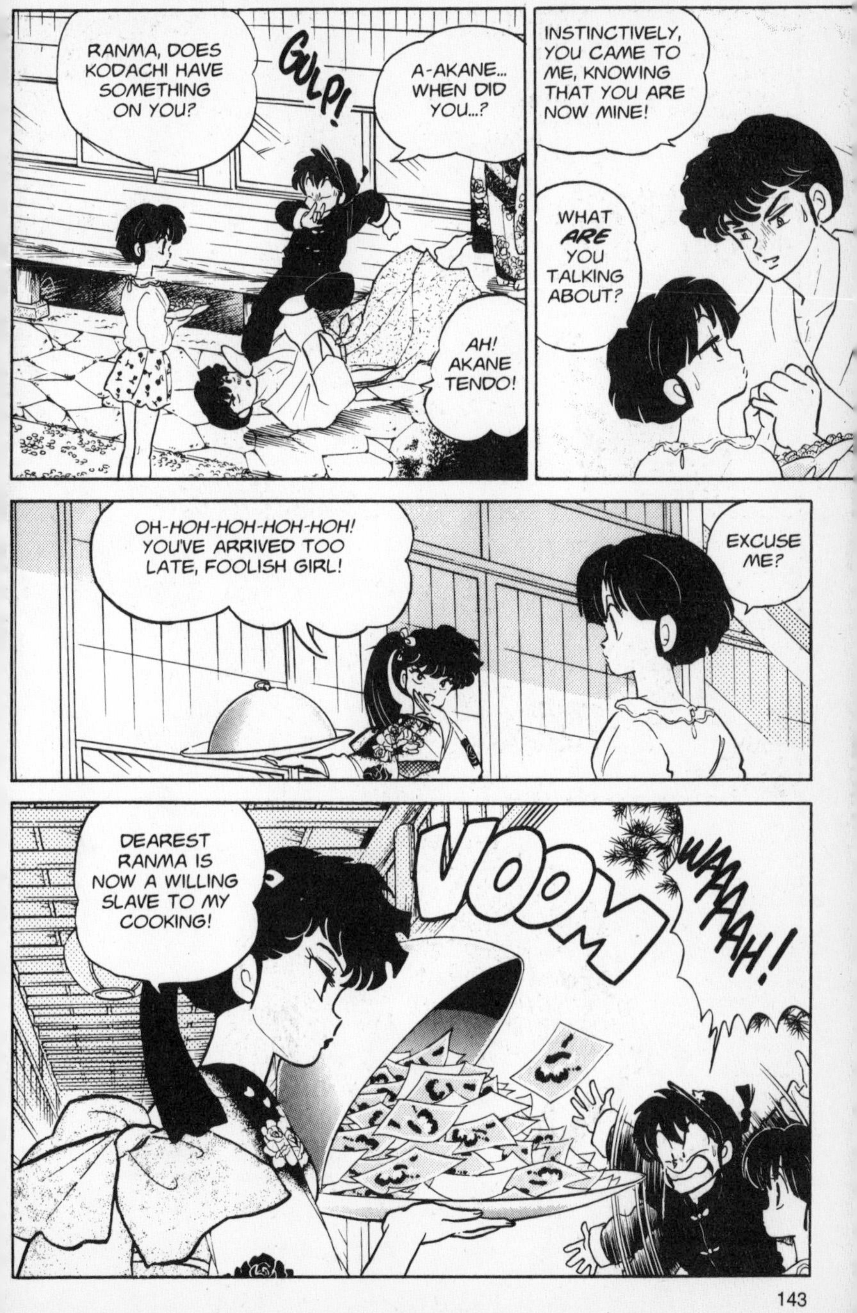
RANMA, DOES KODACHI HAVE SOMETHING ON YOU?
GULP!
A-AKANE... WHEN DID YOU...?
AH! AKANE TENDO!
INSTINCTIVELY, YOU CAME TO ME, KNOWING THAT YOU ARE NOW MINE!
WHAT ARE YOU TALKING ABOUT?
OH-HOH-HOH-HOH-HOH! YOU'VE ARRIVED TOO LATE, FOOLISH GIRL!
EXCUSE ME?
DEAREST RANMA IS NOW A WILLING SLAVE TO MY COOKING!
VOOM
WAAAAAH!

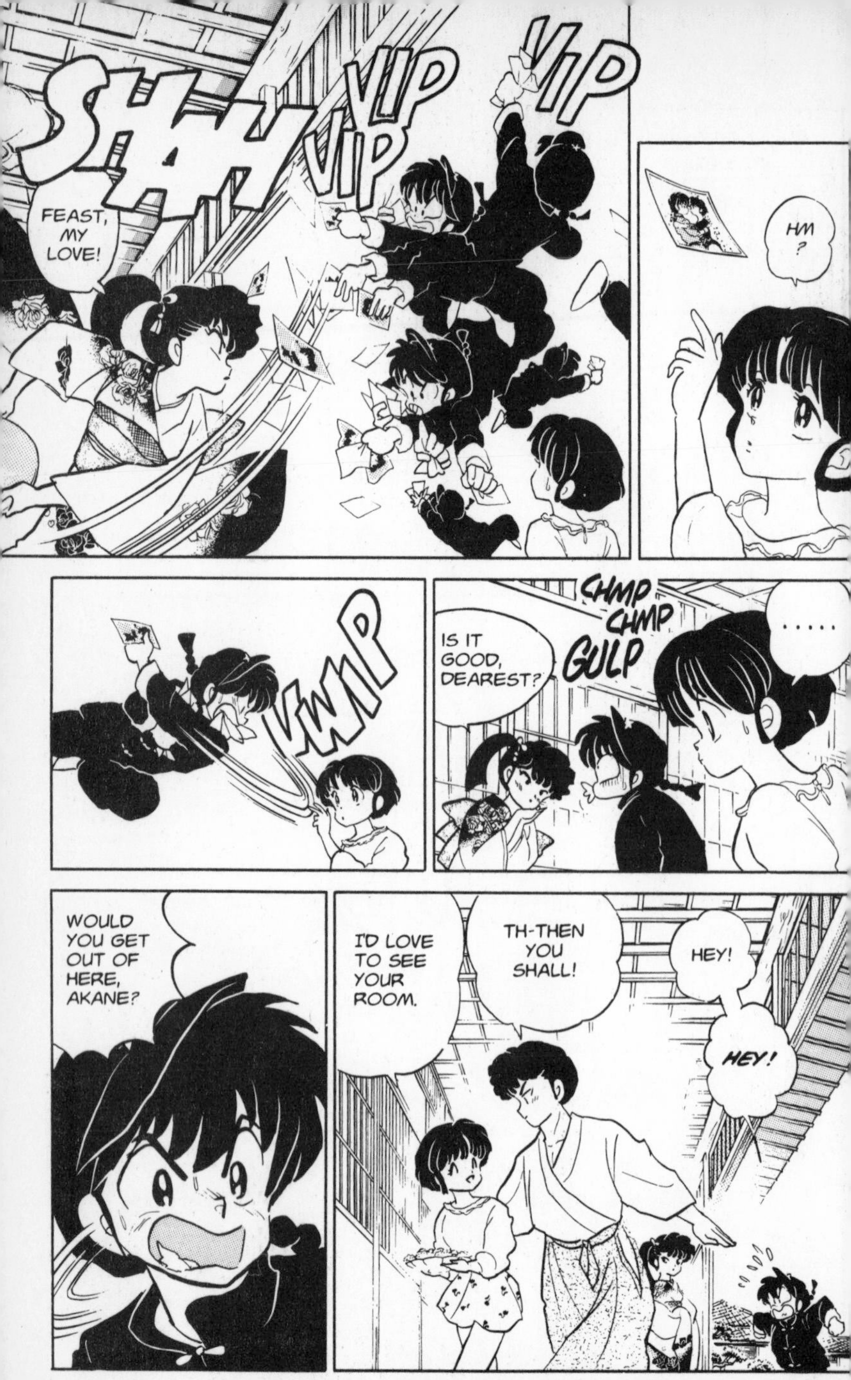
SHAA
VIP VIP
VIP VIP
FEAST, MY LOVE!
HM?
VWIP
IS IT GOOD, DEAREST?
CHMP CHMP
GULP
.....
WOULD YOU GET OUT OF HERE, AKANE?
I'D LOVE TO SEE YOUR ROOM.
TH-THEN YOU SHALL!
HEY!
HEY!

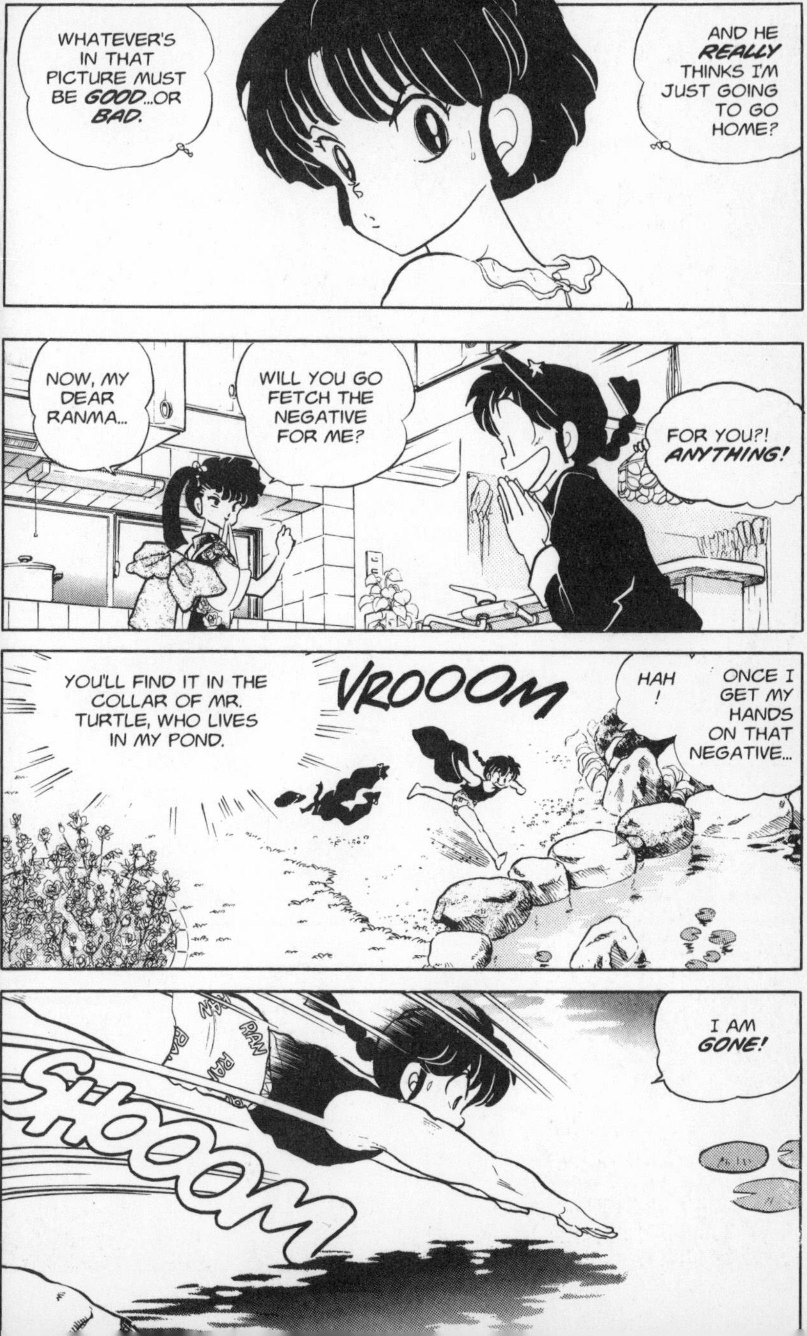
WHATEVER'S IN THAT PICTURE MUST BE GOOD...OR BAD.
AND HE REALLY THINKS I'M JUST GOING TO GO HOME?
NOW, MY DEAR RANMA...
WILL YOU GO FETCH THE NEGATIVE FOR ME?
FOR YOU?! ANYTHING!
YOU'LL FIND IT IN THE COLLAR OF MR. TURTLE, WHO LIVES IN MY POND.
VROOOM
HAH!
ONCE I GET MY HANDS ON THAT NEGATIVE...
SHOOOM
I AM GONE!

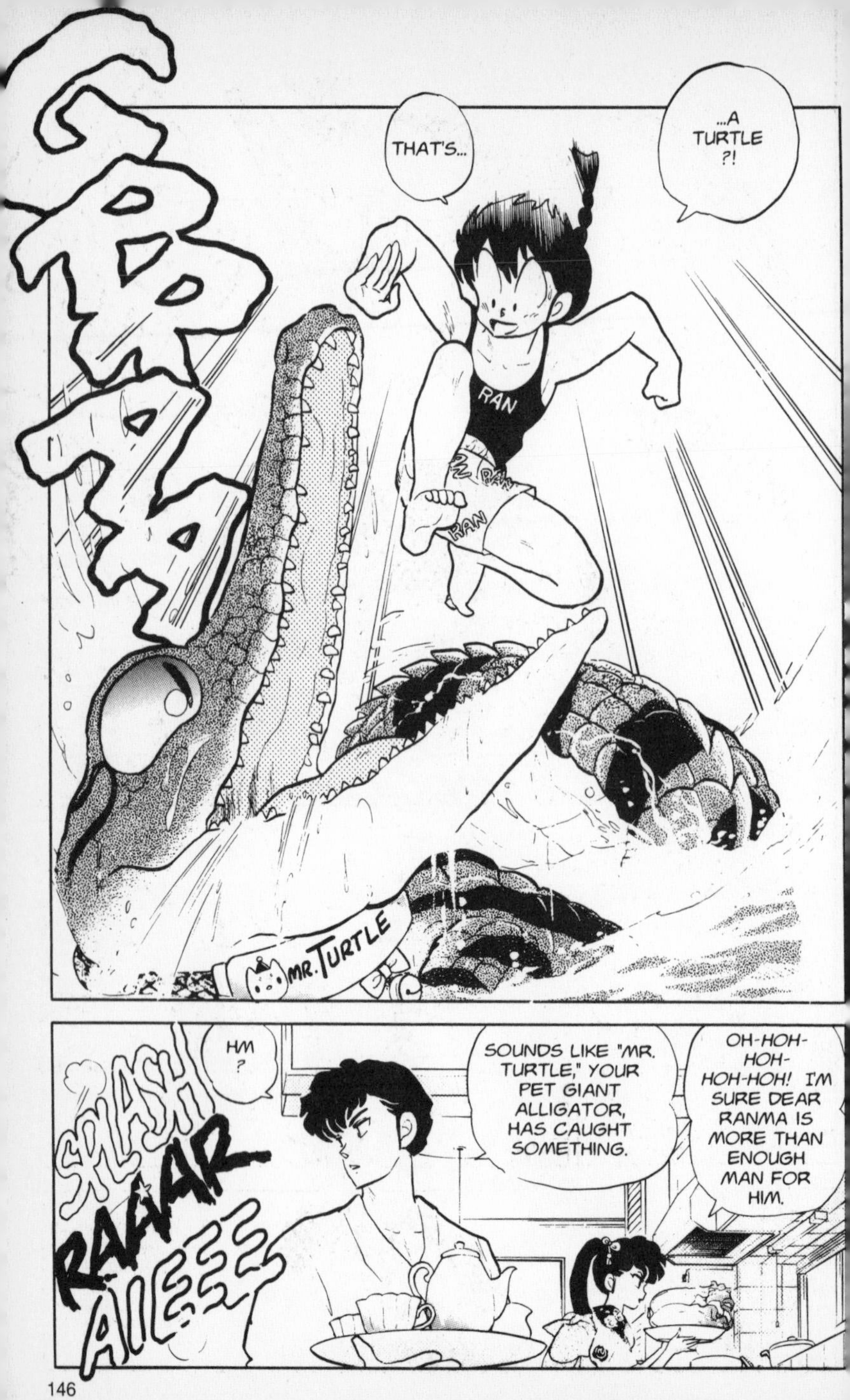
THAT'S...
...A TURTLE ?!
MR. TURTLE
SPLASH
RAAAR
AIEEE
HM ?
SOUNDS LIKE "MR. TURTLE," YOUR PET GIANT ALLIGATOR, HAS CAUGHT SOMETHING.
OH-HOH-HOH-HOH-HOH! I'M SURE DEAR RANMA IS MORE THAN ENOUGH MAN FOR HIM.

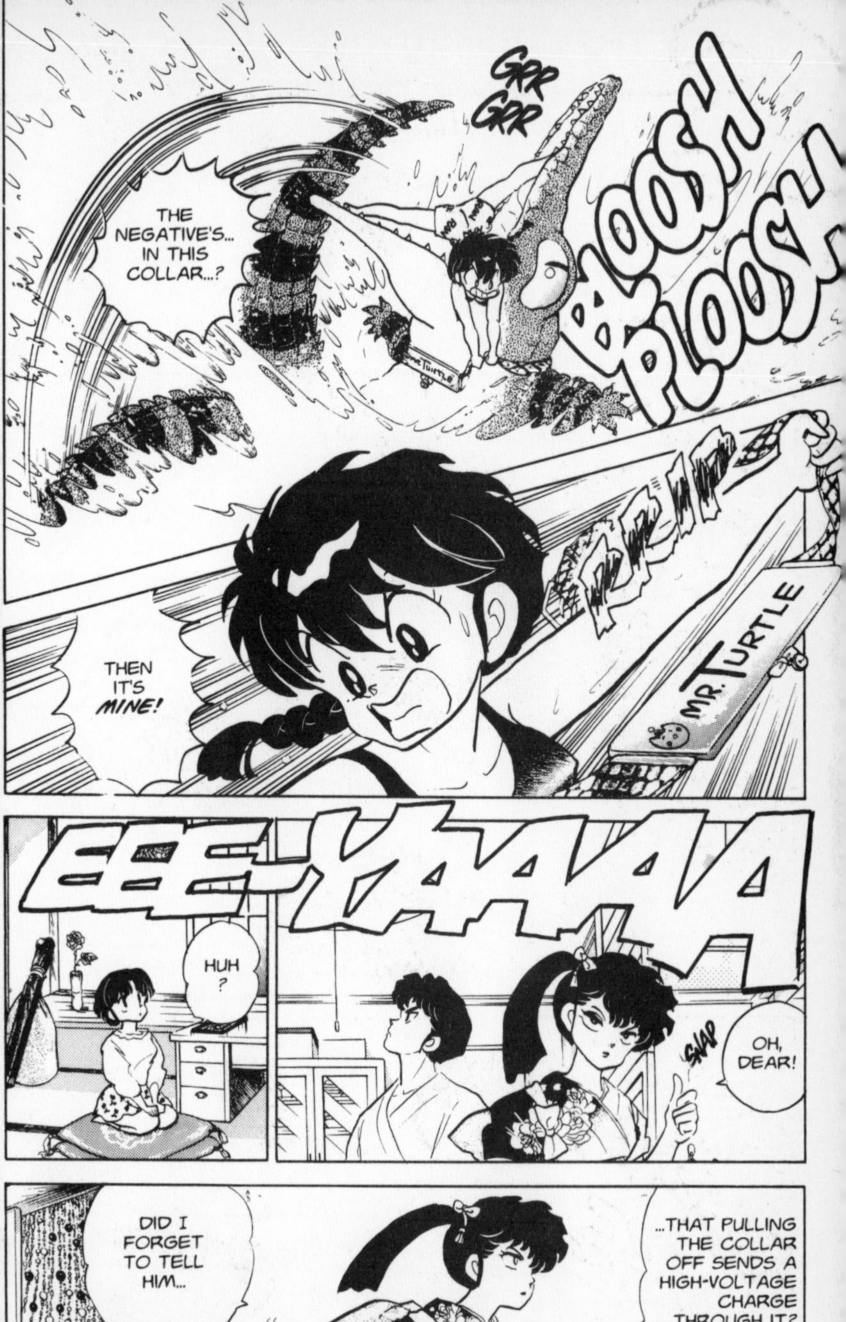
GRR GRR
THE NEGATIVE'S... IN THIS COLLAR...?
BLOOSH BLOOSH
MR. TURTLE
THEN IT'S *MINE!*
MR. TURTLE
EEE-YAAAA
HUH ?
SNAP
OH, DEAR!
DID I FORGET TO TELL HIM...
...THAT PULLING THE COLLAR OFF SENDS A HIGH-VOLTAGE CHARGE THROUGH IT?

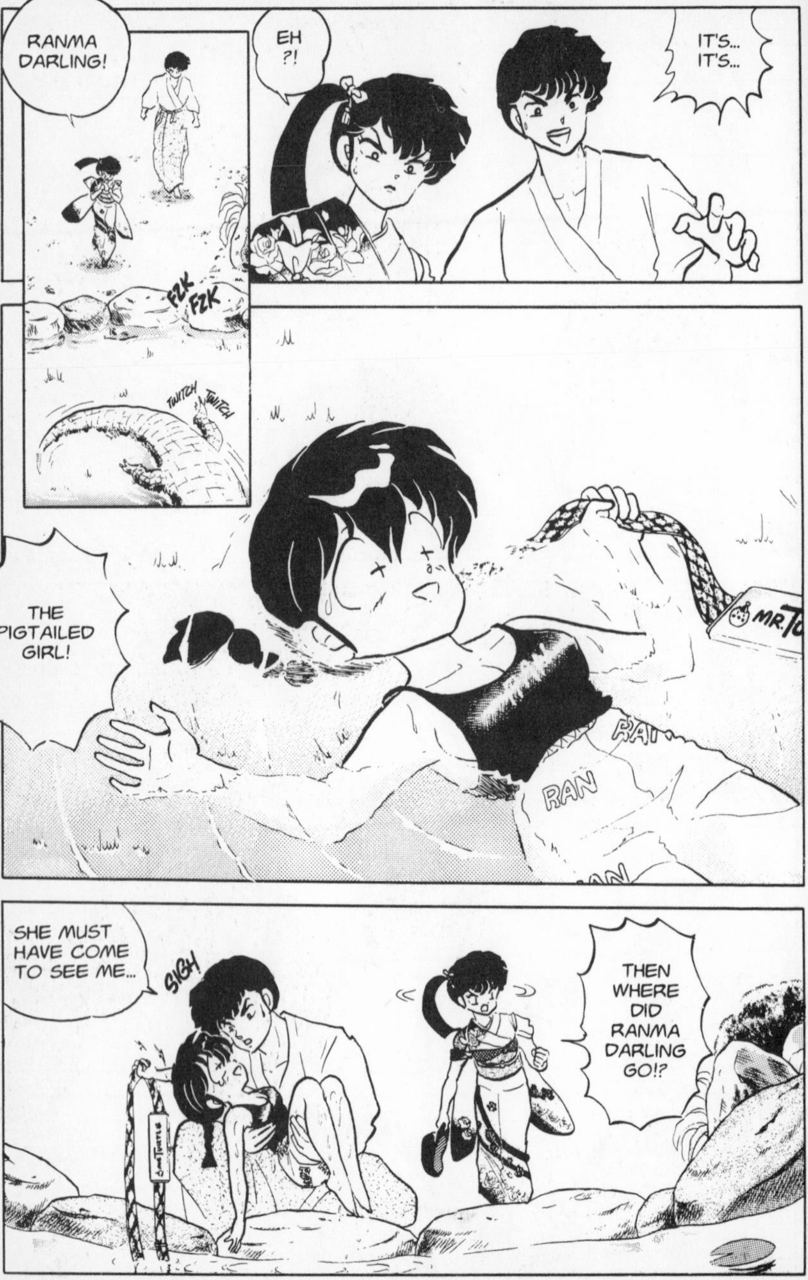
RANMA DARLING!
FZK FZK
TWITCH TWITCH
EH ?!
IT'S... IT'S...
THE PIGTAILED GIRL!
MR.TU
RAN
RAN
SHE MUST HAVE COME TO SEE ME...
SIGH
THEN WHERE DID RANMA DARLING GO!?

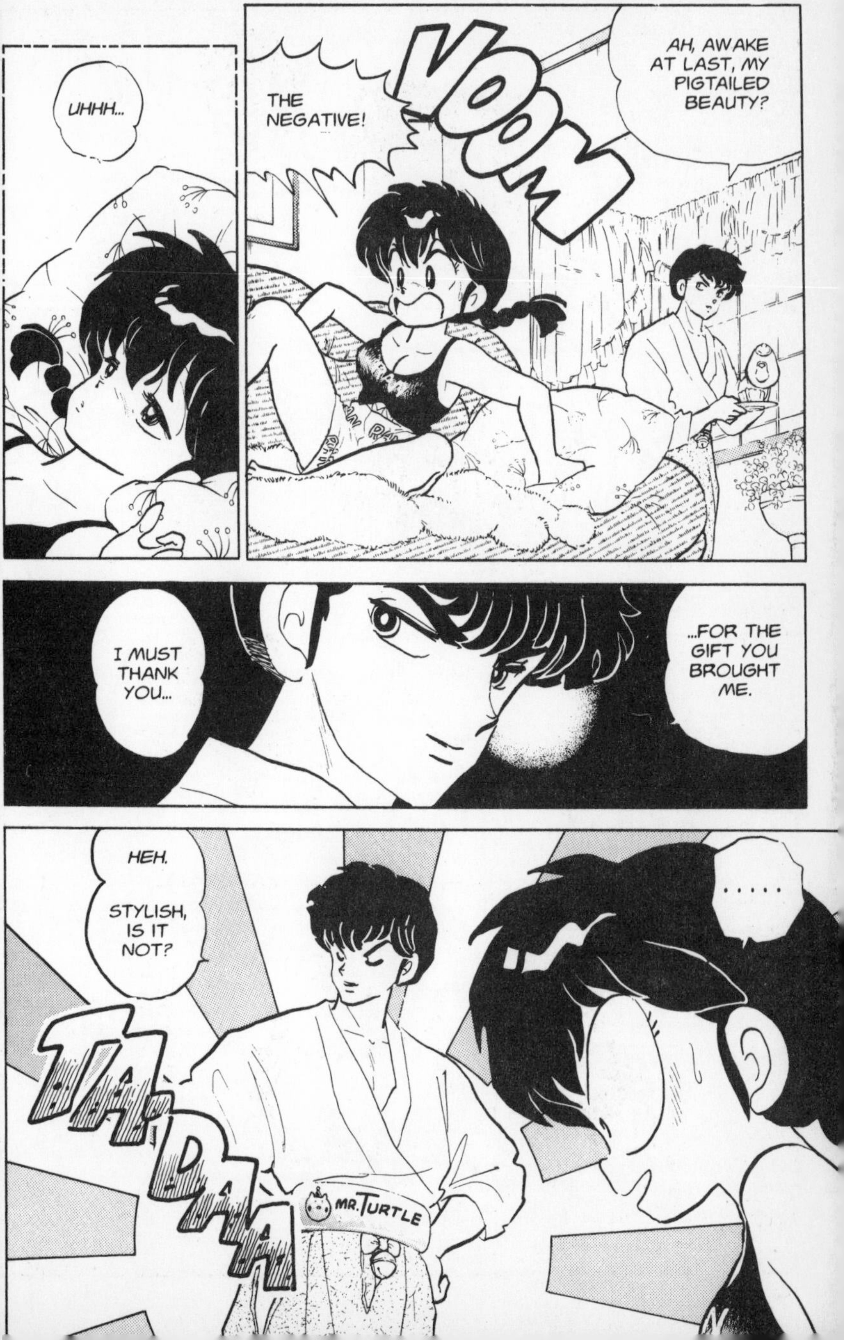
UHHH...
THE NEGATIVE!
VOOOM
AH, AWAKE AT LAST, MY PIGTAILED BEAUTY?
I MUST THANK YOU...
...FOR THE GIFT YOU BROUGHT ME.
HEH.
STYLISH, IS IT NOT?
.....
TA-DA-A-A
MR.TURTLE

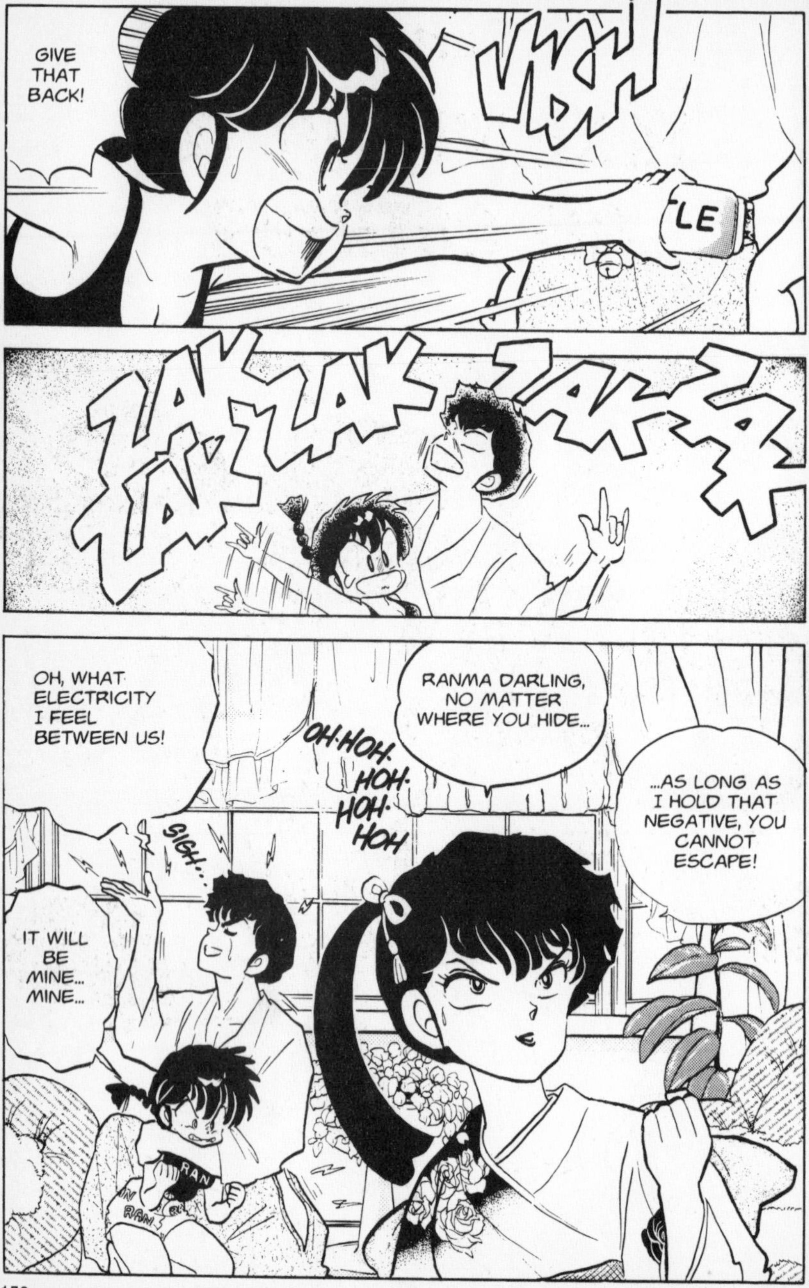

GIVE THAT BACK!
VISH
ZAK ZAK ZAK ZAK ZA
OH, WHAT ELECTRICITY I FEEL BETWEEN US!
RANMA DARLING, NO MATTER WHERE YOU HIDE...
OH·HOH· HOH· HOH· HOH
...AS LONG AS I HOLD THAT NEGATIVE, YOU CANNOT ESCAPE!
SIGH...
IT WILL BE MINE... MINE...

Part 10

TAKE ME OUT TO THE BATHTUB

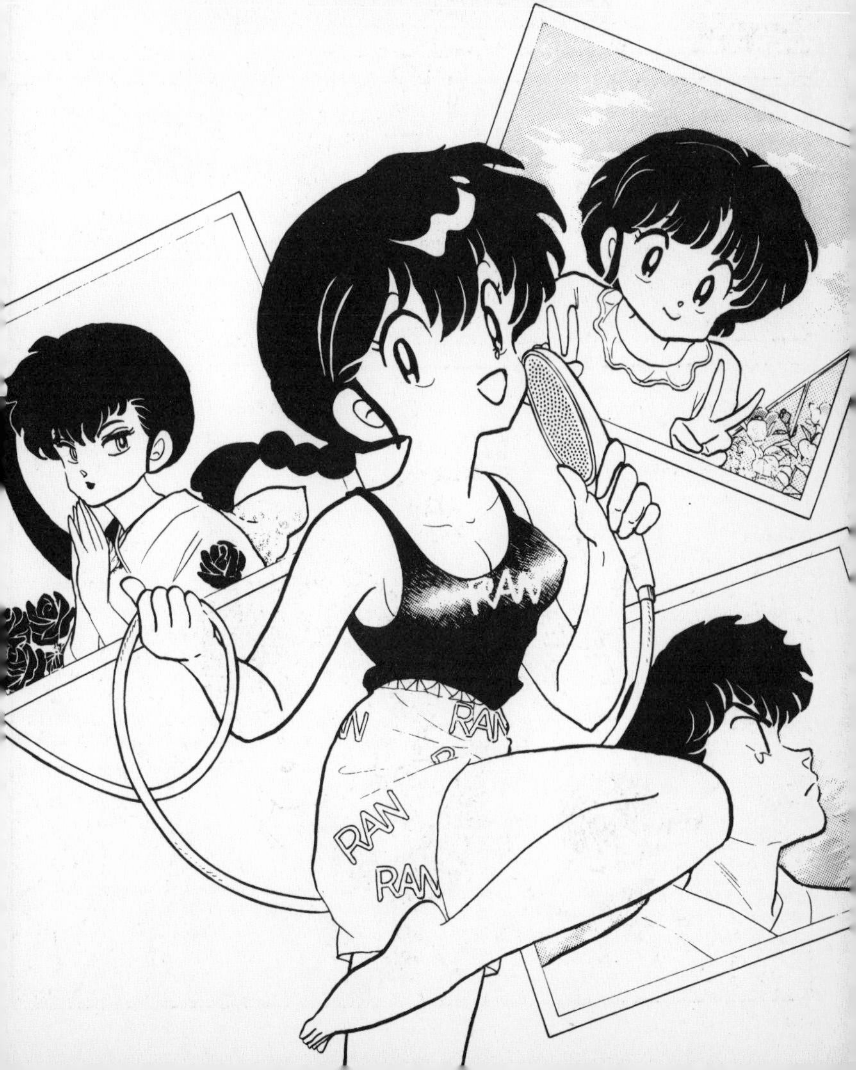
RAN
RAN
RAN
RAN

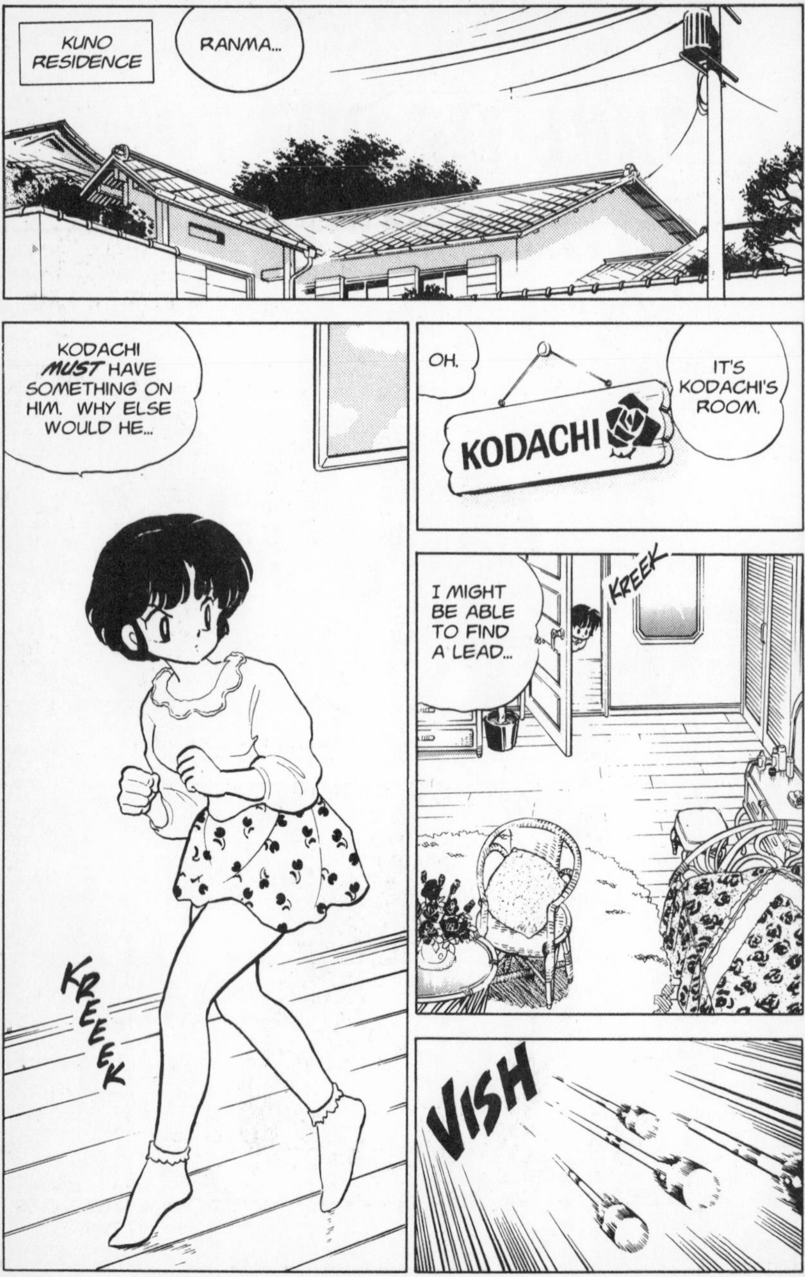
KUNO RESIDENCE
RANMA...
KODACHI *MUST* HAVE SOMETHING ON HIM. WHY ELSE WOULD HE...
KREEEEK
OH.
KODACHI
IT'S KODACHI'S ROOM.
I MIGHT BE ABLE TO FIND A LEAD...
KREEK
VISH

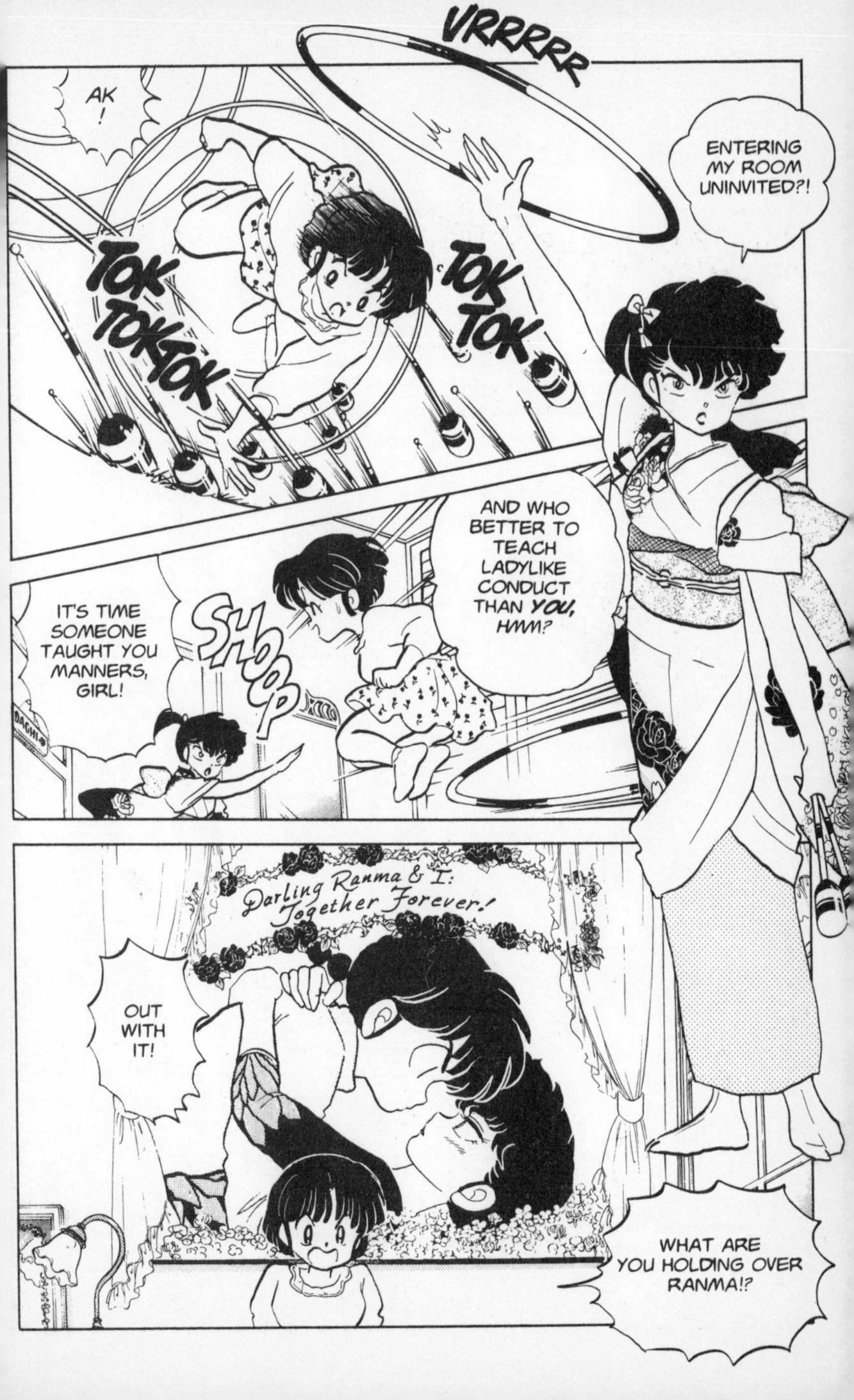
VRRRRR
AK!
TOK TOK TOKTOK
TOK TOK
ENTERING MY ROOM UNINVITED?!
IT'S TIME SOMEONE TAUGHT YOU MANNERS, GIRL!
SHOOOP
AND WHO BETTER TO TEACH LADYLIKE CONDUCT THAN YOU, HMM?
Darling Ranma & I: Together Forever!
OUT WITH IT!
WHAT ARE YOU HOLDING OVER RANMA!?

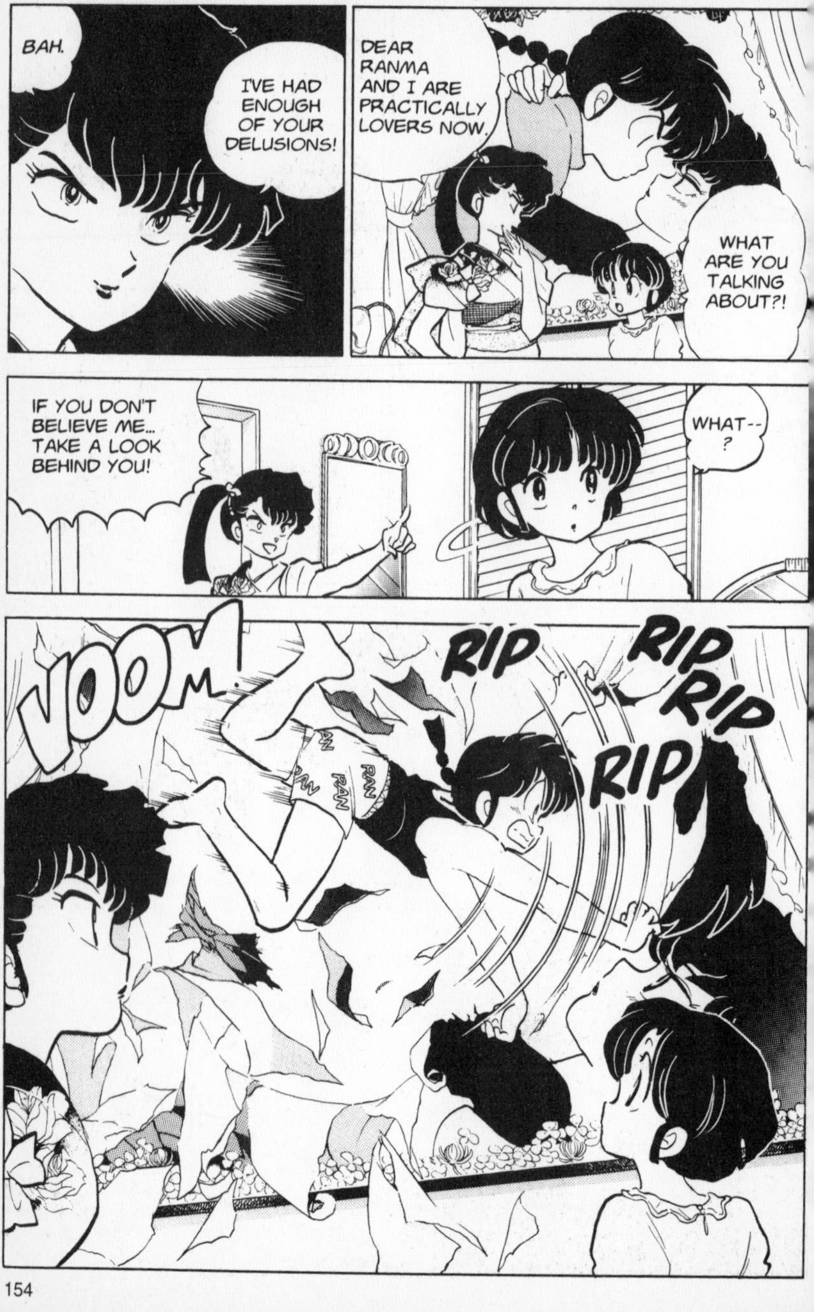
BAH.
I'VE HAD ENOUGH OF YOUR DELUSIONS!
DEAR RANMA AND I ARE PRACTICALLY LOVERS NOW.
WHAT ARE YOU TALKING ABOUT?!
IF YOU DON'T BELIEVE ME... TAKE A LOOK BEHIND YOU!
WHAT--?
VOOM!
RIP
RIP RIP RIP
RIP

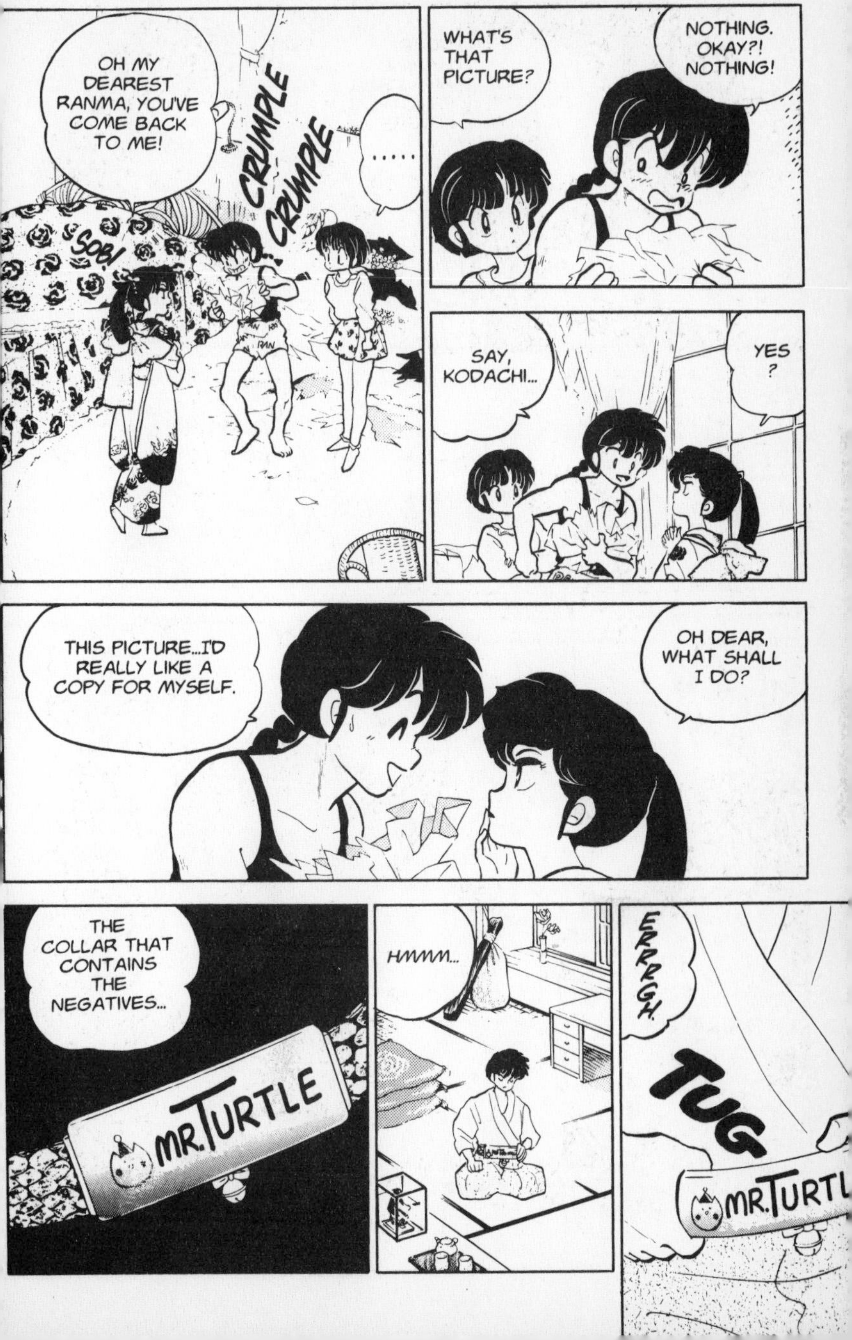
OH MY DEAREST RANMA, YOU'VE COME BACK TO ME!
CRUMPLE
CRUMPLE
SOB!
.....
WHAT'S THAT PICTURE?
NOTHING. OKAY?! NOTHING!
SAY, KODACHI...
YES ?
THIS PICTURE...I'D REALLY LIKE A COPY FOR MYSELF.
OH DEAR, WHAT SHALL I DO?
THE COLLAR THAT CONTAINS THE NEGATIVES...
MR. TURTLE
HMMM...
ERRRGH.
TUG
MR. TURTL

ZAKK ZAKK ZAKK

FEH. SIZZLE

I CAN'T TAKE IT OFF.

THE METAL OF THE BELT...

...IS CALLED "MEMORY METAL."

THE ONLY WAY TO REMOVE IT WITHOUT GETTING SHOCKED...

...IS TO DOUSE IT IN HOT WAT--

VRRRROOM

TOOM TOOM TOOM TOOM

EH?

OH, KUUUU- NO-O- O-O...

ZHOOP

DOES OO WANNA TAKE A BAF WIF WIDDLE ME, HM?

156

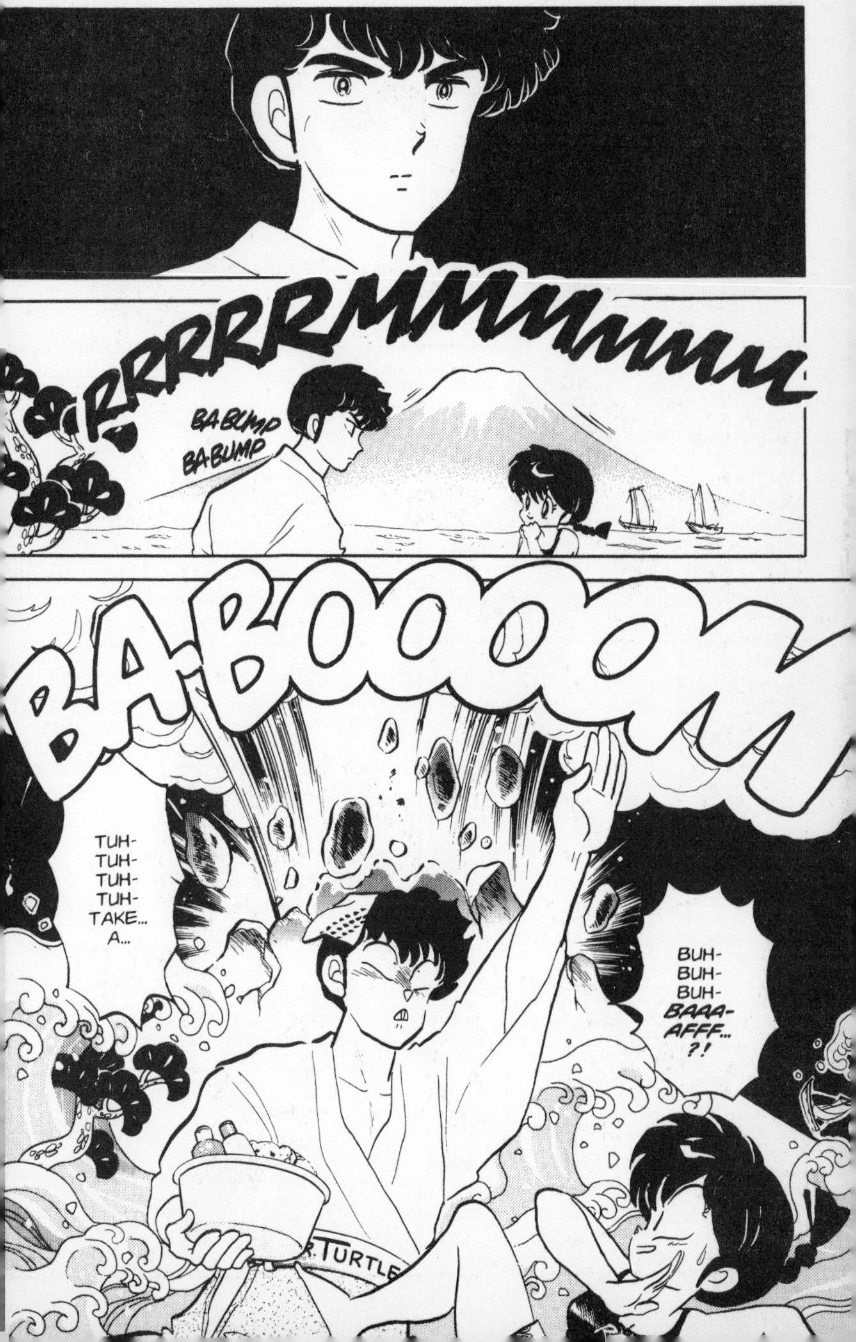
RRRRRMMMMMMM
BA BUMP
BA BUMP
BA-BOOOOM
TUH-
TUH-
TUH-
TUH-
TAKE...
A...
BUH-
BUH-
BUH-
BAAA-
AFFF...
?!
R. TURTLE

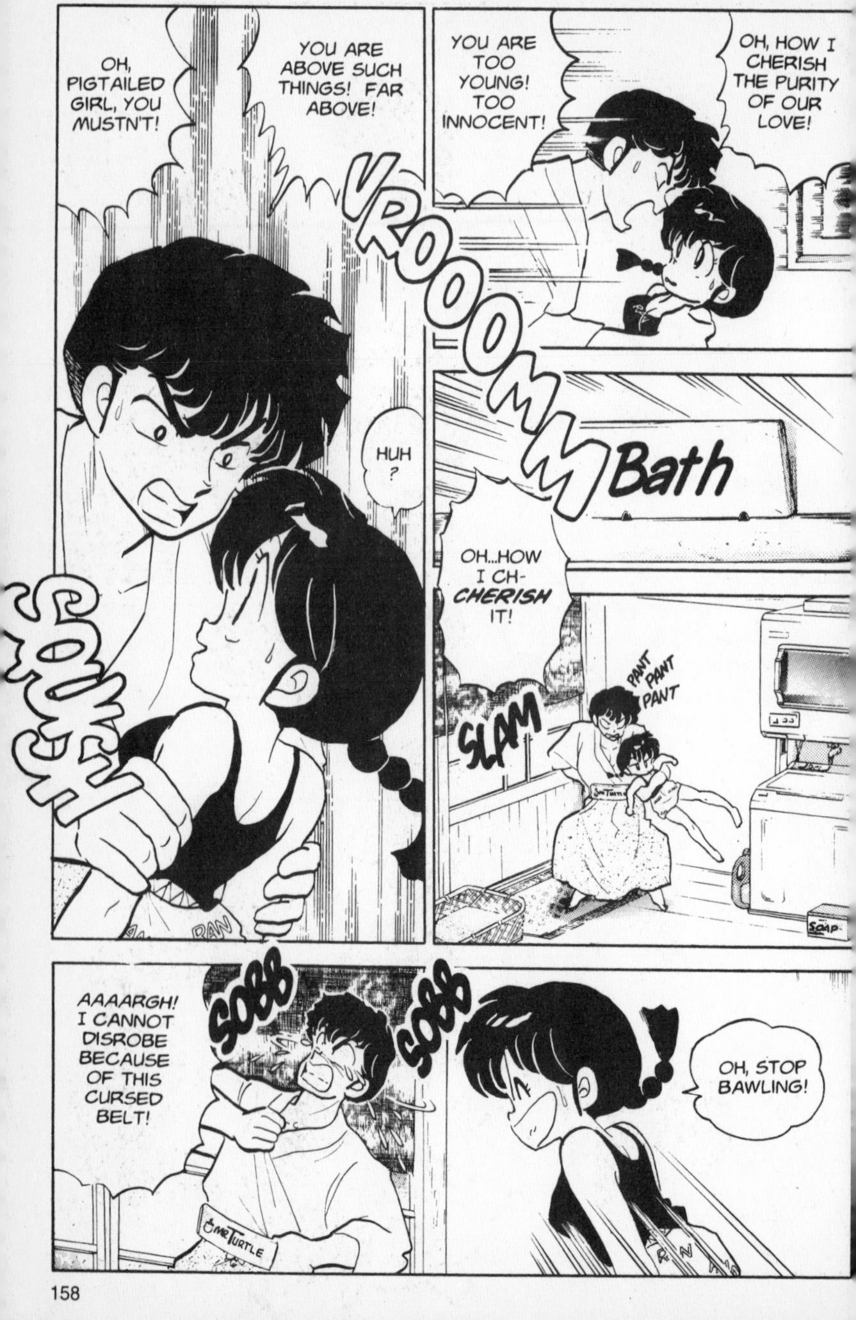

OH, PIGTAILED GIRL, YOU MUSTN'T!
YOU ARE ABOVE SUCH THINGS! FAR ABOVE!
HUH?
SQUICH
YOU ARE TOO YOUNG! TOO INNOCENT!
OH, HOW I CHERISH THE PURITY OF OUR LOVE!
VROOOMMM
Bath
OH...HOW I CH-CHERISH IT!
PANT PANT PANT
SLAM
SOAP
AAAARGH! I CANNOT DISROBE BECAUSE OF THIS CURSED BELT!
SOBB
SOBB
OH, STOP BAWLING!

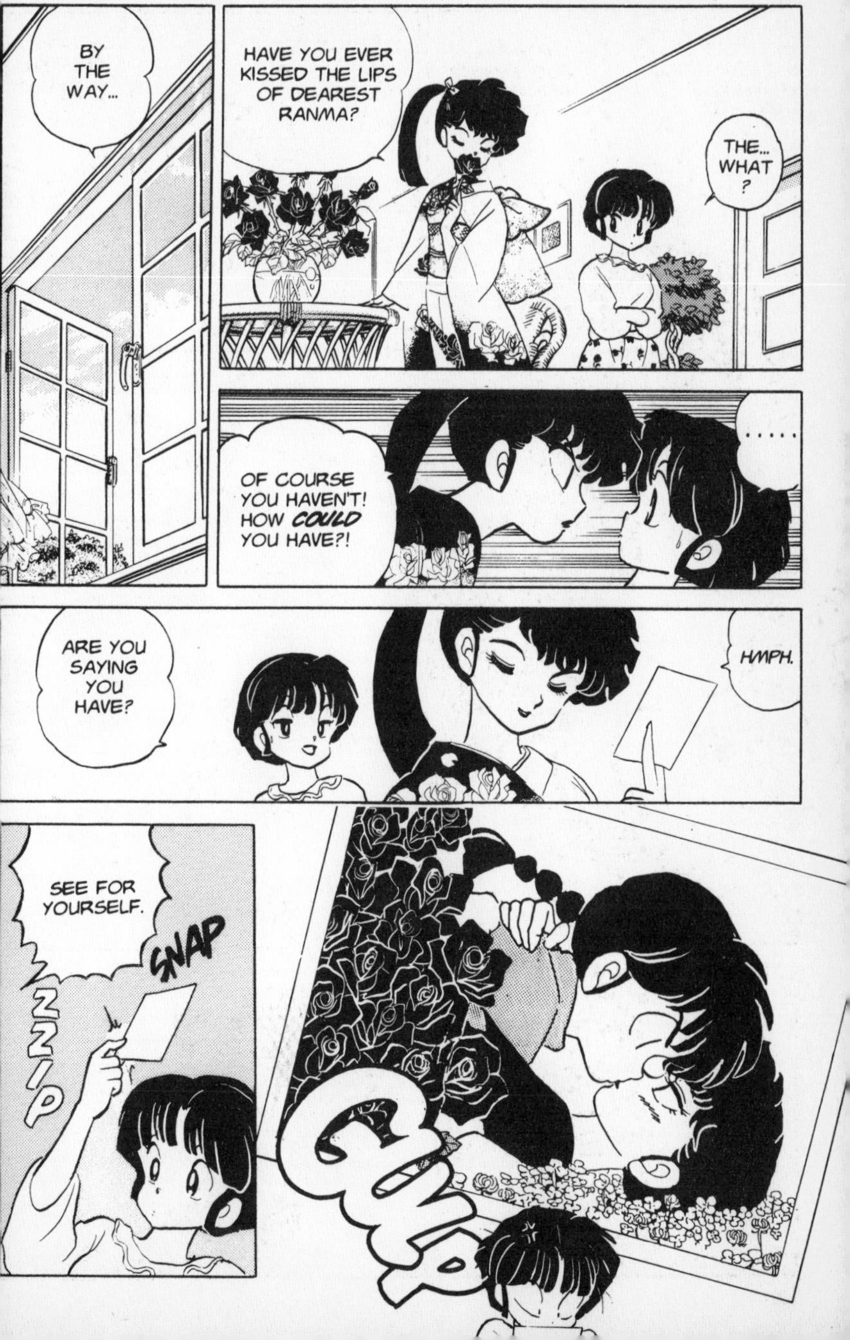
BY THE WAY...
HAVE YOU EVER KISSED THE LIPS OF DEAREST RANMA?
THE... WHAT?
OF COURSE YOU HAVEN'T! HOW *COULD* YOU HAVE?!
.....
ARE YOU SAYING YOU HAVE?
HMPH.
SEE FOR YOURSELF.
SNAP
ZZIP
GRIP

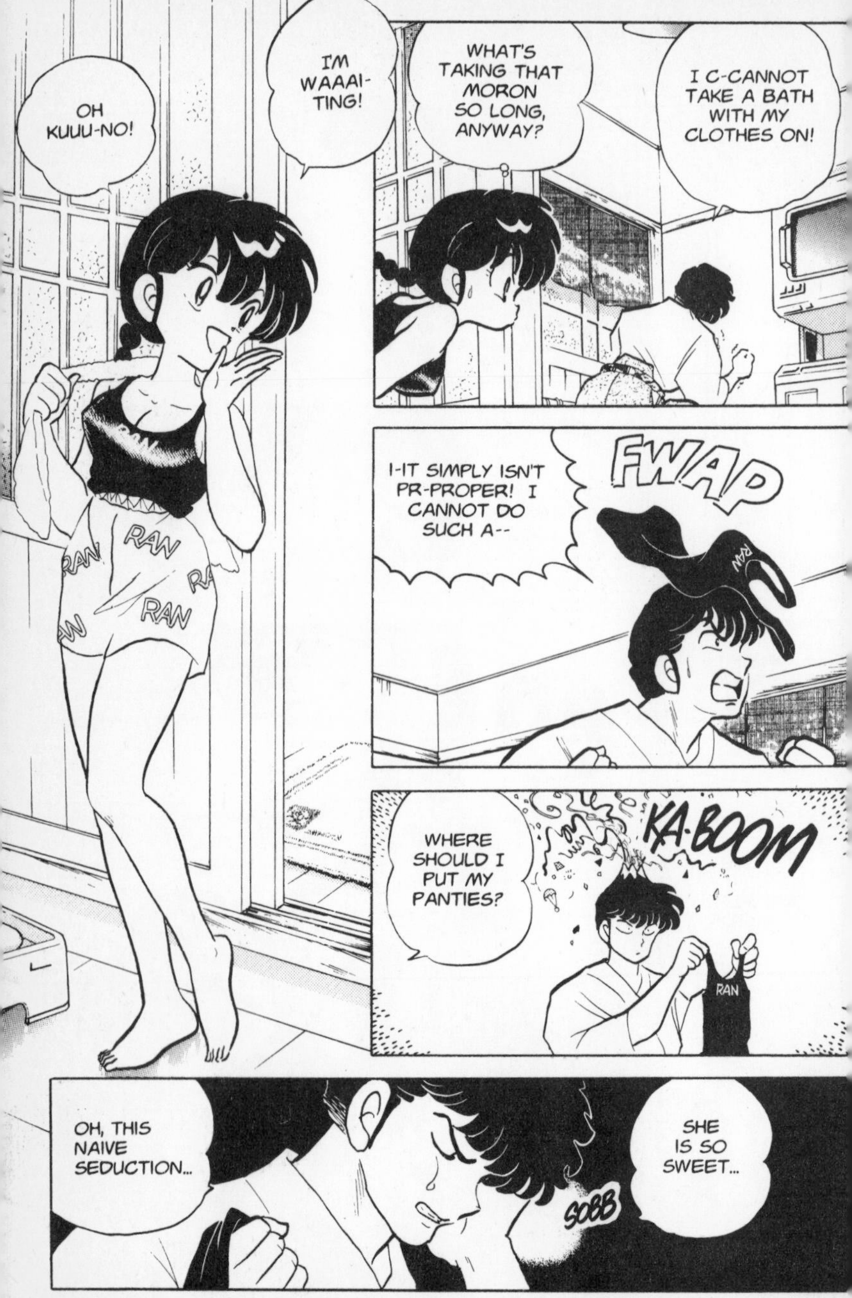
OH KUUU-NO!
I'M WAAAI-TING!
WHAT'S TAKING THAT MORON SO LONG, ANYWAY?
I C-CANNOT TAKE A BATH WITH MY CLOTHES ON!
I-IT SIMPLY ISN'T PR-PROPER! I CANNOT DO SUCH A--
FWAP
WHERE SHOULD I PUT MY PANTIES?
KA-BOOM
OH, THIS NAIVE SEDUCTION...
SOBB
SHE IS SO SWEET...

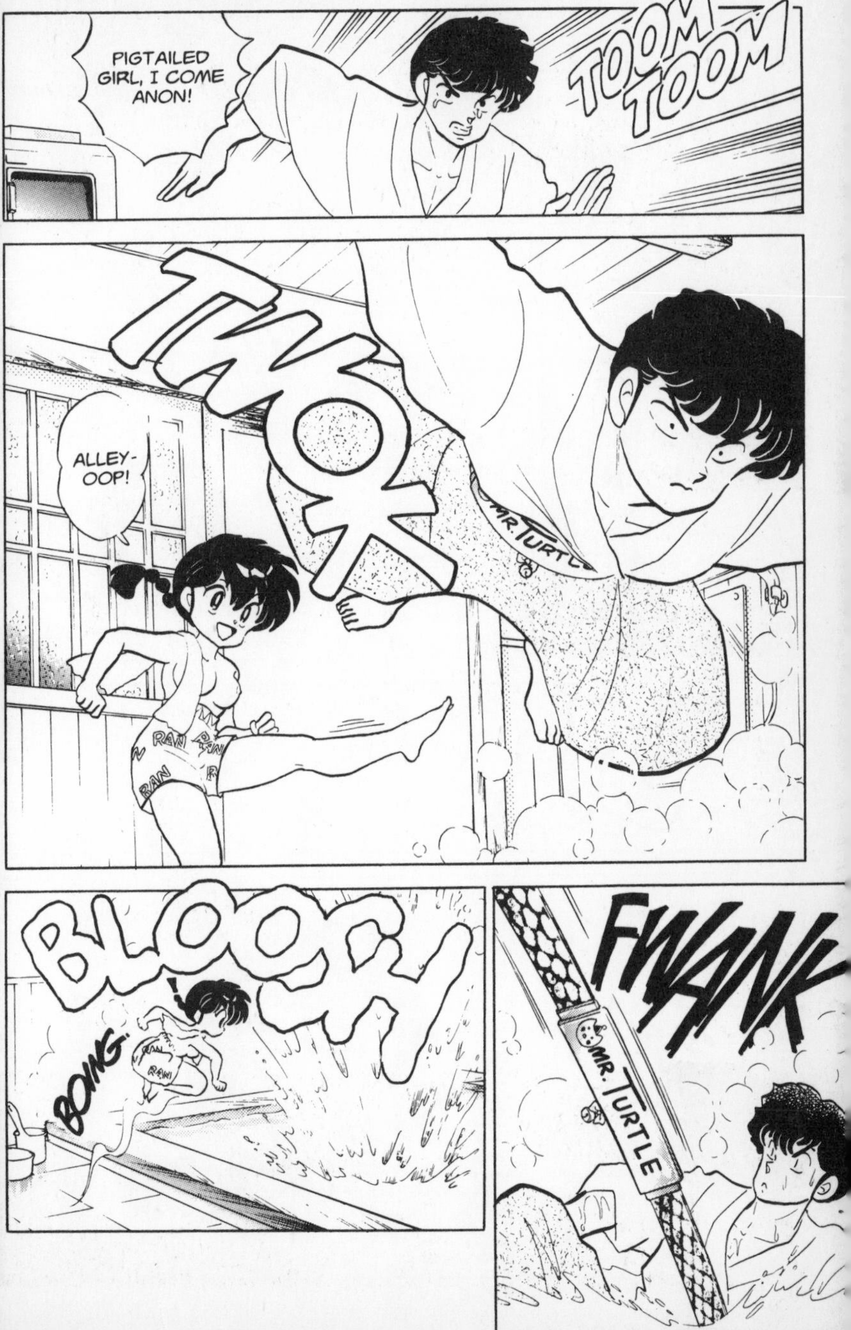
PIGTAILED GIRL, I COME ANON!
TOOM TOOM
TWOK
ALLEY-OOP!
MR. TURTLE
RAN RAN
BLOOP!
BOING
FWANK
MR. TURTLE

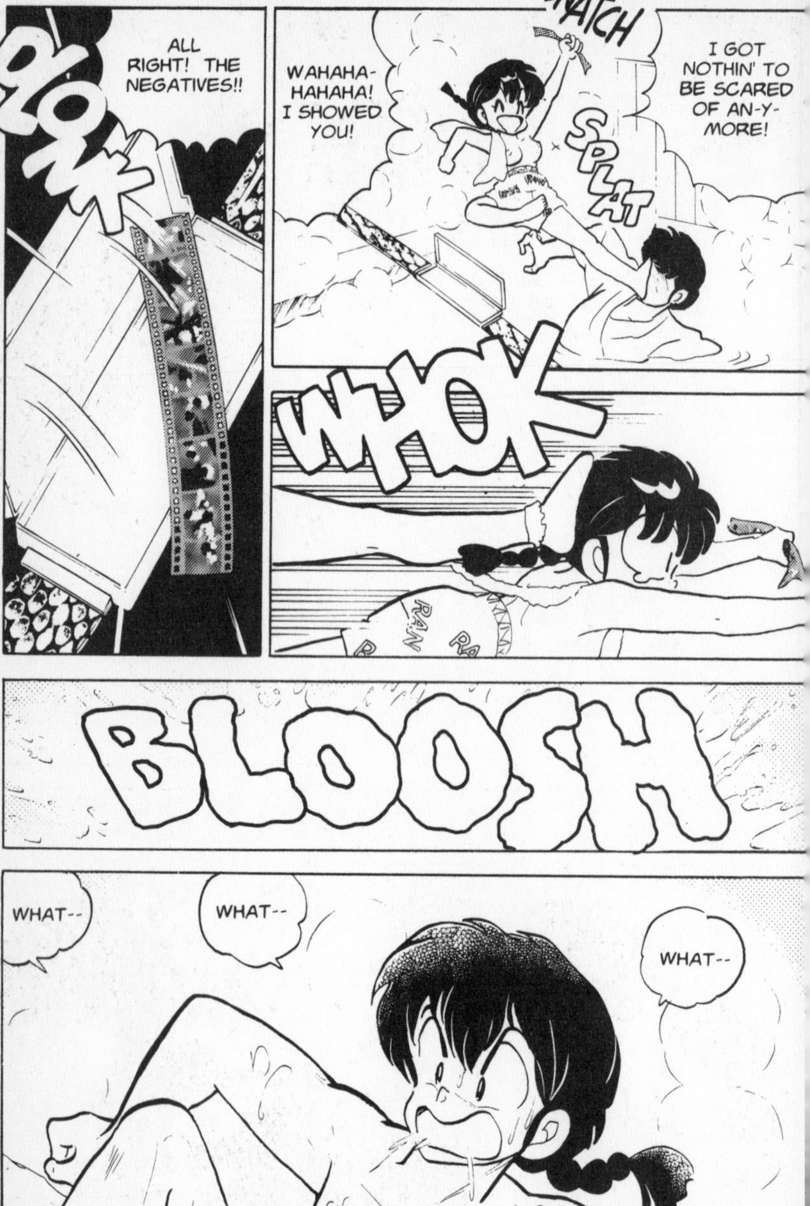
PLONK
ALL RIGHT! THE NEGATIVES!!
SNATCH
WAHAHA-HAHAHA! I SHOWED YOU!
SPLAT
I GOT NOTHIN' TO BE SCARED OF AN-Y-MORE!
WHOK
BLOOSH
WHAT--
WHAT--
WHAT--

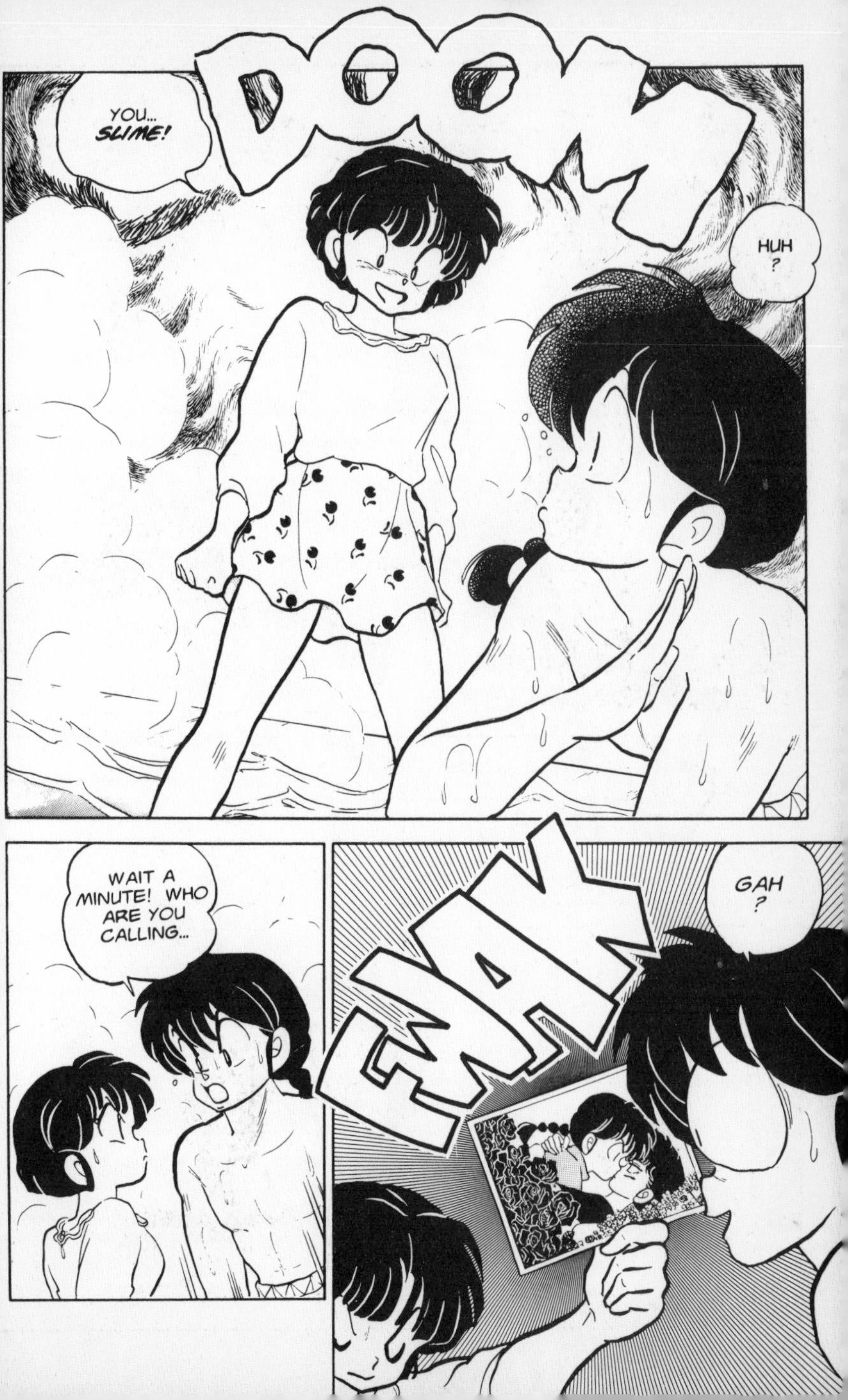
YOU... SLIME!
DOOM
HUH ?
WAIT A MINUTE! WHO ARE YOU CALLING...
FAP
GAH ?

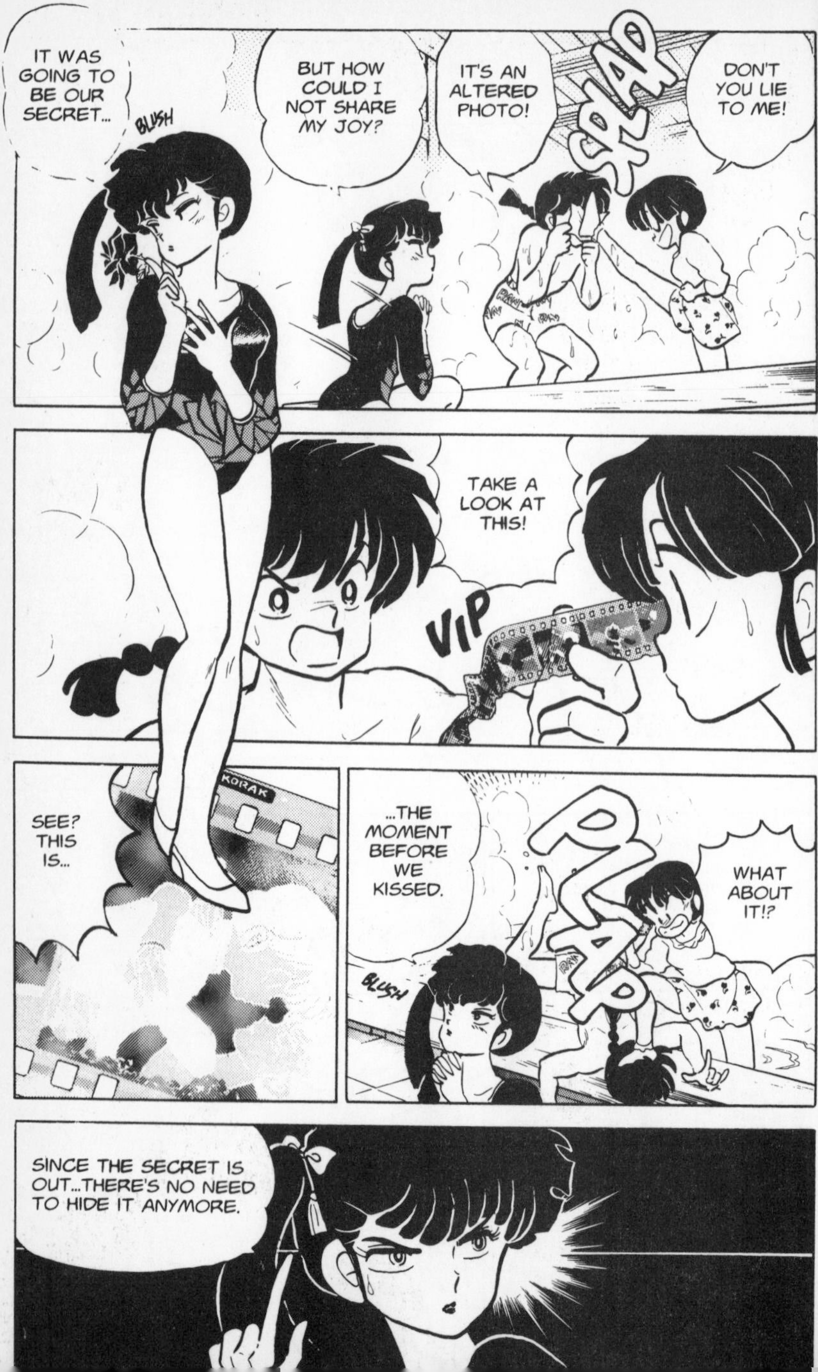
IT WAS GOING TO BE OUR SECRET...
BLUSH
BUT HOW COULD I NOT SHARE MY JOY?
IT'S AN ALTERED PHOTO!
SPLAP
DON'T YOU LIE TO ME!
TAKE A LOOK AT THIS!
VIP
SEE? THIS IS...
KORAK
...THE MOMENT BEFORE WE KISSED.
PLAP
WHAT ABOUT IT!?
BLUSH
SINCE THE SECRET IS OUT...THERE'S NO NEED TO HIDE IT ANYMORE.

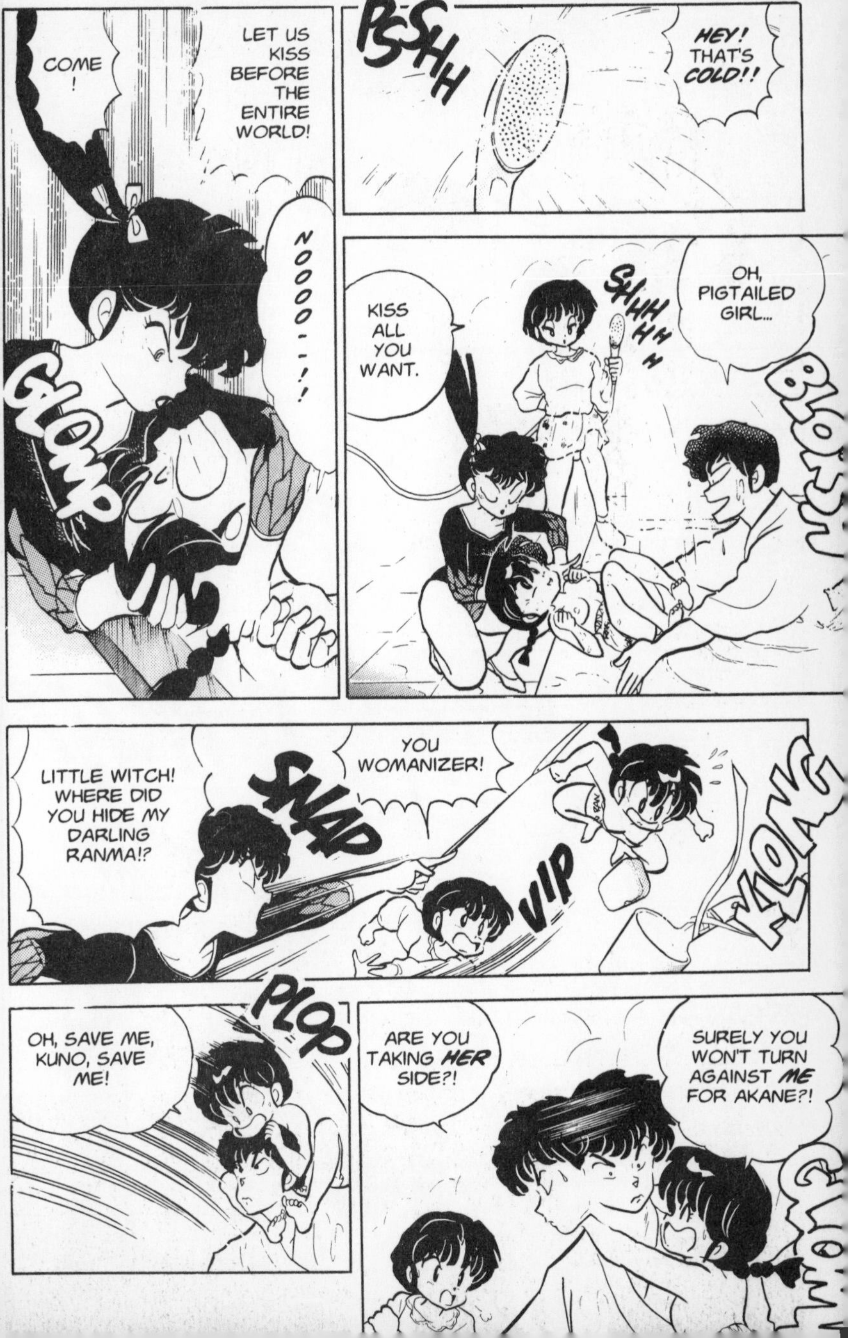
COME!
LET US KISS BEFORE THE ENTIRE WORLD!
NOOOOO--!!
GLOMP
PSSHH
HEY! THAT'S COLD!!
KISS ALL YOU WANT.
SHHHHHH
OH, PIGTAILED GIRL...
BLOTCH
LITTLE WITCH! WHERE DID YOU HIDE MY DARLING RANMA!?
SNAP
YOU WOMANIZER!
VIP
KLONG
OH, SAVE ME, KUNO, SAVE ME!
PLOP
ARE YOU TAKING HER SIDE?!
SURELY YOU WON'T TURN AGAINST ME FOR AKANE?!
GLOM

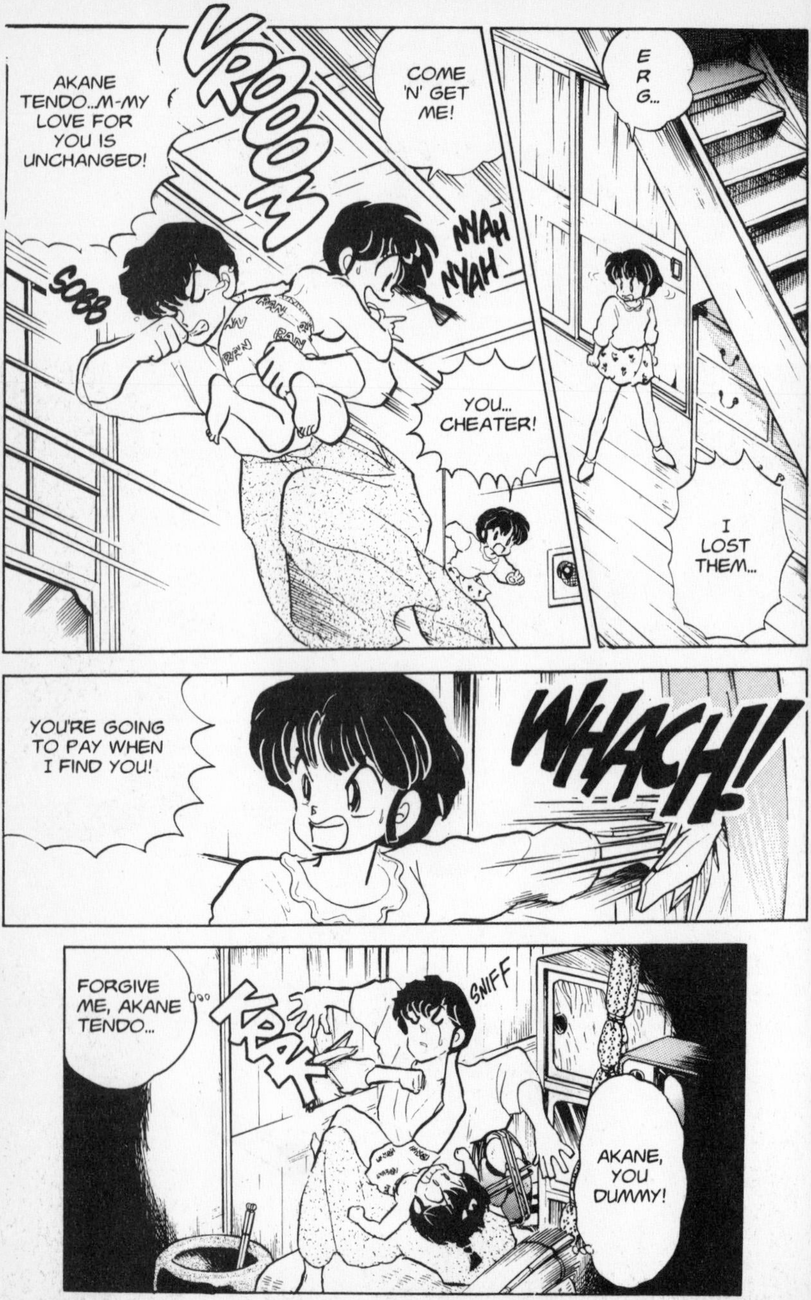
AKANE TENDO...M-MY LOVE FOR YOU IS UNCHANGED!
VROOOOM
COME 'N' GET ME!
SOBB
NYAH NYAH
YOU... CHEATER!
ERG...
I LOST THEM...
YOU'RE GOING TO PAY WHEN I FIND YOU!
WHACH!
FORGIVE ME, AKANE TENDO...
KRAK
SNIFF
AKANE, YOU DUMMY!

Part 11

...I ATE THE WHOLE THING

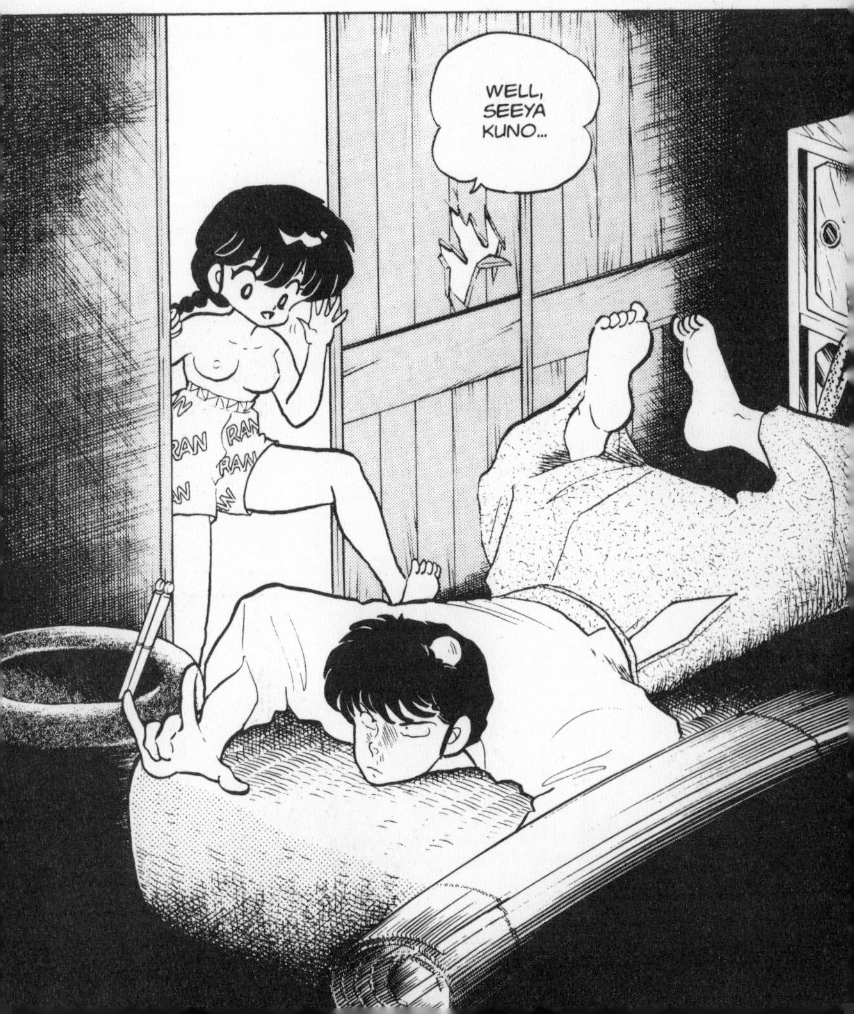
WELL, SEEYA KUNO...

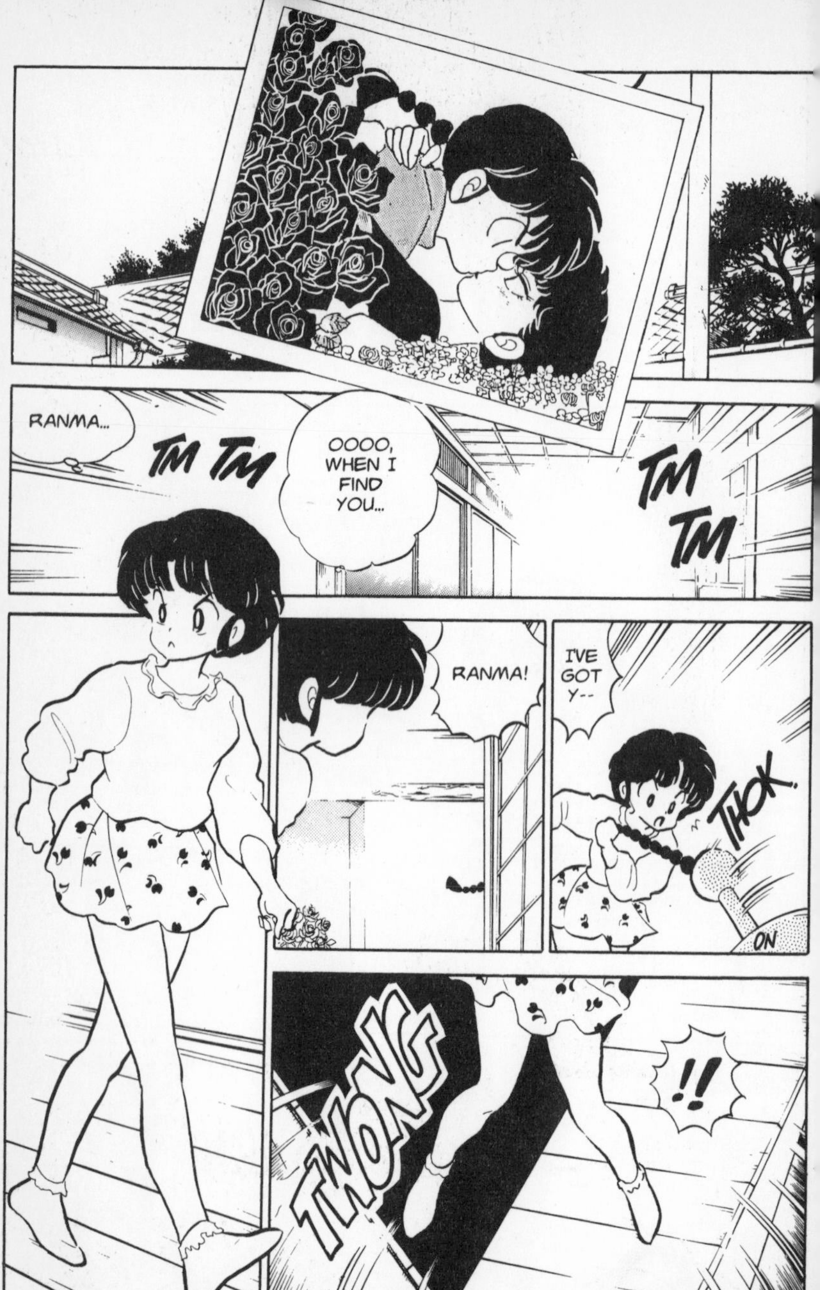

RANMA...
TM TM
OOOO, WHEN I FIND YOU...
TM TM
RANMA!
I'VE GOT Y--
THOK
ON
TWONG
!!

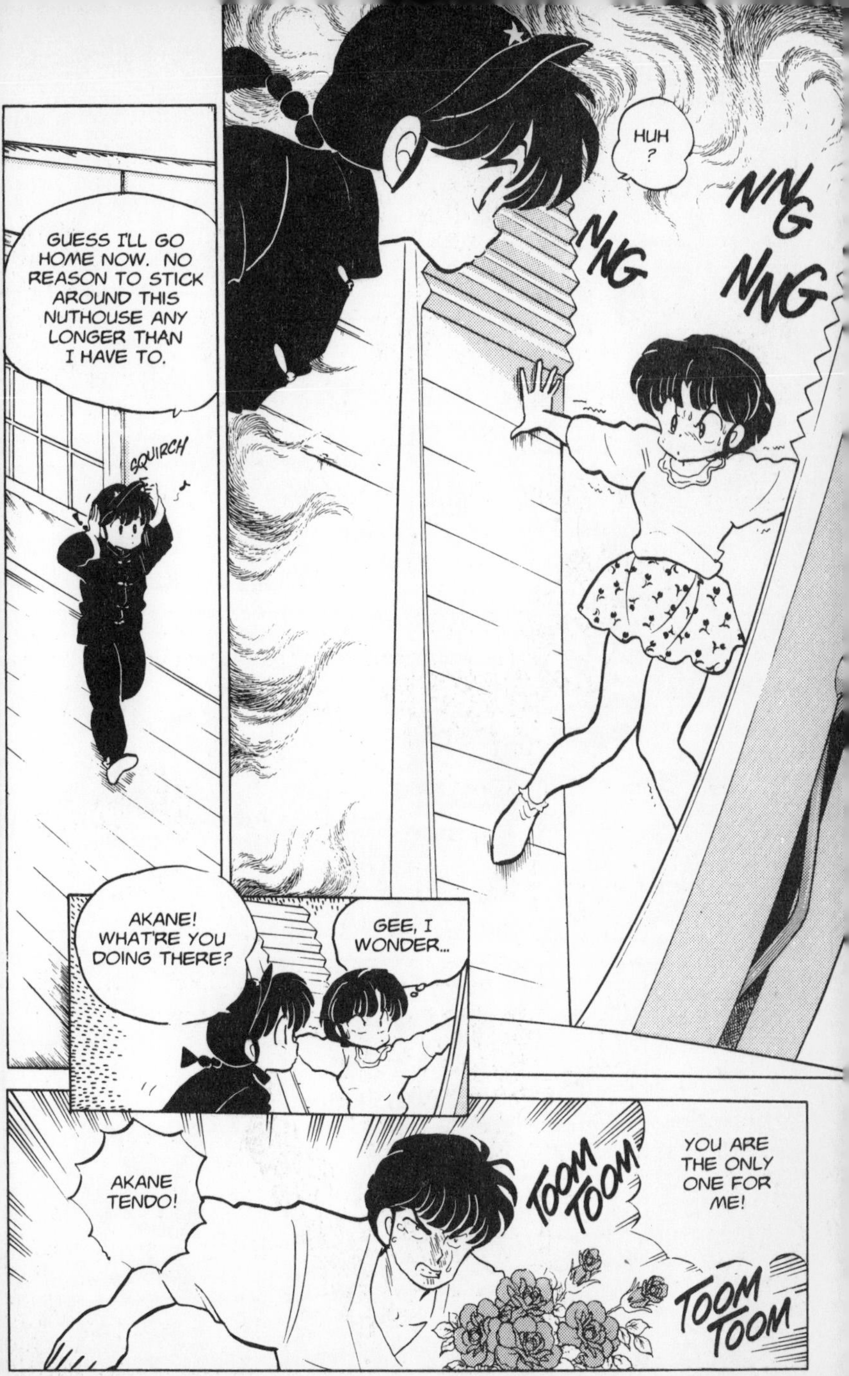
GUESS I'LL GO HOME NOW. NO REASON TO STICK AROUND THIS NUTHOUSE ANY LONGER THAN I HAVE TO.
SQUIRCH
HUH ?
NNG
NNG
NNG
AKANE! WHAT'RE YOU DOING THERE?
GEE, I WONDER...
AKANE TENDO!
TOOM TOOM
YOU ARE THE ONLY ONE FOR ME!
TOOM TOOM

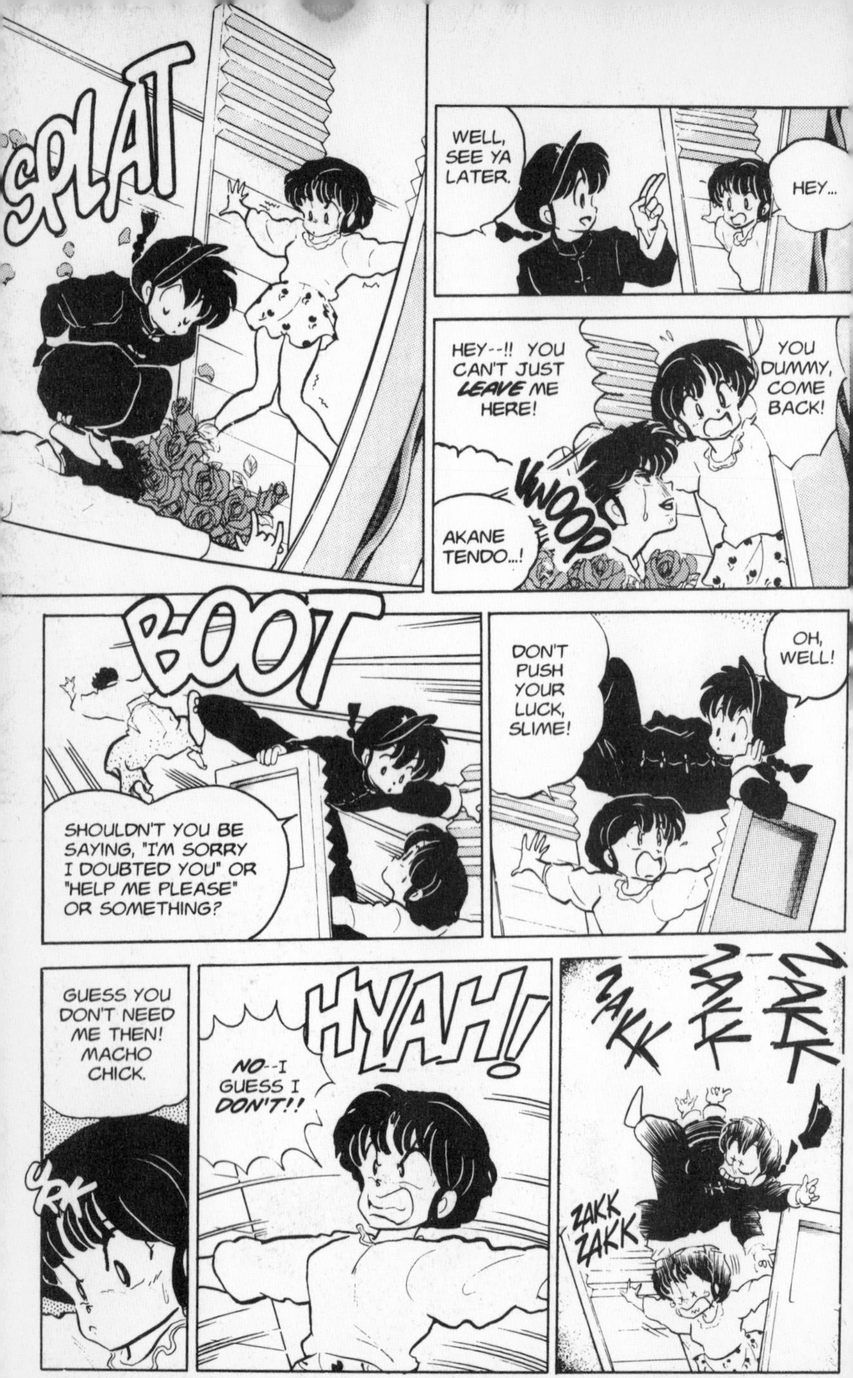
SPLAT
WELL, SEE YA LATER.
HEY...
HEY--!! YOU CAN'T JUST *LEAVE* ME HERE!
YOU DUMMY, COME BACK!
VWOOOP
AKANE TENDO...!
BOOT
SHOULDN'T YOU BE SAYING, "I'M SORRY I DOUBTED YOU" OR "HELP ME PLEASE" OR SOMETHING?
DON'T PUSH YOUR LUCK, SLIME!
OH, WELL!
GUESS YOU DON'T NEED ME THEN! MACHO CHICK.
SRK
HYAH!
NO--I GUESS I *DON'T!!*
ZAKK
ZAKK
ZAKK
ZAKK ZAKK

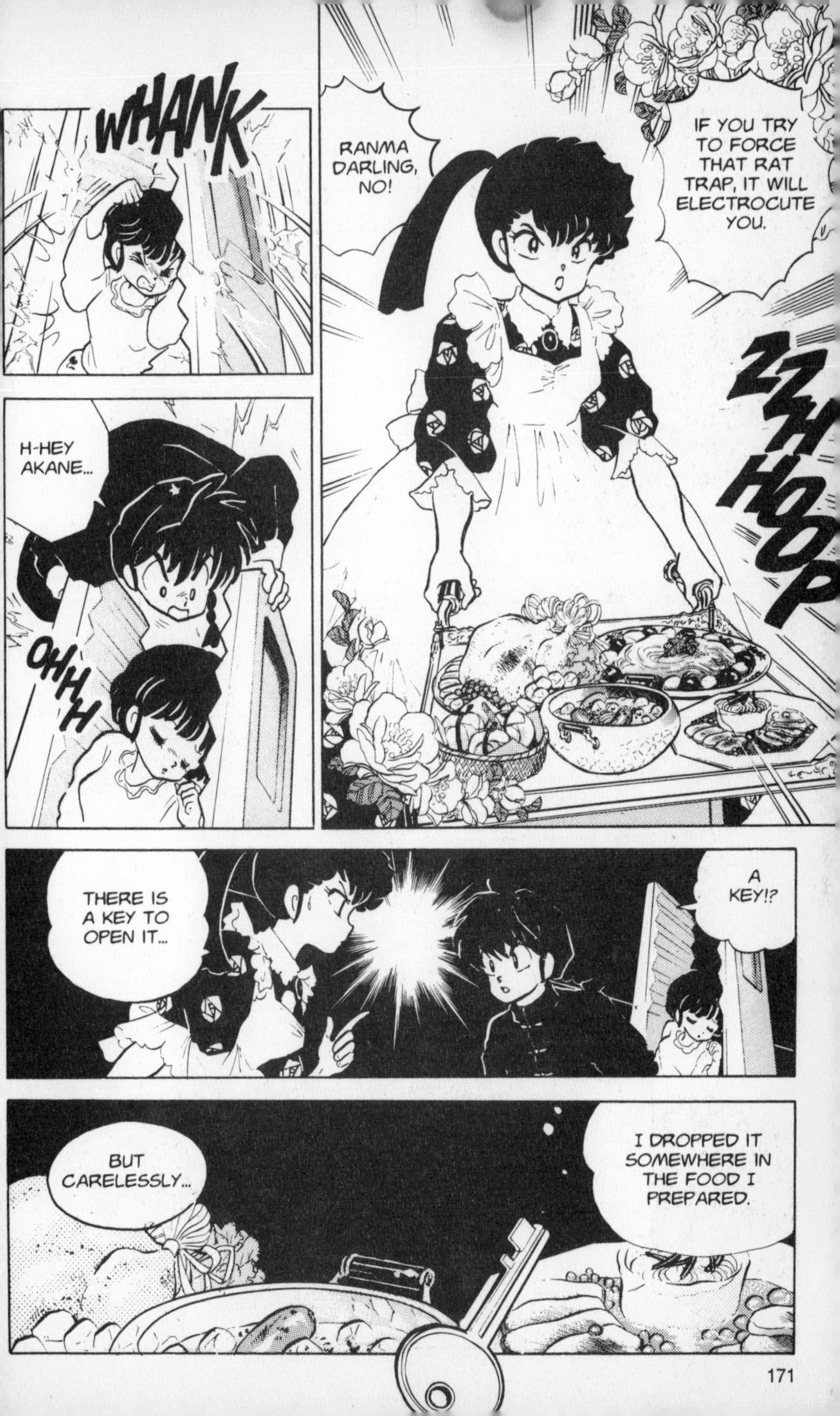
WHANK
H-HEY AKANE...
OHHHH
RANMA DARLING, NO!
IF YOU TRY TO FORCE THAT RAT TRAP, IT WILL ELECTROCUTE YOU.
ZZHHOOP
THERE IS A KEY TO OPEN IT...
A KEY!?
BUT CARELESSLY...
I DROPPED IT SOMEWHERE IN THE FOOD I PREPARED.

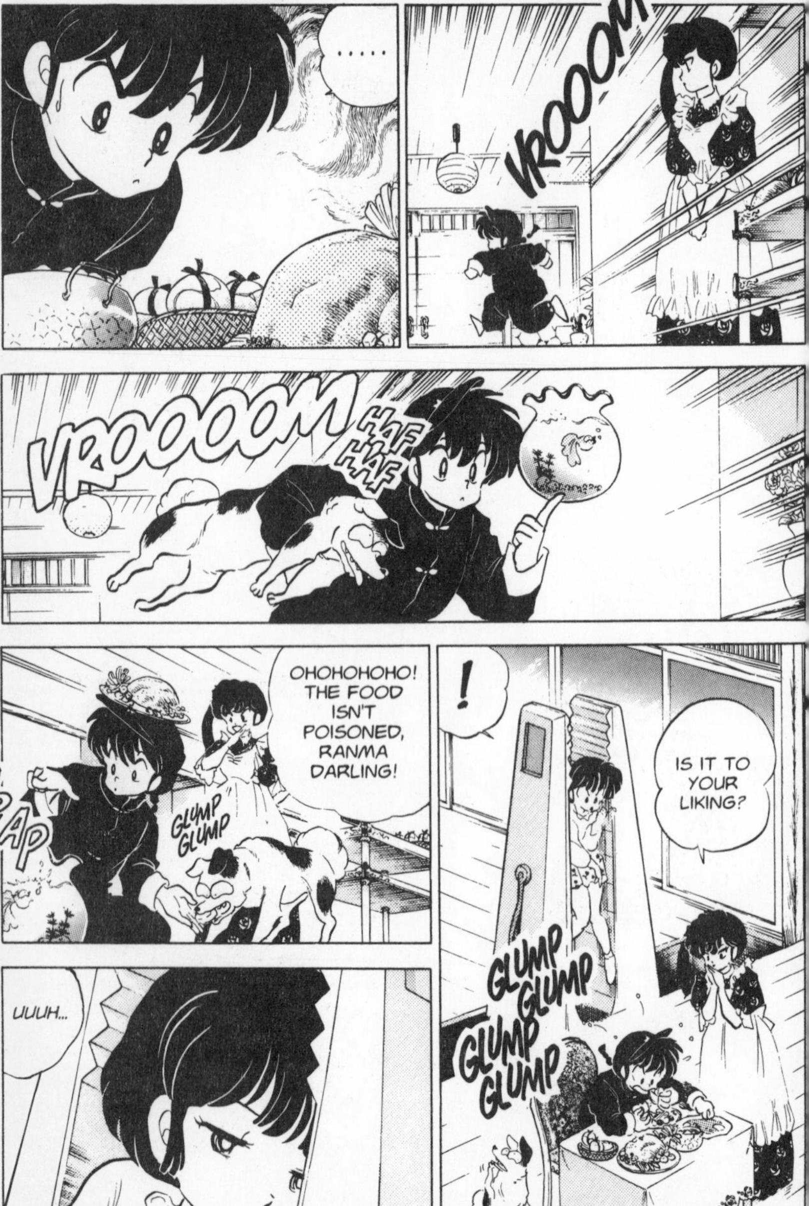
......
VROOOM
VROOOOM
HAF HAF
SPLAP
OHOHOHOHO! THE FOOD ISN'T POISONED, RANMA DARLING!
GLUMP GLUMP
UUUH...
!
IS IT TO YOUR LIKING?
GLUMP GLUMP
GLUMP GLUMP

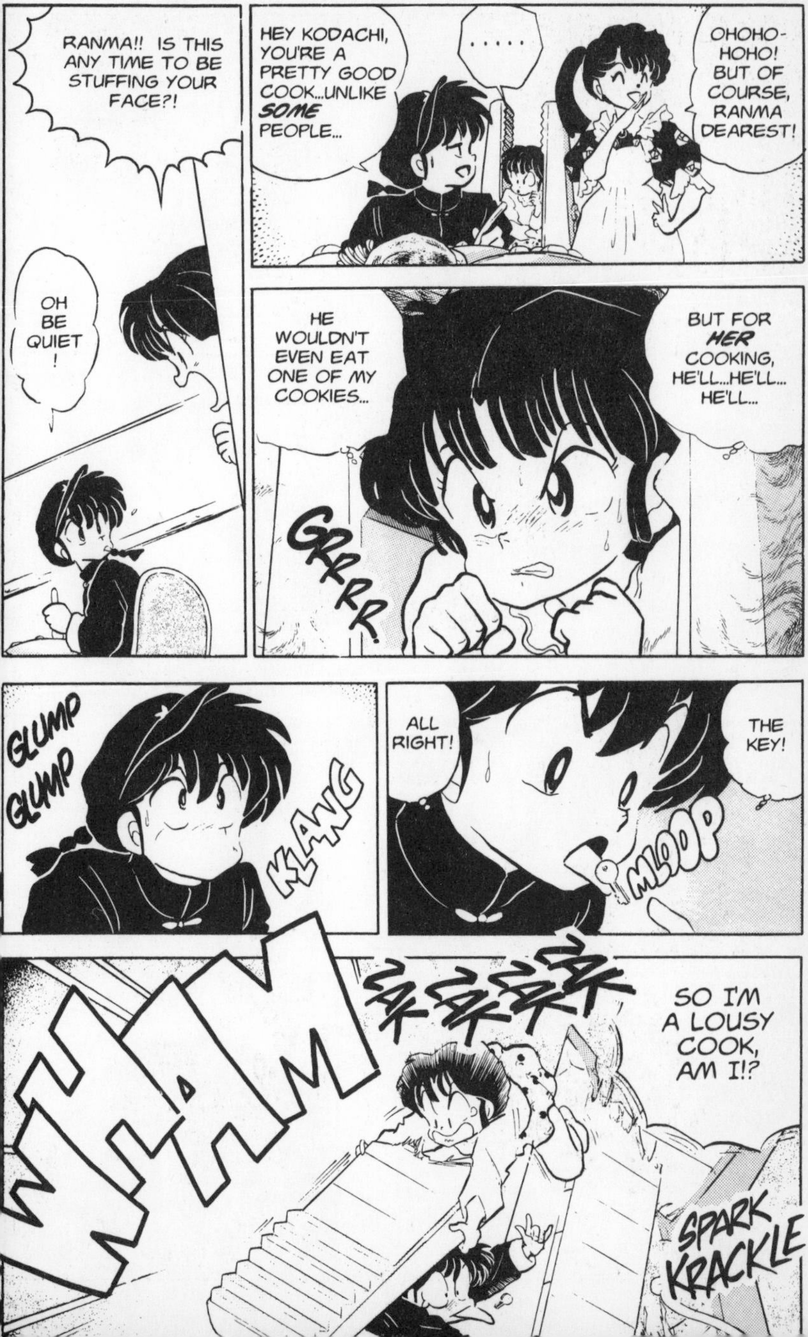
RANMA!! IS THIS ANY TIME TO BE STUFFING YOUR FACE?!
OH BE QUIET!
HEY KODACHI, YOU'RE A PRETTY GOOD COOK...UNLIKE SOME PEOPLE...
......
OHOHO-HOHO! BUT OF COURSE, RANMA DEAREST!
HE WOULDN'T EVEN EAT ONE OF MY COOKIES...
BUT FOR HER COOKING, HE'LL...HE'LL... HE'LL...
GRRRRR
GLUMP GLUMP
KLANG
ALL RIGHT!
THE KEY!
MLOOP
WHAM
ZAK ZAK ZAK ZAK ZAK
SO I'M A LOUSY COOK, AM I!?
SPARK KRACKLE

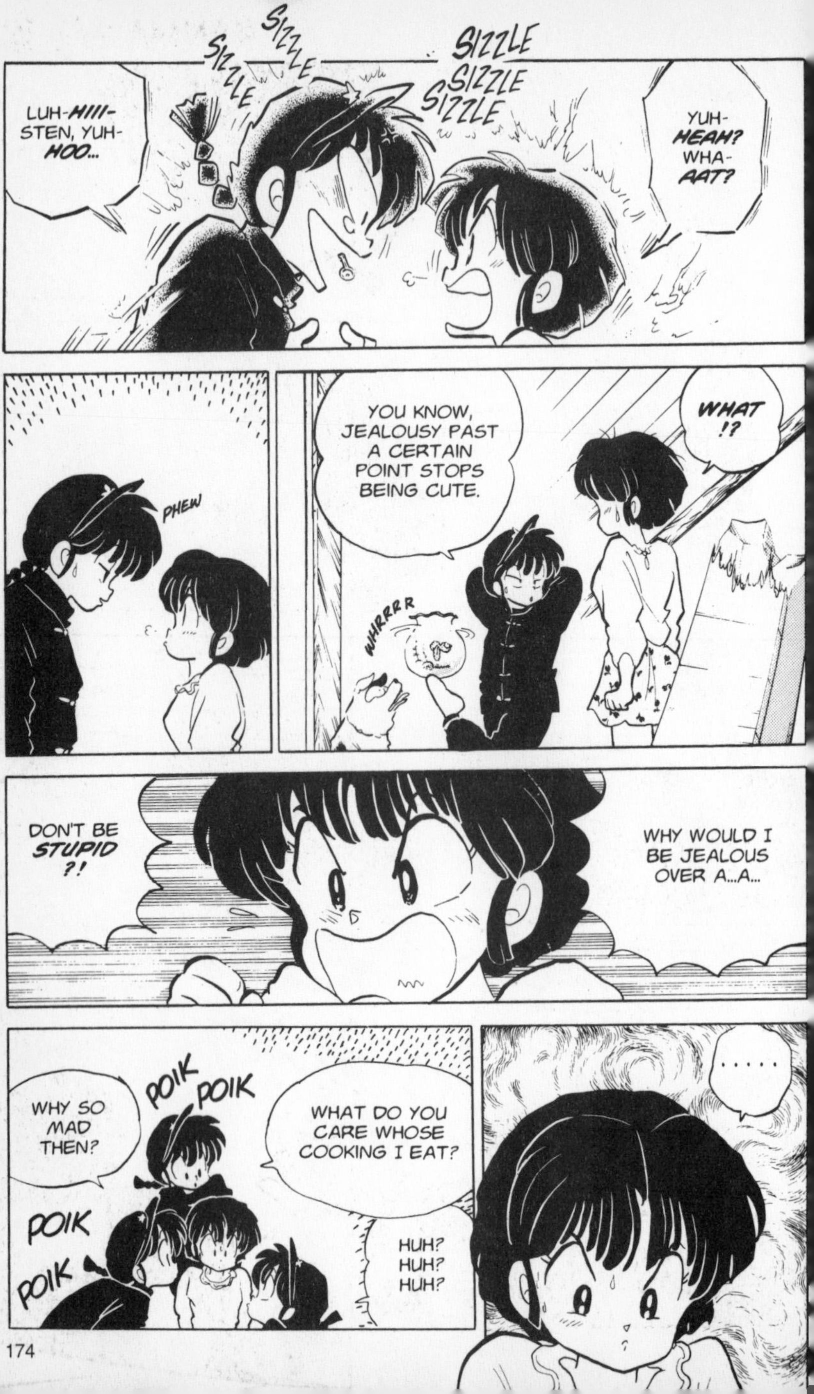
LUH-HIII-STEN, YUH-HOO...
SIZZLE SIZZLE
SIZZLE SIZZLE SIZZLE
YUH-HEAH? WHA-AAT?
PHEW
YOU KNOW, JEALOUSY PAST A CERTAIN POINT STOPS BEING CUTE.
WHRRRR
WHAT!?
DON'T BE STUPID?!
WHY WOULD I BE JEALOUS OVER A...A...
WHY SO MAD THEN?
POIK POIK
WHAT DO YOU CARE WHOSE COOKING I EAT?
POIK
POIK
HUH? HUH? HUH?
.....

FINE, THEN.

I'M GOING HOME...

HUH?

WHAT'S WITH HER...?

TOOM TOOM

. . . . .

AND I AM *NOT*...

...JEALOUS!

TOOM TOOM

BLUNT INSTRUMENT

LOOKS LIKE THE PARALYSIS POTION IN THE FOOD...

HOO HOO HOO

HOO HOO

...IS STARTING TO TAKE EFFECT.

OHHH... NNNNO...

OKAY! FINE! SEE IF I EVER HELP YOU AG....

VOOSH

...GLUG... AGUG... GLUG...

GUH?

FWUMP

BLOOSH

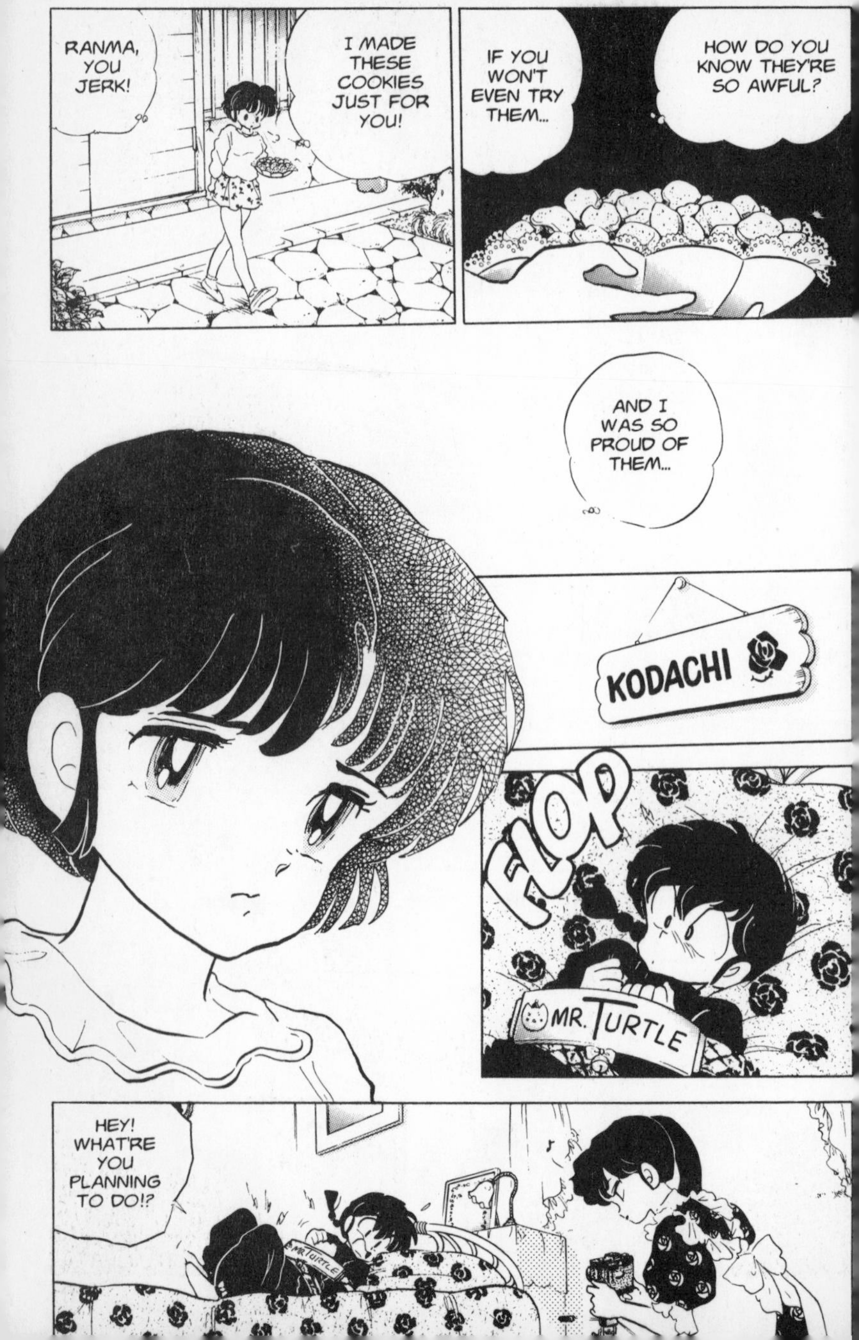
RANMA, YOU JERK!
I MADE THESE COOKIES JUST FOR YOU!
IF YOU WON'T EVEN TRY THEM...
HOW DO YOU KNOW THEY'RE SO AWFUL?
AND I WAS SO PROUD OF THEM...
KODACHI
FLOP
MR. TURTLE
HEY! WHAT'RE YOU PLANNING TO DO!?
MR. TURTLE

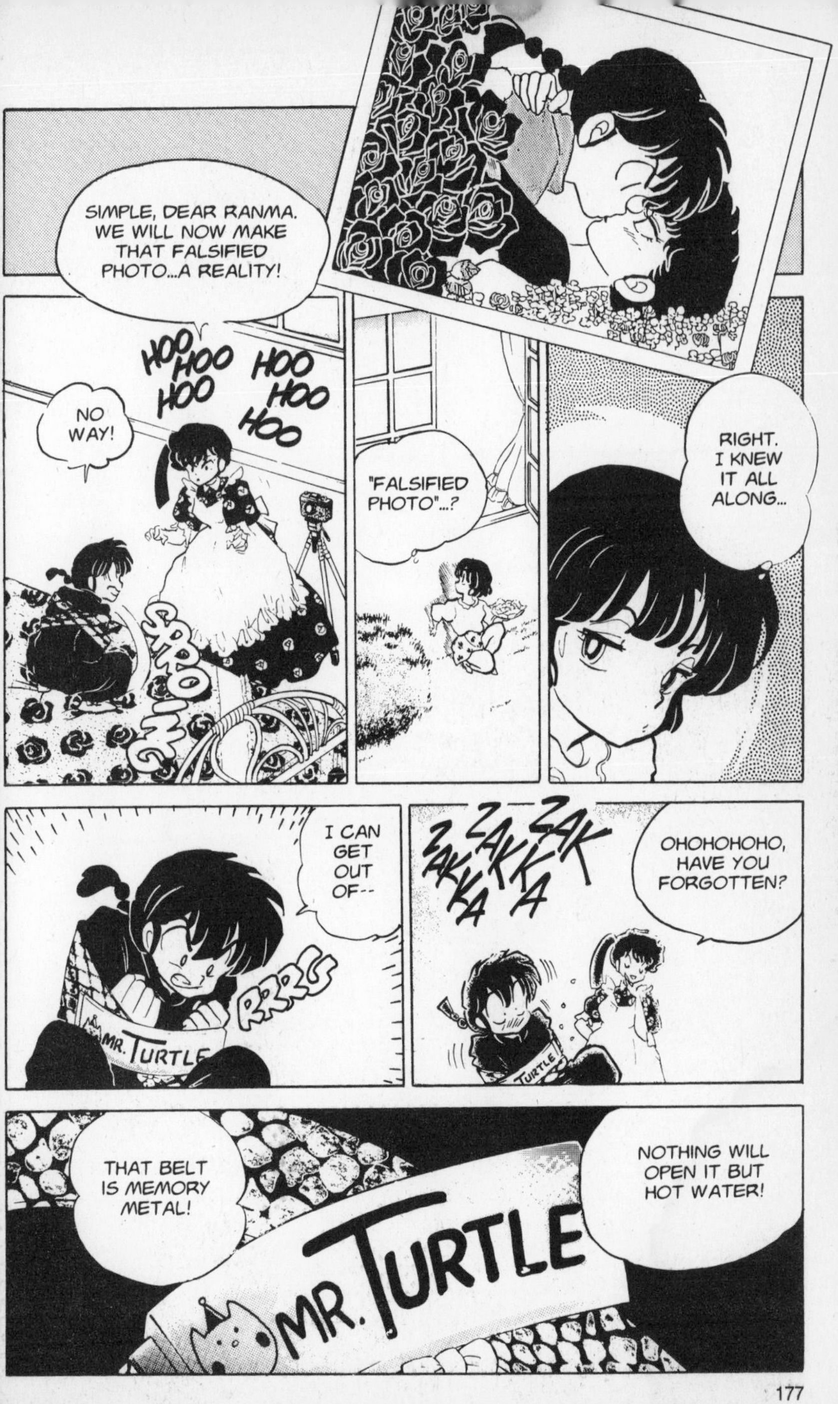
SIMPLE, DEAR RANMA. WE WILL NOW MAKE THAT FALSIFIED PHOTO...A REALITY!
HOO HOO HOO
HOO HOO HOO
NO WAY!
SPROING
"FALSIFIED PHOTO"...?
RIGHT. I KNEW IT ALL ALONG...
I CAN GET OUT OF--
RRRG
MR. TURTLE
ZAKKA ZAKKA ZAK
OHOHOHOHO, HAVE YOU FORGOTTEN?
TURTLE
THAT BELT IS MEMORY METAL!
MR. TURTLE
NOTHING WILL OPEN IT BUT HOT WATER!

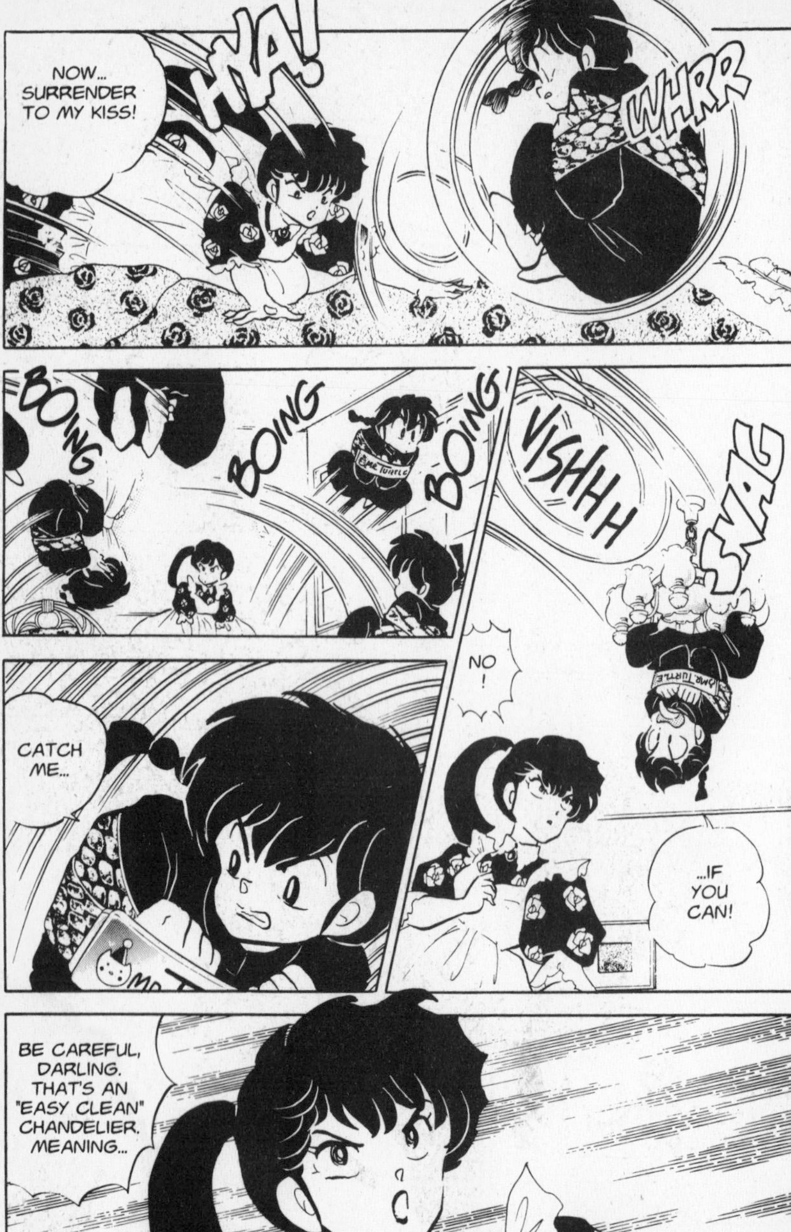
NOW... SURRENDER TO MY KISS!
HYA!
WHRR
BOING
BOING
BOING
CATCH ME...
VISHHH
SNAG
NO!
...IF YOU CAN!
BE CAREFUL, DARLING. THAT'S AN "EASY CLEAN" CHANDELIER. MEANING...

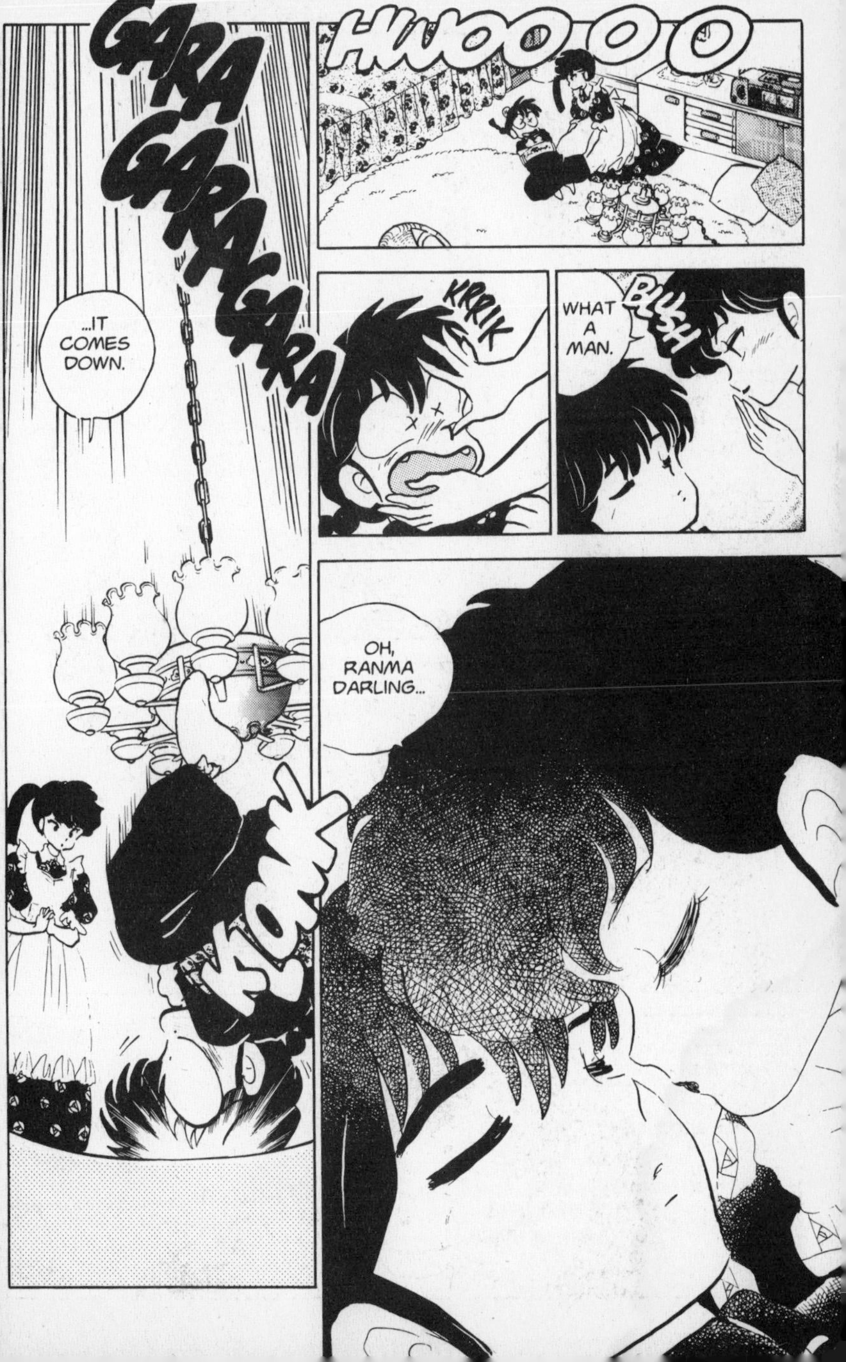
GARA GARAGARA
...IT COMES DOWN.
KLONK
HWOOOOO
KRRIK
WHAT A MAN.
BLUSH
OH, RANMA DARLING...

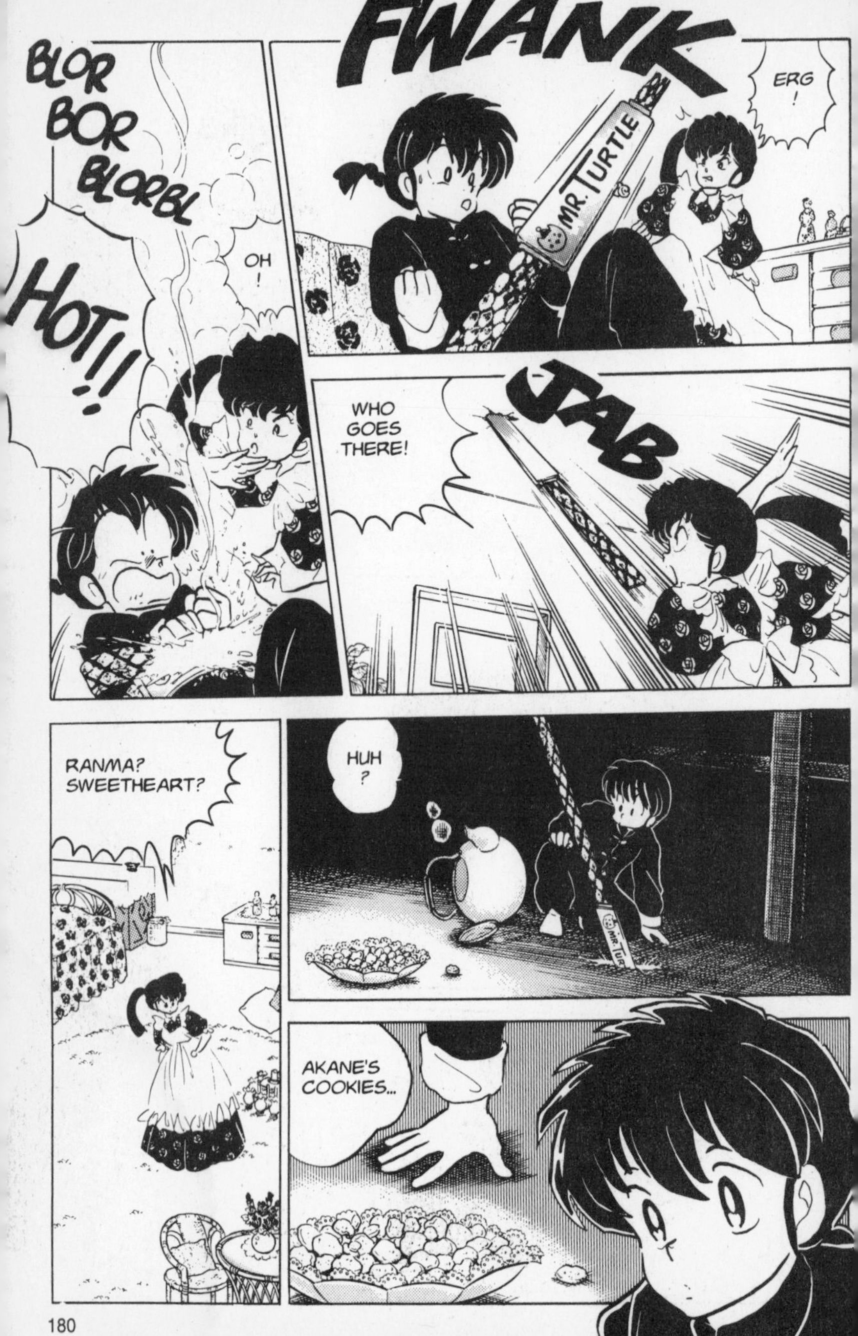
BLOR BOR BLORBL
HOT!!!
OH!
FWANK
MR. TURTLE
ERG!
JAB
WHO GOES THERE!
RANMA? SWEETHEART?
HUH?
MR. TURTLE
AKANE'S COOKIES...

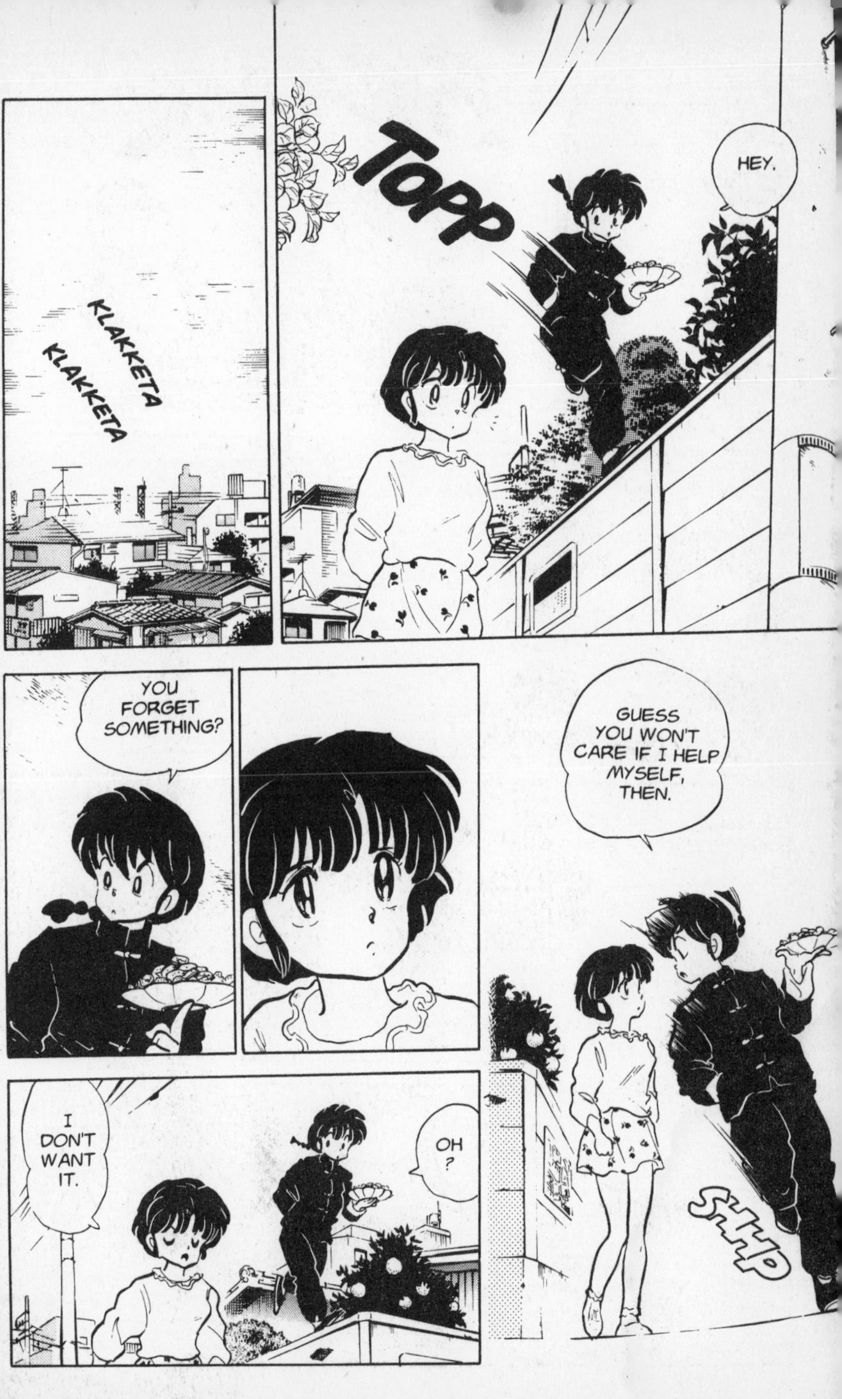
KLAKKETA
KLAKKETA
TOPP
HEY.
YOU FORGET SOMETHING?
I DON'T WANT IT.
OH?
GUESS YOU WON'T CARE IF I HELP MYSELF, THEN.
SHHP

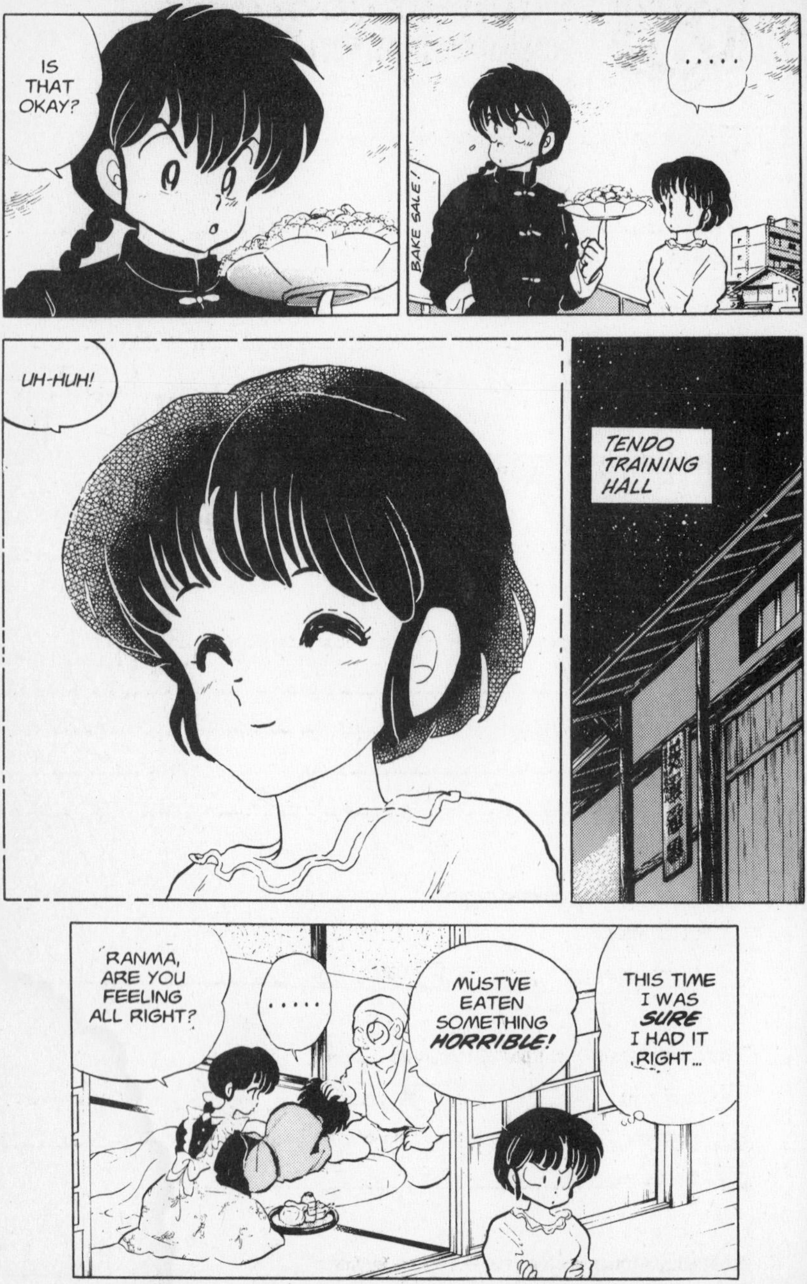
IS THAT OKAY?
BAKE SALE!
.....
UH-HUH!
TENDO TRAINING HALL
RANMA, ARE YOU FEELING ALL RIGHT?
.....
MUST'VE EATEN SOMETHING HORRIBLE!
THIS TIME I WAS SURE I HAD IT RIGHT...

TO BE CONTINUED...

COMPLETE OUR SURVEY AND LET US KNOW WHAT YOU THINK!

☐ Please check here if you DO NOT wish to receive information or future offers from VIZ

Name: _____

Address: _____

City: _____ State: _____ Zip: _____

E-mail: _____

☐ Male ☐ Female   Date of Birth (mm/dd/yyyy): ___/___/___ (Under 13? Parental consent required)

What race/ethnicity do you consider yourself? (please check one)

☐ Asian/Pacific Islander   ☐ Black/African American   ☐ Hispanic/Latino

☐ Native American/Alaskan Native   ☐ White/Caucasian   ☐ Other: _____

What VIZ product did you purchase? (check all that apply and indicate title purchased)

☐ DVD/VHS _____

☐ Graphic Novel _____

☐ Magazines _____

☐ Merchandise _____

Reason for purchase: (check all that apply)

☐ Special offer   ☐ Favorite title   ☐ Gift

☐ Recommendation   ☐ Other _____

Where did you make your purchase? (please check one)

☐ Comic store   ☐ Bookstore   ☐ Mass/Grocery Store

☐ Newsstand   ☐ Video/Video Game Store   ☐ Other: _____

☐ Online (site: _____)

What other VIZ properties have you purchased/own? _____

_____

How many anime and/or manga titles have you purchased in the last year? How many were VIZ titles? **(please check one from each column)**

ANIME	MANGA	VIZ
☐ None	☐ None	☐ None
☐ 1-4	☐ 1-4	☐ 1-4
☐ 5-10	☐ 5-10	☐ 5-10
☐ 11+	☐ 11+	☐ 11+

I find the pricing of VIZ products to be: **(please check one)**

☐ Cheap ☐ Reasonable ☐ Expensive

What genre of manga and anime would you like to see from VIZ? **(please check two)**

☐ Adventure ☐ Comic Strip ☐ Science Fiction ☐ Fighting

☐ Horror ☐ Romance ☐ Fantasy ☐ Sports

What do you think of VIZ's new look?

☐ Love It ☐ It's OK ☐ Hate It ☐ Didn't Notice ☐ No Opinion

Which do you prefer? **(please check one)**

☐ Reading right-to-left

☐ Reading left-to-right

Which do you prefer? **(please check one)**

☐ Sound effects in English

☐ Sound effects in Japanese with English captions

☐ Sound effects in Japanese only with a glossary at the back

THANK YOU! Please send the completed form to:

NJW Research
42 Catharine St.
Poughkeepsie, NY 12601

All information provided will be used for internal purposes only. We promise not to sell or otherwise divulge your information.